GLOBAL
COMMUNICATION

D0473226

Third Edition

GLOBAL
COMMUNICATION
Theories, Stakeholders, and Trends

Thomas L. McPhail

WILEY-BLACKWELL

A John Wiley & Sons, Ltd., Publication

Blackwell Publishing was acquired by John Wiley & Sons in February 2007. Blackwell's publishing program has been merged with Wiley's global Scientific, Technical, and Medical business to form Wiley-Blackwell.

Registered Office
John Wiley & Sons Ltd, The Atrium, Southern Gate, Chichester, West Sussex, PO19 8SQ, United Kingdom

Editorial Offices
350 Main Street, Malden, MA 02148-5020, USA
9600 Garsington Road, Oxford, OX4 2DQ, UK
The Atrium, Southern Gate, Chichester, West Sussex, PO19 8SQ, UK

For details of our global editorial offices, for customer services, and for information about how to apply for permission to reuse the copyright material in this book please see our website at www.wiley.com/wiley-blackwell.

Library of Congress Cataloging-in-Publication data is available for this book.

978-1-4443-3030-4 (paperback)

A catalogue record for this book is available from the British Library.

Set in 10/12.5pt Century by SPi Publisher Services, Pondicherry, India
Printed in Singapore

01   2010

Contents

Figures and Tables

Figures

Tables

Contributors

Junhao Hong is a professor in the Department of Communication, State University of New York at Buffalo. He is also a Research Associate of the Fairbank Center for Chinese Studies at Harvard University. From 2004 to 2006 he was President of the Chinese Communication Association. His research areas include international communication, media and society, and the impact of new communication/information technology. He has published several authored and edited books, dozens of book chapters, and a number of research articles in various international referred journals. He is an expert on Asian communication trends and issues.

Lawrence Pintak is Founding Dean of the Edward R. Murrow College of Communication at Washington State University. Previously, he was Director of the Kamal Adham Center for Journalism Training and Research at The American University in Cairo and publisher/co-editor of the online journal *Arab Media and Society* (www.arabmediasociety.org). He is the author of *The New Arab Journalist: Mission and Identity in a Time of Change* (I. B. Tauris, 2010), and several other books about the media and international affairs. Pintak is a former CBS News Middle East correspondent and he has contributed to many of the world's leading news organizations in his 30-year career in journalism on four continents. His work regularly appears in *The New York Times*, the *International Herald Tribune*, *Columbia Journalism Review* online, *Daily Star* Beirut, *Arab News* and a variety of publications around the world.

Alexa Robertson is Associate Professor in the Department of Political Science, Stockholm University (Sweden), and teaches in the Department of Journalism and Mass Communication, where she is also part of a group working on

Transformations in Screen Culture. Her research focus is on the comparative analysis of television news broadcasts from different European countries, in a theoretical context of globalization and identity. Her book, *Mediated Cosmopolitanism*, is being published by Polity Press in 2010.

Nancy Snow is Associate Professor of public diplomacy at Syracuse University where she teaches in the dual degree masters program in public diplomacy sponsored by the S. I. Newhouse School of Communications and the Maxwell School of Citizenship and Public Affairs. At the time of writing she is on leave as Associate Professor of Communications at California State University, Fullerton, and Adjunct Professor of Communications in the Annenberg School at the University of Southern California. She is the author or co-editor of six books, including the *Routledge Handbook of Public Diplomacy* (with Philip Taylor), *Propaganda, Inc.* and *Information War*. She has taught public diplomacy at Tsinghua University in Beijing, China, and consulted with many other nations on their rebranding efforts, including Israel, Canada, Spain, Germany, and England. She is senior fellow in the USC Center on Public Diplomacy and lifetime member of the Public Diplomacy Council at Georgetown University and Fulbright Association.

Preface

After September 11, 2001 the peaceful satisfaction of many nations that began with the end of the Cold War and the demise of communism came to an early and abrupt end, foreshadowing the rise of a new enemy – global terrorism. Along with this new elusive enemy came new wars and a profound increase in global communication. From embedded journalists with videophones covering the wars, to new media outlets, such as Al-Jazeera, Al-Arabiyya, and Al-Hurra, to photos being sent home and around the world on the internet, the role and scope of international media shifted dramatically. This third edition captures the major aspects of this new and in many cases disturbing era, updates the materials contained in earlier editions, plus contains totally new chapters on the importance of global public diplomacy (Chapter 4), the European scene (Chapter 9), the volatile Arabic media scene (Chapter 13), and China/Asia (Chapter 14).

This book portrays international communication from differing perspectives – it examines a number of major trends, stakeholders, and global activities, while promoting no particular philosophical or ideological school, whether of the left or the right. Rather, it seeks to provide information about major international trends of a theoretical, cultural, economic, public policy, or foreign relations nature. Moreover, in order to provide a framework for understanding the interconnection between the international communication environment and the global economy, *Global Communication* documents major historical events that connect the two. It also highlights communication industry mergers and acquisitions that frequently transcend national boundaries.

Just as the printing press and the assembly line were necessary events for the industrial revolution, so also the internet and modern communication technologies are essential for the international communication revolution. This book traces the influence and roles of major global communication technologies such as satellites, videophones, and personal computers. Collectively, these and other technologies have transformed the international communication environment, making possible the advent of global media systems such as CNN (Cable News Network), MTV (Music Television), the BBC (British Broadcasting Corporation), and the internet.

As part of the background needed to examine global media and related sectors, it is important to understand the history of the international communication debate, which developed initially within the halls of the United Nations Educational, Scientific, and Cultural Organization (UNESCO). This debate about the New World Information and Communication Order (NWICO) is important because it identified two significantly different philosophies, each supported by a different set of scholars and nations. Because the debate reflects much of the concern about the philosophical, cultural, and artistic threats that are of paramount concern to many nation-states, the phenomenon of "electronic colonialism" – the impact and influence of Hollywood feature films and television, plus other media from industrial nations – is also detailed. One large and vocal group supports a free press perspective without regard to its economic and cultural consequences; the other group supports a more interventionist approach, calling on governments and other organizations to be concerned with essentially non-commercial dimensions of the international communication environment. Because of the roles each group played, the policy positions, agencies, and leaders on both sides of the debate are examined extensively. Several new major global stakeholders, including the significant role of the global advertising industry, are also detailed.

A second major theme of the book concerns the economic implications of international communication. Although the economies of the international communications industries cannot be separated from governmental and cultural policy debates, it is important to recognize that most communication organizations are independent, active, commercial, and aggressive players in the international communication arena. They have global influence and they affect the communication environment both at home and abroad. As such, attention is also given to communication enterprises such as the Hollywood feature film industry; media giants such as Time Warner, Disney, Viacom, Bertelsmann, Sony, and News Corporation; as well as the internet, international wire services, such as the Associated Press and Reuters, and several multinational advertising agencies. As will be demonstrated, some of these organizations appear to be oblivious to the global policy debate and are willing to let the marketplace alone determine the winners and losers, whereas others are very concerned about the non-economic aspects of "trade" emerging from international communication.

All major global multimedia conglomerates are based in the United States, Europe, and Japan. Most of the concern about cultural issues emanates from nations in Latin America, Africa, and Asia. Therefore, a world-system theory perspective is outlined in Chapter 1 to decipher some of the structural cleavages in the international communication field. Throughout this book, electronic colonialism and world-system theories are identified as a crucial part for the discussion and analysis concerning global stakeholders in the communication sector. These two theories help unify the various stakeholders as well as identify their collective impact on globalization.

Any book about international communication would be deficient if it examined only one of these two major themes. A review focused solely on NWICO without mention of CNN or the BBC, for example, would ignore the contemporary reality and economic aspects of global communication. Similarly, a book that emphasized the internet and other new communication options and opportunities to the exclusion of the philosophical debate would fail to provide the necessary historical and cultural perspectives. To a surprising extent, the end of the Cold War and the collapse of the Soviet Union have shifted the debate in favor of the trade-focused parties. Only by detailing major themes and examining their interrelationships can a student of international communication come to understand the complexities of the global communication scene and the implications of the rapid change in global communication landscape that continues on a daily basis worldwide.

We should not underestimate the nature and depth of the transformation taking place in global communication. The era of the Enlightenment (*c.* 1600–1800) contributed to the intellectual transformation of Western societies, and so today we are going through a similarly profound alteration in our societies, fueled by the major structural changes in global communication, primarily the internet. Just as the major contributors to the Enlightenment era were Francis Bacon, John Locke, Adam Smith, Jean-Jacques Rousseau, Sir Isaac Newton, Catherine the Great, and others, so also today we have a critical mass of change agents who are forming the intellectual nucleus to create a new type of society with their profound insights and innovations. People such as Marshall McLuhan, Bill Gates, Steve Jobs, Charles Saatchi, Tim Berners-Lee, Margaret Whitman, Carol Bartz, Jim Balsillie, Larry Page and Sergey Brin of Google, and others are collectively providing the intellectual architecture and means to transform and create a new information era. Hundreds more working in their homes, laboratories, or universities in various nations around the world have contributed to the ongoing revolution in international communication. Yet few of these individuals responsible for creating a new media framework or paradigm have truly understood the long-run ramifications of their contributions on the type of society we will have in 50 years' time. In all likelihood, our future society will be dramatically different from the industrial society of even a mere 60 years ago at the end of World War II.

It is important to keep in mind that this intellectual transformation is not limited to economics, politics, trade, or education; rather, it will affect all of these areas as well as transform our concept of self and of community. Yet one major problem with this transformation is appearing already: this new society changed by the media is located only in select parts of the globe; primarily in those core nations that have already benefited from the previous industrial era. This overall intellectual transformation is occurring at the same time a large number of poor nations are still attempting to come to grips with enormous social problems ranging from illiteracy, poverty, subjugation, famine, civil wars, and poor health, particularly HIV/AIDS. As we move forward into a new era transformed by global media, one might also consider dichotomies created by the reality of a relatively small cluster of nations with full access to the internet, digital television, and wireless telephony, and, at the other extreme millions of people on the other side of the "digital divide" who have yet to make a phone call, or read a newspaper, or use a PC "mouse." One cannot be certain how parts of a world so intrinsically linked to media will interact with the vast numbers of individuals who so far have lived without it; we will be watching closely.

Acknowledgments

I would like to thank my friends who tested the materials and provided useful feedback and suggestions. I also want to thank Brenda McPhail for her assistance, patience, and feedback. I also want to thank Rebecca and Ryan McPhail for keeping me abreast of the significance of new media, blogging YouTube, MTV, and the latest in technologies, like the iPod. Kerry Marks undertook several duties in excellent fashion relating to this new edition. Finally, I want to thank my students who survived earlier drafts of the new materials.

Thomas L. McPhail

1

Global Communication
Background

Introduction

The world of international communication has changed rapidly in recent years. Following World War II, global communication was dominated by the tensions arising from the Cold War, pitting the old Soviet Union against the United States (US) and its allies. Much of the rhetoric, news space, face time, and concern dealt with some aspect of government control of mass communication or the impact of governments and other entities on free speech, or the free flow of information, or data across international borders. Likewise, much of international coverage on both sides of the Atlantic had an East–West tone, reflecting a communism versus democracy wedge. With the demise of the former Soviet Union and communism as a major global force, the factors underpinning international communication shifted dramatically. No longer did crises around the globe create major confrontations between two superpowers. What's more, the end of communism spelled the demise of the Soviets as enemies of the free press and the free flow of information. In many editors' and producers' opinions, it also spelled the end, ignoring, or at least downgrading the importance of foreign news coverage. That clearly changed on September 11, 2001.

Today, the US stands alone as the world's only superpower. While other economic entities, such as the European Union and parts of Asia, compete daily with the US in the global marketplace, there is no large-scale foreign military threat to the United States. But today there are new enemies' threats out there. The Taliban, Al-Qaeda, Osama bin Laden, the Islamic Jihad, suicide bombers, extremists, and a vast array of terrorist cells around the world have taken up new weapons to confront the US and other nations. The new weapons are primarily low tech:

smartphones, the internet, social networking sites, video cameras, Twitter, netbooks, and other means. Improvised explosive devices (IEDs) have replaced the nuclear bombs scare of the Cold-War era. This widespread terrorist phenomenon has again seen an editorial shift to greater coverage of international affairs. The "good guys versus bad guys" mentality has returned. Terrorists of many stripes are replacing communism as the evil force. The Middle East and other nations harboring and training extremists are the new Evil Empire. During the 1990s, *Time* magazine, the *New York Times*, and network newscasts had been replacing their foreign bureaus and international coverage with a parochial domestic agenda. Now Afghanistan and Iran are front-page news on an almost daily basis. The terrorism and its followers have put international news back in prime time. In addition to the various government investigations into issues like weapons of mass destruction (WMD), the 9/11 Commission, the Abu Ghraib and Guantanamo Bay prisoner scandals, war crimes, and public safety have led to a new global agenda and media focus, returning coverage to the Cold-War era coverage levels.

International communication refers to the cultural, economic, political, social, and technical analysis of communication and media patterns and effects across and between nation-states. International communication focuses more on global aspects of media and communication systems and technologies and, as a result, less on local or even national aspects or issues. Since the 1990s, this global focus or prism through which interactions are viewed or analyzed has been altered substantially by two related events. The first is the end of the Cold War and the sweeping changes this has brought; this includes political realignments across Europe. The second is increasing global interdependence, which is a fixture of the expanding global economy. The global economic recession demonstrated that the interdependence of economies big, like the US, and small, like Iceland. But this interdependence has more than an economic orientation; it also has a cultural dimension. This cultural dimension, in turn, has three important traits:

1   How much foreign content is contained, absorbed, or assimilated within the cultural domain?
2   How is this foreign content being transmitted (e.g., by books, movies, music, DVDs, television, commercials, mobile appliances, or the internet)?
3   How are domestic or indigenous cultures, including language, being impacted by this foreign content?

These aspects, issues, and questions are what this book is about. *Global Communication* highlights an international or global approach to the broad range of components that collectively make up the discipline of international communication. Because "[w]e live in an era of new cultural conditions that are characterized by faster adoption and assimilation of foreign cultural products than ever before,"[1] this book investigates in some detail who and where these cultural products are coming from and why, and addresses issues and concerns about their impact in foreign lands and in foreign minds.

Historically, the United States government has orchestrated international communication policy and the many activities relating to transborder communication activities. During the 1950s and 1960s, the US State Department, the Central Intelligence Agency (CIA), the National Security Council, and the Pentagon played central roles within international organizations to promote policies to suit Cold War agendas and objectives. This behavior was evident at a number of international conferences, but it was particularly clear in the US position regarding the New World Information and Communication Order (NWICO). Ultimately, the hostile rhetoric became so intense that the United States under President Reagan withdrew from the United Nations Educational, Scientific, and Cultural Organization (UNESCO) in the 1980s. The United States remained outside UNESCO until 2004. The United Kingdom withdrew as well and has also since returned.

When the Soviet Union disintegrated in the early 1990s, the counterpoint to much of the US rhetoric and foreign policy, whether overt or covert, disappeared. The old rationales – Cold-War rhetoric, concern about communism, and fear of nuclear destruction – became less prominent in the new environment of openness and cooperation with Eastern Europe as well as Russia. Foreign trade replaced concern about foreign media initiatives. Hard-line Soviet style journalists were either forced into retirement, or they quickly claimed adherence to free press traditions and practices. Several former Soviet dominated nations had become members of the European Union. This included a move to market economies and a media system supporting a free press.

Yet the current international communication landscape is in a state of flux. The vacuum created by the demise of the old Soviet Union had been filled by an atmosphere of economic determinism influenced by the reality of the increasing global economy. Economic determinism and free market beliefs, including global mergers and the pursuit of foreign markets, moved the focus of power and discussion from Main Street to Wall Street. Even the stock markets became transnational entities. More and more American firms, from Hollywood films, Blockbuster, to music, to Microsoft now earn more than 50 percent of their profits from abroad. Eighty percent of MTV's total audience is non-US and this percentage will only continue to expand as the global economy continues to grow in size and importance. Yet now this economic-based media orientation has to be shared with terrorism topics and the heavy costs associated with covering foreign wars, widely scattered terrorist bombings, or global disasters like the Asian tsunami.

The following are two examples of different global communication issues, one concerning terrorism, and one from Latin America. These vignettes reflect the breath and diversity of global communication issues. There are also complete chapters on media matters across Europe, the Middle East, and Asia later in the book.

Terrorism and September 11, 2001

Not only did the world change as result of the attacks on the World Trade Center and the Pentagon; the global media changed as well. In New York City alone, the estimated costs of the terrorist attack exceeded $17 billion, over 100,000 jobs, and nearly 3,000 lives. All major US news outlets, print and electronic, created special programming or special editions to cover not only the attack itself but also its aftermath. In particular, CNN and the *New York Times* devoted significant coverage, news space, and attention to terrorism. Major television network shows, such as the Emmys, were rescheduled, and Hollywood producers assisted federal government officials in designing media propaganda to counter global terrorism. The US government even created a new high profile Under Secretary of State for Public Diplomacy position. The main goal was to find a way to improve the US's image among the Muslim world. Yet after a series of disastrous foreign tours led by political partisans with little knowledge of Islam or the Arabic language or culture, the effort was doomed. The issue of public diplomacy from a global perspective is now so important that an entire chapter is devoted to it later in this book.

Related events also kept the 9/11 and War on Terrorism themes alive. Events such as Al-Jazeera's showing of various Osama Bin Laden and other Al-Qaeda videotapes became an issue within the Pentagon, as well as major US television outlets. The January 2002 kidnapping and murder of *Wall Street Journal* reporter Daniel Pearl also became part of the terrorism coverage. The wars in Afghanistan and Iraq, the train bombing in Spain, terrorist actions in the Philippines, and the school massacre in Belsen, Russia, the heavy death toll in India as a small group of terrorists attacked two luxury hotels, gave global media outlets a plethora of new material and evidence of an altered and more dangerous world.

The National Commission on Terrorist Attacks upon United States (9/11 Commission) held numerous open hearings and its widely read final report in July 2004 gave further life to the post-9/11 media frenzy. In particular, terrorism expert Richard Clarke's strong statements against the Republican administration also kept the commission and terrorism on the front pages and provided a much needed daily windfall for the all-news networks.

The global media coverage also shifted, putting on the radar renewed emphasis on the Arab–Israeli conflict, Muslim culture and communities, the plight of the Palestinians, and the labeling of Hamas as a terrorist organization. . The mass media also began running pieces about the disastrous Vietnam War and began making quagmire analogies to the Iraq War. The US election of President Obama signaled a policy shift to remove US troops from Iraq but at the same time to redirect and increase efforts in Afghanistan against the war-lords and the Taliban.

The BBC also got caught up in the war coverage issue. The BBC presented a piece about the contentious WMD rationale and interviewed a British expert,

David Kelly. He claimed that the evidence was "sexed up" to support the WMD claim. Shortly thereafter he committed suicide as a direct result of the stress caused by the media frenzy surrounding his testimony. Following that, the BBC management began a formal investigation, known as the Hutton Report, and several lapses in journalistic integrity by the BBC were noted. Senior BBC officials resigned as a result of the report as well.

In terms of the mass media itself, prior to 9/11 much of the literature on network television news focused on the preponderance of bad news. Phrases like "if it bleeds it leads" were common in terms of framing and understanding what was going to dominate the nightly newscasts, both locally and nationally. Post-September 11, this news mantra became the global mantra and other world broadcasters became either enthralled or captivated with the horrors of war and scattered terrorist acts, beginning with Afghanistan and the raids on Taliban-resistance fighters. Iraq and the gruesome beheadings of kidnap victims became common fare on the BBC World Television Service and CNN, as did the horrific pictures and tales of abuse and torture by US military coming out of the Abu Ghraib prison scandal. In fact, the internet was central to exposing the prison scandal. In Iraq US soldiers were sending pictures and e-mails back home to their family and friends. This is how the circulation of pictures moved from the internet to mainstream mass media, such as CBS's *60 Minutes*. The US military also tried to adapt and come up with a reasonable policy, which appeared elusive, concerning soldiers that were blogging their daily activities in Iraq on the internet, much to the chagrin of not only their field commanders, but also the Pentagon in Washington. The Iraq war became known as the first internet war.

In 2005 British soldiers were prosecuted for Abu Ghraib type torture in a jail near Basra. The European media were outraged at the abuse photographs. Some media began referring to the US and British military in Iraq as a coalition of the shameful.

Finally, the post-9/11 media environment, which was dominated by a great deal of sympathy for the position and activities of the Bush administration, has come under some criticism. FOX network, Judith Miller of the *New York Times*, Sinclair Broadcasting and others were labeled as public relation apologists for the White House and Pentagon. There was also the failure by the mainstream media to examine critically the Patriot Act, ghost detainees, or military oversight at the Guantanamo Bay, wire-tapping of American citizens, and basically no tough questioning of Attorneys General, or the FBI and CIA. CBS news anchor Dan Rather openly accused his fellow journalists of lying down and fearing the White House or FBI subpoenas, or other retribution, if they pursued high-profile stories or questioned the War on Terrorism.[2] A notable exception was *The New Yorker*'s Seymour Hersh. He withstood the orchestrated criticism of his magazine pieces and his book, *Chain of Command: The Road from 9/11 to Abu Ghraib*. In the book, he details how the torture and acts of humiliation by the US military in Iraq were an outcome or fallout of the US disregarding the Geneva Convention and proceeding without the United

Nations' full support. Speaking at Columbia University's Graduate School of Journalism in the fall of 2004, Richard Sambrook, Director of the BBC's World Service and Global News Division made critical comments about the US media being less than objective in their post-9/11 coverage, particularly of the war in Iraq (Sambrook, 2004). Seth Lewis and Stephen Reese after studying the framing process at a major American newspaper concerning the coverage of the War on Terror state that:

> In response to the terrorist attacks of September 11, 2001, the Bush administration advanced a War on Terror to justify security policies at home and military intervention abroad, exemplified by continuing conflicts in Iraq and Afghanistan. As a rhetorical device for marshaling resources and defining the terms of the debate, the War on Terror has emerged as a powerful ideological frame.[3]

Basically the new War on Terror represented a quantum change in US foreign policy. Anything done in the name of national security was permissible and any challenge, even by the media, represented weakness and a lack of understanding the new Bush–Cheney war, including torture, ideology.

The lack of a critical stance by the media could also be said about coverage of the war in Afghanistan. But the war in Afghanistan is fundamentally different from the Iraq war. The latter was a war of choice not related to 9/11. The Afghanistan war on the other hand was related to 9/11. Osama Bin Laden and the Taliban were all over various caves and towns across the region. They were a clear terrorist threat. But even the media got caught up in a battle of frames as the US military command pushed one approach and the NATO command pursued another. Michael Phillips of the *Wall Street Journal* calls it a PR war. He reported on June 1, 2009 that the US command was back at providing body counts of enemy Taliban killed in Afghanistan. Phillips states:

> The practice has revealed deep divides in military circles over the value of keeping such a score in a war being waged not over turf, but over the allegiance of the Afghan people. Does it buck up the troops and the home front to let them know the enemy is suffering, too? Or does the focus on killing distract from the goals of generating legitimacy and economic development?[4]

Not since the Vietnam war have body counts become a media strategy for the US military. In contrast, the 42 nation NATO command is solidly against the practice. They want to convince the people of Afghanistan that they were there to aid them, not kill them. The issue came down to a battle for the minds of Afghans being the primary goal of the NATO forces, whereas the US military were concerned more about the minds of the voters and politicians back home in terms of continuing their support for the nearly decade long war with no victory in sight. Body counts and civilian victims were of less importance to the US military command than their public relations push at home. NATO attempted to set the frame or media agenda as one supporting the tenets of a civil society, including a free press; the US command set the frame quite differently employing a tactic from the Vietnam era where the dead played a role in stoking support for the war effort. The public diplomacy aspect and negative fallout in terms of alienating the Afghans, including their prime minister, were ignored by the Pentagon. This is surprising given the efforts of the US State Department to place public diplomacy near the top of its agenda for the Muslim world. More is said about this important aspect in a later chapter of this book.

Latin American Media

Latin American media are significantly different from media markets in North America and Europe. Several countries in Latin America, such as Argentina, Brazil, Chile, Colombia, and Peru have experienced political, economic, and social turmoil since the end of World War II. Some other nations continue to be controlled by dictators with military backing. Given this environment, the radio and television industries in these nations tend to be either government owned and controlled or heavily regulated. In a few cases powerful domestic media conglomerates are controlled by wealthy families, such as Televisa in Mexico or Grupo Globo in Brazil. In other Latin American nations, the independent print press frequently is allied with the political and religious elites. There is little investigative journalism since both the state-owned or commercial media do not favor it and several investigative reports have wound up dead. Although Latin American markets are substantial in terms of population and growing consumer base, they still are relatively underdeveloped compared to their North American and European counterparts but that is changing. Sallie Hughes and Chappell Lawson discuss the obstacles which Latin American media confront on a frequent basis. They identify

> five general barriers to the creation of independent, pluralistic, and assertive media systems in the region.; (a) violence against journalists encouraged by a generalized weakness in the rule of law; (b) holdover authoritarian laws and policies that chill assertive reporting; (c) oligarchic ownership of television, the region's dominant medium; (d) the spottiness of professional journalistic norms; (e) the limited reach of print media, community-based broadcasters, and new communication technologies.[5]

Despite these structural issues the Latin American environment is changing in terms of governments and mass communication. Many governments moved to a more open and democratic way of attempting to improve overall social and economic conditions for the populace. In telecommunications and mass media systems, there was a noticeable liberalization, deregulation, and privatization as reform legislation was passed in many Latin American nations. The growing increases in literacy, access to the internet, and cheaper satellite dishes have collectively moved the debate over media's role in society. Several Latin American countries are clearly at a crossroad; they must decide whether they will follow this new neoliberal path, including broader ownership of the media, or revert to the historical tendency of military coups, government control, and ownership, favoritism to elite families, and heavy censorship.

Despite the uneasy balance between old and new, the Latin American market is characterized by two significant phenomena. First, by virtue of the domination of the Spanish language (with the exception of Brazil, which speaks Portuguese), Latin America has not been as readily inundated with US television shows or films, which carry English language soundtracks. In contrast, English-speaking nations such as Canada, Australia, and Great Britain were easy international markets for, first, Hollywood feature films, and then US television programs, followed by music. This language difference led to a second important Latin American media phenomenon. Because these countries were forced to create their own programming, they created an interesting and successful genre known as telenovelas. They are Spanish soap operas that are extremely popular from Mexico to the tip of South America. They have been successful enough to be exported to Spain, Russia, Cuba, Puerto Rico, and other non-English speaking European countries, as well as Florida and California. Many of the leading actors and actresses are national celebrities, like soccer stars, in the various regions of Latin America. The export market is expanding rapidly for telenovelas because they cost much less to produce than their Hollywood and New York counterparts.

On the feature film front the scene is not as encouraging. Over 60 percent of the theater screens across Latin America regularly show Hollywood films. In Latin America there are few film houses or even nations that can mount and finance blockbuster films to rival Hollywood.

Another difference between North America and Latin America is the role and success of newspapers. In North America, many newspapers have folded over the last decade, and single-newspaper cities are the norm rather than the exception. By contrast, Latin American newspapers are still a substantially growing market, with over 1,000 newspapers in circulation and readership, on a daily basis, in excess of 100 million people. Because of the high circulation figures, newspaper advertising is competitive with radio and television, making it a challenge for start-up private stations to succeed. Finally, because newspapers are privately owned, the publishers and editors generally support the movement toward greater democratization as well as government reforms to privatize the communication sector.

Left-wing Connection: Latin America

In the postwar era, Latin America displayed a unique joint interest among labor unions, priests and nuns pursuing Liberation theology, and academics, which were frequently of like mind as they sought Marxist or left-wing solutions to corrupt regimes, many of which had military connections. Ideological fervor and rhetoric spread across Latin America as unions, clergy, and academics sought to tap the discontent of the peasants to mobilize support for economic and political change. For the most part, their efforts failed, the prime exceptions being Cuba, now Venezuela, and likely El Salvador and Chile. There were occasional major confrontations, such as the uprising in Chiapas, Mexico. In this revolt, the rebels went so far as to exclude the major Mexican broadcaster, Televisa, from their various press conferences. Latin American academics were particularly critical of North American models, such as open markets, free enterprise, private ownership, and advertising-supported media. They frequently attacked the violence of Hollywood feature films or the wasteland of television shows ranging from *The Simpsons*, to *Baywatch*, to reality shows, to MTV videos. They saw American junk culture with the same distain through which they saw American junk food.

With the demise of Marxism and the end of the Cold War, these same Latin American groups have lost steam and credibility. Labor unions are becoming isolated as democratization begins to take hold in several nations, along with greater economic prosperity. Leftist academics are finding fewer opportunities to promote anti-US media criticism as liberalization, privatization, and deregulation takes hold across the communication sectors. Latin American academics tend to write flourishing and lengthy essays critical of American culture with little, if any, empirical data to support their assertions. Today, change is bringing greater media choice, more advertising, less government ownership, and reduced regulatory control of electronic media across Latin America.

The role of media and culture, plus their impact on economic growth in Latin America, has been demonstrated in the literature. Cultural change and economic change are linked, but as David Holman points out, "[T]he 'McDonaldisation' of all societies is possibly inevitable, but it is possible to eat McDonald burgers, and to wear jeans, without losing any of the most cherished aspects of the national culture."[6] Yet historically Latin American communication scholars have been among the most critical and particularly anti-United States, in their writings. The vast majority work from a Marxist platform, which is now stale and suspect with the end of the Cold War. Yet some continue their diatribes, not appreciating how substantially the global communication scene has changed.

What follows is a dramatic example of how the Cold-War atmosphere framed media activities involving Washington and a Latin American nation, in this case Chile.

Chile: US Government Media Interaction

The 1973 military coup in Chile during the Cold War provides an example of the US government's concern, influence, and backstage role in the US media when dealing with foreign events. In this case, as in others, it is important to realize that frequently the US press corps has little background knowledge, local information or sources, cultural awareness, or even native language skills as preparation for breaking foreign stories. In the past, this weakness frequently was addressed by willing and well-trained US embassy staffers who provided background briefings to visiting US journalists in order to furnish them with "off the record" information and help them establish meetings and interviews. The information generally was selected to frame, support, and promote US position and foreign policy objectives abroad. Although there is nothing intrinsically wrong with this practice, problems develop when journalists write their stories or file their video clips without acknowledging the substantial influence or assistance of US embassy personnel.

From 1970 to 1973, the United States government sought to assist in the overthrow of Chile's democratically elected leftist government. The United States was hostile to Chilean president Salvadore Allende, whom US President Richard Nixon had labeled a communist threat. According to the US State Department, Allende had to be removed, or he could set an example and communism could spread across South America. When the Chilean military seized power in September 1973, the US government supported General Augusto Pinochet, despite the fact that he had been associated with many nefarious crimes, including supporting Chilean death squads. Pinochet subsequently ruled Chile for 17 years.

Without detailing the specific role of the Central Intelligence Agency (CIA), it is instructive to examine its relationship with the US media in Chile. Prior to and during the revolution, the CIA directed its Chilean station chief to engage in propaganda. He was to spread misinformation when it suited US objectives. According to the *New York Times*:

> The CIA's propaganda efforts included special intelligence and "inside" briefings given to the US journalist ... Particularly noteworthy in this connection is the *Time* cover story which owed a great deal to written materials provided by the CIA. [Moreover,] CIA briefings in Washington changed the basic thrust of the story in the final stages, according to another *Time* correspondent.[7]

The result of this cozy relationship between US foreign affairs officials and foreign correspondents was a *Time* magazine cover story openly calling for an invasion of Chile to thwart the Marxist president and to stop the spread of communism throughout South America. During this era *Time* was a cheerleader for stopping leftists by any means.

The point of this example is not to debate the role of the CIA in ultimately assisting in the overthrow of a democratically elected leader, but rather to focus on the role of foreign correspondents during the height of the Cold War. The US State Department, Department of Defense, and CIA all actively courted US foreign correspondents. The foreign correspondents in turn were to varying degrees willing to accept advice, leads, and in some cases, copy from US embassies around the world. This situation was particularly true in countries where English-speaking US journalists did not speak the native language. In these cases, embassy staff and CIA operatives had enormous clout and access. They knew which locals spoke English and were sympathetic to the US position. American embassies set up media interviews and assisted journalists with logistics and acquisition of compatible equipment and other necessities for gathering pro-US news in foreign venues.

For over a decade, without the *raison d'être* of the Cold War and the anti-communist fervor that once dominated the agenda and mindset at the US State Department and its network of foreign embassies, CIA operatives have been marginalized and replaced by trade representatives. US ambassadors and their staffs courted economists, investors, and the business community. Journalists no longer received priority access or assistance. Indeed, unless journalists are reporting on successful business ventures by US investors or corporations, they have difficulty getting their phone calls returned.

In the post-Cold-War era, US embassies focused on trade and the provision of the organizational and logistical work necessary for US corporations to expand exports in these countries or regions. Senior embassy personnel spent the majority of their time seeking out investment opportunities, organizing trade fairs, or identifying new export markets while nurturing existing ones. Within the new reality of US embassy culture and foreign policy there is now a shared emphasis. The business press now shares media attention with security, terror, or war issues. Some US journalists abroad deal with foreign policy and terrorism while others still look at foreign profits, mergers, and acquisitions in the post-Cold-War-environment.

The terrorist piece and Chilean example reflect the dramatically changing landscape confronting international communication. This book looks at global media, global communication technologies, such as the internet, global advertising, multimedia organizations, Europe, the Middle East, and Asian media, and global events from post-Cold War and 9/11 vantage points. But some historical themes of concern continue to shape the scope and impact of global communication. These themes are best understood by examining where, why, and in what context New World Information and Communication Order emerged. But before discussing NWICO, from an historical perspective the role and invention of the telegraph in the mid-nineteenth century had profound consequences for international communication. This new technology resulted in a paradigm shift from national to international communication (Hills, 2002).[8] It resulted in information becoming a commodity, particularly for the expanding print press and telegraph traffic. Finally, it also fostered a new breed of journalists – the war correspondent.

History of the War Correspondent

Prior to the Crimean War (1853–6) there had been many wars. What would separate the Crimean War from the others was the impressive fact that this war was the first to be covered by a foreign correspondent. For example an earlier war of 1812, between Canada and Great Britain against the US, ended in 1815. Canada and Great Britain declared victory with the Treaty of Ghent, ending the war. It was signed in Europe in December 1814. But this agreement did not reach North

America until February 1815. With the newly invented telegraph, however, it was possible during the Crimean War for reporters to send daily dispatches. The necessary new technology was the telegraph, which was patented in Europe by Charles Wheatstone in 1838.

The background to the war was a dispute between Russia and France, under Napoleon, over control of the Middle East. The British also had a vested interest in the conflict since they controlled the seas and trade routes, and aspired to continue their colonial expansion in the Middle East region. The Russians lost the Crimean War under the Treaty of Paris. Following this loss the Russians pulled back from their global expansionist goals. They soon sold Alaska in 1867 to the US for $7.2 million.

William Harold Russell was the first foreign war correspondent for the London-based *Times*, which was founded in 1785 and now is controlled by News Corp. Three interesting factors emerged from this coverage. First, Florence Nightingale, the legionary nursing pioneer, complained to the British press about how poorly the British war casualties were treated, and the horrific battlefield conditions compared to the excellent French facilities. The coverage in the *Times* eventually led to the dismissal of the cabinet minister responsible for the conduct of the war. Second, Queen Victoria of Britain called for a Royal Commission on Health and War (1856–7) but Nightingale was not appointed to the Commission because only males were eligible. Third, the impact of the *Times* coverage was so important and explosive that the number of journalists assigned to cover the US Civil War (1861–5) skyrocketed. The London *Times* circulation nearly doubled. In the US, with over half a million deaths, the pictures and accounts were major copy for the infant print press across the north and south. Several foreign correspondents from Europe also covered the Civil War. For example, the UK reporters supported the slavery-afflicted South to protect the cheap source of cotton for British factories. The UK press for centuries has been blindly supportive of the monarchy and the national government's policies, right or wrong. Finally, the massive circulation increases also fueled the demand for greater literacy so that many more people could read the war coverage in the newspapers.

New World Information and Communication Order (NWICO)

The foregoing examples are indicative of some of the major issues in international communication. In the past, much of this debate focused on the New World Information and Communication Order. NWICO dominated the international communication agenda for almost two decades. It represents

1   an evolutionary process seeking a more just and equitable balance in the flow and content of information;

2   a right to national self-determination of domestic communication policies; and

3   at the international level, a two-way information flow reflecting more accurately the aspirations and activities of less developed countries (LDCs).[9]

Despite the fact that some proponents still champion this vision, many believe that NWICO is no longer a serious international issue. Even UNESCO, where much of the debate took place, has abandoned it. Yet NWICO may become a born-again matter because of the deep divisions which emerged from the World Summit on the Information Society (WSIS). The WSIS is covered in more detail later in this book.

An appreciation of its basic premises and of the issues that divided nations remains an important and relevant element in a complete understanding of the different views about international communication. Not everyone views the global media flows and control over aspects of the communication scene the same way.

NWICO's ultimate goal was a restructured system of media and telecommunication priorities in order for LDCs to obtain greater influence over their media, information, economic, cultural, and political systems. For LDCs, or peripheral nations, the current world communication system is an outgrowth of prior colonial patterns reflecting commercial and market imperatives.[10] NWICO was promoted as a way to remove this vestige of colonial control. However, Western governments and news organizations vigorously opposed any such plan, fearing it will bring increased interference with the press, thus ultimately reducing market share and profitability.

In seeking to gain a more balanced flow of information, peripheral regions postulate potential mechanisms that clash with strongly held journalistic traditions and practices in the West. From time to time they called for government control of the media, limited reporter access to events, journalistic codes of ethics, licensing of reporters, and taxation of the broadcast spectrum – all ideas that Western journalists, media owners, and policymakers abhor. Even the call for a "balanced flow" of information, which was approved by UNESCO in the 1970s, was criticized as interference with a free press, free flow, and free market mechanisms. Only an open and free flow of information is viewed as being fully consistent with the goals of a truly free press. Yet the critics maintain that the free flow is really a one-way flow – from core nations to other regions of the world, with little or no reciprocity.

The concerns of the Western press about NWICO are not merely theoretical. Because it legitimates a governmental role in the dissemination of information, several nation-states continue to support and implement policies based on NWICO. In Africa, for example, the government of Liberia, through its Ministry of Information, released an edict restricting press access to the internet. Journalists need a government permit, which limits the information they can cover. Because no permit or license has ever been issued for use of the internet, this activity basically is prohibited.

The nations of Africa are not alone in their attempts to intervene and establish restrictive regulations concerning international websites. For example, in the Middle East, Islamic opposition to media, including the internet, is widespread:

> First satellite television, now the Internet. Computer-literate Saudi citizens, already spoilt for satellite choice, are about to be swamped by a wave of imported material on the Internet. After considerable delay, the government is expected to announce on October 19th [1998] which local companies have been chosen to deliver this Trojan horse of miscellaneous information into Saudi Arabia's pristine households. The Saudi government long ago decided that unfettered access to foreign websites would introduce a torrent of political and religious debate, not all of which would be welcomed by the regime.[11]

Many critics attack the Western press as if it were a monolithic, rational system. They fail to realize that what eventually winds up in Western newspapers, on radio, or on television is determined by a complex, and not entirely consistent, process of decision-making. As Mort Rosenblum explains:

> Correspondents play an important part in selection by determining what to cover in the first place. But most of the process is in the hands of editors at different stages. These are the gatekeepers. Each medium and each type of correspondent operates in a different fashion, but the principle is the same. A correspondent's dispatch first goes to one gatekeeper and then what emerges – if anything – goes on to others. All along the way; the original dispatch may be shortened, lengthened, rewritten, or thrown away entirely. This series of editors determines what is to be eventually shared with the public; and they decide what the American people may never know.[12]

This is an important point. What people in Western or core societies learn about peripheral regions is meager and the result of several gatekeepers. What makes this successive diminution of information about poor nations so paradoxical is that both technically and theoretically there is more international information available today than ever before. The internet, satellites, fax machines, videodiscs, portable computers, radio, smartphones, and direct long-distance dialing have collectively replaced the slow and cumbersome dispatches of the past.

But practically, the story is quite different. There are several contributing factors. The major one is simply the high cost of international reporting. The estimated cost to place and equip a single foreign correspondent abroad for one year is $300,000. This has led to a net reduction in the number of reporters that wire services, networks, or individual papers are willing to post abroad. Second, restrictions range from censorship and outright bans to withholding critical interviews past filing time, threats of physical abuse unless proper slants are evident, jailing, or even death all serve to reduce or limit the amount of available copy. Third, the high turnover of foreign correspondents and the pack journalism phenomenon make editors and publishers reluctant to expend time and money to significantly increase foreign coverage. Fourth, the trend toward "parachute journalism," in which large numbers of foreign correspondents, assorted paparazzi, and belligerent camera crews descend by the planeload on international scenes of conflict or natural disasters, tends to trivialize or sensationalize events that are far more complex than a 30-second clip or a few paragraphs can capture. Finally, the lack of public concern, as reflected in the trend toward light, fluffy, gossipy, and trendy journalism, focusing on celebrities or trivia reduces the incentive for editors to provide in-depth and continuous coverage of a broad range of foreign issues and conflicts. On the print side *The New Yorker* magazine, the *New York Times*, the *Wall Street Journal*, *The Economist*, and the *Washington Post* are clear exceptions.

The reason for this shift in newspapers has been a mix of accounting and fiscal concerns related directly to declining circulation numbers, a movement toward local community journalism, and the internet taking readers and advertisers as well. The policies of the media are increasingly governed by marketing experts, who make news decisions to reflect focus-group results, rather than by editors. Without the Cold War, there was no strong focus for international news. With no counterpoint or dramatic confrontations between East and West, there were no engaging images to attract the public's attention to international coverage. The terrorist attacks of 9/11 and the aftermath of terrorist bombings around the globe has changed all that. But even that coverage and carnage has been decreasing over time.

Clearly, the exceptional and unusual still dominate what is reported. In-depth front-page pieces on population, education, health care, environment, and other development successes are still rare. Rosenblum, in talking about "the System," makes this point:

> Foreign correspondents do often seem to be mad as loons, waiting on some source for hours in the rain so they can write a dispatch which might well end up blotting spilled coffee on an editorial desk back home. Editors seem madder still, suffering hypertension over whether their own man reached some obscure capital in time to duplicate stories available to them by other means. And their combined effort, when it reaches breakfast tables and living rooms across the United States, often appears to be supercilious and sloppy.
>
> This system is geared as much to amuse and divert as it is to inform, and it responds inadequately when suddenly called upon to explain something so complex and menacing as a dollar collapse or a war in Asia. Yet it is the American citizen's only alternative to ignorance about the world.
>
> Because of the system – and in spite of it – most Americans are out of touch with events that directly affect their lives. When crisis impends, they are not warned. When it strikes, they are not prepared. They know little about decisions taken on their behalf which lessen their earnings, restrict their freedoms and threaten their security.[13]

Why is this the case? What are the implications? In an era of so much information, why is there so little useful information? The Western press warns that this situation would worsen under NWICO. The idea of licensing foreign correspondents is seen as the first of many steps that collectively will result in fewer reporters being acceptable to authoritarian nations and only favorable, pro-government news stories being permitted out of many of them. As this book describes in detail, international news coverage is going to change. The question is whether it is going to improve in accuracy, quantity, and quality, or whether gatekeepers will restrict or heavily censor news. That is why awareness of global media issues and positions is central to understanding international communication. That is also why this book has specific chapters on the Middle East and China since they are important players in terms of what Marshall McLuhan labeled the "global village."

Two major theoretical outlooks or theories will assist in organizing and understanding the events, trends, and major stakeholders in the rapidly changing field of international communication. They are electronic colonialism and world system theories. Both are described in the following section, and then their interrelationships are outlined. In addition, throughout *Global Communication* certain examples of the media scene or global operations as they reflect and apply to these underlying two theories are commented on.

Electronic Colonialism Theory (ECT)

Traditionally, mass media research looks either at select micro issues, such as agenda setting, ownership, or violence, or at a specific medium, such as print, radio, television, or the internet. Only occasionally do scholars examine the macro aspects of the overall mass communication system. Harold Innis, Marshall McLuhan, Armand Mattelart, Jacques Ellul, Ben Bagdikian, and George Barnett are representative of the macro research school. The concept of NWICO offers another macro approach. Electronic colonialism theory reflects much of the current global concerns, particularly with reference to culture, and is a good theoretical concept with which to begin. It provides a theoretical frame for examining the stakeholders and transnational issues.

Four Epochs of Global Colonization

Over the course of history, there have been only a few major successful trends in empire building. The first era was characterized by military conquests. These occurred during the Greco-Roman period and witnessed the expansion of the Roman Empire throughout most of what is modern Europe, including North Africa. This early era is labeled military colonialism.

The militant Christianity of the Crusades represented the second era during the Middle Ages. The Crusades, with the Catholic Pope as patron, sought to control territory from Europe, across Northern Africa, to the Middle East. Beginning around 1095, a series of Crusades over 200 years resulted in eastern expansion and the establishment of new European colonies promoting Christianity in the Middle East and across Africa. The territories were seized from Muslims, as Western civilization became the dominant international force or hegemony. Relics and treasures from various nations and the Greek Orthodox Church were plundered and returned to the Vatican as gifts. For example, in 1204 the Crusaders sacked and desecrated Constantinople's holiest cathedrals and shrines. To this day much of the history and treasures of the eastern Greek Orthodox Church are locked in the Vatican's basement. In 2004 Pope John Paul II made a token gesture and returned the bones of two early Greek theologians but many Greeks are still waiting for the plundered gold, silver, and art works from this era. This era is labeled Christian colonialism.

Beginning with the invention of significant mechanical advances in the seventeenth century, the third era – mercantile colonialism – continued untamed until the mid-twentieth century. Spawned by a desire for cheap labor, the importation of raw materials, along with ready export markets, created by colonies, for finished products, the industrial revolution created mercantile colonialism. Asia, Africa, the Caribbean, and the Americas became objects of conquest by European powers. France, Great Britain, Spain, Portugal, The Netherlands, Belgium, Italy, and the Nordic nations systematically set about extending their commercial and political influence. These expanding empires of Europe sought markets, raw materials, and other goods unavailable at home. In return, they sent colonial administrators, immigrants, a foreign language, usually English, educational system, religion, philosophy, high culture, laws, and a lifestyle that frequently were inappropriate for the invaded country. None of this concerned the conquerors, such as the vast British Commonwealth, who thought they were doing the conquered a favor. In the 1700s and 1800s international status was a function of the number and location of one's foreign colonies.

During the latter part of this era, industrialized nations sought to extend their influence through transnational corporations that supplemented and extended more traditional means of control. But the common denominator remained a desire for economic advantage – plentiful raw materials, cheap labor, and expanding markets. Mercantile colonialism also included other commercial imperatives such as advertising, government regulation, and laws, including contract and intellectual property rights, which better suited the larger and more powerful industrialized nations than their weaker foreign colonies of regions. These collective actions began the global economy which the US would master and dominate following World War II.

A key element in the success of mercantile colonialism was the invention of the printing press by Johannes Gutenberg. In the early 1450s, he produced 200 copies of the Gutenberg Bible. Despite their high cost, the bibles completely sold out, ushering in a new era of communication. Although Gutenberg was forced into bankruptcy and eventually died a poor man, his invention provided the means for others to amass incredible wealth and power. Initially, the presses were used to mass-produce religious materials in the vernacular, but soon "penny press" newspapers appeared. Over time the printing press undermined the absolute authority and control of the Roman Catholic Church and European monarchies alike. Also, the demand grew for a literate workforce capable of operating the increasingly sophisticated technology of factory production. The demand for public education

Eras	Dates
Military colonialism	BC–1000 AD
Christian colonialism	1000–1600
Mercantile colonialism	1600–1950
Electronic colonialism	1950–Present

Figure 1.1 Electronic colonialism theory

and the evolution of mass societies created nations with greater literacy and some disposable factory wages. These phenomena permitted the purchase of newspapers, movie tickets, telegrams, books, and eventually radios.

World Wars I and II brought an end to major military expansion and positioned the industrialized nations of the West in command of international organizations, vital trade routes, and global commercial practices. During the 1950s, the business and economic climate encouraged transnational corporations to increase and solidify domestic and foreign markets based on the production of mass-produced goods, from breakfast cereals to cars. As the industrial revolution ran its course, two major changes occurred during the late 1950s and early 1960s that set the stage for the fourth and current era of empire expansion.

The two major changes were the rise of nationalism and decolonization, centered mainly in developing nations, and the shift to a service-based, information economy among core nations. The service economy relies substantially on satellites, telecommunications, and computer technology to analyze, transfer, and communicate information. It renders obsolete traditional national borders and technological barriers to communication. This fact has significant implications for industrial and non-industrial nations alike as the military, religious, and mercantile colonialism of the past was replaced by the "electronic colonialism" of today and tomorrow (Figure 1.1).

Electronic colonialism represents the dependent relationship of poorer regions on the post industrial nations caused and established by the importation of communication hardware and foreign-produced software, along with engineers, technicians, and related information protocols, that establish a set of foreign norms, values, and expectations that, to varying degrees, alter domestic cultures, languages, habits, values, and the socialization process itself. From comic books to satellites, computers to fax machines, CDs and DVDs, smartphones to the internet, a wide range of information technologies make it easy to send and thus receive information.

The issue of how much imported material the receiver retains is critical. The concern is that this new foreign information, frequently favoring the English language, will cause the displacement, rejection, alteration, or forgetting of native or indigenous customs, domestic messages, or cultural history. Now poorer regions fear electronic colonialism as much as, and perhaps even more, than they feared the mercantile colonialism of the eighteenth and nineteenth centuries. Whereas mercantile colonialism sought to control cheap labor and the hands of laborers, electronic colonialism seeks to influence and control the mind. It is aimed at influencing attitudes, desires, beliefs, lifestyles, and consumer behavior. As the citizens of peripheral nations are increasingly viewed through the prism of consumerism, influencing and controlling their values, habits, and purchasing patterns becomes increasingly important to multinational firms.[14]

When viewers watch the television show *Baywatch*, they vicariously learn about Western society and mores. *Baywatch*, which began in 1989, hit a peak in the mid-1990s when more than one billion people a week in nearly 150 countries viewed it. With shows like this, along with *Dallas, Knots Landing, All in the Family, Friends*, or *Fresh Prince of Bel-Air*, foreign viewers began to develop a different mental set and impression of the United States. Another example is *The Simpsons*, the longest running prime-time animated cartoon ever developed. The show has now surpassed 300 episodes and is widely distributed around the globe. It has a leading cartoon character, Homer Simpson, who thrives on being a moron and placing his family and friends in bizarre situations. The show and characters thrive on portraying the distasteful aspects of US life, culture, education, and community. Yet the program has been so successful that not only does it continue, but it has also spawned other weekly animation shows such as *South Park*. Likewise, movies such as *Basic Instinct, Rambo, Scarface, Silence of the Lambs, Natural Born Killers*, and *Texas Chainsaw Massacre* deliver the trappings of an alternative lifestyle, culture, language, economy, or political system that go far beyond the momentary images flickering on the screen. Electronic colonialism theory details the possible the long-term consequences of exposure to these media images and messages to extend the powerful multinational media empires' markets, power, and influence.

Not surprisingly, the recent rise of nationalism in many areas of the world seeks to counter these neo-colonialist effects. Many of these newer nations are former colonies of European powers. Their goal is to maintain political, economic, and cultural control of their own history, images, and national destiny. It is within these cultural issues that students of journalism, cultural studies, communication, and telecommunications find theoretical, policy, and research interest. For example, issues that concern both developing nations and the industrial ones, and frequently find them on opposing sides, are the performance and role of international wire services, global television networks, advertising agencies, and the internet.[15]

History of Electronic Colonialism Theory

Prior to World War I, when international communication consisted primarily of mail, some newspapers were crossing national borders, along with limited electronic communication, which was a mixture of wireless and telegraph systems using Morse code, also crossing international boundaries. There was no international communication theory.[16] Also, the feature film industry was in its infancy, but there were examples of movies created in one nation being shown in another nation. For example, Hollywood exported to both Canada and Mexico some of its major films, even at this early stage. Likewise some European films were exhibited in movie houses in other nations.

This early communication era was dominated by the systematic exploitation by powerful European nations of foreign colonies that were to be a source of cheap labor and raw materials. In turn, these resources were manufactured into finished goods and sent back to the various colonies. Many of the onsite colonial leaders were either government officials or wealthy European families who dispatched many locals to rural or remote areas. Examples of this phenomenon are the Maori tribes in Australia and New Zealand, Native Indians across North America, Zapatistas in Mexico, French Canadians in Québec, and many tribes across Africa. Given the pervasiveness of Great Britain's colonial empire, the non-commercial British Broadcasting Corporation (BBC), which was founded in 1922, was also exported as the operating model for many new radio systems that were being started across the globe. Reuters, then a British wire-service, covered British expeditions for English language newspapers.

During the late 1920s and 30s, there did emerge an alternative workers' culture which promoted a grassroots orientation to art, culture and some local media. Labor organizations sought to promote folk art, decentralize the bourgeoisie orientation of the elite cultural industries, like opera, and promote local media with a non-commercial orientation. During this phase there emerged a European group of critical scholars, now referred to in the literature as the Frankfurt School. A group of philosophers which included Herbert Marcuse, Jurgen Habermas, Max Honkheimer, and Theodor Adorno developed a body of theory critical of power elites. To some extent they planted the seeds of electronic colonialism theory by focusing academic attention on ownership and power issues.

Many labor-based and critical initiatives became mute for two major structural reasons: the Great Depression and World War II. It was only after the end of World War II in 1945 that there was substantial international expansion of the mass media and trans-border activities involving communication as well as cultural products. Global advertising also became a growth area. In addition, many of the academics associated with the Frankfurt School relocated to North American universities and some American critical scholars would take up the cultural imperialism track or viewpoint over time.

After World War II, the United Nations on December 10, 1948 recognized the growing importance of the interaction of culture and the arts within the Universal Declaration of Human Rights. Article 27 of the 30 article proclamation states.

1   Everyone has the right freely to participate in the cultural life of the community, to enjoy the arts and to share in scientific advancement and its benefits.
2   Everyone has the right to the protection of the moral and material interests resulting from any scientific, literary or artistic production of which he is author."[17]

National government media services, such as the BBC, the US's Voice of America, or Canada's Radio Canada International, along with many others, began to expand their activities into multiple languages with a strong desire to promote fundamental concepts of free speech, free press, and democracy, particularly in light of a campaign to thwart, counter, or indeed stop the growing global threat and rise of communism. Most short-`wave, government backed radio services promoted a Cold-War agenda in their broadcasts.

In the late 1960s and throughout the 1970s, the debate about international communication moved to the halls of UNESCO in Paris, France. Certain constituencies, such as the old Soviet Union countries, academics in Nordic and Latin America countries, and some social democratic party forces across Europe, began to express early concern about the negative impact of Western culture and the global economy. Although there was significant support for non-commercial media systems, there was also concern expressed about global syndication of Hollywood films and television shows, along with the impact of music, particularly that emanating from the United Kingdom and the United States, under the banner of rock-and-roll. This debate about the importation of junk culture, much like junk food, hit a responsive chord at UNESCO. A major UNESCO-sponsored research report, which confirmed the imbalances in global media flows, is known as the MacBride Report (1980). The report added momentum to the anti-one-way flow debate. Eventually the debate about NWICO and its various elements by 1985 led the United States and Great Britain to withdraw from UNESCO in protest.

During the 1980s, under the philosophical mantra of US President Ronald Reagan, a new era of privatization, liberalization, and deregulation not only took hold in North America, but also across Europe, strongly promoted by Prime Minister Margaret Thatcher in the United Kingdom. There was a significant emphasis on market forces, free enterprise, and entrepreneurship, and a strong reversal of any type of sympathy or support for non-commercial media, government regulation, or public ownership of telecommunication systems. Market forces also led to a flurry of mergers and acquisitions across the communication sector. Consolidation created global giants and this trend continues. In 2004, WPP, a British-based advertising firm, purchased the US-based Grey Global and Sony of Japan bought MGM. One new global player deserves to be singled out. Namely the creation of a satellite delivered all news network, Cable News Network (CNN) by Ted Turner in 1980, which would come to significantly alter the global news as well as other broadcasting practices.

Finally, during this period, there were three seminal documents that formed the basis for a school of cultural imperialism. To some extent these were forerunners to eventual development of the electronic colonialism theory. In particular, Herbert Schiller's 1969 work entitled *Mass Communication and American Empire*, Tapio Varis' work for UNESCO and his 1974 article entitled "Global Traffic in Television," and Jeremy Tunstall's 1977 book, *The Media are American*, served as a new catalyst and basis for promoting critical research in terms of analyzing international communication flows, impact, and imbalances. Critical scholars such as Dan Schiller and Bob McChesney along with others are still carrying some of the research on. Yet it would not be until the 1990s that a major new group finally emerged as a global non-governmental organization (NGO).

The International Network for Cultural Development (INCD) was established in 1998 to defend cultural expression, cultural diversity, and promote national and multilingual cultural expression. It sought to promote genuine authentic media, rather than or indeed to counter the impact of the dominance of English language mass media which controlled the flow of cultural products across national boundaries. The INCD took up the debate on international communication with new vigor and sought out new global participants, including senior government officials. They were opposed to multinational communication corporations promoting a homogenized global culture. INCD, along with UNESCO, and several academics sought to align themselves with government officials to promote an alternative to the market-based, free enterprise capitalist system, which was clearly dominating global communication and served the interests of mainly American media conglomerates. A major goal of INCD is to promote through the auspices of UNESCO an international convention that now defines and aims to protect cultural and linguistic diversity along with support for open artistic expression.

Much of the dominance that occurred since the middle of the twentieth century has been documented in a 1981 work entitled *Electronic Colonialism: The Future of International Broadcasting and Communication*, with a Foreword by Everett Rogers, which was published by Sage Publishers, with a revised and updated second edition in 1986 (McPhail, 1986). This early work, along with the first edition of *Global Communication*, documented and expanded the literature about international communication. Collectively these works laid the groundwork and further amplified the theory of electronic colonialism. It is this theory to which we now turn and add additional details.

What is Electronic Colonialism Theory (ECT)?

Just as mercantile colonialism focused on empires seeking the toil and soil of others, frequently as colonies, so now ECT looks at how to capture the minds and to some extent the consumer habits of others. ECT focuses on how global media, including advertising, influence how people look, think, and act. The aim of ECT is to account for how the mass media influence the mind. Just as the era of the Industrial Revolution focused on manual labor, raw materials, and then finished products, so also the Information Revolution now seeks to focus on the role and consequences concerning the mind and global consumer behavior.

Consider how culture is conveyed in a multimedia world. Historically grandparents and tribal elders played a central role in recreating, transmitting, and transferring culture. They relied on oral communication along with family, community, or tribal connections. Culture is basically an attitude; it is also learned. It is the learning of shared language and perceptions, which are incorporated in the mind through education, repetition, ritual, history, media, or mimicking. In terms of the media's expanding role, it becomes a shared media culture including influencing perceptions and values. Examples of media systems that attract heavy users are Hollywood movies, MTV, ESPN (Entertainment and Sports Programming Network), soap operas, CNN, the internet, or video games. These systems tend to be the output of global communication giants, such as Time Warner, Disney, Viacom, Sony, and News Corp. Collectively they have the real potential to displace or alter previous cultural values, language, lifestyles or habits, activities, or family rituals. This is particularly true for heavy users of one or two external media. Over time, ECT states that these changes can and usually do impact friends, family, and community ties. A virtual community or new friends who share two things replace the latter. First, a preoccupation with identical media, such as MTV, talk radio, Facebook, or Al-Jazeera, and second, the embedded media culture that involves new or different messages, perception, learning, and habits. An example of this is the new sub-culture of black slang. It is at the core of the new media induced culture for this group. Rap music, movies, concerts, dress, and playgrounds repeat and reinforce this niche linguistic trend.

A way to look at ECT is to think that we go through life wearing various masks. We come to learn how to play out the appropriate roles, such as child, parent, spouse, student, immigrant, minority, athlete, or boss.[18] But with ECT the masks become somewhat invisible because we begin to think and feel different, as we become what we watch, do, or listen to. The media become a veil of collective new images, which we absorb into our minds and eventually, even if subtly, begin to act out, dress, or speak differently as we consume input from the mass media rather than from family, community, or former friends. The socialization process is hijacked by the media empires rather than colonial empires of days gone by. It is as if we have moved with modernization from a tribal state where culture was located in a fixed territory, region, or nation to a mediated state of mind where we might have more in common with someone or some group halfway around the world via the internet or MTV rather than in our own house, school, or neighborhood.

Now with ECT a new culture has emerged that is a global phenomenon driven primarily by large multimedia conglomerates. They control, reproduce, and spread the global flow of words, images, and sounds. They seek to impact the audiences' minds without regard to geography.[19] Their audiovisual products become sold and standardized without regard to time or space. They are marketed to international consumers who come to view their world outlook and buying habits as the logical outcome of a new media culture, as outlined and identified by ECT. For example, many Hollywood films and DVD sales now make more revenue outside the United States than at home; or MTV, Disney, Microsoft, and Google, have more aggressive expansion plans outside the US than inside. A good example is IBM. Over 70 percent of all IBM employees work and live outside the US. For many conglomerates the US domestic market is saturated and thus offshore sales, audiences, consumers, or expansion is a logical trend that is enabled and explained by the phenomenon of ECT. The leading American communication giants describe themselves as global companies and not US companies. Their corporate strategic plans all focus on expanding global markets and developing products and services for international consumption. They position themselves as stakeholders, beneficiaries, and advocates of the global economy. They are the foot-soldiers of electronic colonialism.

World System Theory (WST)

World system theory provides the concepts, ideas, and language for structuring international communication. It was proposed and developed by Immanuel Wallerstein.[20] The theory has also been linked to dependency theory[21] in that some of the criticisms are similar to the rhetoric and writings of the critical school of media scholars. Others have applied world system theory to specific sectors, as Thomas Clayton did to comparative education, or George Barnett did to telecommunications.[22] This chapter develops world system theory as it applies to international communication. The previously explained theory of electronic colonialism applies directly to the actions and reactions in the "semiperiphery" and "periphery" zones, as developed by Wallerstein and others. These zones constitute prime export markets for multimedia firms.

World system theory states that global economic expansion takes place from a relatively small group of core-zone nation-states out to two other zones of nation-states, these being in the semiperipheral and peripheral zones. These three groupings or sectors of nation-states have varying degrees of interaction on economic, political, cultural, media, technical, labor, capital, and social levels. The contemporary world structure follows the logic of economic determinism in which market forces rule in order to place as well as determine the winners and losers whether they are individuals, corporations, or nation-states.[23] It is assumed that the zones exhibit unequal and uneven economic relations, with the core nations being the dominant and controlling economic entity. The core nations have the power and are essentially the major Western industrialized nations. The semiperiphery and periphery nations are in a subordinate position when interacting with core nations. Core nations exert control to their benefit and define the nature and extent of interactions with the other two zones. Core

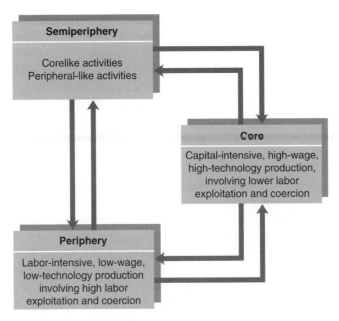

Figure 1.2   Relationships in the capitalist world economy
Source: Thomas Shannon, *An Introduction to the World-System Perspective* (Boulder, CO: Westview Press, 1989), p. 29. © 1989, 1996 by Westview Press. Reprinted by permission of Westview Press, a member of Perseus Books, LLC.

nations define the relations between the core and the semiperiphery as well as the core and the periphery. The core provides technology, software, capital, knowledge, finished goods, and services to the other zones, which function as consumers and markets. The core nations also force a neo-liberal approach concerning free markets and deregulation with the two weaker zones. The semiperiphery and periphery zones engage in the relationship with core nations primarily through providing low-cost labor, raw materials, mass markets, or low-cost venues for feature films. Mass media technology (hardware) or products (software) represent finished goods or services that reinforce and frequently dominate relations between the three sectors. World system theory is useful in examining cultural industries, mass media systems, audiovisual industries, technology transfer, knowledge, regulatory regimes, and activities of the biggest global stakeholders, which pursue interrelated strategies to maximize corporate growth, market share, revenues, and profits.

Thomas Shannon describes the economic, labor, technology, and other processes among the three zones, as shown in Figure 1.2.

Central to these relationships is the learning of appropriate economic values that facilitate modernization. Some of these values are conveyed through advertising as well as in the content of Western core-produced mass media exports. Also central to the relationships among the sectors is a mass communication system that allows the transfer of media materials to create either a broadly based popular culture for a mass market or audience, or alternative cultures for a niche market large enough to encourage imports of select media products or services. The essential point is that despite criticisms of modernization theory and goals, there are nevertheless clear stages and goals that periphery nations need to learn, pass through, adopt, or clear as a precondition for advancing to the next zone, the semiperiphery. The nations in the semiperiphery engage in both core-like and periphery-like economic and media behavior. They strive to emulate core values over periphery values in order to become a core nation over time.

The core nations are generally considered to be the United States of America, the European Union (EU), without the most recent 10 entrants which are considered to still be semi-peripheral nations, Canada, Japan, Norway, Israel, Australia, New Zealand, South Korea, Switzerland, and South Africa.

The semi-peripheral nations are China, Brazil, India, Chile, Turkey, Mexico, Venezuela, Argentina, Russia, Saudi Arabia, Egypt, Oman, Pakistan, Croatia, Iceland, Philippines, and the 10 new members of the EU. They are Cyprus, Czech Republic, Estonia, Hungary, Latvia, Lithuania, Malta, Poland, Slovak Republic, and Slovenia). This latter group was on the fast track to become core nations since the EU provides the necessary leadership and access to capital and consumer markets to rapidly improve their economies as compared to their former status of being small and marginal nations on the world's stage. But with the global economic downturn the pace of economic gains has been slowed, and in some cases, like Hungary, has become negative. Yet over the next few decades China, Brazil, and India are also likely to become core nations and rival both the United States and the EU as world economic powers.

The peripheral nations are the least developed nations, frequently referred to as the Third World or developing countries. Most of Africa, Latin America, large parts of Asia, and the least developed member states of the former Soviet Union are in this third zone. This zone has the least trade, weakest economies, high corruption and health problems, and fewest news stories written or broadcast about them, plus the worst internet connectivity on the planet. The news stories that do appear about these countries are negative, focusing on coups, civil wars, or natural disasters. Industrialization, which is central to the rise of capitalism and capitalists, has yet to reach this peripheral zone. Literacy – the ability to read newspapers, books, or magazines – is also lacking in this last zone. A defining characteristic of the peripheral zone is the agrarian nature of their economies. They lack influence or power in defining their relations with the core, with the major exception of being able to ban all foreign media imports, as Iran and other authoritarian regimes have done (see Figure 1.3).

World system theory explains well the expansion being played out in international communication. Mass media, including television and feature films, are major vehicles (sound, print, video, and data) for conveying and indoctrinating the two subordinate zones. The dominant capitalist ideology is embedded within

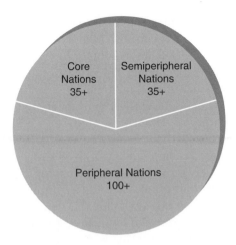

Figure 1.3   Breakdown of nations in the three world-system zones, 2010

the transactional structure, marketing, and strategic plans of the major core cultural industries. The major multinational media conglomerates come from core nations, particularly the United States and the European Union. They seek to influence, expand, and promote their range of cultural products, including books, magazines, movies, music, and so forth, into the two subordinate zones for profit. The software and hardware of international communication are constructed and marketed by core industries and enterprises. They are then sold directly or indirectly (co-productions, minority ownership, licensing agreements, etc.) to semiperipheral and peripheral nations as quickly as markets can absorb and pay for them. Just as the general world-system theory explains that capitalist ideologies are necessary for the working and expansion of the global economy, so also the major multimedia conglomerates have a parallel goal of directly enhancing their performance, both at home and abroad, by promoting and endorsing core-capitalist mechanisms and values within the two subordinate zones. Jim Collins for example, describes Walt Disney as a visionary who used his company's products "to shape society and its values." Collins continues: "From Israel to Brazil, Sweden to Australia, children grow up with the guiding hand of Walt Disney partly shaping their imaginations and world outlook."[24] This is a classic example of what electronic colonialism is all about. The business leaders of core multinational media firms seek to convert and capture the attitudes, minds, and purchasing behavior of global customers in such a fashion that their products or services are purchased first and frequently.

If the economic, social, and cultural values of core nations are not accepted and internalized by the subordinate zones, then the necessary attitudes and required behavior to purchase core-produced CDs, movies, videos, cassettes, DVDs, iPods, and books will not develop. Consumer spending is ultimately required in all zones. Core-based cultural industries and ideologies require the successful sale of core goods and services across the other two zones in order to increase market share as well as join with other core industries such as automobiles, fast food, equipment, airplanes, computers, and so on in enjoying the benefits of an expanding global economy The utilization of advertising campaigns for cultural products, which are in many instances customized for the other zones, is also part of the overall capitalist movement.

Advertising itself represents a mini "case study" of world system theory and is covered in a later chapter. Without going into excessive detail here, it is worth noting that almost all new media outlets worldwide are commercial stations, or networks, which rely solely on advertising revenue for their income and profits. This gives advertising enormous influence and a central role in the ultimate success of new ventures. Further compounding this dependency is the fact that all of the advertising agencies are multinational corporations from core nations. These core headquartered agencies bring with them everything from accounting practices, research, graphics, and artwork, along with placement strategies that are imposed on media customers in the subordinate zones, as part of their comprehensive full-service contracts. Whether the enterprises are in print, radio, television, outdoor billboard, or the internet, multinational advertising agencies frequently rule in the crucial component of the communication enterprise.

World system theory carries an implied belief that prosperity will accrue to the two subordinate zones as they become more pro-capitalist and expand their markets to include the core nations. But a major part of the prosperity problem is that as core nations expand their cultural artifacts and products to the other zones, these economic transactions often do two things. First, they require foreign customers to purchase core products, with the eventual profits returning to the multimedia conglomerates, most of which are based in Europe or the United States. Second, communication products manufactured in core nations usually displace or replace indigenous cultural products with foreign alternatives and values. Local films, music, books, and so forth in the two subordinate zones now must compete with major advertising and promotion campaigns affiliated with the core products that local firms are simply not able to afford. So when discussing prosperity, one needs to ask, prosperity for whom? Who is being rewarded? A local person or a foreign firm? As core enterprises expand into the subordinate zones, it is the multimedia firms that reap the prosperity in a measure not commensurate with their impact on or assistance in the subordinate zones.

One argument in favor of this imbalance of influence makes the case that labor, central to world system research, does benefit in the two subordinate zones. For example, when movies or television series are produced in the subordinate zones, extras, drivers, local restaurants, and merchants of all trades are involved, or when newspapers, magazines, or records are sold, a commission is paid to the local shopkeeper. Many other examples also illustrate that the subordinate zones do profit by being part of core-nation transactions. In fact, core nations actively court other core nations' media firms to undertake business in their countries. Consider the following, which deals with the filming industry and Canada–United States relations, both of which are core nations.

Many Canadian nationalists lament endlessly US media and cultural influences. Since the early introduction of radio in Canada, there has been a constant concern about the US media spillover into Canadian homes, theaters, and minds. Yet as media giants become more concerned about and focused on global markets and profitability, Canada has increasingly welcomed film-making by Hollywood movie studios and US television networks. Montreal, Toronto, and Vancouver are prime locations for US companies producing movies and television series. These productions create thousands of jobs annually and contribute millions to the Canadian economy. Canada, as the core nation physically closest to the leading core nation, the United States, has to accept the growing role that US, particularly Hollywood, studios play in its economy, employment, and culture. As media costs escalate, particularly for leading stars, Canada begins to look like Hollywood North. A *Maclean's* (Canada's weekly newsmagazine) Special Report entitled "Northern Exposure" sums up the situation like this: "Stars want good roles, studios want to save money and create good entertainment. By filming in the Great White North, they can have it all."[25]

Finally, although there is not much specific empirical media research[26] with a world system theory focus, one notable exception is a study by Kyungmo Kim and George Barnett. Their article, "The Determinants of International News Flow: A Network Analysis,"[27] is a good example of the utility of world system theory. They apply both world system and dependency theories. Following a detailed examination of international news flow across 132 nations, they conclude, "[T]he findings of this research reveal the inequality in international news flow between the core and periphery. The Western industrialized countries are at the center, dominating international news flow. Most African, Asian, Latin American, and Oceania countries are at the periphery."[28] Based on a regression analysis of their data, they further conclude:

> This center-periphery structure of the international news flow network has two implications for communication dependency. First, Western industrialized countries are at the position in which they produce and sell international news. In contrast, the peripheral countries consume and depend on their information from the core countries. One way this happens is through the maintenance of historical colonial relationships.[29]

The authors point out that not much truly global research on international news flow has been undertaken for a variety of structural reasons; this study is a major exception. In 2008 Barnett and others produced another empirical piece with a world system framework titled, "The Structure of International Aid flows and Global News." After examining AFP (Agence France Presse), AP (Associated Press), CNN, and Reuters concerning coverage, countries mentioned, and the flow of aid they conclude: "The results indicate that global news coverage is significantly related to aid allocations and relations. Recipient countries with a high level of news coverage receive more aid and have more international relations than those with less coverage."[30]

A similar twist is reported by Clifford Bob in his book, *The Marketing of Rebellion: Insurgents, Media, and International Activism* (2005).[31] After examining 45 activists and NGO leaders he concludes aid goes to those with the most media skills and not necessarily the neediest or most worthy. Getting face time on CNN or the BBC is priceless for an NGO spokesperson during a crisis. Coverage does count. Bob claims that there is a Darwinian struggle for scarce resources among NGOs. Those needed resources could be money, media exposure, or relief aid.

In conclusion, the three zones of WST reflect a world where the living standards are extremely broad. Modernization and globalization have failed to produce the economic and social change that many academics and policy experts predicted. Wallerstein recognizes this aspect when he comments:

> The whole discussion from 1945 to today has been one long effort to take seriously the reality that world-system is not only polarized but polarizing, and that this reality is both morally and politically intolerable. For countries at the bottom, there seemed nothing more urgent than figuring out how to improve their situation, and first of all economically. After all, all these people had to do was to see a movie and they would know that there were other people in the world that were better off, than they were. As for the countries at the top, they realized, however dimly, that the "huddled masses yearning to breathe free" represented a permanent danger to world order and their own prosperity, and that therefore something, somehow had to be done to dampen the tinderbox.[32]

The tinderbox is now loaded with terrorists who have two dominant traits: religious extremism and anti-Western ideologies. The Western or core nations have yet to come to grips collectively to solve this dangerous global phenomenon.

The Connection: Electronic Colonialism and World System Theories

There is a substantial and important link between the electronic colonialism theory and world system theory. ECT posits that when exported the mass media carry with them a broad range of values. These values are economic, social, cultural, and sometimes political or religious in nature. Increasingly they carry with them the English language, in terms of music, movies, or the internet. WST theory elaborates and extends ECT by dividing the nations of the globe into three categories; it then expands on how the core category works to influence the two subordinate categories. Some core nations are concerned about the impact and penetration of ECT as well. Canada, France, Great Britain, Israel, New Zealand, and Australia are prime core nations that continually worry about the Americanization of their domestic cultural industries and consumer behavior.

They realize that with each additional commercial media outlet, there will be more spent on foreign syndicated shows or royalties going elsewhere leaving even less money for indigenous productions of all genres.

Nations in the subordinate categories, mainly the semiperiphery and periphery, have a multitude of reasons, whether they be economic, social, cultural, or moral, to be concerned about the implications of ECT. Dependency theory, when referring to attitudinal shifts brought about by repetitive interactions with core businesses, is an example of ECT. For example, since the 1980s there has been a steady stream of research from Latin America on the structural impact, mostly negative, of relations with core nations, particularly the United States, but also with former colonial powers in Europe, particularly Spain. Although much of this research failed to utilize or identify either EC or WS theories as being relevant, in retrospect both theoretical constructs have much to offer in terms of organizing and explaining Latin American research and theory.

Just as WST applies to all three zones, so also ECT has different applications in each zone. Utilizing appropriate aspects of both theories will significantly enhance future research in international communication. ECT, with its cultural lens, and WST, with an economic lens, are well suited for examining jointly the global activities of multinational cultural industries.

Communication Forces among Nations

International communication as a commercial sector acts as an ideal case study of the application of world system theory. Multinational communication conglomerates, major wire-services, as well as major advertising agencies are all based in the core zone. When operating in other core nations, or in semiperipheral and peripheral nations, they do so with a well-refined and strategically set agenda drawn from the capitalist economic system. The semiperipheral and peripheral zones are viewed as prime potential markets for core-based multimedia corporations, which define the relations among the semiperiphery and periphery nations. Part of the corporate goal is to influence the attitudes and values of potential customers as explained by the theory of electronic colonialism. There is no threat of force, such as military conquest, yet marketing strategies, research, advertising, and economic savvy permit core-zone businesses to influence consumer behavior by creating appropriate global mind-sets toward their cultural products and services. Core nations thrive on market-based activities since they make the rules.

To understand the post-Cold-War global communication environment, it is necessary to understand the evolution of the two quite different views of the core-industrialized nations, and the peripheral regions are, after decades of modernization efforts, still locked into the peripheral zone. Indeed, some peripheral nations are now worse off than they were when they had European colonial masters. Their situation – in terms of economy, health, education, indigenous media, and technology – has only deteriorated over time. In order to understand this lag and fundamental dichotomy, it is necessary to review the role UNESCO played as the major global forum for many of the stakeholders to set out their views, take sides, and establish how deep-seated and structurally different their views and concerns are about international communication.

Also, during the 1990s the movements toward liberalization and privatization witnessed many nations' state-controlled and owned media monopolies under siege. The siege was not from an armed military intruder; rather, it was a mix of three new strong hegemonic communication forces. These forces were

1   expansion of cable and satellite broadcasting systems;
2   an avalanche of Western, primarily American, television and movie programming; and
3   the collective rules of the World Trade Organization, the World Bank, and the International Monetary Fund.

The three forces, hardware, software, and free market rules radically altered the media environment and balance in a vast number of core and semiperipheral nations between 1980 and today. Whereas only one or two public television channels were the norm for years, suddenly dozens of new channels and choices appeared on television sets as cable or satellite services became available around the globe. The impact was to create electronic colonies, built mostly around US shows or music, out of a new generation of viewers and listeners around the world.

For years, public-broadcasting systems, particularly in Europe, had attempted to enlighten and inform their audiences. But with new channels came new opportunities to promote entertainment, advertising, market forces, and the clear goal of making a profit. Commercial channels sought out popular programming ranging from *Big Brother*, *Millionaire*, *Weakest Link*, *Survivor*, *The Simpsons*, to soap operas and reality shows, to *Baywatch*. In their wake, they left smaller audiences for the public broadcasters, which in turn were coming under increasing pressure from politicians and regulatory authorities to do something about their shrinking audiences. At the same time, many commercial broadcasters were seeking increased revenues from public sources. Every new commercial channel that is introduced steals away a portion, even if it is small, of the audience from the public channels. The public networks find themselves being challenged seriously by three forces which in many cases are beyond their control: financial, technological, and regulatory. The new forces all emanate from core nations to the semiperipheral and peripheral zones. In these latter nations, the consumption of media from local, sometimes bland, monopolies is frequently being replaced with Western media and foreign values that have had considerable cultural, economic, regulatory, and political repercussions over time.

Breadth of the Problem

The range of global communication activities is extensive indeed. At one end of the spectrum is the large group of developing, or peripheral, nations concerned about basic communication infrastructures, such as the introduction of radio or telephone services. At the other end are core nations, some of which have been industrialized for over a century and others are concerned about their own survival in the rapidly evolving information age. They do not want to become information colonies of other nations. Communication issues related to mergers, transnational data flows, computers, censorship, privacy, and employment in cultural industries are central policy concerns for several industrialized nations, particularly across Europe. This is highlighted by the fact that today more than 50 percent of the US gross national product (GNP) depends on information-based services and industries. This means that future high skilled employment is directly related to the ability to supply all aspects of the information chain – hardware, software, and research and development – necessary to participate and be a net winner in the information age.

Clearly, for Western core nations, such as Canada, France, Switzerland, Australia, the Nordic countries and others, the notion is that they may become electronic colonies of the US. This represents a serious threat and challenge to their culture, identity, and employment opportunities in the communication sector. It is forcing a rethinking of national media philosophies and public support, including subsidies to the arts. Issues related to national sovereignty, culture, language, and electronic colonialism are once again raising questions about the appropriate role of government intervention, fiscal assistance to cultural industries, and media ownership regulations. The emergence of the electronic newspaper, interactive cable, the internet, smartphones, and direct satellite broadcasting is raising questions about the role of regulation and the concept of national borders or boundaries Although the specific questions may differ, the basic issues are not far removed from the scope of concerns that peripheral nations experience about their communication disparities and problems.

Another issue for industrialized countries relates to the growing conflict between economic and national security imperatives. From the beginning, competitive and commercial pressures have affected information flows as media outlets tried to silence the voices of their competitors. Today, the major supporters of the free-flow philosophy are governments responding to pressures from multinational corporate interests, ranging from American Express to Microsoft, IBM, and Time Warner that are seeking to protect or extend their corporate and not necessarily US national interests. What is good for IBM in selling computer systems to Iran, China, Russia, or Venezuela for example, may not necessarily be good for the national, or indeed international, interests of the United States. Yet these corporations and their advertising agencies rely on open borders and open markets, backed by the World Trade Organization, in order to compete effectively in the global economy.

Finally, it should be recognized that much of the pressure and support for the free-flow philosophy is coming from print media, both daily newspapers and major weekly magazines. Their concern is intense and historically genuine. But technology is quickly moving them toward government involvement in the dissemination of their messages. Although print and electronic media are still running on separate legal and regulatory tracks, their paths are expected to converge as print media increasingly rely on electronic information systems such as the internet to take their messages to consumers. The current wave of newspapers in distress or going out of business will continue. Their fate was predicted as early as 1980.[33] Although always regulated to some degree,[34] the print media will find themselves increasingly restrained by legislative, regulatory, or court actions that are clearly inconsistent with the spirit of the United States' First Amendment rights.

What is significant, then, is that international communication is no longer solely focused on the role of the print press and the newsgathering habits of the international news agencies, such as AP and Reuters. It is growing to encompass a broad range of issues that arise from the emergence of global broadcasting, global advertising, and the global economy. The further economic deterioration of LDCs, the pervasiveness of satellite-delivered television programming, and the ability of the internet to defy traditional means of control are all reigniting the debate about the appropriate environment for international communication, along with the appropriate role of government in global communication policy. This role is no longer limited to national governments but has clearly moved into international forums, particularly the specialized agencies of the United Nations.[35]

Format for the Balance of the Book

The foregoing highlights the general themes of this book. It examines broadcasting, mass media, and news services ranging from MSNBC, MTV, and CNN to television sitcoms and Hollywood export markets. It investigates the roles of the major players, whether they are News Corp., Sony, the BBC, Disney, Bertelsmann, Viacom, or Time Warner. It probes the role of advertising and the influences as well as future of the internet and their ability to transcend national boundaries and beliefs.

The growing importance and significance of other major regions is reflected in new chapters dealing with the Middle East media, particularly Al-Jazeera, Europe, and Asia. There is also a new chapter on public diplomacy. It focuses on the important issue of US public diplomacy in a global world of ideas and ideologies.

Global communication of all types is undergoing major reexamination. In order to be knowledgeable and understand the various factors influencing the processes of international communication, we need to know who the major stakeholders are and how certain economic and technical forces are changing the global media landscape. This book details the changes in the nature, flow, and control of all types of international communication, including news, in the future.

In order to accomplish this, the remainder of *Global Communication* outlines the major institutions, individuals, corporations, technologies, and issues that are altering the international information, telecommunication, and broadcasting order. This includes all types of media activities – wire services, internet, fax machines, electronic data, satellites, journalists, film, radio, television, cell phones, and advertising. Traditional assumptions about media flows and priorities are being challenged and altered daily. What follows is a descriptive and analytical portrayal of how certain events, some very recent, are affecting the domestic and foreign information environments of today and tomorrow. Central to the discussion are the collapse of communism, the importance of global media and communication organizations, the global wars and their coverage, the influence of global advertisers, and, finally, the substantial and somewhat unanticipated impact of personal computers, mobile devices, and the internet.

These issues are explained and interpreted through three major theories or movements: NWICO, electronic colonialism, and world system theories. Collectively, they help organize or frame the trends, economics, technologies, and stakeholders involved in the dynamic, globally significant, and expanding role of international communication. Part of the dynamic is the pace of mergers and acquisitions affecting several of the global communication stakeholders. As the global economy evolves and increases in influence, international communication moves in unison with it. The other part is the rapid pace of innovation of technologies which support and to a large extent make easier global communication. International communication will have a greater impact on the future of the planet than exploration and transportation combined.

Notes

1. Hong-Won Park, "A Gramacian Approach to Interpreting International Communication," *Journal of Communication* 48(4) (1998): 79.
2. *USA Today* (September 16, 2004): 7A.
3. Seth Lewis and Stephen Reese, "What is the War on Terror? Framing through the Eyes of Journalists," *Journalism and Mass Communication Quarterly*, 86 (spring 2009): 85.
4. Michael Phillips, "Army Deploys Old Tactic in PR War," *Wall Street Journal* (June 1, 2009): 1A.
5. Sallie Hughes and Chappell, "The Barriers to Media Opening in Latin America, *Political Communication* 22 (2005): 9–10.
6. David Holman, "Economic Policy and Latin America Culture: Is a Virtuous Circle Possible?" *Journal of Latin American Studies* 31 (February 1999): 176.
7. *New York Times* (September 13, 1998), sec. WK: 7
8. Jill Hills, *The Struggle for Control of Global Communication: The Formative Century*, Urbana, IL: University of Illinois Press, 2002.

9. There are several ways of defining and categorizing the nations of the world. Frequent dichotomies include North–South, East–West, developed–underdeveloped, socialist–capitalist, industrialized–Third World. Another system categorizes according to core, semiperipheral, and peripheral. Although the system is far from perfect, this book will use the following: Western nations include the industrialized nations, which according to the World Bank are Australia, Great Britain, Canada, Finland, France, Italy, Japan, The Netherlands, Sweden, Switzerland, United States, and Germany. Most of these are situated in the North and are core nations. The peripheral nations are located mainly in Asia, Africa, and Latin America-generally to the South.

    It also should be noted that nations are continually obtaining independence or moving back and forth on both the political and economic continua. Examples include Russia, Indonesia, Iran, Iraq, Mexico, Brazil, former Yugoslavia, Venezuela, and Poland. No definition will fit accurately over time. Therefore, the terms are used for the sake of convenience because they reflect the major global parties involved in the NWICO debate. These categories also apply to the theories of electronic colonialism and world system that will be detailed later.

10. Ha-Joon Chang, *Bad Samaritans: The Myth of Free Trade and the Secret History of Capitalism*, New York: Bloomsbury Press, 2008.

11. *The Economist* (October 17, 1998): 50.

12. Morton Rosenblum, *Coups and Earthquake*, New York: Harper & Row, 1979, pp. 1–2.

13. Ibid.

14. Cultural reproduction theorists view international media initiatives as a means of reproducing and socializing students in peripheral nations into knowledge systems that make them more compatible with Western ideals and, equally important, Western consumer values. Cultural reproduction theorists see foreign mass media as reproducing and socializing the populace of other nations into a knowledge system or frame of mind that will make them more compatible with or sympathetic to foreign ideas and consumer values. See Alan Hedley, "Technological Diffusion or Cultural Imperialism? Measuring the Information Revolution," *International Journal of Comparative Sociology*, 39(2) (June 1998): 198–213. Hedley states, "Also flowing from this analysis is the potential for cultural dominance that the information revolution may foster. However, unlike previous technological revolutions, what are at stake are the very minds and thought processes of those dominated. Only powerful nations currently have the ability to choose the type of information society most compatible with their cultural institutions" (p. 210). Edward Goldsmith, "Development as Colonialism," *The Ecologist*, 27(2) (March–April 1997): 69–78, focuses on the role of transnational corporations and their expanding development of the global economy. He concludes, "The new corporate colonialism is thus likely to be far more cynical and more ruthless than anything we have seen so far. It is likely to dispossess, impoverish and marginalize more people, destroy more cultures and cause more environmental devastation than either the colonialism of old or the development of the last 50 years. The only question is. How long can it last?" (p. 76).

15. The major global stakeholders for all these sectors are detailed in later chapters. Some readers may want to refer to these chapters now.

16. Hills, Jill. *The Struggle for Control of Global Communication*, Chicago: University of Illinois Press, 2002.

17. United Nations, *Universal Declaration of Human Rights*, 1948.

18. Napier, David. *Righting the Passage: Perceptions of Change after Modernity*, Philadelphia: University of Pennsylvania Press, 2004.

19. Al Reis and Jack Trout, *Positioning: The Battle for Your Mind*, New York: McGraw Hill, 2001.

20 Immanuel Wallerstein, *The Modern World System*, New York: Academic Press, 1974, *The Modern World System III*, San Diego Academic Press, 1989, and "National Development and the World System at the End of the Cold War" in A. Inkeles and M. Sasaki (eds.), *Comparing Nations and Cultures: Readings in a Cross-disciplinary Perspective*, Englewood Cliffs: Prentice-Hall, 1996, pp. 484–97. A definition of world system theory, along with a fine review of research trends, is contained in Thomas Hall's "The World-System Perspective a Small Sample from a Large Universe," *Sociological Inquiry*, 66(4) (November 1996): 440–54.

21. André Frank, *Capitalism and Underdevelopment in Latin America* (New York: Monthly Review Press, 1969), Barnett Singer and John Langdon, "France's Imperial Legacy," *Contemporary Review*, 27(2) (May 1998): 231–8; Alvin So, *Social Change and Development: Modernization, Dependency, and World System Theory*, Newbury Park: Sage, 1990.

22. Thomas Clayton, "Beyond Mystification: Reconnecting World System Theory for Comparative Education," *Comparative Education Review*, 42 (November 1998): 479–94; George Barnett and Young Choi, "Physical Distance and Language as Determinants of the International Telecommunications Network," *International Political Science Review*, 16(3) (1995): 249–5.

23. Or groups of nation-states such as those in NAFTA, the European Union, ASEAN, or MERCOSUR.

24. Jim Collins, "Shaping Society," *USA Today* (September 23, 1999): 19A.

25. "Northern Exposure," *Macleans* (October 11, 1999): 71.

26. John Comer, Philip Schlesinger, and Roger Silverstone (eds.), *International Media Research: A Critical Survey*, London: Routledge, 1997.

27. Kyungmo Kim and George Barnett, "The Determinants of International News Flow: A Network Analysis," *Communication Research*, 23 (June 1996): 323–52, G. Barnett, T. Jacobson, and S. Sun-Millar, "An Examination of the International Communication Network, *Journal of International Communication*, 3(3) (1996): 19–43; G. Barnett, "A Longitudinal Analysis of the International Telecommunications Network: 1978–1996." *American Behavioral Scientist*, 44(10) (June 2001): 1638–55; G. Barnett, B. S. Chon, and D. Rosen, "The Structure of International Internet Flows in Cyberspace," *NETCOM (Network and Communication Studies)*, 15(1–2) (September 2001): 61–80.

28. Yon Soo Lim, George Barnett, and Jang Hyun Kim, *Journal of International Communication*, 14(2) (2008): 139.

29. Kim and Barnett, 1996, p. 344.

30. Kim and Barnett, 1996, p. 346.

31. Clifford Bob, *Marketing of Rebellion: Insurgents, Media, and International Activism*, New York: Cambridge University Press, 2005.

32. Immanuel Wallerstein, "After Developmentalism and Globalization, What?" *Social Forces* (March 2005) 83(3): 1265–6.

33. In 1980, after examining a series of emerging video-text systems across North America, I realized that newspaper industry was a prime target for eventual competition from a coalescing of electronic inventions. For example, in Chapter 1 of a public policy study, which was titled "The Electronic Newspaper," I predicted in prescient fashion basically what is unfolding today.

   What does all this mean, or what should it mean, for daily newspaper people? Basically, it means the door-to-door newspaper as we know it today is on the skids.

While it is difficult, if not impossible, to determine the rate of transition to the electronically disseminated newspaper, it is reasonable to believe that a major part of this transition will occur within this century. Clearly, it will not be an overnight change. However, certain newspaper services will slowly be transferred to a computerized videotext system. As more and more of these services leave the prototype stage and begin operating as subscription services, the financial viability of the newspaper will become increasingly challenged. At the same time, the financial ability of information providers to develop and to encourage additional information services will increase, T. L. McPhail, *The Future of the Daily Newspaper: Public Policy Issues*, Institute for Research on Public Policy, Montreal, Canada, 1980, pp. 5–6.

34. This refers to journalistic limitations. Most agree that there should be no limitations on the political, economic, or social consequences of investigative journalism, but clearly there are legal limitations. These include the laws related to libel, slander, defamation, obscenity, and so forth that do constrain what is printed or aired. For example, in 2004 US Federal officials in order to charge journalists from major media outlets with illegal activities used the Intelligence Identities Protection Act of 1982.

35. Another forum is the 46 nations International Network for Cultural Diversity (INCD), which began with a meeting in Canada in 1998, followed by meetings in Mexico, Greece, Switzerland, South Africa, and Croatia, plus a growing number of regional meetings. These meetings focus on cultural identity, cultural policy, and the impact of cultural globalization. A growing concern of the member nations is the treatment of cultural industries, particularly television, film, and magazines by the World Trade Organization (WTO). The INCD group, which does not include the United States, views the WTO's policies as favoring the one way flow of Hollywood and New York products around the globe to the detriment of local cultures. One policy option being floated at INCD meetings is to remove cultural goods and services from WTO agreements. This initiative has major implications concerning global trade for the major stakeholders detailed in future chapters.

Finally, Canada is providing leadership for the INCD group for the obvious reason that it is on the cutting edge of becoming an electronic colony of the United States to a very large extent. It has become a branch plant of US media empires. The foreign content of Canada's mass media is staggering. Consider the following 98 percent of theater revenues are for foreign, mainly Hollywood, films; 83 percent of magazines, such as *Time*, *Newsweek*, and *Sports Illustrated*, sold are foreign, 80 percent of music sales in all formats are foreign; and more than 60 percent of television programming on the three national networks comes from other nations, despite decades of electronic media content regulations, along with handsome financial subsidies, from the Canadian federal government.

2

Development Research Traditions and Global Communication

Introduction

The chapter looks at the changing area of development communication. This area has focused on Third World issues and how modernization has essentially failed to deliver change in developing nations or regions. The lack of telephone service, illiteracy, few indigenous media successes, and lack of connectivity to the internet all come into play. After six decades of development, the Third World or peripheral nations still lack access to modern telecommunications and mass media. This chapter addresses the history, major approaches or theories, the role of NGOs, the competition for resources, "the CNN effect," and the paradigm shift underway at the time of writing.

It is this shift which will be the focus of this chapter. The key aspect is that for decades the old paradigm of modernization had an economic focus or lens decades whereas the new focus is on policy matters with a social and cultural lens. One of the emerging roles is how are media and telecom systems promoting democracy as well as broader quality of life/environment issues. Part of the change is a bottom-up or grass roots approach rather than top down which has dominated the field since the end of World War II. Much of the early emphasis, projects, and funding was motivated by a desire to thwart the growth of communism around the globe, particularly in underdeveloped nations.[1]

Over the past decade some objections to globalization have emerged. Not all see the same benefits, if any. The benefits of globalization are not evenly shared by all. Compounding this criticism is the post-Cold-War fear of the United States becoming a hegemonic power and defining aid and international policies to suit donor nation goals, and not receiving nation's needs and goals. The area of family planning and the role of women is a particularly sensitive area. There has been a significant increase in feminist scholarship dealing with the media within a development context during this same time frame. Other factors include what is now being referred to as coercive democracy where the USA is combining its post-Cold-War military power with its hegemonic economic power to set conditions on foreign aid or international treaties that cripple weak nations or regions. The bulk of the benefits from aid and treaties tend to go to Western nations while others in the Third World see little improvement.

During the 1980s, several factors came together to further the movement questioning Western aid, globalization, free market values, and the impact of foreign media. Among these factors was the failure and subsequent rejection of the theory of modernization promulgated by major industrialized, core nations, and aid agencies since the close of World War II. Implementation of that model had failed to produce positive economic results in the eyes of peripheral nations. In reality, after decades of core-based modernization attempts, some peripheral nations were worse off and others had made little progress. Within the overall theoretical framework, the mass communication system was a substantial component among the mix of factors that cumulatively should have moved peripheral nations to at least semiperipheral status and then to industrialization and modernization. Herein lays the connection between modernization theory and development communication. In theory, development communication should work in concert with other growth factors to lead poorer nations to modernization or, at least, to move them from the peripheral zone to the semiperipheral zone. In practice, those peripheral nations that did invest in media infrastructures realized too late that these systems were bringing in more foreign, not local, content. For example, where cable or satellite media were introduced, affluent locals watched CNN, the BBC, or MTV rather than domestic broadcasters.[2]

In retrospect, just as educational television in the West failed to bring about the projected revolution in the classroom, the prediction that broadcasting was the means by which poor nations could rapidly transform into industrialized nations was similarly off course. Indeed, during the last decade, some peripheral nations moved in the opposite direction with regard to their housing, environment, currency, literacy, and health care, particularly with the spread of AIDS (acquired immune deficency syndrome).

Some poor nations, for example, assumed that the introduction of color television is the appropriate medium to foster economic and cultural development. But color television is expensive and has limited uses and applications. In peripheral nations where color television broadcasting is available, few households even have access to black-and-white television sets. Digital television, which is now the standard in core nations, is raising a new issue and barrier. This new technology will render existing analog broadcasting systems and their receivers obsolete. In their eagerness to "measure up," many peripheral nations are likely to desire the digital format and related new technology, but its costly introduction is likely to set back, rather than promote, development.

The balance of this chapter traces the various streams of the major theories of communication, both American and European, as well as major research trends that underpin the knowledge base for students of international communication. Beginning with development theory, the review highlights major contributions to the theoretical and applied international media research literature. The chapter concludes with a discussion of the application and implications of the theories of electronic colonialism and world-system theory.

Development Journalism/Communication

Development journalism and communication are attempts to counterbalance the thrust toward electronic colonialism. They acknowledge that the demands of an infant press differ from those of a mature press. To impose the legal, economic, or regulatory models of one onto the other results in a failure to appreciate the underlying fundamental differences that are a result of a combination of historical and cultural factors. Development journalism is the concept that attempts to deal with the needs, strengths, and aspirations of journalistic endeavors in the emerging developing nation-states.[3] It is a media theory that encourages an engineered press – a press committed to government set priorities and objectives. It assumes that all efforts, including local media, need to work in unison to support national goals. Totalitarian and military regimes in a substantial number of peripheral nations follow and enforce this media theory and approach.

Consequently, development journalism essentially serves to promote the needs of developing countries. It encourages indigenous media and discourages reproduction of Western media models, which debase, challenge, or marginalize local and traditional cultures. Most peripheral media systems are underdeveloped, with few newspapers, some radio outlets, and usually one television system, at most. Access to the internet is very limited. Under these conditions, administrators, editors, and reporters in peripheral regions find little relevance in Western media values and systems, which do not serve the needs of peripheral nations or highlight their interests or concerns. Except for the occasional political coup or natural disaster, all focusing on bad news, few of their stories are told in the mainstream media and even less is revealed from the peripheral nations' own perspective. In fact, research indicates that the vast majority of international media offerings emanate from a few core nations as sources. Consider the following:

1. Major Western news agencies such as the Associated Press, Bloomberg, Reuters, and Agence France Presse provide about 90 percent of the entire world's wire service information. They are all based in core nations.
2. Major Western newspapers, magazines, and journals are virtually all published in the United States or Europe. In Europe, most of these media come from foreign colonial powers and still enjoy significant sales in current or former colonies.

3. International radio programming such as Voice of America (United States), the BBC (United Kingdom), Deutsche Welle (Germany), and other Western short-wave services transmit programming specifically designed for international audiences. The perspective is invariably that of the Western core industrial nations, but the majority of the global audience is in non-core nations.

4. Global television news, newsreels, photos supplied by firms such as CNN, BBC, AP, Getty, and Reuters have established worldwide markets for their products using material produced or designed for initial use in the United States, Europe, or other Western media and communication systems.

5. Television programming and feature films are almost exclusively the province of Western nations. Over two-thirds of available global video programming comes from the United States alone.

6. All major global advertising agencies are based in the United States, Europe, or Japan. If there is any physical presence of agencies at all in semiperipheral or peripheral nations, it is only in the form of small branch offices of the leading global agencies.

7. Getty Images is now another major provider of photographs and imagery, along with the wire-services, so that the visual imagery or lens has a Western bias. Getty Images basically moved the fragmented stock photography industry into the digital age.

Although the seeds of a theory of development journalism were sown shortly after World War II, it was decades before the debate about the role of the mass media reached the West. Originally, the dominant paradigm for development communication reflected a mainstream consensus of opinion among all stakeholders that encouraged both economic and industrial growth. It was assumed that as the gross domestic product (GDP) increased, so too would communication activities of all types, including the development of telecommunication as well as mass media systems. This economic-based "growth is good" model or mantra was the underpinning for modernization theory. It ignored the fact that enormous capital investment was required to finance sustainable communication development. Without adequate domestic professional and fiscal resources, peripheral nations found themselves even more dependent on external foreign aid, which invariably had strings attached. Also many of the aid projects had cultural baggage associated with them, such as abandoning certain cultural traditions, but this was ignored or downplayed.

Over time, piecemeal programs evolved to encourage development. However, it soon became clear that foreign aid turned out to be little more than a weapon on the Cold-War battlefield. The Soviet Union supported communist-oriented nations and regions, and the United States assisted fledgling democracies ostensibly committed to a free enterprise model. Moreover, uncounted sums of this aid were skimmed off by corrupt regimes, military officials, or wasted by inept, untrained bureaucrats with good intentions but little experience with large-scale development projects. This blatant failure to improve the conditions in developing countries led to a rethinking of development communication.

The immediate result of such rethinking was manifest in sensitivity to the structural and cultural constraints on the impact of communication, in addition to conscious awareness that the mass media were just a part of the total communication infrastructure. It became evident that successful and effective use of communication in any community requires adequate knowledge of the availability, accessibility, relationships, and utilization of communication infrastructure and software in that community.[4]

The problems were not limited to the lack of communication progress in developing nations; some critics found fault with Western researchers who ignored indigenous media and failed to stress the importance of sustaining local cultures. African scholar Kwasi Ansu-Kyeremeh states, "[T]he paltry literature regarding various interpretations of indigenous communication systems elsewhere and in Africa"[5] is a problem in itself. And this lack of relevant models is only part of the problem in peripheral nations. Ank Linden points out, "Governmental authorities in Third World countries often seem to be more interested in maintaining the status quo than in strengthening the communication capacity of the people."[6] Many peripheral leaders did not want external help which could jeopardize their control of the people along with the ability to skim off much of the foreign aid. When this happened American and other officials were willing to look the other way as long as the regimes were anticommunist. Concern about the sociology and culture of communication, whether in the form of folklore transmitted orally or as color television transmitted live via satellite, heightened the need for a revised vision of cultural development and the role of communication in it. Whereas the Western media valued freedom of the press, free speech, and the free flow of information, most peripheral nations began to reject these and related values as luxuries they could not afford. They had no multitude of competing views and media systems. Most of these countries were fortunate to have a single electronic medium, usually radio. What is more, as illiteracy on a world scale continues to increase, a widely accessible printed press remains a distant dream, if not an illusion, for many emerging nation-states. Finally, of course, virtually all peripheral regions lack the necessary telecommunications infrastructure required for modern media systems, including cellular phones and access to the internet.

Moreover, the position of peripheral nations on the role of government control conflicted with that of the core and democratic nations. In some cases, development media initiatives sought the support of local governments, and in others the governments imposed rigid controls. In both situations, the media had little choice but to accept and repeat the messages those in control wished to disseminate. The result was two diametrically opposed journalist philosophies about the relationship between the media and government. The Western journalists favored a free press, and LDC journalists followed a development journalism approach.

Development journalism/communication is a pivotal concept in this new environment. Its proponents are newly emerging nations, all in the periphery, primarily in Africa, Latin America, and Asia, with low income, high illiteracy rates, and virtually no modern media systems. The infrastructure and finances to support an advanced telecommunications system simply do not exist. Where they do exist, they are controlled by the ruling elites. As the poor countries see it, in order to rapidly improve the economic and social position of peripheral nations, a concerted effort by both government and media is required. The "luxury" of competing and critical views on government policies and programs within the national media is viewed as detrimental to the colossal task of "catching up."

In order to correct the imbalances and mistaken impressions created by the Western press, peripheral nations continue to promote their media theory of development journalism. At a practical level, they reject neutrality and objectivity in favor of active roles as promoters of government objectives. They engage in advocacy journalism. Their reporting reflects the stated objectives of their governments, and they see no conflict with this. In some instances, some countries attempt to limit any positive reporting of Western activities. In some cases only negative stories are disseminated in order to reinforce the view of the West as the "Great Satan." Unfortunately, in doing so, the development press commits the same grievous crime it so readily attributes to the Western press.

Finally, many media corporations based in Europe and North America have reduced their number of reporters in Africa, Asia, and Latin America in particular for three significant reasons (see Figure 2.1). First, the cost of stationing full-time reporters in foreign bureaus has increased dramatically. These media corporations are profit driven and they seek ways to reduce costs, so they close foreign bureaus. Second, with the lack of Cold-War tension, there is at least a perception of a lack of interest on the part of editors and management about events in distant lands. Less space and time is allotted to foreign news. Many media corporations based in Europe and North America have reduced the numbers of reporters in Africa, Asia, and Latin America across all media. Third, core-based editors realize that when a mostly negative major news story breaks somewhere in a peripheral nation, they can dispatch a crew and reporters in a relatively short period of time owing to the ease of airline travel and the portability of equipment. This phenomenon further exacerbates the criticism and antagonizes the critics of Western media because it contributes to the largely negative media coverage of peripheral nations and regions. A tsunami, coup, earthquake, or riots where American tourists are involved is what gets covered.

Historically, the notion of development and progress was intertwined with economic issues and measurements; so now we turn to a consideration of economic models of growth and modernization.

Many media corporations based in Europe and North America have
reduced the numbers of reporters in Africa, Asian, and Latin America

Figure 2.1 Declining foreign bureaus, 2010

The Economic Growth Model

Perhaps the best-known categorization of stages of development is the one
advanced by US economist Walter Rostow in *The Stages of Economic Growth*.
This was one of the central early works which set modernization theory on an
economic trajectory. Other were by Daniel Lerner, *The Passing of Traditional
Society*, Everett Rogers, *The Diffusion of Innovations*, and Wilbur Schramm,
Mass Media and National Development.

Walter Rostow asserted that the development process can be divided into five
clearly defined stages: traditional society, establishment of preconditions to
takeoff, takeoff into sustained growth, the drive to maturity, and the age of high
mass consumption (see Figure 2.2).[7] In most versions of this scheme, traditional
and modern societies are placed at opposite ends of an evolutionary economic
scale. Development is viewed as evolution beyond or out of traditional structures and ways that supposedly cannot accommodate rapid social change or
produce sufficient economic growth. The new attitudes, values, and social relationships that support social change and industrialization are frequently conveyed through mass media as well as educational systems.

The economic growth model assumes development to be irreversible, like biological evolution. Modernization occurred when the necessary conditions for
change were established, and the process continued inexorably. Societies
absorbed the stress and change as they adapted themselves and their institutions
to the new order and ways of doing things in order to prosper. In reality, however, this dominant paradigm of development following a modernization track
did not produce the success stories that governments, foundations, and aid agencies had promised. The complex processes and depth of traditional behaviors
rendered most development efforts futile. Corrupt regimes did little to help the
situation as well. Criticism of the model mounted and continues today.

To understand the role that mass media was thought to play in development
under the dominant paradigm, it is important to note that one of the most
prominent features of the paradigm was the assumption that development

| Stage 1 ⟶ Traditional society |
| Stage 2 ⟶ Establishment of preconditions to takeoff |
| Stage 3 ⟶ Takeoff into sustained growth |
| Stage 4 ⟶ Drive to maturity |
| Stage 5 ⟶ High mass consumption |

Figure 2.2   Walter Rostow's stages of economic growth

could be equated with economic growth, the type of rapid growth that core nations experienced through capital-intensive, technology-driven industrialization. As Everett Rogers points out, "economists were firmly in the driver's seat of development programs. They defined the problem of underdevelopment largely in economic terms, and in turn this perception of the problem as predominantly economic in nature helped to put and to keep economists in charge."[8] Despite criticisms, theorists and aid practitioners continued to be preoccupied with the economic determinism of Western models of modernization, in large part because they produced measurable phenomena. Non-economic factors, such as culture, language, customs, and the role of women, were largely ignored.

Yet, as nations struggled to move from the peripheral to the semiperipheral zone and finally to elite core status, the nations and their citizens needed to adopt the trappings and values of a modernized state. Embedded in the modernization process is the ever-pervasive and influential role of mass media and communication technologies. Anthony Giddens states:

> The media, printed and electronic, obviously play a central role in this respect. Mediated experience, since the first experience of writing, has long influenced both self-identity and the basic organization of social relations. With the development of mass communication, particularly electronic communication, the interpenetration of self-development and social systems up to and including global systems becomes even more pronounced.[9]

To some extent, Giddens is speculating that modernization will ultimately lead to Marshall McLuhan's "global village," where communication systems are capable of importing images, data, and sounds from around the corner or around the globe, with similar technologies and similar effects. One of the most profound effects will be that the language of the "global village" will be English.[10]

In summary, development has been viewed as "a type of social change in which new ideas are introduced into a social system in order to produce higher per capita incomes and levels of living through modern product methods and improved social organization."[11] But after decades, a growing chorus of critics began to make themselves heard.

The Inadequacy of the Economic Growth Model

For the most part, attempts at direct social and economic change in peripheral regions never materialized, and the effort of core nations to engineer social change in poorer regions of the world have been largely unsuccessful. In fact, a World Bank *World Development Report*[12] points out that developing countries are still relatively worse off, vis-à-vis the core nations, in terms of growth. One only has to look at the relative penetration of information technologies or internet access per capita to glean how far behind peripheral nations are in participating in the information revolution and global economy. Some critics go so far as to claim that the World Bank and the International Monetary Fund (IMF) have been counterproductive in terms of global development (Danaher, 2001). Critics, such as those opposing trade agreements, point out that economic life simply has not improved through World Bank intervention and that local private enterprises in peripheral nations are frequently squeezed out by large IMF projects or multinational conglomerates entering peripheral regions in cooperation with the IMF or other aid agencies.[13]

Another major problem is illiteracy. Along with economic stagnation, many peripheral nations have increasing illiteracy rates. Poor regions are defined in part by their high illiteracy rates. Illiteracy makes access to consumption of certain mass media such as newspapers, magazines, and books irrelevant to a large proportion of the population in peripheral areas, particularly the younger generation. Nations with high birth rates see themselves moving downwards in terms of both literacy and overall economic status.

Many peripheral-based critics began questioning the entire functional school of media theory. In general, the functional theorists uncritically accepted the position of media elites and the reinforcement of the status quo as legitimate and rational behavior for the media systems. But today, the relevant questions about placing communication systems in peripheral nations are "functional for what purpose and for whom?"

Imported economic practices, technologies, and media often created confusion because traditional systems were unable to support the required change. In turn, some analysts shifted to non-economic explanations of development, identifying variables such as mass media exposure, telecommunications, political and social structural changes, social mobility, population control, along with individual psychology and commitment as preconditions for positive development and eventual modernization.

The development of mass communication was portrayed under the dominant paradigm as part of a universal, inevitable sequence of changes that traditional societies undergo in the transition to modernity. Mass communication was thought to function best in the service of centralized government development agencies when geared toward raising the public's aspirations and facilitating the acceptance of new ideas, values, and inventions for the purpose of overall economic growth and higher gross national product (GNP). Critical questions about the impact on traditions, tastes, values, language, history, role models, or cultures inherent in foreign mass media were simply not addressed.

The Research Traditions

When communication researchers turned their attention to development and modernity, they had a dual heritage. First, they were influenced strongly by the body of theory on the development process that had been built up in other fields, particularly economics, political science, and sociology. But equally strong influences on development communication research were the well established traditions and orientation of social science research in the communication field. The following sections briefly review the major research traditions in the discipline of communication-functionalism, structuralism, and professionalism. Almost the entire body of literature dealing with international communication since the post-World War II era was guided and influenced by these schools of thought. (Critical theory which had its roots in the Frankfurt School which looked at power and other variables did not seriously challenge the dominant paradigms.)

Functionalism

The traditions of functionalism began to take shape with the commercially oriented, early mass communication research of the 1930s and 1940s in the United States. Functionalism reflected the marketing concerns of a consumer society. Lazarsfeld, one of the pioneers of mass communication research, described this type of work as "administrative research."[14]

Historically, US mass communication research isolated specific media purposes, messages, or effects from the overall social process. It did not attempt to relate communication to the social, ideological, political, cultural, and economic systems in which it operated. Explanations about the specific communication data were seldom discussed in terms of the larger communication system, or from a macro-theoretical perspective. A linear, onetime analysis was typical of the early stages of research and still afflicts the discipline today.

US mass communication researchers concentrated on collecting and classifying data in order to illuminate new forms of social control, persuasion, or attitude change. They did not see it as their function to interpret these facts or build grand theories about structural and systemic determinants of the communication process. This early trend continues, with a focus on quantitative, empirical, behavioral science methods as opposed to highly conceptual, speculative, theoretical, or philosophically discursive approaches to mass communication research. There are a few noticeable exceptions.[15]

This emphasis on quantitative, empirical methodology at the micro level is not surprising considering that most early mass communication research studies were commissioned by broadcast, government agencies, foundations, or large advertising organizations. They were to deal primarily with specifically defined concerns about message effectiveness. These sponsors or agencies wanted to know what kind of political propaganda or persuasion technique would produce the desired effect. They were interested in the influence of such things as votes, purchases, attitudes, or behavior change of individuals. In terms of studies in the Third World, the subjects were mostly male farmers. Sponsoring organizations wanted hard data about the impact of particular messages. They had no interest in how these findings fit into a greater social, ideological, or cultural scheme. Melvin Defleur and Sandra Ball-Rokeach note that as a result, the study of audiences to discover effects almost monopolized mass communication research.[16] Following the functionalism approach, US researchers have tended to accept the system as a given and implicitly endorse it by failing to examine how their understanding of communication could be enriched by questioning other basic characteristics of the system, such as ownership, power, or the role of women.

A final note; much of the data gathering was undertaken by disparate groups of graduate students under the supervision of major American academics. But once the field data were collected the teams of researchers would return to their universities and the subjects across the peripheral regions would be left with nothing.

Structuralism

Some critics, such as Herbert and Dan Schiller, Dallas Smythe, Bob McChesney and Howard Frederick, probed more deeply into the question of who communicates with whom and for what purposes. They found that the real shaper of peripheral nations' communication systems and the messages they produce is media from core nations. Most peripheral regimes do not have the expertise or resources to establish domestic communication systems that genuinely reflect their history, needs, concerns, values, and culture. Consequently, they rely on the transfer (usually through foreign aid programs) of core-nation communication technology and software. Imported TV series, sitcoms, feature films, and wire-service copy are far cheaper to acquire than the equivalent domestically produced media fare.

In addition, it is important to note that most of the international communication industry is owned and controlled by giant core nations, mainly in the form of European, US, or Japanese transnational communication conglomerates. Good examples are Time Warner, Disney, Viacom, General Electric (NBC), the News Corporation (FOX and the Wall Street Journal), Google, Amazon, Microsoft, Sony, and Bertelsmann. These corporations are tied closely into a subtle and invisible network of core-based political, ideological, and economic elites, and they use the communication industry to perpetuate certain "needs," tastes, values, and attitudes so as to increase profits. Sales and market share are the defining matrices. When a peripheral nation imports, either through purchase, loan, or donation, communication technologies (from simple short-wave radio equipment, to printing presses, to ground stations for color television by means of satellite or the internet), plus software, it imports an alternative way of life. Herbert Schiller and others on the left described this as cultural imperialism and followers currently claim that it is becoming steadily more important in the exercise of global power:

> The marketing system developed to sell industry's outpouring of (largely inauthentic) consumer goods is now applied as well to globally selling ideas, tastes, preferences, and beliefs. In fact, in advanced capitalism's present stage, the production and dissemination of what it likes to term "information" become major and indispensable activities, by any measure, in the overall system. Made-in-America messages, imagery, lifestyles, and information techniques are being internationally circulated and, equally important, globally imitated. Multinational media corporations are major players in the world economy. Information and communications are vital components in the system of administration and control. Communication, it needs to be said, includes much more than messages and the recognizable circuits through which the messages flow. It defines social reality and thus influences the organization of work, the character of technology, the curriculum of the educational system, formal and informal, and the use of "free" time – actually, the basic social arrangements of living.[17]

A substantial body of literature deals with the central concept of cultural imperialism,[18] which usually applies either to specific peripheral nations or to specific communication industries such as feature films, advertising, television sitcoms, or mass circulation magazines. The central finding of the research is that exporting corporations establish ground rules in such a way that the peripheral nations are at a structural disadvantage from the start. Yet this is considered a crucial process in world-system theory. Somehow, this imbalance is supposed to exist in order for core nations to grow and succeed even more.

A good example of this process is reflected by a leader in video, DVDs, and video games rentals, the US retailer Blockbuster. In addition to its US stores, Blockbuster has more than 2,600 stores in 23 foreign nations. Many of these stores are in semiperipheral and peripheral nations. One can easily imagine what happens to a small, local, family owned and operated video store in peripheral nations such as Thailand, Argentina, Brazil, Mexico, or Chile when a Blockbuster store opens in the same community. Finally, as it seeks to become the leading global in the rental market, Blockbuster also brings with it a vast library of Hollywood feature films, American music, and US marketing and advertising expertise, with little room or interest for low-quantity video or DVD rentals of foreign indigenous productions.

Another example is Wal-Mart. It has close to 4,000 stores internationally, where Mexico alone has over 1,200 stores. These foreign venues greet 50 million customers per week and produced close to 100 billion in annual revenue. These stores have a Home Entertainment Area which sells consumers electronics of all types, DVDs, video games, and e-books. Wal-Mart is one of the largest sellers of video and music in the world. Finally, Wal-Mart has come out with strong support for the United Nation's eight Millennium Development Goals (MDG). The MDG have both direct and indirect application to development communication.

Professionalism

An integral but seldom discussed instrument of cultural imperialism is the technocratic baggage, including technicians, engineers, producers, directors, behind-the-scenes personnel, and writers, that are required for the technical maintenance and operation of an imported communication infrastructure. These technocrats, along with their manuals, usually are on loan from the industrialized nations or are trained and educated in core nations. They bring to peripheral countries value systems and attitudes associated with Western professionalism about how communication systems should be properly run. This socialization frequently adds another layer to the software that portrays a foreign culture. Moreover, technological personnel are frequently in the employ of various core nation aid agencies – governmental, educational, or religious organizations – that also are heavily value-laden enterprises with a proselytizing agenda.

These realities may help to explain why the introduction of mass media in many peripheral nations failed to produce substantial results. Although there were some efforts to promote cultural sovereignty and indigenous productions, in the final analysis, these efforts produced little of substance on a national level. A noted authority in the field, Robert Stevenson, states: "Development journalism – very much a part of the New World Information Order debate at the United Nations Educational, Scientific and Cultural Organization (UNESCO) in the 1970s – now has a record, and it is not impressive."[19]

Given its preoccupation with audience research, US communication studies have not investigated the ties that bind media institutions to other sources and structures of power, whether domestic or international. In essence, communication experts have taken for granted that more modern technology, including communication hardware and software, will be beneficial and will promote more economic growth. In fact, the policies they support do not necessarily advance development, or improve their quality of life, but tend to foster a neocolonial-like dependence on organizations from core nations. Increasing amounts of media and information technologies often contribute to the already unbalanced distribution of benefits by concentrating additional communication power in the hands of ruling elites. These elites may be political, religious, or military in nature. This further creates tension and frustration in peripheral regions by promoting inappropriate and inaccessible consumer products and values, further expanding the economic gap between core and peripheral nations.

Professionalism, as a body of research, did not have a parallel counterpart in European communication studies. The European tradition differs in two dramatic ways. First, many of the studies undertaken by European communication scholars deal with either critical theory emerging from the Frankfurt School of the 1930s, or with cultural studies that examine issues from a far different perspective than the North American traditions. Furthermore, practicing media professionals in Europe have distinctly different training than their US counterparts.

Whereas most US professionals are required to have a university degree, preferably from one of the leading schools of journalism, European media outlets prefer to train their personnel through apprenticeships at regional media outlets, particularly provincial newspapers. Thus, European media professionals learn their craft by doing rather than by studying.

Despite the substantial difference between European and US socialization of media professionals and technicians, it is important to note that the critical school frequently examines ownership by media elites or economic aspects of the industry. These European researchers often reach conclusions similar to those of US scholars. Basically they have found dysfunctional elements in the exportation of considerable amounts of communication hardware, software, and related cultural products.

Western Research Failings

More exhaustive approaches focusing on structural, contextual, and procedural determinants of communication have been low priority research concerns in the United States. US students of communication have never sought a conceptual inventory that would provide a complete basis for explaining communication in the context of an overall social system. This failure to recognize communication as inextricably tied to social structure and power has hampered the field. Even the diffusion of innovation research tradition has flawed assumptions. Luis Beltran writes,

> One basic assumption of the diffusion approach is that communication by itself can generate development, regardless of socioeconomic and political conditions. Another assumption is that increased production and consumption of goods and services constitute the essence of development, and that a fair distribution of income and opportunities will necessarily derive in due time. A third assumption is that the key to increased productivity is technological innovation, regardless of whom it may benefit and whom it may harm.[20]

The dominant research tools of diffusion studies – interview, sample survey, and content analysis – are another obstacle to the exploration of social structure as a key factor in the communication process. A preoccupation with methodological precision and small samples has taken precedence over macro-theoretical formulations.

This brings us to another feature of communication research that militates against the adoption of a macro-social approach that encompasses the roles of structural and organizational variables. Most theoretical models of development tend to locate internal sources of problems in developing countries and seldom look at external agencies or practices, such as the World Bank or World Trade Organization or at foreign ownership of media, ad agencies, and telecommunication systems. Many of the peripheral nations have simply been glad to be the recipients of foreign aid or to have a global corporation build a plant or office in their country and create new employment opportunities.

It was suggested earlier that the lack of an adequate focus on structure in development communication research in particular, and US communication studies in general, is related to researchers' acceptance of the premise that the system is in synch. Basically, researchers did not question the system since they viewed it as working for everyone's benefit. This acceptance makes it difficult for researchers to question the structure and organization of that system, instead encouraging them to concentrate their attention on how mass communication could act on audiences in a way that promotes conformity, purchases, and adjustment to a larger consumption driven social order.

One could argue that the lack of a structural focus stems also from the empirical, quantitative slant of US communication research and a corresponding reluctance to theorize at the macro level, as Marshall McLuhan did. The influences of communication on ideological and value systems, patterns of social organization, or subtle, difficult-to-measure matrices of power and social interaction are much harder to handle with empirical precision. These variables are less subject to rigorous measurements than the effects of specific messages on specific audiences. Study of those influences necessarily involves some theorizing, hypothesizing, and a speculative thinking not always firmly rooted in hard data. But such modes of understanding run against the grain of the exactness of the behavioral science tradition of US communication research as promoted and reinforced at universities.

A decade ago, the claim of scientific neutrality and objectivity was being challenged by a growing number of critics in the communication and journalism fields. Some comparative research is also appearing. In the foreword to *Images of the US around the World: A Multicultural Perspective*, Majid Tehranian makes the following point concerning the image of the United States in a global context:

> The image of the United States thus gradually deteriorated from a friend to a foe. In the meantime, however, the flow of American soft power in the spread of its cultural influence around the world through its cultural exports (English language, books, films, music, radio and TV programs, blue jeans, Coca-Cola, Madonna, and Michael Jackson) has seduced the younger generation nearly everywhere into emulating the American ways. The repugnance against Americanization has led some critics of US cultural influences to call it westoxification. Just like intoxication, the afflicted not only fall victim to its influence but revel in it.[21]

New Departures

Current students of the discipline have found development communication theory and research methodology wanting in several respects, and they are undergoing a reexamination. To overcome these limitations, efforts are underway to find more sophisticated tools for measuring the influence of social structure; for example, the non-economic variables of social life and culture, at both macro and micro levels.

In addition, Marxist theories of communication and development gained attention during the 1960s and 1970s. In these models, the causes of underdevelopment are traced back to international imbalances caused by the dominance of capitalist systems and the imperialist control they exercise over peripheral regions. There is a growing consciousness of the role that multinationals play in perpetuating colonial dependence both culturally and ideologically through their economic and political control of the international communication industry. This understanding is reflected in many new models that consider the influence of global political and economic power structures on development in their attempts to describe the causes of and solutions to underdevelopment. But in the early 1990s, with the failure of communism and its champion, the Soviet Union, much of the interest in and research with a Marxist underpinning quickly lost advocates and viability. The Marxist body of communication literature became stale. Still, the predominately European-based critical school of cultural studies is gaining broader attention. Although it offers a significant alternative, the problems of operationalizing its premises make large-scale research projects difficult and very costly.

For decades, communication scholars such as Schiller and Rogers pointed out the centrality of communication in the development process, but their research and scholarship had little impact outside the discipline of communication. Most of the aid agencies, foundations, and government organizations responsible for implementing development policies are controlled and dominated by economists or political scientists, and these academics failed to understand the crucial role of communication in the development cycle. They bring a silo mentality or viewpoint to the tasks at hand. If they had incorporated the role of communication, they might have been more successful, and the voices of criticism might have been fewer and less vociferous.

The good news is that there is evidence of a growing movement toward change. The World Bank provides a good example. Long focused on the more easily measured economic indices of development such as miles of asphalt or tons of concrete, the World Bank is reconsidering its focus. It has discovered the centrality of communication within the overall development process. Each year the World Bank publishes its *World Development Report*, which identifies factors that promote sustainable development. It also reflects the thinking of the bank's senior staff. Historically, the reports have focused on large-scale projects, some of which relate to transportation and agrarian infrastructures. However, the 1998 report marks a dramatic shift by including communication as central to future development:

The Report suggests three lessons that are particularly important to the welfare of the billions of people in developing countries.

1. First, developing countries must institute policies that enable them to narrow the knowledge gaps separating poor countries from rich.
2. Second, developing country governments, multilateral institutions, non-governmental organizations, and the private sector must work together to strengthen the institutions needed to address the information problems that cause markets and governments to fail.

3. Third, no matter how effective these endeavors are, problems with knowledge will persist. But recognizing that knowledge is at the core of all our development effort will allow us to discover unexpected solutions to seemingly intractable problems.[22]

In the face of its critics, the World Bank is attempting to reposition itself as an institution that understands and fosters the central role of information, knowledge, and communication in its expanding global mandate.

Finally, a new movement under the umbrella of participatory communication has emerged. It seeks to use communication as a tool at the grass roots level. A goal is to bring about social change by using non-formal education methods. Non-governmental organizations (NGOs), in particular, attempt to work with local people in peripheral regions to share efforts and goals. This approach seeks to promote ownership at the community level. Participatory communication is not top down but aims at being sensitive to local traditions, culture, and language by engaging locals at every stage of both planning and implementation.[23] The regions of Africa, Latin America, and Asia have attempted with varying degrees of success to implement social change along the lines of participatory communication strategies.

Postscript

As noted earlier, the criticisms identified here created widespread cause for concern among academics, professionals, and policymakers. Some are calling for a new definition of development journalism/communication in light of the failure of dominant models.[24] The many nations in the peripheral zone are still stuck in that most marginal, least desirable zone, with little if any power. In a later chapter, we will examine the role of UNESCO in bringing communication concerns to the forefront of the international arena. Although NWICO is not a research methodology, it does represent some theoretical alternatives for media flows, indigenous practices, and cultural sovereignty. These issues deserve the attention of students of development and the media, as well as professionals actively involved in the collection, observation, and reporting of foreign news, cultures, and viewpoints.

In its infancy, discussions about NWICO were marginal, manifesting themselves in a few academic departments and marginal textbooks. But when UNESCO championed the cause for a reexamination of international communication flows, the debates surrounding NWICO took on a life of their own. By introducing communication issues into global political discourse, UNESCO simultaneously found both supporters and detractors. Whereas some nations recognized the validity of the arguments and concerns, others interpreted them in terms of Cold-War rhetoric and divisions. In fact, the latter position ultimately led to the withdrawal from UNESCO of the United Kingdom, under Prime Minister Margaret Thatcher, and the United States, under President Ronald Reagan.

Both countries have now returned to UNESCO. Finally, as the NWICO debate faded at UNESCO it has been "born again." The World Summit on the Information Society (WSIS), in the early and middle part of this decade, once again saw the rhetoric of imbalances, one way flows, and imperialistic hegemony being bantered about. More is said about the significance of the WSIS later in this book.

The main point is that communication research with an international focus is changing, complex, and in some cases controversial. Previous theories and approaches appear limited, which is why the application of world system theory, as well as the theory of electronic colonialism, to global communication trends is a welcome addition to the discipline. Electronic colonialism theory examines the cultural forces influencing individual's attitudes and behaviors in foreign countries, whereas world system theory attempts to explain and separate the different nations or regions of the world into a three-stage or platform construct emphasizing economic variables or conditions.

We now turn to major global stakeholders, including US and foreign multimedia conglomerates. An important point to keep in mind is that new digital technologies are blurring the old boundaries between software and hardware, between broadcasting and telecommunication. Old divisions and distinctions are becoming meaningless as giant communication firms morph into digital providers of a broad array of products and services to end users – customers – around the globe without concern for national boundaries. The convergence of delivery systems in a broadband or wireless environment are forcing regulators and multimedia conglomerates to rethink their global strategies. Convergence, involving the interlocking of digital technologies, computing, telephony, and global networks, is rapidly changing the commercial environments with new stakeholders entering on an almost daily basis. Think Google, iPods, Twitter, Facebook, or YouTube and one quickly sees the pace of change involved.

Notes

1. A landmark document which established the framework, concerns, vision, and mandate for what would become the extensive involvement of the United States in both development communication projects as well as a plethora of anti-communism activities is President Harry Truman's inaugural address of January 20, 1949.

   The address was a mix of concern for the less fortunate of the world, particularly following World War II, and the early fear of the potential spread of communism which would eventually lead to the Cold War. In his address, Truman under "Point 4" called for a new program aimed at spreading the economic and scientific benefits of the US to underdeveloped countries. This would soon translate into a massive amount of talent and aid for projects which had a modernization focus; several of these projects had a communication or media related dimension. For a more detailed discussion, see Thomas McPhail, *Development Communication: Reframing the Role of the Media*, London: Wiley-Blackwell, 2009.

2. Normandy Madden, "Cable, Satellite Media Lure Influential Viewers," *Advertising Age International* (October 1999): 36.
3. The history of development journalism may be traced to the Department of Development Communication in the College of Agriculture at the University of the Philippines. It was established in 1973 for the purpose of training students to assist in the communication process of transmitting, by way of the media, the government's policies on agricultural development projects.
4. Andrew Moemeka, "Development Communication: A Historical and Conceptual Overview," in Andrew Moemeka (ed.), *Communication for Development*, Albany: State University of New York Press, 1994, p. 7.
5. Kwasi Ansu-Kyeremeh, "Indigenous Communication in Africa: A Conceptual Framework" in Kwasi Ansu-Kyeremeh (ed.), *Perspective on Indigenous Communication in Africa*, Legon, Ghana: School of Communication Studies Printing Press, 1998, p. 1.
6. Ank Linden, "Overt Intentions and Covert Agendas;" *Gazette* (1999) 61(2): 153.
7. Walter Rostow, *The Stages of Economic Growth*, New York: Cambridge University Press, 1960.
8. Everett Rogers, "Communication and Development: The Passing of the Dominant Paradigm," *Communication Research*, 3 (1976): 215. Rogers wrote the "Introduction" to the first edition of *Electronic Colonialism*. He died in 2004.
9. Anthony Giddens, *Modernity and Self-Identity*, Stanford, CA: Stanford University Press, 1991, p. 4.
10. David Crystal, *English as a Global Language*, Cambridge: Cambridge University Press, 1997.
11. Everett Rogers, *Modernization among Peasants: The Impact of Communication*, New York: Holt, Rinehart, and Winston, 1969, pp. 8–9.
12. *World Development Report 1998/99 Knowledge for Development*, New York; Oxford University Press, 1998.
13. See, for example, the following collection of essays, which dissect the role of the World Bank and the International Monetary Fund in promoting the politicization of economic life, inhibiting private enterprise, and delaying the emergence from poverty. The contributions argue that because of the nature of their structure, the World Bank and the IMF cannot change pro-market policies. Doug Bandow and Ian Vasques, *Perpetuating Poverty: The World Bank, the IMF, and the Developing World*, Washington, DC: Cato Institute, 1994, p. 362. Also Kevin Danaher, *10 Reasons to Abolish the IMF and World Bank*, New York: Seven Stories Press, 2001.
14. Paul Lazarsfeld, "Remarks on Administrative and Critical Communication Research," *Studies in Philosophy and Social Science* 9 (1941): 2–16.
15. Two of the most notable exceptions are Kyungmo Kim and George Barnett, "The Determinants of International News Flows: A Network Analysis," *Communication Research*, 23(3) June 1996): 323–52, and Jianguo Zhu, "Comparing the Effects of Mass Media and Telecommunications on Economic Development: A Pooling Time Series Analysis," *Gazette*, 57 (1996): 17–28.
16. Melvin Defleur and Sandra Ball-Rokeach, *Theories of Mass Communication*, New York Longman, 1975.
17. Herbert Schiller, *Communication and Cultural Domination*, White Plains, NY: International Arts and Sciences Press, 1976, p. 3.

18. Some scholars see this substantial body of literature as being overly representative of the body of knowledge in international communication. One critic refers to this aspect in the following way: "The root of the problem is that the research paradigm of the field of international communication is dominantly critical" (p. 382). After applying a meta-analysis, the author claimed that the majority of writers used polemics rather than empirical evidence to support their conclusions. Many of the pieces are authored by academics in the semi-peripheral and peripheral regions. In the same article, the author also called for the utilization of more meta-analysis in order to move the field of international communication to a higher plateau. Michael G. Elasmar, "Opportunities and Challenges of Using Meta-Analysis in the Field of International Communication," *Critical Studies in Mass Communication*, 16(3) (September 1999): 379–84.

19. Robert Stevenson, *Global Communication in the Twenty-first Century*, New York: Longman Publishing Group, 1994, p. 13.

20. Luis Beltran, "Alien Premises, Objects and Methods in Latin American Communication Research," *Communication Research*, 3 (1976): 107–34.

21. Majid Tehranian, "Foreword," in Y. Kamalipour (ed.), *Images of the US around the World: A Multicultural Perspective*, Albany: State University of New York Press, 1999, pp. xvi–xvii.

22. World Bank, *World Development Report 1998/99: Knowledge for Development*, p. 1.

23. Hermant Shah, "Modernization, Marginalization, and Emancipation: Toward a Normative Model of Journalism and National Development," *Communication Theory*, 6(2) (May 1998): 143–67.

24. For further details see J. Servaes, T. Jacobson, and S. White (eds.), *Participatory Communication for Social Change*, London: Sage Publications, 1996, and T. Jacobson and J. Servaes (eds.), *Theoretical Approaches to Participatory Communication*, Cresskill, NJ: Hampton Press, 1999.

3

The Message
The Role of International Organizations

Introduction

Historically, the United Nations Educational, Scientific, and Cultural Organization (UNESCO) has tried to avoid controversy. Yet its role, profile, and focus in the international information and communication debate are unmistakable. UNESCO, a specialized agency of the United Nations based in Paris, sponsored crucial international conferences that focused on the global communication debate and also directed its research program toward promoting new initiatives such as the New World International and Communication Order (NWICO). Initially UNESCO invested much, backstage as well as publicly, in NWICO. This eventually led to major problems for the agency, the greatest of which was the withdrawal during the 1980s of the United States and the United Kingdom from UNESCO membership. When they left, they also took their crucial financial support, which had been about one-third of UNESCO's total budget. UNESCO put its efforts and credibility into supporting a call for NWICO, but with the demise of the Cold War, UNESCO was found wanting. It had made a strategic mistake in relying extensively on Soviet support for NWICO.

Before describing the critical historical meetings and stakeholders in the NWICO debate, it is important to note that the global media have two rather distinct origins. In the United States, their origins are strongly rooted in commercial media systems in which advertising and market forces play crucial roles. Initially with newspapers, radio and now with television, telecommunications, and the internet, the US model is one of corporate influence with private ownership and control. The US model treats media and culture as economic commodities. By contrast, in Europe and in most countries of the world, the historical model is one of government ownership or government control of the mass media. The

BBC is a good example of a non-commercial radio and television networks sub-sidized by both the government and listeners or viewers, who pay annual licens-ing fees. In most of the world, radio evolved as a government medium without commercials or the influence of marketplace competition. The role of electronic media was to inform, educate, and entertain – not to make money from advertis-ers. Broadcasting monopolies were the early pervasive global model. When tel-evision technology emerged, these same government approved outlets took responsibility for television broadcasting. For several decades they limited the number of national television networks to only one or two, much as they did with radio. They viewed the media as cultural partners that were necessary to promote a nation's history, culture, education, and the arts. When commercial television emerged, a mixed model was accepted in Europe and in many other countries. The commercial model of the United States was frowned upon until vast audiences began viewing the shows presented by new alternative commer-cial television stations. With deregulation and the advancement of cable and sat-ellite technologies, several competing commercial broadcasting systems were born. These new stations, systems, or networks frequently are foreign media giants, such as Disney or FOX, and frequently reach larger audiences than the original government controlled networks.

It is important to keep this duality of approach in mind when considering the following NWICO debates. The debates themselves tended to move along two different tracks, the one track being more commercial, market driven, and free enterprise in orientation, the other being non-commercial, publicly funded, and government controlled and regulated in the public interest in orientation. The following sections review the history of the international communication debates, illustrating the global and fundamental differences in the origins, phi-losophies, roles, and environments in which global communication stakeholders have operated and, in some monopolistic, government-regulated environments, continue to operate. More than half of the nations in the world – those in the peripheral regions – still place some type of restriction on journalists or media outlets. Even though the commercial, advertiser-supported networks have attracted by far the largest audiences internationally, there is still a dedicated and loyal niche audience supporting public broadcasting, led by outlets such as the BBC. Many non-Americans view the international communication debate from a much different perspective. "Decolonization in itself has not made the world more just and peaceful. The evidence shows more news and images come from the Western world and the access to non-Western culture in terms of infor-mation, knowledge, entertainment and images becomes more scarce."[1]

UNESCO: Backdrop for the NWICO Debates

Acknowledging in its constitution that "since wars begin in the minds of men, it is in the minds of men that the defenses of peace must be constructed," UNESCO origi-nated in Great Britain in 1945. Based on this lofty ideal, UNESCO has transformed itself, from a passive force into an active force, in international affairs. It views its mission as that of a catalyst for and supporter of development:

> Both on the theoretical and the practical level, UNESCO has a vital role to play ... The current economic relations between industrialized and developing countries must, certainly, be transformed, but they cannot on their own change the political and socio-cultural factors, which shape integrated developments. Thus UNESCO has the task of helping: to enlarge the scientific and technological bases which permit each country to use its natural resources better;   to increase and improve communications and information systems; ... to promote the progress of social sciences so that each society can undertake its own studies and utilize the instruments of change without losing its own identity.[2]

Formally established as a specialized agency of the United Nations in 1946, UNESCO entered the international arena with 20 member states, the vast majority being core nations. Its budget is drawn from a levy imposed on each member state. Its General Assembly, comprised of all member states, meets every two years to determine the agency's programs and budget. A 45-member Executive Board supervises the implementation of the programs, and the day-to-day operations of the agency are carried out by the Secretariat. Although based in Paris, the Secretariat draws its personnel from all member states.[3] In the early years, all members were core or semiperipheral nations. Peripheral nations began joining UNESCO after World War II. Many were former colonies of European core nations – this created a tense working environment. Today, delegates from several peripheral nations hold senior positions in UNESCO. To a large extent most peripheral nations view UNESCO as the one specialized agency of the UN, which promotes their needs and agenda with its focus on a broad range of development initiatives.

UNESCO's mandate is broad, covering educational, scientific, cultural, and communication programs and research projects around the globe. The convening and sponsoring of international ministerial and research conferences to discuss various aspects of this broad mandate is one of UNESCO's most important and time-consuming tasks. In fact, it is through this role that UNESCO became a major player in the international communication debates leading to NWICO.

Originally, the Western nations, particularly Britain, France, and the United States dominated UNESCO. However, beginning in the 1950s and continuing today, power and influence shifted as a result of the continual addition of former colonies. Almost all were former colonies of some European nation addition of newly emerging nations, primarily from Asia, Africa, and other peripheral areas. Almost all were former colonies of some European nation. The one-country-one-vote procedures that govern the agency have provided the peripheral nations with a voice and power. During the 1960s, the shared ideological and economic conditions of several of these peripheral nations led to the development of a power bloc or lobby known as the Group of 77. Although this bloc has grown to include well over 100 nations, its role and that of these newly emerged nations within UNESCO is fraught with contradictions. As UNESCO expert Richard Hoggart explains "The new nations, who were, in general, creations of the early sixties, tend to take the UN seriously though ambiguously. Since the UN was set up by the victorious allied powers, it has the stamp of Western ways of thinking. On the other hand, its record in anticolonialism is good and it has made a considerable contribution to the emergence of some new states. Their relationship to the UN is therefore rich in ambiguities."[4]

This ambiguity is no better illustrated than in their attitudes toward global communication. On the one hand, many of these nations want, some desperately, to become modern industrialized countries with color digital television, personal computers, cellular phones, and all the media trappings that money and technology permit. Yet, as noted earlier, most lack even the basic telecommunication infrastructures for telephone, let alone sophisticated ground terminals for satellite television transmission, or broadband cable for internet access. At the same time, many of these nations reject Western culture – Hollywood films, Madison Avenue commercials, and core-nation or foreign-produced television programming. For many in the peripheral zone, only pure, indigenous domestic media products are acceptable. The dilemma, of course, is that core-nation technology and shows are easily accessible and cheaper than the production or creation of high quality indigenous systems or software.

Throughout its existence, UNESCO has had its critics. Part of that criticism is a result of the periodic negative assessment of its parent, the United Nations. Another flash point, during the mid-1970s, was a decision that excluded Israel from the European regional grouping, creating a barrage of criticism from the Western press, and leading the United States to temporarily withhold its contribution to UNESCO, an amount equal to about 25 percent of the agency's total budget.

Paradoxically, another cause for criticism was the consistent demand of peripheral countries for better development initiatives. UNESCO's initial response to critics was to focus on education, which culminated in the publication of the 1972 Faure Commission report, *Learning to Be*.[5] But with the completion of that major effort, a substantive policy vacuum developed that permitted the introduction of a series of resolutions by republics of the Soviet Union concerning the development of national media and communication policies. UNESCO, core governments, and multinational media corporations largely ignored the issues and questions being raised because they underestimated the strength, determination, voting power, and depth of animosity felt by peripheral nations. These peripheral nations had a long list of grievances about international media flows. The lack of substantive policy permitted the Soviets and several peripheral nations to hijack UNESCO's planning agenda in the late 1970s. The result was the eruption of the NWICO debates, which dominated the activities of UNESCO for more than two decades. This chapter highlights the major forums in which the media and communication debates crystallized. Even today, many nations around the world are critical and concerned about the impact of foreign software on their domestic values, attitudes, and beliefs. A good example is the concern of the American dominated Internet Corporation for Assigned Names and Numbers (ICANN).

It is based in California and its main task is to globally manage the allocation of internet domain names and addresses. Several critics want to turn over ICANN to a new UN agency and remove it from the hegemonic control of the US government.

Identifying the Issues and Taking Sides

The debate officially began in 1970[6] when UNESCO's General Assembly outlined the need to articulate national communication policies and a series of publications dealing with this issue began to emerge. This examination, by the peripheral nations in particular, led to increased documentation and greater awareness of the one-way flow of media messages from core to peripheral nations. It also became apparent that national communication development policies for semi-peripheral and peripheral nations could not be produced when so much of their media were produced or controlled by foreign firms based in London, Paris, New York, or Los Angeles.

Subsequently, three significant resolutions were introduced that increased the visibility and divisiveness of the global media issue. The first related to the rapid development of direct broadcast satellite (DBS) technology. DBS allowed media outlets to transmit their messages directly to receiving sets throughout the world. Whereas traditional ground station broadcasting signals could be controlled or blocked to prevent the widespread transmission of alien messages, DBS signals could easily circumvent these restrictions and procedures. In response, UNESCO passed a resolution – by a vote of 100 to 1, with the United States as the only dissenter – to require satellite broadcasters to obtain the prior consent of national governments and their regulators before transmitting messages to a foreign territory. Even though there was no technical way to enforce the resolution, its passage represented a bold-faced rejection of US "free press" and "free flow" rhetoric and business practices.

The second resolution called for regional meetings of experts to discuss national communication policies. This resolution received the unanimous support of the General Assembly, but dissension arose when it was decided to hold these meetings in peripheral regions and not in the core industrialized nations, as had been UNESCO's tradition. A few of the key early meetings were held in Latin America.

The third contentious resolution, which was introduced by the USSR, sought to acknowledge both the right and the responsibility of national governments to control the media messages availability to their citizenry. Although the resolution failed to pass, it was attractive to many peripheral nations, which were heartened to have the support of at least one of the superpowers. Although peripheral nations had achieved a significant presence in UNESCO, this Soviet "sharing of the minds" with respect to communication policy lent strength to their votes, opinions, and influence. For their part, the Soviets had no journalistic qualms or ethical dilemmas about extending international government control of media; clearly, their major objective was to aggravate the United States, Europe, and other core nations.

The Non-aligned Movement

As the process of decolonization continued to transfer newly emerging nations from the foreign-policy mandates of their former colonizers, now many Third World nations began to fear becoming satellites or pawns of the one of the two superpowers, the United States or the Soviet Union. Consequently, a new political pressure group emerged. In 1973 a summit meeting of foreign ministers of non-aligned countries met in Algiers. During this meeting, participating nations acknowledged their desire to develop a unique foreign-policy stance independent of both the United States and the USSR. They wanted to create a "third option" to reflect their independence. Many of the policy positions postulated sought to overcome the consequences of past colonization. Among these was a demand for the decolonization of information and an end to the one way flow of media.

A series of non-aligned conferences followed in Peru, Tunisia, Mexico, India, and Sri Lanka. At each successive meeting, the rhetoric and action progressed from attacking transnational communication corporations to developing an action plan for the establishment of a wire service, Inter Press Services, which would begin as a pool of contributing government information services. Additional issues included debate about the New International Economic Order (NIEO) and awareness of the growing power of a nucleus of oil-rich, non-aligned countries in the Middle East, known as the Organization of Petroleum Exporting Countries (OPEC).

In addition to the non-aligned summit meetings, a crucial seminar was held at the University of Tampere in Finland. Finland's President Urho Kekkonen, in addressing the issue of cultural imperialism, asserted that the theory of the "free" flow of information was really a rationale for a "one-way" flow. Not coincidentally, a major research study also was presented at the conference that documented the pervasive influence of US and British television program sales internationally.[7] As research increasingly revealed evidence of the one-way flow of media products, particularly wire services, anti-Western rhetoric escalated.

Latin America Meetings

While the non-aligned countries proceeded to articulate their complaints and develop communication strategies, several UNESCO-sponsored meetings were convened to investigate the disparities in international information flows and participation in national communication policy development. The major issues quickly became the relationship between communication policies and economic, social, and cultural development, and the role of governments in promoting the latter by controlling the former. A major conference to examine these questions was set for July 1976 in San Jose, Costa Rica, but two background meetings were held in Bogota, Colombia, July 4–13, 1974, and Quito, Ecuador, June 24–30, 1975. These meetings provided significant impetus and research for critics of Western media. Background papers, data, and research documents were presented out lining several grievances about a broad range of international communication issues. Foreign wire services, particularly those headquartered in New York, London, and Paris, came in for considerable criticism about their coverage of Latin America.

It should be emphasized that all parties to the debate understood that these regional conferences were creating momentum for a major international conference focusing on media and information flow issues. Global information flows and media policies dominated the debate at UNESCO just as education had in the 1960s. However, while there had been a general consensus about the positive role and impact of education, a strong and highly divisive polarity of opinion (free press versus government control) was developing concerning global information policies.

19th UNESCO General Assembly, Nairobi, 1976

The vital role of information and the debate about how to promote development through information policies were the focus of the 19th UNESCO General Assembly. By this time, most peripheral countries had abandoned the desire for and rhetoric about a free press in favor of a development press, one that would assist in the positive development of their poor nation-states. They wanted a cultural stamp of their own making and not one imported from core nations or "Made in the USA." The director general of UNESCO, Amadou-Mahtar M'Bow from Senegal, Africa, could not have agreed more.

The major document before delegates at the Nairobi conference was a resolution similar to the one that had been introduced by the Soviet Union in 1971 entitled "Draft Declaration of Fundamental Principles Governing the Use of the Mass Media in Strengthening Peace and International Understanding and in Combating War, Propaganda, Racialism and Apartheid." This declaration, specifically Article 12 requiring that national governments take responsibility for all media systems, guaranteed extensive attention from the Western press. Once again, the Western media coverage of UNESCO was negative. The negative focus affected the leadership role of Director-General M'Bow as well as the media debate.

Before outlining the major events in Nairobi, it is necessary to remind readers of a situation during the early 1970s that again cemented Western, particularly

US, faith in the value of a free press. Without dwelling on the details, two junior reporters for the Washington Post, Carl Bernstein and Bob Woodward, pursued a lead that ultimately resulted in the resignation of Richard Nixon as president of the United States. Like nothing else might have, the Watergate scandal reinvigorated a latent distrust of government regulations and demonstrated to the people of the United States and other core nations the need for a press free from government control. Even the mere suggestion of increased government control of the media was anathema to the US public and Western journalists. In a similar fashion, British control of the national press during the Falkland Islands invasion in 1982 irritated many British reporters and publishers as well as the British public. Consequently, the Western model of the press as the "fourth estate" had been strongly reinforced in advance of the Nairobi conference.

After years of preliminary discussions concerning the role of the media, the Nairobi debate boiled down to a signal draft declaration consisting of 12 articles. Given the heightened profile of the issue within UNESCO and on the news agenda of the global wire services, a means to avoid a direct confrontation between East and West was sought. Leaving aside other issues, it was Article 12, calling for state responsibility for media activities that dominated the conference. In the "spirit of Nairobi," a compromise was reached, mainly backstage, to shelve the draft declaration and to reduce pressure among the peripheral nations and non-aligned militants by forming a new group to study the issue further. UNESCO created the International Commission for the Study of Communication Problems, headed by Senator Sean MacBride of Ireland.

Having accurately analyzed the strong Western objection to development journalism and government oversight or control of press activities, Director-General M'Bow wanted to avoid an outright showdown, as well as save his career. Although he was able to delay the debate and critical vote until UNESCO's next General Assembly, to be held in Paris in 1978, he also exacerbated the problem by linking the debate over a new international information order to the proposed new international economic order.

New International Economic Order (NIEO)

In order to provide a complete picture of the rise of the non-aligned movement, it is necessary to describe the development of the New International Economic Order (NIEO). During the early 1970s, the United Nations and its member agencies became major vehicles for change, offering hope to emerging peripheral nations. Many observers were surprised by the extent to which the resolve and the magnitude of change adopted by the United Nations was misanalyzed not only in terms of NWICO, but also with respect to the underlying NIEO. It took Western economists several years to come to grips with NIEO, and only a few understood its link to international communication and

NWICO. This point is highlighted in a report published by UNESCO, which also addressed the changing balance of power within the international agency, and across the UN system.

Just what was the NIEO that the United Nations, and therefore UNESCO, were supporting? In effect, it represents a major change for the West, which traditionally controlled the United Nations and its organizations. This is clearly not the case any longer. When 146 nations met in Paris for five weeks of UNESCO meetings in the fall of 1978, the largest group, 106 Member States, represented Third World, and many were also part of the so-called non-aligned, nations. They were originally labeled the "Group of 77" and this label is still used despite continually increasing size and influence.[8]

Given the shift, it should not be surprising that the pressure for changes to enhance the development opportunities of peripheral nations became a pressing issue on the agendas of the United Nations and its specialized agencies. In response, on May 1, 1974, the United Nations General Assembly passed a resolution to adopt a major program of action establishing a New International Economic Order. The declaration encouraged member states to:

> work urgently for the establishment of a New International Economic Order based on "equity, sovereign equality, interdependence, common interest and cooperation among all states," irrespective of their economic and social systems which shall correct inequalities and redress existing injustices, make it possible to eliminate the widening gap between the developed and the developing countries and ensure steadily accelerating economic and social development and peace and justice for future generations.[9]

The result was a flurry of research and conferences conducted to clarify the issues and develop strategies for achieving the goal.[10]

Despite all the activity, enhanced economic development for peripheral nations failed to occur. However, the peripheral nations found an unexpected opportunity for change when the Organization of Petroleum Exporting Countries (OPEC), originally founded in Baghdad in 1960, was able to force a substantial increase in the price of oil, a basic commodity throughout the world.[11] During the 1970s, OPEC quickly became a model for peripheral nations to emulate in hopes of obtaining the economic concessions and achieving the financial growth that had escaped them over decades of foreign control.

The changes in economic orientation and philosophy brought about by NIEO influenced all aspects of the UN and UNESCO. Everything from the influence of transnational corporations to the role of the major wire services and the impact of popular culture was examined in light of either NIEO or NWICO. The anti-colonial rhetoric of the new order was harsh. Colonial domination, neocolonialism, racial discrimination, apartheid, media images, cultural imperialism, Western hegemony, and violations of human rights were all subject to severe criticism. Although the goals of the new order were lofty, its real objective was to shift international power from Western, core nations to a loose coalition of peripheral regions, Arab OPEC regions, non-aligned nations, and socialist (namely, the

USSR) countries. The next goal was to effect a change in sociocultural priorities under the protection or guidance of NWICO.

The Debate Begins in Earnest

As UNESCO prepared for the next general meeting, the future of Director General M'Bow rested on how he handled the contentious draft declaration on the mass media. He realized that the "spirit of Nairobi" was a false one built on acrimony and distrust. The agreement to establish the MacBride International Commission as a means of buying time and reducing the building pressure had been worked out backstage at the last moment to avoid a walkout by Western delegations. That compromise was no longer sufficient to withstand the mounting strain.

M'Bow also had to do something to polish UNESCO's image, which had become severely tarnished. UNESCO's Secretariat perceived the problem as one created by the Western press, which had emphasized negative aspects of UNESCO's leadership, initiatives, and programs. In reality, however, UNESCO's public image was more negatively affected by its shift from a passive, pro-Western agency to an activist, pro-development, peripheral oriented agency. Its ideological commitment to fundamental change, through NIEO, for example, was little understood and was perceived as a threat to the free markets and economic security that core nations had taken for granted since UNESCO's inception in the 1940s. But new peripheral nations looked to this specialized agency of the United Nations to take care of their international grievances.

As for the plight of peripheral nations, "it was as though they had moved from military colonialism to technological neocolonialism without a thought beyond the purely practical and profitable."[12] Many peripheral nations had rushed to accept Western technology and software designed for other cultures and other needs, and now conceded that Western-controlled aid was not the answer to their problems. They had seen aspects of electronic colonialism and they did not like what they were seeing. They did not want to be consumers of a foreign and alien culture. As a result, peripheral nations approached the media and culture debate with a call for greater distributive justice bolstered by their five-year discussions of the need for a NIEO. They had flexed their muscles, voted, received attention, and won; now they were prepared to go after the Western mass media.

In his opening address to the 1978 General Assembly, Director-General M'Bow set the framework for UNESCO's future agenda. Noting that "the establishment of a new international economic order constitutes ... one of the major contexts, and no doubt the largest, within which the activities of the Organization will take place," M'Bow continued by asserting that the imbalances between the West and the peripheral nations were not limited to "solely the production and exchange of information and knowledge.[13] In this way, M'Bow ensured that NWICO would become further intertwined with the NIEO. After reviewing several other

UNESCO activities including human rights, education, disarmament, and science and technology, M'Bow turned to communication. He acknowledged "the task awaiting the international community in this field over the next few years represents a real challenge, since it is a task which is at one and the same time immense, complex, essential and urgent.[14] Then M'Bow proceeded to review the MacBride Commission and highlighted specific areas that required further research and clarification, including disparities in global communication.

In closing, M'Bow criticized his opponents and urged them to adopt NWICO:

> I believe very sincerely that the draft now before you could meet with a large measure of agreement, provided that it is read objectively and dispassionately, and that form of words are patiently sought which dispel the ambiguities of hidden motives that some people still read into it. In this way, the large measure of agreement that the General Conference considers necessary could be achieved.[15]

M'Bow lost ground quickly as Western nations, in response to his address, spoke against the submitted draft declaration. Activities in plenary sessions, in corridors, and in media briefings cumulatively portrayed UNESCO as divided along East–West lines, with the East (socialist) receiving support from many peripheral and OPEC nations. It was clear that the controversial draft declaration on the role of the mass media would have significant implications. It represented a distinct change from the free flow of information policy established by the United Nations and formally supported by the United States since the 1940s.

Moreover, peripheral nations clung to their objections to the Western media. Their criticisms reflected three primary issues. The first argument was a straightforward anticapitalist approach that criticized the commercial orientation of the press, radio, television, and film industries. The second line of attack focused on the one-way flow of information from the United States, through wire services, television programming, and Hollywood productions, to other nations, with little if any reciprocal trade. Some peripheral nations, particularly those in Africa, that were former colonies of European powers, also attacked the BBC, Reuters, and Spanish and French broadcasting interests, although less vociferously. Fear of electronic colonialism motivated the third argument, which featured a dislike of the history, norms, morals, language, lifestyles, and cultural aspects conveyed through the content of core nations' press, radio, television, advertising, and film productions.

For many Western delegates, the issue boiled down to one of state control over the mass media. Secretary of State for Canada John Roberts, MP, delivered one of the strongest speeches during the entire assembly. In explaining Canada's reservations about the Declaration, Roberts stated:

> I am making no secret of my disquiet, and that of the Government of which I am a member, concerning the Draft Declaration on the Mass Media … On every continent there are some people who think that governments should regulate journalists, should tell them, in the public interest, what to write, or should pass judgment on their accuracy. Canadians do not believe that either politicians or public servants should have anything to say in

the management, direction or correction of the media. Quite the contrary. In their view, only a free press can guarantee that the decisions of the state power are in harmony with the wishes of the people. Governments have no means of knowing what the needs of society are for its own well-being, unless they are told by an informed public.[16]

Roberts went on to list reasons for a postponement of the adoption of the contentious text. The address was well received, and because Canada has stature in UNESCO, the Western wire services gave coverage to Robert's remarks. In response, Dr. Phillip Muscat from Malta summed up the major peripheral nations' grievances:

> The service that emanates from the big international press and news agencies sometimes tends to be slanted against the developing countries of the Third World and their leaders. Great prominence is given to certain news items of minor importance, while national achievements in vital sectors are barely mentioned or wrongly reported. Moreover, in certain instances the international press is used as a destabilizing factor against the governments whose only crime is generally that of standing up for their rights, their sovereignty and independence.[17]

Following the plenary session, M'Bow began, as he always did, by criticizing Western press coverage of the issue. He then called for the development of a universal journalistic code of ethics to govern the actions of media and journalists. Many feared that such a code would lead to some type of system that ultimately could be used to restrict journalists' freedom. The Soviets and authoritarian nations thought they had an ally in M'Bow and an issue, NWICO, with which to restrict the Western media.

Ultimately, UNESCO's 20th General Assembly approved a compromise draft declaration on the mass media that endorsed freedom of the press. This represented a significant diplomatic reversal in favor of the West and moderate developing nations and a temporary reprieve for Director General M'Bow. Although it was M'Bow who initially presented, endorsed, and pushed the first controversial draft declaration, the Western press uniformly and correctly blamed the Soviet bloc for the attack on their free-press philosophy. One suspects that M'Bow, finding his back against the wall and his career on the line, abandoned what he had cherished in October to pacify the Western nations and thereby retain their substantial funding. Of course, it is likely that M'Bow also recognized that the forthcoming final MacBride International Commission Report and the next UNESCO General Assembly provided opportunities for him to regroup and present his NWICO tenets once again.

UNESCO in the 1980s

As described in the previous section, it took a reluctantly accepted 11th-hour compromise to pull the 20th General Assembly's session on mass communication out of the fire in 1978. Yet the delegates to UNESCO general assemblies continued to put at least the face of consensus and unanimity on the international communication discussions that invariably tottered on the brink of open warfare and collapse. Once again, this time in Belgrade in 1980, the General Assembly adopted a mass media resolution by consensus when nobody called for a vote on it. As unbelievable as it may seem, that resolution actually won approval because it simultaneously advocated proposals based on the principles of both sides of the debate. The result was an uneven and inconsistent declaration.

Despite its equivocal language, reciprocal concessions, and unanimous approval, the resolution was "one of the most bitterly fought over in UNESCO's history."[18] It revealed the extent to which the Western and developing world positions on NWICO were irreconcilable. Even though concessions were made by both sides, the peripheral nations, acting with the support of the Soviet bloc, seemed to get the better of the West. According to several observers, their advantage appeared to turn on the inclusion of some principles that could be interpreted as anti-free press.

The launching at the 21st General Assembly of the International Programme for the Development of Communication (IPDC) also created a great deal of controversy and suspicion. A 39-member intergovernmental council was established to administer the program and set out its priorities and policies. IPDC continues today with the goal of aiding communication projects in peripheral nations. Because council members were to be elected on a rotating basis to ensure regional representation, peripheral nations would have considerable leverage within IPDC. Another controversial issue concerned the funding for IPDC. Many peripheral nations wanted an international fund to be established within the UNESCO framework. The United States refused to pledge to such a fund and suggested that the money needed to initiate the program should be diverted from UNESCO's regular mass communication budget.

In retrospect, the 21st General Assembly was remarkable for the decisions made. It not only approved a version of the NWICO, but it also accepted the MacBride Commission report, which clearly endorsed activities that would promote development journalism and communication, and it created the IPDC to implement some of those policies. What was unclear at the time was the degree to which the hostility brewing against Director General M'Bow would, by mid-decade, reach sufficient intensity to justify the withdrawal of both the United Kingdom and the United States from UNESCO.

The 22nd General Assembly of UNESCO convened in Paris on October 25, 1983. One hundred and sixty-one countries participated in the five-week conference, which turned out to be one of the most critical in the history of UNESCO. Just a few weeks after the meetings were adjourned, US State Department dissatisfaction with a number of UNESCO issues led to the announcement of their intention to withdraw from UNESCO at the end of 1984 unless its demands for substantial change were met. The United States did withdraw.

The meetings began with the presentation of "The Draft Programme and Budget for 1984–1985," which was prepared by the UNESCO Secretariat on the basis of the consensus reached by the delegates. Of most relevance to this discussion is "Major Programme III, Communication in the Service of Man," outlined below:

Programme 111.1 Studies on Communication:

a   to simulate the development of research, especially concerning the sociocultural impact of new communication technologies, the democratization of communication and the future of books and reading;
b   to further elaborate the concepts of "the right to communicate" and access to and participation in communication, and to continue to study the idea of the responsibility in communicators;
c   to continue the study of methods for planning, programming and financing of communication, with special reference to the communication industries.[19]

The program continued by encouraging the reduction of current international communication imbalances through the development of a plurality of information sources and through cooperation and collaboration. It acknowledged that the activities listed in the program would "facilitate a detailed examination of a new information and communication order, with a view to promoting its establishment."[20] The proposed budget for the three major programs listed in Programme III was almost $30 million, an increase of more than 33 percent over the previous budget. So much for the cost-containment sought by the United States and the United Kingdom.

It had been hoped that the freedom of the press issue and NWICO, which had divided UNESCO for over a decade, might be only a minor topic at this meeting. On the first day of debate, however, two serious and contentious issues arose. The first was the substantial increase in the budget for communications. The second was a Soviet Union proposal calling for curbs on press freedom as part of NWICO.

The Soviet delegation realized that the First Amendment was sacred in the eyes of the US press, and its intention was to aggravate the US and other Western delegations. The Soviet draft urged UNESCO to draw up a list of "mass media organs" whose reporting had violated the guidelines that the organization had enunciated earlier. These were the same guidelines that most Western governments had criticized as hostile to the freedom of the press. The Soviets were forced to withdraw their contentious resolution, but its introduction had heightened distrust of NWICO by providing a concrete illustration of its threats to press freedom.

Although the media debate was a key issue, the size of the budget increase created another serious problem for the United States. The United States was the only one of the 161 nations to vote against the $374.4 million budget. At the final vote, 10 other countries abstained after asking for a budgetary freeze. The final budget adopted was about $12 million less than that first proposed, but the cuts did not go deep enough for the United States, which had been seeking "zero growth" in all UN agencies.

Although the United States failed to achieve as much as it had hoped, it certainly was more successful than it had been in the past decade. It had curbed the development of NWICO, and there was an emerging shift toward the Western perspective on press matters. Although the final budget did not represent zero growth, it was only 2.5 percent higher than the previous one. What, therefore, prompted the US decision to pull out of UNESCO less than one month later?

Shortly after the close of the 22nd General Assembly, stories began appearing in the US press about the possible withdrawal of the United States from UNESCO. According to a *New York Times* report, the proposal was being considered in the State Department and a decision was expected soon.[21] Gregory J. Newell, Assistant Secretary of State for International Organization Affairs, said that his office had conducted a study of the performance of some 19 organizations and noted that in addition to mismanagement and lack of budgetary restraint, there were problems of politicization within many UN agencies. He asserted that internal studies had shown what the Reagan administration viewed as improvement in many UN multilateral agencies, but that UNESCO had responded inadequately. Newell then ordered a complete review of UNESCO that would later justify US withdrawal.

Opponents of the withdrawal pointed to the improvements made at the 22nd General Assembly. They feared that withdrawal would leave the organization vulnerable to those who opposed US interests. Moreover, the United States Commission for UNESCO, although acknowledging problems, voted by an overwhelming majority to continue membership and fight for change from within. But Newell recognized the vulnerability of UNESCO and used it to condemn and threaten the entire UN system.

Following the reviews, the US State Department recommended, on December 21, 1983, that the United States file notice of its intention to withdraw from UNESCO on January 1, 1985. The decision had to be made by December 31, but the US would have one year in which to reassess the situation. President Ronald Reagan sent a formal letter of withdrawal to Director-General M'Bow on December 29, making it clear that the departure was temporary and that the United States retained the right to rejoin. According to a State Department spokesperson, the decision was taken because "UNESCO has extraneously politicized virtually every subject it deals with, has exhibited hostility toward the basic institutions of a free society, especially a free market and a free press, and has demonstrated unrestrained budgetary expansion."[22] Under President Reagan the White House and the Department of State had ignored the UN and UNESCO and now they were trying to punish the UN system for promoting policies that questioned the US's role as a global commercial power.

Officially; the State Department recommendation to withdraw from UNESCO was based on what it identified as three major behavioral problems:

1. the politicization of issues;
2. the promulgation of statist concepts; and
3. mismanagement and fiscal irresponsibility.

The United States officially withdrew from UNESCO in January 1985. (It returned under President Bush in 2002 and now has an ambassador in Paris and a National Commission in Washington.)

UNESCO without the United States

By the time the 23rd session of the UNESCO General Assembly was convened in Bulgaria on October 8, 1985, not only had the United States withdrawn from the organization, but the United Kingdom also was reconsidering its membership. Given this Western power void, the socialist bloc was anxious to put its own stamp on the meetings.

In fact, the selection of Sofia, Bulgaria, as the site for meeting was part of a Soviet strategy to enhance its own power and position within UNESCO. Given the budgetary limitations facing the agency, it made fiscal sense to hold the conference at UNESCO headquarters in Paris where it would not be necessary to house and feed 1,000 UNESCO employees for the six-week assembly. But it was precisely that expenditure, in addition to the revenues generated by the presence of 3,000 additional delegates to the conference that caused the Soviet Union to lobby strongly on behalf of the Sofia site. Moreover, by convening in Bulgaria without an official US delegation, many socialist countries saw this as an opportunity to strengthen their role within UNESCO and use it as a vehicle to promote anti-West projects and administrators.

Once again, the most sensitive issue to emerge during the General Assembly was the discussion of NWICO. NWICO emphasized the disparities among nations and suggested means, sometimes contradictory and contentious, for reaching a new order and balance in international information, media, and communication flows. Although NWICO was still a relatively modest concept, the major problem was the fact that it was systematically perceived as being structurally different by the two major groups of nation-states. Western, core nations viewed NWICO as troublesome, vague, and potentially harmful. On the other hand, the socialist bloc, peripheral nations, and non-aligned nations contended that NWICO was both a practical program and a theoretical concept to encourage and legitimize a more activist indigenous production capacity. It was considered to be a paradigm from which to facilitate infrastructure developments along pro-peripheral nation lines. This cleavage was reinforced by the US withdrawal from UNESCO.

The United Kingdom played an interesting role at the 23rd General Assembly. Basically, the UK's position was a difficult one because it had given notice in December 1984 that it intended to withdraw from UNESCO at the end of 1985. As a result, the British were almost as powerless within UNESCO as the United States. As diplomatic eunuchs, their efforts to exert influence became somewhat melodramatic. Most of the peripheral nations saw no reason to consider the UK's views, complaints, or objectives, and even its Western allies and Commonwealth partners realized that its actions were intended to legitimize its decision to withdraw as of January 1986.

New Era, Leaders, and Strategy

M'Bow left the Director-General position at UNESCO in 1986. He also left apolitically weakened and fiscally poor UN agency to his successor, Federico Mayor, from Barcelona, Spain. Mayor was elected as the new Director-General of UNESCO in 1987 and held the office until 1999. During his UNESCO tenure, he altered the agency's role and did not support NWICO.

Mayor assumed the leadership of UNESCO at arguably the lowest point in the agency's history. Its budget had been slashed as a result of the withdrawal of the United States and the United Kingdom; and particularly negative Western newspapers, magazines, and other media coverage had tarnished its reputation. Director-General Mayor's immediate goal was to establish a climate of trust in the hope that the United States and the United Kingdom would return to full membership. He also sought to decrease the size of the bureaucracy and improve administrative management. By the late 1990s, Mayor convinced Great Britain to return but had little else to show for his efforts at significant reform.

At the 25th UNESCO General Assembly in 1989, Director-General Mayor issued a new communication strategy. This new approach stressed the Western principles of freedom of press, freedom of expression, and the development of an independent and pluralistic media. This philosophical and ideological shift was not only more attractive to the West, but it also coincided with the fall of the Berlin Wall in November 1989, which had raised expectations for an independent press throughout central and Eastern Europe.

In order to implement the new communication proposals, Mayor announced that a series of UNESCO meetings would be convened in Namibia, Kazakhstan, Chile, and Yemen. At each of these regional meetings, UNESCO's free-press communication proposal was to be enunciated, and ideas to promote press freedom and media pluralism in the regions would be explored. For example, the Windhoek Resolution, emerging from the 1991 Namibia conference to promote a pluralistic and free African press, declared that:

1. Consistent with article 19 of the Universal Declaration of Human Rights, the establishment, maintenance and fostering of an independent, pluralistic and free press is essential to the development and maintenance of democracy in a nation, and for economic development.
2. By an independent press, we mean a press independent from governmental, political or economic control or from control of materials and infrastructure essential for the production and dissemination of newspapers, magazines, and periodicals.

3. By a pluralistic press, we mean the end of monopolies of any kind and the existence of the greatest possible number of newspapers, magazines and periodicals reflecting the widest possible range of opinion within the community.
4. The welcome changes that an increasing number of African States are now undergoing towards multiparty democracies provide the climate in which an independent pluralistic press can emerge.
5. The worldwide trend towards democracy and freedom of information and expression is a fundamental contribution to the fulfillment of human aspirations.[23]

Wherever Director-General Mayor went during the 1990s, he promoted the new UNESCO communication strategy. His activities and comments were directed toward persuading two audiences: the current UNESCO member-ship and the United States. Not only did he advocate resolutions supporting new free and pluralistic press initiatives throughout the regions of the world, but he also sought to convince the United States that UNESCO's communica-tion policy was very much in line with the US free-press traditions and that they should return. Plus the support for NWICO also came down with the Berlin Wall.

For example, in his opening address to the conference in Bulgaria in September 1997, Mayor asserted:

> The indisputable success of that Round Table certainly gave new impetus to UNESCO's work for the development of independent and pluralistic media in both the public and private sector and encouraged us to continue along the same lines in other parts of the world-firstly in Africa (Windhoek, Namibia, May 1991), then in Asia (Almaty, Kazakhstan, October 1993), in Latin America and the Caribbean (Santiago de Chile, May 1994), and in the Arab region (Sana'a, Yemen, January 1996). The four Declarations and the corre-sponding plans of action adopted at those meetings have become real milestones in UNESCO's struggle for freedom of expression and of the press.[24]

He proceeded to emphasize this point and went on to stipulate the steps that must be taken to achieve the goal:

> The most crucial requirements today include: Building up pluralistic and independent media public and private alike-to replace the former monopolistic state-controlled news agencies, newspapers, and radio and television networks; Transforming media legisla-tion unsuited to democratic requirements; roviding the skills and know-how to meet the challenges of a democratic and competitive society including new areas of specializa-tion such as marketing, advertising, media management and public relations.[25]

This revised communication policy at UNESCO paved the way for the return of the United Kingdom, but it did not persuade the United States. In fact, UNESCO's critics in Congress, the State Department, and outside of government remained adamant that the United States stay out of UNESCO. For example, in 1995, despite the positive changes undertaken by Mayor and the return of the United Kingdom, the ultra-conservative Heritage Foundation argued, "Rejoining UNESCO ... would be a serious mistake."[26] Its rationales were delineated in "Executive Memorandum #403." They are:

1. UNESCO has serious management shortcomings.
2. Rejoining UNESCO would send the wrong signal about UN management reform.
3. UNESCO's mission lacks focus.
4. UNESCO activities are redundant.
5. The United States already benefits from the best of UNESCO.[27]

The memorandum concludes with a plea to the US government to spend elsewhere the $65 million annual dues due UNESCO. President Clinton stated in 1995 "I assure you that US membership in UNESCO remains on my list of priorities for the future."[28] Also on his list for the 1990s was paying back the $1.6 billion in dues owed to the United Nations that Congress had refused for years to approve but finally relented to do in 1999.

UNESCO in the 1990s

In the early 1990s, as a result of dramatic but peaceful political revolutions, the former Soviet Union and its client states rapidly abandoned totalitarian structures, including their press systems. Consequently, many journalists and editors from newly independent states of eastern and central Europe began to participate in the new communication strategy debate within UNESCO. The general conferences, which continued to be held every two years, produced several resolutions supporting the goals of the new strategy. In particular, there was considerable support for independent and free media along the lines of the Western model. In addition, the International Programme for the Development of Communication (IPDC) encouraged proposals that facilitated the founding of free and open press activities in peripheral nations. Director-General Mayor also created a new unit within UNESCO entitled "Freedom of Expression and Democracy." Its goal was just that – to promote freedom of expression and other democratic ideas, including a free and pluralistic press. Moreover, under Mayor's leadership, UNESCO began to work against the imprisonment and expulsion of journalists around the world. In response to these policy changes, the United Kingdom rejoined UNESCO in 1997.

The United States's Reaction

Director-General Mayor's efforts and the revised international communication policy did not go unnoticed in the United States. When the US National Security

Council established an interagency working group in 1993 to examine UNESCO, all relevant activities ranging from the administration of the agency to its media-related strategies underwent thorough scrutiny. The working group's findings were positive, and it recommended that the United States rejoin UNESCO by mid-decade. Simultaneously, a small group in the US House of Representatives initiated favorable discussions concerning UNESCO and suggested that it was time for the United States to return. Educators also began to lobby informally for US reentry. Mayor also traveled extensively in the United States to promote good relations between UNESCO and the US. Despite the goodwill created by Mayor, his successor, and UNESCO's free-press initiatives it was not until 2002, under President Bush, that the US rejoined UNESCO.

A New Focus

In the late 1990s, UNESCO produced a major document titled *World Information Report* that began to chronicle information resources in almost 200 countries around the globe. Its publication marked a change in emphasis within UNESCO to the examination of the global information highway, including the internet. The *World Information Report* provided extensive documentation of computer-based information processing, including the shift toward multimedia, telecommunications, and electronic databases.

The report is divided into three parts. The first section describes the information services in individual countries or regions. The second section details the infrastructures for information industries and focuses on technical issues including multimedia and telecommunications. The final section discusses issues and trends such as the emergence of the information society, information highways, economic implications, copyright matters, and other social or legal questions. The report concludes with a chapter outlining the necessity for international cooperation in order to ensure access for all through the interconnection of global information technologies. Mayor emphasized the importance of these issues and UNESCO's new direction in 1998:

> We need to make a new start, founded on the principles and values enshrined in UNESCO's Constitution, which stipulates that, for a lust and lasting peace, "intellectual and moral solidarity" is a necessary condition. Here, the new communication technologies and especially the development of the information highways have the potential to give concrete form to global solidarity by including the excluded, because the networks they form can reach all human beings, wherever they live.[29]

Part of the new focus is to promote practical and concrete programs that can help peripheral regions. For example, now in UNESCO documents the push concerning communication is to provide "equal access to information and communication technologies."[30] UNESCO is also sponsoring regional conferences focusing on a free and pluralistic press.

Mayor's Successor: An Asian Leader

In October 1999, two important events occurred in UNESCO. First, a new Director-General was elected after major candidates had emerged from Australia, Saudi Arabia, Egypt, and Japan. Ultimately, the Japanese ambassador to France, Koichiro Matsuura, was elected. He began his six-year term immediately and presided over the annual budget of $300 million; this budget is now closer to $500 million since the United States and United Kingdom have rejoined. The DG was re-elected to a second term. Since the last two DGs are from core nations, Spain and Japan, it is likely that the next DG would likely be from a peripheral or semi-peripheral nation.

The second event concerned allegations of cronyism and mismanagement, specifically that the French government had used the Paris-based UNESCO to place former government aides on UNESCO's payroll throughout the 1990s. The UK paper *The Guardian* ran extensive stories documenting the administrative problems, going so far as to report that almost half of UNESCO's appointments in the 1990s failed to meet the administrative criteria for credentials and for fair and open competition for senior appointments.[31]

In 2004 DG Matsuura organized a meeting to draft a global convention on the protection of cultural diversity and artistic expression. This followed an earlier 2004 meeting with over 600 delegates from 132 UNESCO Member States, plus numerous NGOs, that discussed the protection of cultural goods and services. This includes the mass media for many of the participating nations. This Convention on the Protection and Promotion of the Diversity of Cultural Expressions puts UNESCO on a likely collision course with the World Trade Organization (WTO).

The Convention was approved by UNESCO in 2005, with the US voting against it. The Convention seeks to affirm the rights of nations to set their own cultural policies, plus recognize that culture is linked to identity, values, and concept of self. Basically the Convention does not see culture as a commercial good to be bought and sold, like cars or wheat. It is distinct and in many cases unique and thus needs to be protected from electronic colonialism. The Convention covers the five related activities including creation, production, distribution, access to, and enjoyment of cultural expressions and activities. Finally, it also seeks to protect languages and the protection of diverse or indigenous languages.

The WTO is seeking to expand its mandate by including cultural industries in such a way as to reduce all protectionist measures – such as quotas, grants, subsidies, license fees, and a host of other protectionist tariffs. This entire matter has the potential to become a major global public policy issue. The US will be on one side and the cultural nationalists on the other.

Finally, UNESCO is also heavily involved in the World Summit on the Information Society (more is discussed about the WSIS in chapter 5). UNESCO is providing assistance for many of the WSIS action plan areas under the umbrella of UNESCO's major initiative labeled "Knowledge Societies." Some critics of the WSIS claim that it seeks to promote governments having a role in media oversight and to them it sounds like a phase or stage two for the discredited NWICO. Given that the second meeting of WSIS was in anti-free press and authoritarian Tunisia, the outlook is dim for all agencies, including the ITU and UNESCO, which sponsored WSIS and supported the bizarre selection of the location of Tunisia for a major international conference dealing with the media and communication.

Conclusions

Although the UNESCO General Assembly has always addressed 13 major programs, beginning with the 1976 meeting in Nairobi its conferences have been dominated by the single communication program, NWICO, and its fallout. Like a lightning rod, NWICO attracted all the media attention. Not only was it an issue of distinct interest to the media, but it also polarized the delegates to the point that the United States and the United Kingdom withdrew. It also created significant public image problems for the agency and threatened its internal operations and financial stability. Today, UNESCO still has major fiscal and image problems. Historically, the debate was about aspects of electronic colonialism that the core nations did not want to hear about, deal with, or come to terms with. Peripheral nations were concerned that their cultures, values, languages, and influence were being displaced by slick, heavily advertised sounds and images from a few core nations.

Although there is little doubt among those familiar with UNESCO that the organization does sound work in several areas ranging from literacy and environmental concerns to scientific and educational topics, these efforts receive scant attention at the general assemblies and in global media. This imbalance is clear when one realizes that UNESCO's communication sector receives less than 10 percent of the agency's budget, but clearly receives well over 90 percent of its media coverage. The problem is complicated further because that coverage, particularly in Western nations, is overwhelmingly negative. It is difficult, therefore, for concerned individuals and governments to be supportive of UNESCO when the public at large is not favorably impressed, and when the uninitiated believe that all UNESCO does is debate communication and promote anti-free press policies.

The historical role of the Soviet Union is also clear. It was obvious to many that the Soviet Union was promoting an anti-free press agenda and that it had considerable rein within the halls of UNESCO. To a large extent, without the United Kingdom or the United States at the negotiating table, UNESCO became a captive of the socialist nations that offered token support to peripheral nations. A second challenge related to internal leadership. After 11 years as director-general, M'Bow had failed to respond to the growing negative perception of UNESCO, even within the UN system. His term came to an abrupt end in 1987. Finally, and perhaps most surprising, was the implosion of the Soviet Union, which spelled the end of its role as the great benefactor, champion, and savior of UNESCO and NWICO. When the USSR exited from the world stage, so too did the influence and funds it lent to UNESCO.

Despite the problems NWICO created, the overall debate in UNESCO has been informative. It not only forced a reanalysis and reaffirmation of values, but it also accentuated the need for hard data and planning practical strategies in order to enhance communication development throughout the world. NWICO continues to evolve in its search for practical and applied measures aimed at redressing media imbalances and promoting greater concern for cultural sensitivity and indigenous software. The peripheral nations still cling to NWICO in the face of greater core-nation media pressure to adopt Western philosophies, products, and practices. Director-General Matsuura wants none of the divisive rhetoric and is promoting a media-friendly UNESCO. Finally, a small group of academics and journalists from around the globe continue to promote the aims of NWICO. Under the banner of the MacBride Round Table, they meet every two years to examine the state of affairs in peripheral nations.[32] They are an advocacy group created in 1989 to examine the global communication imbalances identified in the 1980 MacBride Report, titled *Many Voices, One World*,[33] commissioned by UNESCO. They are expanding the research agenda to include internet issues as part of the NWICO legacy.

Finally, UNESCO is moving into two areas loaded with contention. They are a global convention on cultural diversity[34] and strong affiliation with the WSIS. Either of these hot button issues could once again see major donor nations reexamine their commitment to UNESCO and its programs.[35]

Notes

1. Ali Mohammadi, *International Communication and Globalization*, London: Sage, 1997, p. 2.
2. UNESCO, "What Is UNESCO," Paris: UNESCO, 1977.
3. For an excellent look at the internal workings and problems of UNESCO's Secretariat, see former Assistant Director-General Richard Hoggart's *An Idea and Its Servants: UNESCO from Within*, London: Chatto and Windus, 1978.
4. Richard Hoggart, *An Idea and Its Servants: UNESCO from Within*, London: Chatto and Windus, 1978, p. 64.
5. Faure Commission report, *Learning to Be*, Paris: UNESCO, 1972.
6. Some analysts date the beginning of the NWICO debate to 1968, when the Declaration on Human Rights was amended to include the notion of a balanced and free flow of information. Given the subsequent differences in interpretation, policy decisions, and political maneuvering related to this phrase, it is interesting to note that it was the United Slates that first introduced the amendment.

7. Kaarle Nordenstreng and Tapio Varis, "Television Traffic: A One Way Street? A Survey and Analysis of the International Plow of Television," Paris: UNESCO, 1974.

8. Brenda Pavlic and Cees Hamelink, *The New International Economic Order: Links between Economies and Communications*, Reports and Papers on Mass Communication 98, Paris: UNESCO, 1985.

9. United Nations, *Declaration on the Establishment of a New International Economic Order*, G. A. Res. 3201, Sixth Special Session, UN Supp. (No. 1), UN Doc. A/9559.

10. See, for example, UNESCO, *Moving towards Change: Some Thoughts on the New International Economic Order*, Paris: UNESCO, 1976.

11. The history of OPEC is also viewed by communication scholars as a classic case study of initial Western media inattention, and then biased reporting, once OPEC was able to establish itself as a major instrument of political and commercial power – extending to the gas pump.

12. Hoggart, 1978, p. 193.

13. UNESCO 20C/Inf. 9, October 28, Paris: Author, 1978, p. 4. Reprinted by permission of UNESCO.

14. Ibid., p. 14.

15. Ibid., p. 15.

16. John Roberts, UNESCO document 20C/vr (prov), November 6, 1978, press release, reprinted by permission of UNESCO.

17. Phillip Muscat, UNESCO document 20C/vr (prov), November 4, 1978, press release, reprinted by permission of UNESCO.

18. *New York Times* (October 25, 1980: 14).

19. UNESCO, Draft Programme and Budget for 1984–1985, 111 Communication in the Service of Man, 22C/5, Paris: Author, 1983, p. 2.

20. UNESCO, Draft Programme and Budget for 1984–1985, 111 Communication in the Service of Man, 22C/5, Paris: Author, 1983, p. 3.

21. *New York Times* (15 December 1983: D1).

22. *New York Times* (30 December 1983: D4).

23. UNESCO, "Declarations on Promoting Independent and Pluralist Media: Declaration of Windhoek," Paris: UNESCO, May 3, 1991, mimeographed, p. 4.

24. Federico Mayor, "Address at the Opening of the European Seminar to Promote Pluralistic and Independent Media," Paris: UNESCO, September 10, 1997, mimeographed, p 1.

25. Ibid., p. 2.fc

26. Thomas P. Sheehy, "Executive Memorandum #403: Stay out of UNESCO," Washington, DC: Heritage Foundation, January 1, 1995, mimeographed, p. 1.

27. Ibid.," p. 1,

28. www.Reuters, Information Service, November 15, 1995.

29. Federico Mayor, "Opening Address: Human Rights on the Eve of the 21st Century," Paris: UNESCO, December 17, 1998, mimeographed, p.2.

30. UNESCO 160 EX/48. *Final Report of the Task Force on UNESCO in the Twenty-First Century*, October 11, Paris: UNESCO, 2000, p. 6.

31. Jon Henley, *The Guardian*, October 18, 19, 21, 1999.

32. This group seeks to examine issues of access, ownership, equality, and trends in global communication in the tradition of the MacBride Report. See, for example,

Richard Vincent, Kaarle Nordenstreng, and Michael Traber (eds.), *Towards Equity in Global Communication*, Crosskill, NJ: Hampton Press, 1999.

33. Sean MacBride, *Many Voices, One World*, New York: Unipub, 1980.
34. The entire background, related activities, and future plans/meetings of the convention are available at: www.unesco.org/culture/en/diversity/convention.
35. Events at UNESCO are a lot like history on the run. To keep up with matters discussed in this chapter, including the agenda of the new Director General, Irine Bokova, see www.unesco.org/.

4

Public Diplomacy
New Dimensions and Implications

Nancy Snow

Introduction

In global communications, ideas matter. But ideas alone can't make any measurable difference if they are not properly marketed to an audience, be it a consumer or citizen. Consider one relatively unknown junior senator from Chicago, Illinois, who used outstanding marketing and persuasion skills, along with internet savvy, to package his ideas effectively enough to win the American presidency in 2008. In many respects, Barack Obama is the ultimate public diplomat. He is the new "gold standard." He used his powerful oratory skills to convey his beliefs and ideals to the American people. In the process, he became an international celebrity who illustrated a new globally-minded United States (US) president, sensitive to not just what others think about the US nation and its people, but also committed to changing unpopular foreign policies like pledging to close Guantanamo Bay prison in Cuba and ending the post-September 11 slogan, Global War on Terror (GWOT), that predicated the wars in Afghanistan and Iraq.

The Personal is Political in Public Diplomacy

Public diplomacy, with its emphasis on political power relations, has a strong tie to national security and foreign policy outcomes. This translates into distinct public diplomacy agendas driven by specific administrations and their leaders in power. While President Obama may emphasize a more collaborative public diplomacy style that brings together global partners in mutual endeavors, his predecessor President George W. Bush brought attention to a unilateral style of public diplomacy through his administration's emphasis on winning the US-led War on Terror. Bush asked the nation, "Why do they hate us?"[1] and instituted international communication campaigns that would attempt to overcome the animus that led to terrorist attacks in 2001.

James Glassman was the final and only male Under Secretary of State for public diplomacy and public affairs for President Bush. His predecessor, Karen Hughes, was President George W. Bush's chief adviser on all things persuasion and communications and was once described by the *Dallas Morning News* as "the most powerful woman ever to serve in the White House."[2] Margaret Tutwiler, former ambassador to Morocco and protégé of Secretary of State James Baker, though serving a short five months in the position, offered a memorable statement that echoed the frustrations associated with being a nation's image czar: "There is not one magic bullet, magic program or magic solution. As much as we would like to think Washington knows best, we have to be honest and admit we do not necessarily always have all the answers."[3]

Tutwiler emphasized active listening on the part of the US government – including listening to its diplomats serving on the frontlines – and expanding the discussion of American values and policies to public venues outside of traditional elites in diplomacy and government. "We only have to look at the activities of US corporations overseas to see the value of being present and engaged in neighborhoods that we in government have for too long neglected."[4] She also announced a slight increase in educational exchanges, particularly youth exchanges, focused primarily on the Middle East. When Tutwiler suddenly announced her switch from government public relations to the New York Stock Exchange executive suites, one could not help but notice that the move occurred during the week that the first brutal images of abused Iraqi prisoners in Abu Ghraib were released worldwide, rendering her youth exchange program from the Middle East – Partnerships for Learning, with its less than 200 participants – a drop of hope in an ocean of anger and resentment.[5]

Glassman, Hughes, Tutwiler, and the most noted Under Secretary, Charlotte Beers, were tasked with carrying out a public mission to communicate with global publics in the service of national security and foreign policy objectives of the United States. Charlotte Beers, who once headed J. Walter Thompson and Ogilvy & Mather, is considered a legend in the advertising world. Known as the "Queen of Branding" and the "Steel Magnolia of Advertising," the Texas-born Beers convinced then Secretary of State Colin Powell that America needed a rebranding campaign on US foreign policy in the post-9/11 environment. As Powell explained his decision to the Senate Foreign Relations Committee, "Well guess what? She got me to buy Uncle Ben's rice and so there is nothing wrong with getting somebody who knows how to sell something."[6]

From Uncle Ben to Uncle Sam

The suggestion that selling Uncle Sam was as seamless a sales job as packaging instant rice did not sit well with many observers in the press and public. Andrew Alexander of the *London Daily Mail* wrote, "One shouldn't laugh, really, but

I must confess to a short guffaw on reading that Washington's new war propaganda chief is a woman head of an advertising agency whose personal triumphs included Uncle Ben's rice and Head and Shoulders shampoo." Columnist Frank Rich of the *New York Times* cracked: "The Bush appointee in charge of the propaganda effort is a CEO (from Madison Avenue) chosen not for her expertise in policy or politics but for her salesmanship on behalf of domestic products like Head and Shoulders shampoo. If we can't effectively fight anthrax, I guess it's reassuring to know we can always win the war on dandruff." Steve Lopez of the *Los Angeles Times* joked that the White House decision to choose Beers as chief propaganda queen led to his "second out-of-body experience" since the onset of the war in Afghanistan on October 7, 2001. (His first out-of-body experience was the White House decision to choose the project title Operation Infinite Justice, which was quickly dumped for the more modest Operation Enduring Freedom.) At first befuddled that the White House would put an ad executive in charge of America's image war, Lopez sarcastically snipped: "Who knows? Maybe they're onto something. Just the other day I took a sip of Coke and began singing, 'I'd like to teach the world to sing in perfect harmony.' How could anyone hate a nation of peace-loving simpletons for whom the best part of waking up is Folger's in your cup?"[7]

Despite the media grumblings, Beers came into her office with much fanfare and high expectations for accomplishing the main Brand America mission to diffuse harsh global opinion attitudes toward the United States, particularly in the Arab Middle East, but also in Europe and Latin America. Charlotte Beers quickly identified George Bush and Colin Powell as the "poster people" of American public diplomacy in the world.[8] Her tenure was marked by the rather dubious outcome of the US State Department sponsored advertising campaign called "Shared Values," that consisted of two-minute clips of Muslim Americans talking about their positive lives in the United States.[9] Beers resigned from her position in March 2003, just weeks before the US invasion of Iraq. Her male successor, James Glassman, said that the American public diplomacy mission was a global war of ideas:

> Our mission today in the war of ideas is highly focused. It is to use the tools of ideological engagement – words, deeds, and images – to create an environment hostile to violent extremism. We want to break the linkages between groups like Al Qaeda and their target audiences. Indeed, in the war of ideas, our core task is not how to fix foreigners' perceptions of the United States but how to isolate and reduce the threat of violent extremism. Our task is not to build our brand but to help destroy theirs.[10]

Barack Obama's first Under Secretary for public diplomacy is Judith McHale. Appointed in May 2009, she has not received the same media attention as Charlotte Beers or Karen Hughes. In her first major speech, McHale emphasized the people-to-people diplomacy (P2P) of her new boss, Hillary Clinton:

> This is not a propaganda contest – it is a relationship race. And we have got to get back in the game. So how do we rebuild our national credibility and renew our engagement

with the people of the world? We need to develop a multidimensional, results-oriented approach that combines traditional outreach with cutting-edge technology to engage with people at all levels of society. Broadly speaking, public diplomacy operates on two levels. First, communication. This is the air game, the radio and TV broadcasts, the websites and media outreach that all seek to explain and provide context for US policies and action; and second, engagement, the ground game of direct people-to-people exchanges, speakers, and embassy-sponsored cultural events that build personal relationships.[11]

McHale's first address was titled, "Public Diplomacy: A National Security Imperative," and she referenced Secretary of Defense Robert Gates, the point man in both the Bush and Obama administrations to elevate public diplomacy to the level of national security.

We are not the only ones who see the significance of increased engagement. Friends, competitors, and adversaries are moving quickly. The Chinese are building infrastructure and cultural centers across the world, developing long-term relationships in Africa, Latin America, and elsewhere. The Iranian public diplomacy network in the Middle East and beyond includes satellite television and radio networks in several languages, more than 100 newspapers and magazines, and thousands of websites and blogs. And of course Al-Qaeda and other extremists continue to engage aggressively using a range of new and old media.[12]

Public Diplomacy and Global Communication

It is clear from these previous statements that public diplomacy is a new subfield of global communication with old constituent ties to social influence, rhetoric, persuasive communication and international exchange and engagement. As a modern concept, it is firmly ensconced in the Cold-War ideological struggle of the twentieth century between the United States and the USSR; this was the era when public opinion management and winning hearts and minds of global publics outside the two spheres, such as non-aligned nations, was supreme.

The continuum of persuasion between information and engagement has traditionally been the exclusive domain of governments in support of foreign policy interests. Traditional diplomacy is about relationships of state officials. It is top-down, elite, and driven by government officials who meet often in private where business and negotiation take part with little contact or communication with the public. Public diplomacy (PD) refers to global communication efforts to inform, influence, and engage global publics in support of national interests. As opposed to traditional diplomacy efforts that take place behind closed doors and lead to sometimes-awkward staged handshakes before the credentialed press, public diplomacy efforts are designed to be transparent in their mission and open-sourced in their function. It is the support of the overseas public, in particular, non-official target groups, individuals and organizations that a nation seeks, not just one head of state or foreign minister.

Public diplomacy is a global process oriented toward diplomacy to publics. Open communication, interaction, and reaching out to publics through news and opinion management are expected in public diplomacy. Unlike traditional diplomacy that has a small network of advanced trained and educated individuals, public diplomacy's mission is open to everyone. It is a function and concern of all nations and citizens, including multinational organizations such as the European Union, UNESCO, and Medécins Sans Frontières (Doctors Without Borders). In the short-term, public diplomacy is about getting one's message out to foreign publics in a timely and understood fashion; at its core, the best public diplomacy is about relationship building to build mutual understanding between the parties engaged in a communication exchange.

Public Diplomacy History

The Cold War (1948–91) between the United States and the Soviet Union played a primary role in maintaining public diplomacy's government mission. By the early 1990s with the rise of global citizen activism and global media in service of such activism, public diplomacy took on a new patina, much more person-to-person and public-to-public in activity and outcome. With an emboldened sense of purpose at having contributed to the demise of the Cold War, global citizens refused to remain sidelined in the post-Cold-War era. Many took it upon themselves to shape attitudes and opinions of their foreign compatriots outside the official channels of governments. By September 2001, with the declaration of a US-led global war on terror and the decline of traditional media's influence, global citizens created their own websites, e-mail lists, and online meetings to educate, inform, influence, and engage on foreign policies which directly affected their livelihoods.

Public diplomacy's etymology has an American heritage, though its communicative attributes predate its twentieth-century origins wherever nations with ambition or at war cared about what others outside their national borders thought of them. Public diplomacy is like old wine in new bottles, those new bottles being democratization of information and new information and communication technologies that have shrunk, if not collapsed, borders between global publics. Though public diplomacy has a dominant American patina, public diplomacy is an ancient phenomenon. As scholar Jan Melissen notes:

> Image cultivation, propaganda, and activities that we would now label as public diplomacy are nearly as old as diplomacy itself. Even in ancient times, prestige-conscious princes and their representatives never completely ignored the potential and pitfalls of public opinion in foreign lands. References to the nation and its image go as far back as the Bible, and international relations in ancient Greece and Rome, Byzantium and the Italian Renaissance were familiar with diplomatic activity aimed at foreign publics.[13]

Edmund Gullion, dean emeritus of the Fletcher School of Law and Diplomacy (1964–78) at Tufts University in Massachusetts (USA) is credited with first elevating the term in 1965 at the time of the dedication of the Edward R. Murrow Center of Public Diplomacy. It had been twelve years since the founding of the independent federal agency responsible for public diplomacy activities, the United States Information Agency (USIA) in 1953 by Dwight D. Eisenhower. Gullion sought a term that would accomplish two functions:

1. disassociate public diplomacy from the loaded term propaganda with all its negative associations from World War II; and
2. elevate the role of the diplomat serving the public in the foreign service from that of a government public relations or advertising "sales" agent.[14]

Gullion was a highly decorated foreign diplomat who retired during the Lyndon Baines Johnson administration as US Ambassador to the Congo. The new Murrow Center emphasized direct communications and mutual understanding between the people of the United States and those in other countries. An early brochure described public diplomacy this way:

> Public diplomacy ... deals with the influence of public attitudes on the formation and execution of foreign policies. It encompasses dimensions of international relations beyond traditional diplomacy; the cultivation by governments of public opinion in other countries; the interaction of private groups and interests in one country with those of another; the reporting of foreign affairs and its impact on policy; communication between those whose job is communication, as between diplomats and foreign correspondents; and the processes of intercultural communications.[15]

Traditional Public Diplomacy (TPD) has several features:

- Government to Publics (G2P);
- official in nature;
- necessary evil as technology and new media democratized international relations;
- linked to foreign policy/national security outcomes;
- one-way informational and two-way asymmetric (unequal partners in communication);
- give us your best and brightest feature players;
- passive public role; and
- crisis-driven and reactive (let's put out fires, come in on crash landings).

The retired broadcast journalist Murrow was named director of the United States Information Agency (USIA) by President John F. Kennedy in 1961 and served in that position until January 1964. To this day, Murrow remains the iconic, if not ironic, face of public diplomacy. Though world famous as a foreign war correspondent who always reported the facts on the ground, Murrow had to transition from objective narrator of the Fourth Estate to the opinion management style required of a federal agency head tasked with "telling America's story to the world." While Murrow viewed public diplomacy as a focus of non-governmental interactions that presented unofficial and diverse views of private individuals and organizations, he was also associated with a presidential administration that emphasized counterinsurgency and covert operations in developing countries.[16] The respected journalist said that harnessing the national interest overseas required credibility and integrity on the part of public officials:

> American traditions and the American ethic require us to be truthful, but the most impor-
> tant reason is that truth is the best propaganda and lies are the worst. To be persuasive,
> we must be believable; to be believable we must be credible; to be credible we must be
> truthful. It is as simple as that.[17]

After Murrow was kept out of the Kennedy Administration's secret Bay of Pigs invasion plans for Cuba in 1961, he said that USIA must be brought in "on the take-offs and not just the crash landings." Murrow sought to place the public diplomacy activities of the US Information Agency firmly in the domain of policy decision-making inside the White House. Edward R. Murrow along with Walter Cronkite were better known as the patron saints of broadcast journalism in the United States. To public diplomacy scholars and practitioners, he is the lesser-known face of ethical and responsible public diplomacy. Murrow was a visionary who understood that public diplomacy, like politics, is local and personal. The Murrowism, "to be credible, we must be truthful," still holds today.

Defining Public Diplomacy

When it comes to defining public diplomacy today, there is no one accepted definition of what it means, but rather every nation has its own definition that works for its stated goals and objectives. USIA described it succinctly: "Public Diplomacy seeks to promote the national interest of the United States through understanding, informing and influencing foreign audiences."[18] A good elevator ride definition is the following: Public Diplomacy is "an international actor's attempt to advance the ends of policy by engaging with foreign publics."[19]

In that second definition, a new dimension of public diplomacy is that it need not include just official public diplomacy representatives of governments. Today's global media and global celebritydom can elevate a person without any formal elite education in foreign policy onto a platform that can reach more global publics than any foreign minister or most heads of state. For example, the technological phenomenon known as Twitter has allowed Hollywood actors like Ashton Kutcher to compete for followers of his tweets with CNN broadcast journalists like Larry King and Anderson Cooper. If Kutcher wants to make a statement about foreign policy of the United States, he can tweet a short statement of some 140 characters and allow his voice to instantly become part of the global conversation. On April 25, 2009, Kutcher did just that. He posted a tweet asking all his followers to in turn tweet the following: "Every 30 seconds a child dies from Malaria. Nets save lives. Support World Malaria Day."[20] Given the reach of social media and social networking sites today like Twitter, Facebook, and MySpace, there are few, if any, government officials who have the virtual star power of a television or movie star to influence the global public agenda.

From James Glassman to Brangelina

Who is more influential:

1. a professional athlete, international film star, famous musician, or author; or
2. the Under Secretary of State for Public Diplomacy and Public Affairs?

There is no question today that a person who is world famous for something outside of influencing public policy has the opportunity to be more influential as a public diplomat than a person working the corridors of national governments. We live in a mediated environment dominated by infotainment and the comings and goings of celebrities around the clock. Should a celebrity – simply a person famous for being famous – decide to weigh in on some foreign policy issue, the mass media are likely to report on it. This does not mean that foreign secretaries are going to give up making speeches or issuing press statements. But they will more likely follow the example of the new American president and make sure that everything that is said has a multimedia delivery system that favors the internet and social media.

While public diplomacy traditionally involves actors like public affairs and public information officers of governments, government broadcasters, and cultural mediators like sponsored exchange students and field workers, new public diplomacy actors include anyone who challenges dominant assumptions in international relations and foreign policies of government. They may include international terrorists, sports stars, celebrities, and other highly visible global public figures as well as non-governmental (NGO) and private voluntary organizations (PVO). James Glassman, Charlotte Beers, and Karen Hughes and the newest Judith McHale may be the American government faces of public diplomacy; they are hardly its chief influence agents. Brad Pitt's work with Global Green USA building eco-friendly houses in the Ninth Ward of New Orleans or Angelina Jolie's work on behalf of refugees with the United Nations is more influential public diplomacy on behalf of the United States image in the world. They are the new public diplomats of today.

New Public Diplomacy (NPD) includes these features:

- Publics to Publics (P2P);
- unofficial (NGOs, private citizens, practitioners);
- everyone's doing it;
- active and participatory public;
- dialogic and exchange oriented, two-way symmetric;

- generally more long-term in reference to behavioral change; and
- based on relationship, systems and network theories.

No one knows if Angelina Jolie identifies herself as a public diplomat, but she has become the most recognized celebrity member of the foreign policy establishment. Since 2001, Jolie has served as the "face" of global refugees. A Goodwill Ambassador for the United Nations High Commission for Refugees (UNHCR) who has traveled to over 20 countries to speak out on behalf of refugees and internally displaced persons, Jolie was inducted into the Council on Foreign Relations in 2007. The Council, publisher of *Foreign Affairs* magazine, is the most influential think tank of foreign relations in the world. Its select group of over 4,000 individual members includes ex-presidents, secretaries of state, CEOs, and elite media representatives, of which just 1,000 are women. Term members like Angelina Jolie must be under 40 years old and serve five years, after which they can be nominated for life membership. Corporate members (250) include ABC News, AIG, Halliburton, PepsiCo, and Pfizer. Both Angelina Jolie and her partner Brad Pitt live their lives as actors on a world stage.

Compare the global attention paid to these two celebrities and a person in charge of public diplomacy at the State Department or Ministry of Foreign Affairs. Under Secretary of State for Public Diplomacy and Public Affairs James K. Glassman is an international actor, but unlike "Brangelina," he could never garner the same attention to his causes. Glassman, who served as Under Secretary from June 2008 to January 2009, linked public diplomacy to the war against violent extremism. James Glassman's public diplomacy focus is strategic: "Unlike traditional functions of public diplomacy like education and cultural exchanges, the aim of the war of ideas is not to persuade foreign populations to adopt more favorable views of America and its policies. Instead, the war of ideas tries to ensure that negative sentiments and day-to-day grievances toward America and its allies do not manifest themselves in the form of violent extremism."[21] He likened successful public diplomacy as a competition between orange juice and lemonade:

> Think of America's values and political system as orange juice; think of the Al-Qaeda system of violent extremism as lemonade. Our job for the short term is not to put all of our efforts into getting people to drink orange juice, but to get them not to drink lemonade. They can drink anything else they want: milk, ginger ale, tomato juice, Coke. We are confident that, ultimately, they will come around to orange juice or something close to it, but inthe meantime, we want them to stay away from lemonade.[22]

Global Public Diplomacy

A country like Costa Rica with no standing army will have a scaled down public diplomacy to that of countries with major militaries like the United States. North Korea and China have their own public diplomacy objectives that are often indistinguishable from state propaganda goals. In many countries outside the United States, public diplomacy is used interchangeably with propaganda or strategic communication since such activities involve mass communication efforts to change minds in service of behavioral changes that favor the sponsoring country. In order to fully understand public diplomacy, it calls upon global communication practitioners and scholars to consider other perspectives and test your own cultural assumptions. A broad mind and intercultural orientation is helpful in order to transcend the dominance of the United States and Great Britain that have dominated public diplomacy schools of thought. Numerous parameters shape global public diplomacy. These include the following:

Layers of Public Diplomacy

The three main layers of engagement in public diplomacy are monologic (one-way) communication, dialogic (two-way or multidirectional) and collaborative (group ventures/joint projects). An example of monologic communication in the service of public diplomacy involves public pronouncements with global lasting effects, like the words of American president John F. Kennedy who stood at Berlin's City Hall on June 26, 1963 and proudly declared himself a citizen of Berlin:

> Two thousand years ago, the proudest boast was *civis romanus sum* (I am a Roman citizen). Today, in the world of freedom, the proudest boast is "Ich bin ein Berliner." All free men, wherever they may live, are citizens of Berlin, and therefore, as a free man, I take pride in the words "Ich bin ein Berliner!"[23]

These words were meant to inspire all citizens living within the influence of the Soviet Union and behind the Iron Curtain, including those families divided into East and West Berlin by the Berlin Wall. A quarter of a century later, another American president Ronald Reagan would once again stand in Berlin and say, "Mr. Gorbachev, tear down this wall!" On July 24, 2008, Democratic hopeful Barack Obama stood in Berlin and gave his own statement about the promise of freedom to several hundred thousand people who knew very well the significance of Berlin to iconic monologic moments in history:

> Yes, there have been differences between America and Europe. No doubt, there will be differences in the future. But the burdens of global citizenship continue to bind us together. A change of leadership in Washington will not lift this burden. In this new century, Americans and Europeans alike will be required to do more – not less. Partnership and cooperation among nations is not a choice; it is the one way, the only way, to protect our common security and advance our common humanity. That is why the greatest danger of all is to allow new walls to divide us from one another. The walls between old

allies on either side of the Atlantic cannot stand. The walls between the countries with the most and those with the least cannot stand. The walls between races and tribes; natives and immigrants; Christian and Muslim and Jew cannot stand. These now are the walls we must tear down.[24]

One-way communication strategies include international television and radio broadcasting networks like Voice of America (United States), Deutsche Welle (Germany) and the British Broadcasting Corporation (United Kingdom). Following the attacks of September 11, 2001, the US Government spent most of its State Department public diplomacy budget on international broadcasting efforts in the service of the war on terror. Under the auspices of the Broadcasting Board of Governors, the US Government launched Radio Sawa, a 24-hour radio broadcast to the Arab Middle East. Its format was to blend one-third news with two-thirds light music fare, mostly pop music in English, Arabic and Spanish that would appeal to young people (mainly males) under the age of 30. Critics referred to Radio Sawa as using Britney Spears in the information warfare strategies of the United States. Al-Hurra Television (in Arabic, "The Free One") was launched on February 14, 2004. Like Sawa, Al-Hurra has suffered its own credibility problems, most notably, its symbolic brand. If a network calls itself the freedom network, then it puts its target audience on the defensive. If the sponsor of the network is free, does this make the viewing audience unfree? In the case of the Middle East marketplace for Al-Hurra, there is no question that by and large the governments are autocratic and authoritarian in orientation; nevertheless, the people of the Middle East generally delineate their status as free-thinking individuals from their controlling state bodies.

Two-way communication, or dialogue, is obviously important to international political engagement. Much of traditional diplomacy involves dialogue between principals. In public diplomacy, dialogue is expanded to the exchange of information and ideas across social and cultural boundaries.

The third layer of public diplomacy, collaboration, is often the least noted mode of communicative engagement in the literature, but it is no less important to our understanding of how public diplomacy operates in the global communication environment. As Cowan and Arsenault state, "Collaborative projects almost without exception include dialogue between participants and stakeholders, but they also include concrete and typically easily identifiable goals and outcomes that provide a useful basis and structure upon which to form more lasting relationships."[25] Collaboration is similar to the concept of superordinate goals in conflict resolution situations.

Many public diplomats in a dialogic or collaborative context view their roles as cultural mediators or peace negotiators engaged in Track Two citizen-based diplomacy. Track One diplomacy, the arena for formal, official, government-to-government interaction by designated representatives of sovereign states, is complimented by Track Two diplomacy, which refers to non-governmental, informal, and unofficial ties between private citizens and groups that relate to each other outside the constraints of formal power. Often these encounters are designed to bring people together who are in some type of conflict and require mediation. John McDonald, a 40-year diplomat and co-founder of the Institute for Multi-Track Diplomacy, says,

> Track Two aims to reduce or resolve conflict by decreasing the anger, tension, and fear between peoples by improving the communication and understanding of the other side's point of view. In no way is Track Two a substitute for Track One; instead, it complements and parallels the goals of Track One.[26]

Elevation of Exchanges

One of the most important parameters of public diplomacy today is the valuing of person-to-person exchanges. Many universities host international visitors and tout the merits of overseas study in order to expand one's knowledge but also to promote a global understanding of political and social problems. On July 22, 2009, US Secretary of State Hillary Clinton was asked at a Town Hall meeting in Thailand which US foreign policy initiative had the most positive impact on Thailand and Thai education. Her response was no surprise:

> We have been working together for 176 years, and there have been a number of important initiatives over that long period of time. But I think educational exchanges and student exchanges are among the most important, and I would like to see even more of them. I'd like more American students coming to Thailand. I'd like more American faculty coming to Thailand, and I'd like more students and faculty from Thailand coming to the United States.

She later added:

> I think there's no substitute for person-to-person connection, because we are fighting against cultural media stereotypes. The media paints a picture of the United States which very often has not got anything to do with reality. And for a lot of people in Thailand, that's all they will know about the United States unless we create educational and cultural exchanges and opportunities. So that's what I'd like to see more of.[27]

Clinton's emphasis on educational and cultural exchanges over mass media to improve bilateral relations between Thailand and the United States illustrates a longtime tradition favoring what Edward R. Murrow referred to as "the last three feet" of communication. Mass media, for all their dominance, have limited impact in changing attitudes and opinions in global populations. They serve more to reinforce preexisting dispositions.[28]

Interpersonal communication is now viewed as more influential in changing attitudes, beliefs, and behaviors because it provides a two-way (transactive) exchange of information. Media operate within a nexus of influences, including interpersonal forms like family, friends, and social network. While mass media can be independently successful in bringing attention to important issues, greater and longer lasting effects typically follow from interpersonal communication support for public communication campaigns.[29]

Public Diplomacy Goes Public

Public diplomacy is a function and concern of all nations and their citizens, including multinational security organizations such as NATO or non-governmental human rights organizations such as Amnesty International. Today, any international organization has to be mindful of its public diplomacy mission and include some understanding of its purpose in the external and internal communication mission. Gone are the days when nations can rely solely on trained diplomats from the most prestigious universities to represent the interests and concerns of their respective nations abroad. Likewise, international non-governmental organizations must be aware of their own brand image in an increasingly cluttered international information environment.

Public Diplomacy Actors

Traditional public diplomacy actors include public affairs and public information officers of the government, government broadcasters, and cultural mediators like sponsored exchange students and field workers in development who work closely with local citizens. It is easy to see how a Fulbright or Rhodes Scholar could be viewed as a public diplomat. A sponsored exchangee is funded by nation-states with a vested interest in the international education of that person. During the Kennedy administration, the Peace Corps was envisioned as an international development exchange program that would help to brand young Americans as international humanitarians in projects that helped the development needs of the poorest nations. New public diplomacy actors include those who challenge dominant assumptions in international relations and foreign policies of government (international terrorists, sports stars, celebrities, NGOs). The new public diplomats do not toe the government line, but are often just as important influence agents as those who run governments; they are also more often the targets of public diplomacy campaigns run by official sources.

Country Profiles

Germany

On November 9, 2009, Germany recognizes the 20-year anniversary since the fall of the Berlin Wall. The German magazine, *Der Spiegel*, captures the essence of the new Germany in its online photo essay with a 60-year timeline of the state (1949–2009):

Sixty years later, Germans are living in peace with their neighbors. Together they share a common currency – the euro – as well as the political institutions of the European Union. From a heap of bomb-destroyed ruins, Germany has evolved into the world's third-largest industrial nation and the world's leading exporter.[30]

Germany, like so many powerful nation-states with a mixed history, is seeking to improve its image in the world through an orchestrated program of nation branding, presenting Germany as a modern European nation of culture and a "Land of Ideas." Land of Ideas is a far cry from the World War II era symbols of swastikas, concentration camps, and National Socialism. As German scholar Oliver Zöllner writes, "The wording expresses a wealth of positive arguments and associations with Germany both within Germany and abroad: nation of science and culture – the land of poets and thinkers, innovative products that are 'Made in Germany.'"[31] Engaging foreign target groups in dialogues is the fashionable current *leitmotif* of German public diplomacy.

China

China's concern about its national image did not take off with the 2008 Olympics in Beijing, though in the years preceding it became a hot topic. While soft power is a well-known concept among academia, government and the media, public diplomacy is not. More common are the concepts *wai xuan* (external propaganda) referring to China's image overseas or *xuan chuan* (propaganda), which unlike in the United States, has a positive connotation and is used interchangeably with words like advertising and publicity.[32] In practice, Chinese public diplomacy is not unlike the French approach, with a strong emphasis on cultural exchange and diplomacy, seen in the development of culture years such as the Chinese–French Cultural Year in 2004 and the Chinese–Indian Friend Year in 2006 as well as the several hundred overseas Confucius Institutes.

The Chinese government established a division for public diplomacy in 2004 in the Information Department of the Ministry of Foreign Affairs. At its founding, Chinese officials placed a strong emphasis on courting the opinion of the Chinese people than that of an overseas public: "The basic goal of public diplomacy is to enhance the exchanges and interaction with the public in order to guide and win the understanding and support of the public for foreign policies."[33] In an interview with the *People's Daily*, Foreign Minister Zhaoxing Li said that "Inside China, we pay high attention to public diplomacy, often explain to the public China's diplomatic policies and practice, learn from the people how to improve our work, and have received more and more understanding and support from the people."[34] Zhao Qizheng of the CPPCC wrote in an op-ed that good public diplomacy required confronting Western media bias;

we can't expect foreign media to portray China justly, or close the opinion gap they have created. China must present an accurate picture of itself to the world. The expansion of reform and opening up is necessary for the nation's peaceful development. In this regard, China should not only listen, but talk back."[35]

Just six months away from the Beijing Olympics in March 2008, Foreign Minister Yang Jiechi defined the image of China to the rest of the world:

China is working to build a harmonious world of lasting peace and common prosperity. I believe this is also the goal mankind pursues. In ancient China, the idea of "peace and cooperation bring harmony" was already a popular one. We should strengthen our exchanges and cooperation to reduce elements of discord and increase elements of concord so as to promote cooperation among nations. This is a long-term goal for China, and we are working to achieve it. We willwork with other countries for a more harmonious and better world.[36]

Despite these lofty words of peace, harmony, and China's promoted "peaceful rise" image over "global threat," its national leaders continue to highlight economic growth and preserving the prestige of the Chinese national government over culture power. One of China's misconceptions about international image cultivation, according to Yiwei Wang, is that "China has focused on expanding its economy internationally while neglecting culture, or – when culture has been considered – the Chinese government has just focused on expanding the traditional culture and ignored the cultivation of civil society abroad through cultural exchange."[37]

Israel

In 2008, the state of Israel celebrated its 60th anniversary, but not without a recognition that the Palestinian–Israeli conflict persisted. In January 2009, the conflict in Gaza between Hamas and the Israeli Defense Forces heightened global attention to Israel as a conflict-ridden state. Like Germany, the state of Israel is seen through the world's eyes as a country with a mixed reputation and history. Throughout much of Israeli's history, the global public opinion exhibited a great deal of support for the new state, including during the 1991 Gulf War when Israeli citizens donned gas masks following threats from Saddam Hussein.[38] Over the last decade, not only in the Arab Middle East but throughout most of the world, sympathy and solidarity rest solidly with the Palestinian minority in Israel in pursuit of a Palestinian state, not with the Israeli government, military, or Jewish settlers.

Many academics, media, and officials in Israel have been working toward a "new" Israel image, one that acknowledges the continuation of the strife in the region but which also highlights the technological, educational, and cultural merits of the area. Nevertheless, Israel, though strongly supported by the United States, retains an image of a conflict state often criticized by international non-governmental organizations like Amnesty International and Human Rights Watch.

In an effort to overcome an information gap about the modern state of Israel, the country has begun to promote more international tourism, not just religious pilgrimages. It has sponsored media tours to show reporters and young bloggers how multicultural and secular Israel is, in an effort to confront the mediated image of Israel as a place where just religious extremists or warring parties reside. David Saranga, media consultant at the Israeli consulate in New York City, explained the youth and new media emphasis in rebranding Israel:

> The work is open-source, and transparent – as it has to be, to engage a younger genera-
> tion. We are experimenting with what works, and encouraging interaction. With over
> 1,000 friends on Facebook, and 600 unique visitors a day to the isRealli blog, the num-
> bers logging on are respectable, but not massive. However, what is happening on
> YouTube is noteworthy. Previously, if you searched for "Israel" on the video-sharing site,
> the vast majority of films found would be negative or anti-Zionist. Now you are just as
> likely to see positive depictions of the country. These are not "propaganda" films pro-
> duced by the consulate, but are user-generated content.[39]

Tzipi Livni, the head of the more moderate Kadima Party, has been involved in rebranding Israel, including encouraging more young Israelis to conduct civilian-based diplomacy through posting videos about life in Israel on YouTube. Despite these recent efforts, Israel's global image is dominated by hard power over soft power images and its military and economic alliance with the United States, particularly during the Bush–Cheney administration, did nothing to help promote a new image of Israel separate from the world's sole superpower. Nevertheless, Israel has moved forward in recognizing the need to promote a more accurate and balanced image of its people, history, and culture and it has an enormous advantage that the United States is lacking – enormous curiosity on the part of the global civil society to learn more about the modern state of Israel. The US dominates global media coverage, while Israel dominates only during conflict situations. The lack of good information about real life in Israel, including family life, school life, shopping, eating out, is an enormous opportunity for this modern state to take advantage of its rebranding.

Conclusions

The future of public diplomacy will take on new dimensions; it will not be US-centric but defined by global civil society actors working with and without government partners. It will be more personal or *guanxi* than strictly nation-state or government directed. The concept of guanxi is a core personal and social relationship network principle in Chinese society that is often defined as "connections" in English. It has been compared to social capital values advanced by Robert Putnam in his insightful book, *Bowling Alone* to the intermediary concept known as *wasta* in Middle Eastern culture. A person with "good guanxi" is someone who, through the influence of his or her personal contacts, can resolve a problem or take care of a requested need quickly. The principle of reciprocity is a core value in good guanxi. One does not operate in a social vacuum but extends help and favors in order to receive such favors in the future, not necessarily from the same person helped. Public diplomacy's new dimensions will recognize and work within the parameters of a pay-it-forward global society where good social actors will be rewarded and bad social actors will be punished by the global civil society.

In the future, public diplomacy will become more ad hoc, spontaneous, and chaotic than stateroom formal, as new social networks emerge to challenge the growing impotence of the nation-state system to resolve global conflicts or fairly represent the aspirations of their citizens. Iran's presidential election in June 2009 illustrates the power of private citizens to reach out across national and virtual boundaries to challenge the power of the state. Though some would characterize the silencing of the Iranian street demonstrations as reinforcing state power, the documentation of these protests on YouTube and Twitter serves as a model of freedom and independence from both government and traditional media power.

We are in the age of a new mindset in public diplomacy. The focus has shifted from traditional one-way informational diplomatic objectives to two-way interactive public exchanges. Exchanges are being emphasized now more than ever, though support for exchanges still remains more rhetoric than resource-driven. Exchanges support reciprocity, establish rapport, show personal commitment, build continuity and trust over the long term. Person-to-person exchanges allow more room to agree with a "target public" when you can and shows liking better than mass media campaigns. They also defuse mistrust, a sentiment that a nation's public diplomacy is just propaganda or a marketing campaign in a new guise. These positive outcomes of exchanges in the long-term are what make many countries jump on the mass mediated bandwagon in crisis situations. Nevertheless, public diplomacy today is more personal than ever and it is likely that collaborative approaches in public diplomacy will become more dominant in the twenty-first century as nations realize that do-it-alone management is neither practical, effective, nor affordable.

In Chapter 16 "Summary and Conclusions," more is written about the connection between public diplomacy and electronic colonialism theory (ECT).

Notes

1. http://archives.cnn.com/2001/US/09/20/gen.bush.transcript/.
2. Barbara Burrell, *Women and Political Participation: A Reference Handbook*, Santa Barbara, CA: ABC-CLIO, 2004, p. 160.
3. Margaret Tutwiler, "Testimony before the Senate Foreign Relations Committee," Washington, DC, October 29, 2003.
4. Margaret Tutwiler, Testimony before the House Committee on Government Reform Subcommittee on National Security, Emerging Threats and International Relations, February 10, 2004.

5. Nancy Snow, "US Public Diplomacy: A Tale of Two Who Jumped the Ship of State," Special Report, Foreign Policy in Focus, May 27, 2004. Available online at www.fpif. org/papers/0405taleoftwo_body.html.

6 Margaret Carlson, "Can Charlotte Beers Sell Uncle Sam?" *Time* (November 14, 2001).

7. Snow, 2004.

8. Charlotte Beers, Under Secretary of State for Public Diplomacy and Public Affairs; Richard Boucher, Assistant Secretary of State for Public Affairs, "Public Diplomacy in Support of the International Coalition," Foreign Press Center, Washington, DC, November 9, 2001. Available online at http://2002–2009-fpc.state.gov/7533.htm.

9. www.archive.org/details/SharedValues.

10. James Glassman, "Winning the War of Ideas, The Washington Institute for Near East Policy, July 8, 2008," www.washingtoninstitute.org/templateC07.php?CID=408.

11. Judith McHale, "Public Diplomacy: A National Security Imperative," Center for a New American Security, Washington, DC, June 11, 2009.

12. Ibid.

13. Jan Melissen, "Wielding Soft Power: The New Public Diplomacy," *Clingendael Diplomacy Papers No. 2*, May 2005, p. 1.

14. Geoffrey Cowan and Nicholas J. Cull, "Public Diplomacy in a Changing World," ANNALS, *AAPSS*, March 2008, p. 6.

15. Public Diplomacy Alumni Association, "Origins of the Term Public Diplomacy," www. publicdiplomacy.org/1.htm.

16. Edward R. Murrow Center, online exhibit, Fletcher School of Law and Diplomacy, Tufts University.

17. Edward R. Murrow, testimony to Congressional Appropriations Committee, quoted in Alexander Kendrick, *Prime Time: The Life of Edward R. Murrow*, Boston: Little, Brown and Co., 1969, p. 466; also quoted in Nicholas J. Cull, *The Cold War and the United States Information Agency*, New York: Cambridge University Press, 2008, p. 189.

18. Planning group for integration of USIA into the Department of State, June 20, 1997.

19. Geoffrey Cowan and Nicholas J. Cull, "Public Diplomacy in a Changing World," ANNALS, *AAPSS*, March 2008, p. 6.

20. "Ashton Kutcher Takes on Malaria with Twitter," Malaria Policy Center, April 8, 2009.

21. James Glassman, "Winning the War of Ideas," *New York Sun* (July 23, 2008), www. nysun.com/opinion/winning-the-war-of-ideas/82438/.

22. James Glassman, The Washington Institute for Near East Policy, July 2008.

23. Suzy Platt, *Respectfully Quoted: A Dictionary of Quotations*, Washington, DC, Barnes and Noble, 1993.

24. "Organizing for America: Remarks of Senator Barack Obama in Berlin, Germany"; available online at http://my.barackobama.com/page/community/post/obamaroad-blog/gGxyd4.

25. Geoffrey Cowan and Amelia Arsenault, "Moving from Monologue to Dialogue to Collaboration: The Three Layers of Public Diplomacy," in Geoffrey Cowan and Nicholas J. Cull (special editors), *Public Diplomacy in a Changing World, The Annals*, March 2008, p. 21.

26. John McDonald, "The Track Not Taken," *Harvard International Review*, 22(3) (2000): 68.

27. www.state.gov/secretary/rm/2009a/july/126335.htm.

28. Joseph T. Klapper, "The Effects of Mass Communication: An Analysis of Research on the Effectiveness and Limitations of Mass Media in Influencing the Opinions, Values and Behavior of Their Audiences," *American Sociological Review*, 27(1) (1962).

29. R. E. Rice and C. Atkin, Principles of successful public communication campaigns. In J. Bryant and D. Zillmann (eds.), *Media Effects: Advances in Theory and Research*, Hillsdale, NJ: Lawrence Erlbaum Associates, pp. 365–87.

30. www.spiegel.de/international/germany/0,1518,626308,00.html.

31. Zöllner, Oliver. "German Public Diplomacy: The Dialogue of Cultures." In N. Snow and P. M. Taylor (eds.), *Routledge Handbook of Public Diplomacy*. New York: Routledge, pp. 262–9, 2009.

32. Yiwei Wang, "Public Diplomacy and the Rise of Chinese Soft Power, ANNALS," *AAPSS*, March 2008, p. 259.

33. Ministry of Foreign Affairs of the People's Republic of China, academic seminar on China's public diplomacy, 2004.

34. Foreign Minister Li Zhaoxing, interview with *People's Daily*, December 16, 2004; www.fmprc.gov.cn/eng/zxxx/t175545.htm.

35. Zhao Qizheng, "Better Public Diplomacy to Present a Truer Picture of China," *People's Daily Online*, March 30, 2007, http://english.peopledaily.com.cn/200703/30/eng2007 0330_362496.html.

36. Foreign Minister Yang Jiechi Meets the Press, March 14, 2008; www.fmprc.gov.cn/eng/zxxx/t414877.htm.

37. Wang, 2008, p. 261.

38. Etyan Gilboa, "Public Diplomacy: The Missing Component in Israel's Foreign Policy," *Israel Affairs*, 12(4) (October 2006): 715.

39. David Russell, "Meet David Saranga, The Man Whose Campaigns Are Rebranding Israel," *The Jewish Chronicle* (May 23, 2008), www.thejc.com/articles/meet-david-saranga-man-whose-campaigns-are-rebranding-israel.

40. Robert Putnam, *Bowling Alone: The Collapse and Revival of American Community*, New York: Simon & Schuster, 2000.

5

The Medium
Global Technologies
and Organizations

Introduction

Although most of the concern about global broadcasting and communication focuses on ownership, content, impact, flows, or cultural issues, the global telecommunications infrastructure, or the medium by which content is transmitted, is a significant topic as well. Global information superhighways are not without their socioeconomic consequences. The access and penetration of satellite dishes, the laying of fiber optic cables, broadband, the internet, wireless telephony, and the deployment of cell telephones are all part of Marshall McLuhan's "global village." Facebook, YouTube, and twitter all rely on the telecommunication infrastructure. This chapter seeks to detail the major stakeholders in the evolution of telecommunication systems around the globe. As core nations continue to move further into the Information Revolution, their telecommunication systems are central to their success. The global telecommunication system is the central nervous system of the global economy. Global broadcasting could not exist without an internationally functioning technical transmission system or infrastructure. Global commerce relies on the same infrastructure.

The primary global telecommunication agency is the International Telecommunication Union (ITU), a specialized United Nations agency. However, there are other major players, such as Intelsat, that bring to the telecommunications table a mix of philosophical, ownership, technical, and public policy perspectives. Core nations have long dominated ITU, but now semiperipheral and peripheral nations are calling for major structural changes to reflect their needs and concerns.

International Telecommunication Union (ITU)

Today the struggle between core and peripheral nations over the question of NWICO is at an uneasy compromise. The sense of victory felt by core nations over minimizing major tenets of NWICO has been short-lived. Observers note that another arena, the International Telecommunication Union (ITU), based in Switzerland, has become a battlefield between core and peripheral nations. The ITU sponsors major global conferences that look at global technical standards and other issues affecting global telecommunications. At these meetings, participants confer to assign worldwide frequencies from the usable electromagnetic spectrum available for broadcasting and a wide variety of communication services.[1] Historically, these meetings attracted little attention as technicians and engineers from various nations around the world divided the spectrum with great concern for technical harmony. Issues such as radio microwave interference among neighboring nations, technical standards, or equipment interconnection protocols dominated the meetings. When nations sent delegates to ITU meetings, industrial nations assumed that a highly technical and engineering delegation would suffice. Little attention was paid to social, cultural, or economic concerns. But times have changed. Peripheral nations now want a major voice at ITU. They want their concerns on the agenda.

Global conferences are convened and organized by ITU, which is charged with coordinating the international use of telecommunication systems worldwide. The nations represented at these global conferences are members of the ITU. These conferences review and amend existing ITU international radio regulations. For instance, conference participants are empowered to amend regulatory procedures for settling differences between nations and for notifying, coordinating, and registering radio frequency assignments. They also are authorized to set new rules concerning technical and performance standards of telecommunication systems, including satellite issues. Probably the most significant set of regulations the general conferences review is the international Table of Frequency Allocation.

By virtue of the range of their global authority, all ITU conferences are profoundly significant events. During the years between ITU conferences, technological innovations such as satellite communications or cellular phones, and methods for using more and more of the high ranges of the spectrum, particularly microwave frequencies, have revolutionized telecommunications. Major ITU conferences have been held twice in North America: in 1949 in Atlantic City, New Jersey, and in 1998 in Minneapolis, Minnesota. The 1998 conference lasted four weeks and set the ITU's general policies, adopted strategic and financial plans, and elected members of the ITU council.

New developments in communication exercise a profound influence on social, cultural, economic, and political organizations and have so radically transformed the way most people live and interact with each other and their environment that the present era has come to be known as the "information age." All core nations have the latest in communication technologies, whereas the peripheral nations have few computers, cable systems, or digital services.[2] A nation or region cannot be considered "modern" without a sophisticated, technically advanced, and globally interconnected telecommunication network.

History and Structure of the ITU

In 1865 the International Telegraph Union, the ITU's forerunner, was formed under the International Telegraph Convention signed by 20 European nations in Paris. This makes the ITU the oldest international organization surviving today. At that time, the organization dealt exclusively with technical problems. The establishment of international standards for the Morse code was among its first endeavors.

The invention and implementation of wireless systems such as the telegraph, radio and cross border telephoning complicated the process of setting international regulations. In 1885 the Union established the first international rules governing telephony. At the 1906 Berlin conference, the first international conference to deal with radio and to set standards for equipment and technical uniformity, certain sections of the radio frequency spectrum were allocated to specific radio services, most notably the wireless frequencies used by ships at sea. The sinking of the *Titanic* in 1912 led to mandatory 24-hour wireless operators being stationed on all large passenger ships. The 1927 International Radio Telegraph Conference decided the next major advance in radio spectrum management. At this conference, a Table of Frequency Allocation was created.

John Howkins points out the rather simple procedures involved in early ITU activities:

> Users notified the union about the frequencies, which they were already using or wished to use, and the union registered these in its master list. Neither the union nor the user owned the frequency. What happened was that, through the union's processes of registration, the user had a squatter's right to a specific frequency. Furthermore, the union's recognition of a particular usage gave the user some protection in international law.[3]

This simple squatter's right on a first-come, first-served basis did not, however, take into account the limited nature of the resource. Also, the first comers were mainly from North America and Europe, core nations. This procedure has been largely responsible for the congestion in some popular frequency bands, a problem that today makes efficient allocation a difficult proposition requiring regional meetings to sort out conflicting claims.

Initially, spectrum usage was confined to maritime activities such as radio navigation and ship-to-shore communication. During the 1920s, owing to technological advances that provided new means of utilizing higher frequencies, the types of services that the radio spectrum enjoyed multiplied rapidly. As new commercial and public radio services began to compete for spectrum space, fears grew that unless each new type of service was given a separate and distinct band within the spectrum, overcrowding and interference among the services would occur.

The ITU responded to this concern at the 1929 World Administrative Radio Council (WARC), resolving that the various uses of the spectrum be coordinated by allocating a certain stretch or band of frequencies to each particular service. By the 1947 Atlantic City conference, further advances in telecommunications capacity necessitated revision of procedures for registering and securing recognition of spectrum uses. More detailed plans for services were adopted for each of the three newly created regions: Region 1 for Europe and Africa, Region 2 for the Americas, and Region 3 for Asia and the South Pacific.

As early as 1959, the ITU's approach to telecommunications management came under criticism. Critics noted that huge areas of the spectrum, such as the high-frequency bands, were unplanned, and they pointed out that the ITU stepped in to coordinate national assignments of frequencies only after congestion and conflicting uses had occurred. Generally, the ITU gave priority to those nations that had the economic and technological sophistication to occupy a frequency first. These were not necessarily the nations that needed the frequency the most. The fortunate nations were primarily core nations that relied on the squatter's rights tradition to claim prime spectrum positions.

Misgivings about the basic machinery of the ITU escalated in the 1980s and 1990s. The regulations the ITU had originally adopted to make international telecommunications manageable were becoming either overextended or obsolete with the rapid introduction of new demands such as frequency space for cellular telephones and other wireless devices.

To restate the original point, the history of the ITU has been punctuated by problems and doubts about the efficiency of its structural framework. The problems and doubts turn on questions that are essentially of a technical or administrative nature. One prime reason for this technical orientation was articulated in *The Economist*, which noted, "the ITU is full of engineers terrified of controversy and terrified of the press."[4] This fundamental fact is part of ITU's culture today. The current ITU works through four major sectors (see Figure 5.1).

In recent years, critics of ITU have cautioned that although this narrow technical focus may have been tolerable when decisions about telecommunications were of concern only to a limited circle of specialists within the industry, it is no longer adequate. In an age in which telecommunications have become highly politicized because of their profound effects on the complexion of national and international roles, many nations are not only concerned about which medium or frequency they are carried on, but they are also concerned about many nontechnical matters. Semiperipheral and peripheral nations are aware of the pivotal role telecommunications play in the global economy. They also are demanding prime spectrum allocations well in advance of their actual use.

ITU has received prompting from many quarters to implement structural and administrative reforms designed to furnish mechanisms for recognizing and

> 1 Radiocommunication – focuses on satellite orbit issues and the international radio spectrum
> 2 Standardization – focuses on internationally compatible rules and standards
> 3 Development – recently established to provide greater leadership and concern for ICT matters affecting the peripheral regions
> 4 ITU Telecom – leaders from government and industry working together on major policy matters

Figure 5.1   ITU major sectors, 2010

absorbing political and socioeconomic input. At the time of writing, ITU has developed neither the ability to deal with political or ideological concerns nor the necessary administrative structure through which such conflicts could be channeled without crippling itself.

When peripheral nations threaten to turn ITU conferences into ideological and rhetorical contests, they trigger much apprehension. With no experience in dealing with such developments, ITU talks could collapse before technical issues could be resolved. This would jeopardize global spectrum management decisions and leave matters in an uncomfortable state of suspension. Of course, this is the last thing core nations want, with billions invested in global telecommunications systems. These systems represent the central nervous system of the global economy. Therefore, core nations have a keen interest in maintaining a manageable and predictable telecommunications environment through ITU.

Current Concerns

Two chief reasons that the international community devoted more attention and preparation to recent ITU conferences were the increase in the number of countries represented and the fact that peripheral nations, which accounted for almost all the increase, now constitute a majority in the ITU. In the 1950s, fewer than 100 nations were members of ITU. But by 2010, there were 191 nations in the ITU family. The level of preparation and negotiating skill required to manage a meeting of over 2,000 delegates, some 50 NGOs, and 700 sector members dealing with issues of unusual technical and social complexity was unprecedented in ITU's 145 year history. They are also being confronted with the rapid pace of innovation in the telecom and information technologies sectors.

The new majority status of the peripheral nations contributes to the high profile of these conferences, and these nations have been the source of a feature previously unheard of at ITU meetings – namely, the use of political and ideological criteria in arriving at decisions concerning the Digital Divide, spectrum management and allocations, as well as other issues which impact peripheral regions. Decisions at ITU are made on an one-nation, one vote basis. Core nations worry that if peripheral nations act in unison they will be able, by virtue of the majority they command, to push through measures relating to NWICO and thereby guarantee access for the developing world to highly desired spectrum space and geo-stationary orbits for satellites, as well as committing funds to reduce the Digital Divide. Many of the proposals concern the core nations, particularly the US, which will have a great deal to lose or which will have to bear the brunt of new expenditures. A new issue that the US is pushing, cybersecurity, has so far not captured the imagination of the developing nations.

Because the more prominent issues associated with NWICO concern cultural imperialism, such as concentration of ownership, growing private control of media, deregulation, and imbalances in news flow, peripheral nations are quick to point out imbalances in spectrum allocations.

Currently, a major initiative at ITU is promoting a global international mobile system called IMT-2000. This initiative will provide wireless access to the global telecommunication system through application of both satellite and terrestrial systems. It will provide guidance for coordinating related technological developments in order to promote conversion in technical standard for wireless access technologies. This initiative also seeks to coordinate both public and private networks, which are emerging at various rates in different regions of the world.

The role of ITU has expanded enormously owing to technological innovation and the multiplicity of new stakeholders ranging from governments, to broadcasters, to manufacturers, so that it has become the major global organization dealing with the substantial telecommunications sector. Many of the member states and related organizations now expect the ITU to take into account the cultural, social, and non-economic dimensions of the world in making allocations and other major decisions.

Geo-stationary Orbits

Technically, the most effective positioning of a communication satellite is 22,300 miles above the equator in a geo-stationary or geo-synchronous orbit (see Figure 5.2). At such an altitude, a satellite completes one orbit of the earth in the same time it takes the earth to revolve once around its axis, that is, once every 24 hours. Because the satellite is traveling at the identical speed as the earth, it is always hovering over the same area and thus can provide continuous communication service to the same region. Satellites placed at lower or higher altitudes such as 15,000 or 30,000 miles above the earth do not travel at the same speed as the earth and thus over time disappear over the horizon. To provide continuous communication with such satellites, as one satellite disappears over the horizon, another satellite must simultaneously appear to replace it. This requires expensive and elaborate antennae or receivers that can track this new satellite as it enters into view. Because synchronous satellites are always

Figure 5.2   A satellite orbiting Earth

over the same spot on earth, simple receivers or ground stations are able to pick up their signals. Moreover, because of the altitude of synchronous satellites, their beams cover much greater amounts of territory, called a footprint, than lower altitude counterparts.

Unfortunately, there is limited space for satellites in the thin slice 22,300 miles above the equator in which such satellites can operate or park for their lifetime. This is why the question of allotting orbital slots in advance, on a country-by-country basis, has become a pressing issue for peripheral nations, which trail far behind in satellite technology. If and when they catch up, there will not be sufficient usable prime parking spots remaining for their additional geo-stationary satellites.

The issue of geo-stationary parking spots took on additional symbolic meaning in the 1980s. Because the only position for these satellites was above the equator, and because the equator covers parts of peripheral regions in Latin America and Africa, some delegates from these regions seized on this important point. They began to express the idea at ITU meetings that the outer space above these nations should be reserved for them so that they would have appropriate parking spots for future satellite deployment. As already mentioned, these allocations historically have been awarded on a first-come, first-serve basis, which meant that core nations and the former Soviet Union came first to the table to make specific requests for operational satellite parking spots. By the time peripheral nations, even those at the equator, are ready to operate satellites at some future point, there will be no prime parking spots available, only sub-optimal spots. And these sub-optimal spots will be over some other nation, not the prime spots above their own nation-states. Naturally, the traditional operating mode of first-come, first-serve displeased peripheral delegates not only about satellite orbital spaces, but also about spectrum allocation and management. The peripheral regions wanted to replace the first-come, first-serve process of ITU's spectrum management with a new system whereby they could reserve frequencies of all types for their own future use. They argued that this strategy would promote fair and equitable access to the international radio spectrum. Because older industrialized nations entered the field of radio telecommunications at a much earlier date than many newly emerging peripheral nations, core nations by default obtained the rights to all prime frequencies. Just as naturally, industrialized nations, led by the US, objected to any shift in criteria for allocation issues coming before ITU conferences. Core nations claimed that the new policy would leave many allotted frequencies and orbital slots empty, awaiting some future point in time when the peripheral nations would be able to afford new technology.

The outcome of the push by peripheral nations for greater consideration in the allocation of the international communication spectrum, including orbital parking spots, eventually saw substantial compromise. Even the US agreed to allow Intelsat (discussed later in this chapter) to promote the deployment of satellite communications in an equitable fashion across the world. This meant that peripheral nations would have appropriate ground stations for both unlinking and down-linking signals from the vast number of Intelsat satellites deployed around the world.

The Maitland Commission

A number of factors discouraged peripheral nations from pushing NWICO at the ITU. First, they realized there would be other global meetings sponsored by the ITU at which they could state their case and make gains in their movement toward a fairer share of the radio spectrum and orbital parking spaces. Second, many nations, particularly the US, applied pressure and collected on debts to ensure that an orderly spectrum remained intact, particularly for satellites. Third, almost all nations have some type of domestic system, regardless of how rudimentary, and want to see it continue operating without major adjustments. Fourth, divergent and often conflicting national interests among peripheral nations prevented the formation of a powerful, united, and well orchestrated voting bloc that could have presented resolutions and amendments demanding radical changes in ITU policies and procedures.

Although industrialized nations sought to avoid the coming controversy over the crucial role that telecommunications play in economic, cultural, and social developments, peripheral nations persisted in their criticism of the ITU. In response, during the 1980s the ITU established the Maitland Commission, chaired by Sir Donald Maitland of the United Kingdom. The formal title of the study group was the Independent Commission for Worldwide Telecommunications Development.[5] The two-year study submitted its report to the ITU in January

1985. The report addressed the inequities in the distribution of telecommunications systems and services between core and other nations. It looked, for example, at telephone penetration levels and made some startling comparisons. Three-quarters of the world's population lives in countries with fewer than 10 telephones per 100 people, and more than one-half of the globe has access to less than one telephone per 100 people. In the Western core industrialized world, however, individuals enjoy the use of more than one telephone per two people. The commission concluded that this imbalance could no longer be tolerated: "It cannot be right that in the latter part of the twentieth century a minority of the human race should enjoy the benefits of the new technology while a majority live in comparative isolation."[6] Moreover, the commission highlighted the benefits to the entire world if the disparities were removed:

> Given the vital role telecommunications play not only in such obvious fields as emergency, health, and other social services, administration, and commerce, but also in stimulating economic growth and enhancing the quality of life, creating effective networks world wide will bring immense benefits. An increase in international traffic will generate funds, which could be devoted to the further improvement and development of telecommunications services. The increased flow of trade and information will contribute to better international relationships. The process of creating effective networks worldwide will provide new markets for the high technology and other industries, some of which are already suffering the effects of surplus productive capacity. The interest industrialized and developing countries share in the world-wide development of telecommunications is as great as in the exploitation of new sources of energy. And yet it is far less appreciated.[7]

The Maitland Commission argued that although telecommunications systems were once considered a luxury, they are now viewed as essential components of development. Indeed, one may argue that a telecommunications infrastructure is a prerequisite for any type of social or economic development in peripheral nations. For example, the benefits of telecommunications include increased economic, commercial, and administrative efficiency; improved social and emergency services; and more equitable distribution of the social, cultural, and economic benefits of development. In addition, "The absence of a system which enables timely information to be sent and received engenders a sense of isolation and frustration, and so raises a barrier between different sections of the population. This cannot but undermine the process of development."[8] The Maitland Commission concluded that the best way to redress the imbalance and enhance the telecommunications ability of the developing world was through the expansion of telecommunications networks.

A final set of recommendations involved the role of the ITU and how it might be strengthened. The commission reasserted that telecommunications development should be given a higher priority. It charged the Secretary-General of the ITU with monitoring the implementation of the recommendations offered in the report, reporting on the progress made, and stimulating further progress where necessary. The report concluded:

There is no single remedy. A range of actions over a wide front and at different levels is required. Progress will be made only in stages. But, if the effort is sustained, the situation worldwide could be transformed in 20 years. All mankind could be brought within easy reach of a telephone by the early part of next century and our objective achieved.[9]

Maitland Follow-up

The Maitland Commission forever altered the traditional role of ITU. No longer was ITU a simple technical and engineering meeting. In the future, it would have to take into account the peripheral nations' concerns about issues such as access to and equitable distribution of the radio spectrum and other issues. The Maitland Report focused on the inequities among nations, particularly the fact that core nations control telecommunications research, manufacturing, and fiscal resources. Although everyone knew that a telecommunications infrastructure was necessary for the promotion of telemedicine, education, banking, tourism, and eventually access to the internet, peripheral nations realized they were not going to become part of the electronic global village if they did not receive support from ITU. Therefore, peripheral nations did not want to tear down the ITU, but rather reform it from within. Many of these reforms and genuine concerns become prevalent at ITU in the 1990s and up to the present. But new major issues emerged involving the role of the private telecommunications sector within ITU's decision-making apparatus, along with discussions about the privatization of major stakeholders such as Comsat and Intelsat. These crucial matters are dealt with in the following sections.

International Telecommunications Satellite Organization (Intelsat)

Intelsat was formed in 1965 to provide international satellite communication services. From the beginning, the United States was the major participant in Intelsat and the leading core nation in the ITU. Intelsat was controlled and owned by 144 member nations. It provided the satellite technology necessary to complete the global communication systems that were in place by 1969. Intelsat global satellite systems bring video, audio, voice, data, and internet services to users in more than 200 nations around the globe. Basically, Intelsat operates as a wholesaler providing satellite services to users through Intelsat members in each country. The US member was Comsat Corporation. Intelsat achieves this by operating a system of high-powered spacecraft in orbit as well as thousands of earth stations around the world. Intelsat customers are primarily major telecommunications operators in each nation throughout the world. In addition, Intelsat provides satellite communication services to major broadcasters, airlines, banks, multinational corporations, and international newspaper distributors, as well as disaster relief, health care, and telemedicine organizations around the globe.

In the mid-1960s, Intelsat launched the world's first communication satellite, and by 1969 it provided global television coverage of the moon landing to an audience estimated to exceed 500 million people. In 1978, Intelsat linked the World Cup football matches to over 1 billion TV viewers in 42 countries. By 1997, Intelsat had established three regional support centers to increase market awareness and develop further telecommunications business. These offices are in the Pacific Rim, Southeast Asia, and Europe. In 2000, Intelsat made possible the broadcast of the Sydney Olympic Games to a record four billion people around the world, using 10 of its satellites.

In July 2001 Intelsat became a private company incorporated in Bermuda. Before it could issue shares to the public it was acquired by a group of private investors in 2005. This new consortium plans to expand the fixed satellite services beyond the current 200 nations and territories. The investors view Intelsat as the "gold standard" in the fixed satellite services sector.

In a major move under new ownership Intelsat acquired the major US-based Comsat General Corporation. This purchase brought not only private business but also governments which with greater frequently rely on satellites to communicate with their embassies around the world. It does this with a fleet of over 50 communication satellites and a series of fiber optic cables.

Separately in 2001 ViaSat acquired Comsat Laboratories, Comsat's think tank and technical laboratories. This new division of ViaSat provides a broad range of engineering and technical advice for both wireless and satellite clients.

Intelsat Competition

Part of the global telecommunications environment Intelsat faces is the reality of two new strong competing forces. First, there are a series of other satellite providers now operating in direct competition with Intelsat. For example, several companies now provide satellite centric telecommunications services to a range of clients and compete directly with Intelsat for high-volume users and transoceanic telecommunications business. The second major competitor is transoceanic fiber-optic cable systems. These cables have exceptional broadband width, reliability, and speed, and the systems now account for substantial amounts of telecommunications traffic over high-volume routes. These two competing groups service those routes that provide considerable profitability. They do not serve peripheral nations, less populated areas, or low-profit routes where there is little demand for high-capacity, high-speed digital communications. Intelsat is the lifeline provider for universal access to satellite service thanks to its historic ownership and participatory structure. Clearly, however, this field of telecommunications could radically change with deregulation and privatization.

Eutelsat Communications

Eutelsat was established in 1977 to operate satellite systems for Europe. It became a private French-based company in 2001. Currently it has expanded to the Middle East, Africa, Asia, and the Americas where it offers a broad range of information and broadcasting services. It is the major telecommunications service provider for Eurovision, the trans-Europe television network.

Inmarsat

The mobile satellite service company Inmarsat was founded in 1979. It began as providing ships at sea with telephone service via satellite. Using new technologies it now provides a broad range of customers – ships, airlines, media, oil platforms, governments, and NGOs – with global satellite services. It is based in England and is a private company listed on the London stock exchange.

The Future of Intelsat

After 30 years, Intelsat is confronting a new reality. The competitive and regulatory international environment for satellites is substantially different from the environment of a global central monopoly that was present when Intelsat was first formed in the 1960s. Now the environment is rife with deregulation, competition, liberalization, and privatization. The original 144 partners in Intelsat find themselves with increasingly different goals, owners, and domestic policies. Many of the national partners have or will be privatized. This is happening at a time when the other global partners are vigorously advocating their own, different business goals and policies. One aspect of particular policy concern is the total privatization of Intelsat, which occurred in 2001. Intelsat functioned as an intergovernmental operating organization based on a consensus that followed a series of negotiated global agreements. Because there is no global regulator of international telecommunications services or prices, Intelsat tended to promote agreements that would protect all members – core, semiperipheral, and peripheral alike. But now the peripheral group is fearful that its interests would be totally neglected in a privatized environment in which the sheer weight of economics and profitability will dominate future decision-making. Some peripheral nations could even lose their lifeline access to Intelsat's satellites. Without access to Intelsat's infrastructures, they could lose connection to the outside world. In times of national disasters, such as the Asian tsunami or the Iranian election fallout, such lack of connectivity to the outside world could make a crisis even greater.

ITU's Changing Role and Expectations

When ITU was founded in 1865, it was established to coordinate agreements between 20 nations concerning interconnecting telegraph networks for international telegraph traffic. Over time other nations joined, and equipment manufacturers and telecommunication carriers from both the public and private sectors participated in working groups to assist ITU in establishing appropriate technical standards. The private sector firms never had any voting authority but provided needed technical studies so that ITU could develop appropriate international agreements to permit the orderly deployment of telecommunications technologies.

During the first decades of ITU's existence, most telecommunication carriers were monopoly providers already owned by governments of various nations. For example, the government of France owned the Office of the Post Telegraph and Telecommunication, known as PTT. But with the rapid expansion of the global economy, along with rapid innovations in the telecommunications sector, a new environment confronts ITU. The demands of the information society and global economy find telecommunications systems and services being privatized in an era of deregulation. Liberalization, along with new stakeholders who have little or no connection to their own governments through ownership, oversight, or control, is now part of the telecommunications landscape. Thus, the balance of power has shifted with the liberalization of the telecommunications environment to the private sector. This movement is further complicated by the conversion of traditionally distinct analog technologies to digital communications. Telecommunications firms and broadcasting and computer corporations work with essentially the same basic digital technologies. Now Hewlett-Packard, Microsoft, Intel, IBM, and others are some of ITU's private-sector members. They are providing the much-needed technical expertise as both wireless telecommunications and satellite technologies continue to evolve. The current situation in the ITU is becoming awkward, with the private-sector members estimated to provide over 90 percent of the intellectual and technical contribution that underpin ITU's recommendations and technical standards. This new reality needs to be dealt with in order for ITU to retain its global technical decision-making role. Speed and broad participation is not a hallmark of ITU's style of bureaucratic management, yet the private sector wants greater influence at future conferences, and these firms want a say in ITU's future directions. Faced with this growing private-sector call for shared power arrangements, ITU has been slow to respond even though liberalization and privatization have been part of the global information economy for over a decade. In 1998, at ITU's Minneapolis conference, the new environment confronting ITU was discussed in conference materials. Documents supplied to delegates state:

> With an increasing number of new fora created by the market itself, many users and experts now question the relevance of a slow-moving body such as the ITU, where all power is vested in government representatives rather than in those organizations who are investing in and developing new technologies.
>
> However, before writing off the ITU one should bear in mind that it is the only truly global impartial organization whose membership spans all aspects of the industry, from PTOs to manufacturers to satellite system operators to service providers and even user

groups. Even in its current form ITU can largely take single-handed credit for the successful development of the world's current telecommunications networks over the last 100 years.[10]

ITU's slow and cumbersome procedures could cause regional groups to take over its technical standards-setting role. The same document goes on to state:

> Most ITU Members – State and Sector – at least agree that a declining role for the ITU is not desirable. Despite the burgeoning growth of industry- and technology-specific forums and lobby groups, the ITU still represents the only truly global, impartial telecommunications organization. It has no vested interests, represents the needs of the poor as well as the rich countries, and has succeeded where all other industry groups have failed – that is, in pulling together competing organizations and governments in a spirit of cooperation. And, in the ITU's case, this cooperative effort is much more than mere words; it has led to almost faultless interconnection of the global telecommunications network and a shared approach to radio frequency spectrum use for radio communications.[11]

Finally, peripheral nations enjoy their voting status at ITU and do not want to see it diluted by adding private-sector voting rights. They are also concerned that private-sector voting rights will go to multinational corporations based in core regions such as the United States, Europe, or Japan. Over time the marginal voices of the peripheral nations could become even weaker if ITU takes heed of the private sector's discontent with its current status. Yet ITU realizes that if it fails to respond, many major telecommunications players could shift their interests, role, and advice to other regional groups-to the ultimate detriment of ITU in the twenty-first century.

ITU has not been blind to the calls for reform. In developing a strategic plan for 1999–2003, ITU's major planning document recognizes the crucial role that international telecommunications play within the broader context of the global economy. The strategic planning document notes, for example, the following trends within the telecommunications sector:

- rapid technological developments which improve the efficiency of existing products, systems and services and permit innovation in all these areas;
- sharply declining costs for information processing and transmission capacity, accompanied by sharply rising costs for software, marketing and customer service;
- the privatization of government telecommunication operators (between 1984 and 1996, some 44 PTOs (Public Telecommunication Organizations) were privatized);
- the establishment of independent regulatory bodies; the liberalization of domestic and international markets for telecommunication products and services under sector-specific policies and regulations;
- the emergence of "global" telecommunication operators capable of providing end-to-end services across national borders either by establishing a

commercial presence through subsidiaries, acquisitions, partnerships and strategic alliances, or by supplying services across borders;

- the increasingly important role being played in the telecommunication sector by general competition, trade and commercial policies and regulations, most notably through the work of the World Trade Organization Group on Basic Telecommunications (WTO/GBT), which has recently reached agreement on a set of fundamental principals that will serve as the bass for a global telecommunication regulatory framework; and

- the convergence of telecommunication, computer, broadcasting and information technology, which is leading to competition between these previously distinct industry sectors, and raising questions about how to reconcile the different policy and regulatory frameworks which have governed these sectors in the past.[12]

The document does show concern for the increasing gap between "the information rich" and "the information poor," or the Digital Divide as the literature now refers to it. Yet at the same time, as ITU is attempting to reposition itself in the international telecommunications debate, it appears to be a potential big loser as large organizations such as Comsat and Intelsat are privatized. If this occurs, these organizations will have to answer directly to their shareholders rather than seek solutions that take into account the needs of other nations.

World Summit on the Information Society (WSIS)

The United Nations (UN) endorsed the WSIS in 2001. The summit was held in two phases: the first phase was held in Geneva, Switzerland in 2003 and the second phase was held in Tunis, Tunisia in late 2005.[13] Both phases were coordinated by the ITU.

In general the Summit was to take a global approach to the impact of the Information Society (IS). It sought ways to make the IS equitable and inclusive by discussing issues such as access, capacity, and connectivity. Particular attention was paid to e-learning/education, e-governance, e-media, and e-trade. A final plan of action aimed at reducing the digital divide emerged from the second phase, but there are already two areas of contention.

The first issue deals with NWICO. As discussed in earlier chapters, UNESCO, the ITU, and the UN all played some part in the contentious debate about NWICO. Yet, even in the tamer confines of the first phase in Geneva, issues such as reducing imbalances in IT systems and calls for greater diversity of media ownership appeared in the declaration of principles. These and other claims of imbalances clearly reflect aspects of the earlier NWICO feud.

The second and perhaps more explosive issue deals with the governance of the internet. As detailed in the chapter dealing with the internet, the current assignment of internet names is being performed by the Internet Corporation for Assigned Names and Numbers (ICANN). But the WSIS took up the issue and want changes so that the American centric ICANN becomes a global agency where peripheral regions have some influence in future decisions. As WSIS expert Wolfgang Kleinwachter accurately notes there is a growing concern about America's hegemonic control of the internet. He states,

> When the WSIS process started, a number of governments, mainly from the third world, began to question the legitimacy of ICANN. They pointed out that the digital divide was reflected in the distribution of domain names and IP addresses. They felt that they were unable to participate in ICANN's decision-making processes. And they criticized the role of the US government. Some governments suggested that the internet, like telecommunications and broadcasting, should be regulated top-down in order to protect national and political interests"[14]

For an update on this evolving issue visit the internet Governance Forum or www.itu.int/wsis.

World Trade Organization (WTO)

In 1947 most of the industrialized nations established the General Agreement on Tariffs and Trade (GATT), the basic aim of which was to establish international rules for promoting freer trade by reducing tariffs, government grants, or subsidies. The agreements were multilateral in focus, meaning that several nations agreed to a certain timetable to mutually reduce tariffs in order to facilitate growth in trade and the global economy. On January 1, 1995, the World Trade Organization (WTO) succeeded GATT. Currently, the WTO has 153 member nations and is headquartered in Geneva, Switzerland. The entry of China represents a significant market for all core nations. It is also a clear signal to the world that China is on a march to become a core nation.

As global trade increases, including a substantial number of mergers and acquisitions internationally in the communications sector, the roles and influence of WTO have taken on additional importance. Yet the roles played by WTO are not without controversy or consequence. The 1999 meeting in Seattle, Washington, saw substantial protest from environmental activists, labor groups, and anarchists. Although the protest focused on environmental and labor issues, several of the peripheral nations' delegates complained that the imposition of US environmental regulations or salary and working conditions mandated by US labor unions was merely another form of imperialism, which the peripheral nations rejected. Peripheral nations, as well as some core and semiperipheral nations, were also concerned about the impact and relevance of the US labor practices on their cultural industries. An important point of contention is that the United States views media properties such as film, books, and magazines as economic entities, whereas many other nations view these products as central to their history, national identity, language, and culture. As a result, several parties outside the US vigorously defend their right to exclude cultural industries and products from WTO negotiations. The critics fear that the WTO is a pawn of American hegemonic intentions to grasp even greater global control for US-based communication conglomerates, such as Disney or Viacom.

The major NGO contesting WTO's attempts to include audiovisual or cultural industries is the International Network for Cultural Diversity (INCD).[15] INCD seeks to counter the homogenizing effects of the globalization and commercialization of culture. It seeks to preserve diversity and promote choice in the cultural marketplace. This includes the production and distribution of indigenous goods.[16] The INCD is a citizen's movement with over 500 members from 70 nations. It is a prime mover in terms of supporting UNESCO's convention on the protection of the promotion of cultural diversity. This Convention legitimates government's subsidies, grants, etc., to their cultural industries and opposes the WTO's commercialization of this sector. Another active group opposing the WTO's potential adverse move on cultural matters is Croatia-based Culturelink.

A related controversial issue facing the WTO is intellectual property rights. Intellectual property refers to artistic and literary creations, most of which are protected by copyright. With the expansion of global communication corporations, the ability to reward and determine ownership of creative works is becoming more problematic. And with the expansion of international commerce, the WTO's role in establishing ground rules for all trade is receiving much greater attention.

Currently the WTO appears stuck on the Doha Round, which focuses on agriculture because core nations will not drop tariffs which would permit access to key core markets for peripheral nations. India and Brazil have provided the leadership at WTO meetings in terms of forwarding the agrarian demands of the LDCs. Disputes among nations may be resolved through a complicated dispute settlement process. Such a process is clearly preferable to that of earlier times when colonial disputes about trade frequently led to skirmishes, some escalating into open warfare.

Organization for Economic Cooperation and Development (OECD)

OECD was established immediately following World War II. Canadian and US foreign aid under the Marshall Plan was initially administered by the Organization for European Economic Cooperation (OEEC). The goal of this organization was to rebuild Europe, which had been devastated by the war. Much of the motivation for funding what was a successful program was the effort to stop communism from spreading across Europe, which had been devastated by the war. As a follow-up the Organization for Economic Cooperation and Development (OECD) was formed by 20 nations in Europe and North America in 1961. Since then, 10 additional nations have entered, including the Slovak Republic in 2000. The OECD also has relations with 70 other nations and several NGOs. Under the leadership of the former Secretary-General Donald Johnson, a Canadian, the OECD has been attempting to add more development activities to its research agenda.

The member nations and the date of entry in OECD are as follows:

Australia 1971	Korea 1996
Austria 1961	Luxembourg 1961
Belgium 1961	Mexico 1994
Canada 1961	The Netherlands 1961
Czech Republic 1995	New Zealand 1973
Denmark 1961	Norway 1961
Finland 1969	Poland 1996
France 1961	Portugal 1961
Germany 1961	Slovak Republic 2000
Greece 1961	Spain 1961
Hungary 1996	Sweden 1961
Iceland 1961	Switzerland 1961
Ireland 1961	Turkey 1961
Italy 1961	United Kingdom 1961
Japan 1964	United States 1961

OECD members support research to develop international economic and social policy research. They investigate a broad spectrum of public policy issues that seek to identify the impact of national policies on the international economy. Currently, much of their work focuses on the impact of global trade, including everything from video to the internet. For example, the OECD provides member nations with cutting-edge research and data on a variety of topics relating to the mass media. Figure 5.3 gives examples from the over 50 reports produced by the

1   Media mergers
2   New social and economic approaches to a multimedia world
3   The implications of convergence
4   Global information infrastructure
5   Competition and regulation in broadcasting
6   Competition law and policy
7   Telecommunications regulations: institutional structures and responsibilities

Figure 5.3   Examples of OECD's mass media research reports, 2010

OECD which seek to assist member nations in planning for various aspects of media policy and emerging trends.

Two other sectors within their research divisions, which impact global communication, are first, Information and Communication Technologies, and second, Digital Economy and the Information Society.

OECD attempts to forecast macroeconomic developments on behalf of the 30 member countries, which produce two-thirds of the world's goods and services. In a way, OECD is a global think tank for core and some semiperipheral nations. It provides them with expert advice on how to further frame and expand international trade rules so that the cooperation among member nations as well as others increases and creates a stable and expanding global economy. Most of their work is from an economic perspective. New members are admitted to OECD, which tends to be an exclusive club, as long as the new members have a commitment to a democratic system of national government and function with a market economy. There are two groups seeking accession to the exclusive OECD club. The next in line group which will lead to enlargement of OECD and its substantial power consists of Russia, Chile, Estonia, Slovenia, and Israel. A second group which will be addressed after the first group is resolved consists of the three largest semi-peripheral nations, China, India (the largest democracy in the world), and Brazil. All these potential new entrants realize that the OECD provides world class advice in term of forwarding modernization and economic development. The nations that are excluded have no equivalent economic "think-tank" with access to data and best practice policies to aid them in increasing their role and influence in the global economy.

Conclusions

The US withdrawal from UNESCO was not an isolated event; in fact, it reflected the widespread and somewhat negative view of all UN multilateral agencies in which the United States should play a vital role. In addition to problems with UNESCO, which hosted anti-Western projects, particularly with reference to NWICO, the United States has expressed similar concerns about ITU.

US withdrawal from ITU would be a disaster for the long-term development of national and international communication. The fact that an individual can place a call between almost any pair of telephones in the world is no small feat of international coordination, both technical and political: it represents one of the unambiguously constructive achievements of any UN agency. The importance of international coordination is demonstrated by the fact that in the one area where coordination has failed – namely, high frequency broadcasting – chaotic interference has ensued. If the United States were to leave ITU, it has been suggested that the United States could continue to collaborate with the technical committees on standards and on spectrum competition. This ignores the politically charged nature of all intergovernmental agencies; ITU is no exception. With only 4 percent of the world's population, the United States is the largest user of global telecommunications systems and services, made possible, in large part, by the ITU.

ITU is no longer the most private domain of technicians and engineers dealing with communication technology from a purely technical point of view. It is part of the international concern that sees economic, social, cultural, development and political aspects as part of the global decision-making process. ITU's character shift has, of course, drawn sharp criticism from those who either used to benefit from or control the "clubby" technical atmosphere that core nations fostered. Some critics downplay the role of ITU as well as its current changes, but a proper analysis indicates that ITU is not only central to the future of international telecommunications, but also central to the global economy. On any scale, the United States is the major net beneficiary of the global economy. Telecommunications is the central nervous system of the global economy, and the United States would be the biggest loser should ITU fail in its various roles. Yet several peripheral nations within ITU push a parochial agenda that continues to frustrate core nations.

A global village with a fractured ITU, or an Intelsat weakened because of privatization, would set the scene for potential chaotic, conflicting, and competing assignments of the international frequencies related to the electromagnetic spectrum. Even though such a situation would adversely affect other nations, this would pale in comparison to the turmoil and commercial losses that core governments would suffer, as well as their vast private sector, which relies on instantaneous telecommunications every second of every hour without end. More attention to ITU issues by core nations will be required because the consequences of neglect could cripple the global economy.

Basically the ITU is seeking to retain global leadership as the pre-eminent intergovernmental organization where public (government) and private businesses work to develop global telecommunications and information services networks in an orderly and fair manner. This is no small challenge.

Finally, the impact and long term outcome of the WSIS is still to be written. Some critics, particularly the group claiming that it is a back-door attempt to resurrect aspects of the NWICO saga, are concerned. If this resurgence of NWICO happens then the ITU, its major patron, will be blind-sided and this could hasten its demise. The other area of possible contention is the idea of UNESCO promoting an international convention on cultural diversity at the same time the WTO is looking at cultural industries as a new frontier for its commercial trade rules. These rules could one day make subsidies, grants, radio, television, and film content regulations, and screen quotas illegal. This has the potential to even ensnare the publicly funded BBC.

Notes

1. It is appropriate here to introduce the concept of digital communication. Digital communication represents the emerging technological standard for the transmission of voice, video, audio, graphics, and data. As a technology, it decodes incoming

messages into electronic bytes that are then transmitted via a telecommunication medium, whether a wired system, such as fiber optics, or a wireless technology, such as satellite or cellular. The receiving technology reconstructs the digital information into the appropriate original format, such as a color telecast of an international media event such as the Olympics, or data being transferred from one multinational corporation to its various subsidiaries around the globe. Over time all current analog-based technologies will migrate to a digital format. This digitalization of telecommunications will eventually mean that traditional telephone companies will be able to broadcast television services or carry the internet, and vice versa. This is a large part of the engine of change that is propelling so many mergers across broadcasting and telecommunication entities that historically were separate. The convergence phenomenon began to overtake many regulatory bodies and their rule making in the 1990s. In the twenty-first century, both national and international regulatory agencies will be found wanting as digital technologies and other technical innovations simply outpace the ability of regulators to devise appropriate guidelines to provide appropriate oversight or structure to a plethora of competing global digital services.

2. Documentation of the interconnection of global communication networks, trade, and services is contained in George Barnett et al, "Globalization and International Communication: An Examination of Monetary, Telecommunications and Trade Networks" *Journal of International Communication*, 6(2) (December 1999): 7–19; Kyungmo Kim and George Barnett, "The Structure of the International Telecommunications Regime in Transition: A Network Analysis of International Organizations," *International Interactions*, 26(1) 2000: 91–127; Anthony McGrew and David Held (eds.), *Governing Globalization: Power, Authority and Global Governance*. London: Wiley/Polity, 2002.

3. John Howkins, "How the ITU Works;" *Inter Media*, 7(5) (1979): 22–3.

4. "Will You Keep My Space?" *The Economist*, September 1978, p. 18.

5. Independent Commission for WorldWide Telecommunications Development Report: *The Missing Link*, Geneva: ITU, 1985.

6. Ibid., p. 31.

7. Ibid., p. 65.

8. Ibid., pp. 7–8.

9. Ibid., p. 69.

10. www.du.intl, "Opening Documents, ITC Press and Public Information Service, October 12, 1998," p. 6.

11. "Opening Documents," p. 6.

12. ITU Document, "Towards a Draft Strategic Plan for the Union 1999–2003," pp. 5–11.

13. For more up to date information on the summit see http:/www.itu.int/wsis.

14. Wolfgang Kleinwachter," Internet governance: ICANN vs. ITU?" *Intermedia*, 32(1) (2004): 18.

15. For additional information on the INCD see http:/www.incd.net/.

16. For a comprehensive discussion of the impact of globalization on popular culture see Peter Grant and Chris Wood, *Blockbusters and Trade Wars*, Toronto: Douglas and McIntyre, 2004.

6

Internet
The Evolving Frontier

Introduction

The internet is to the information age what the automobile was to the industrial age. The internet is now a mass medium in many nations and has created a new dimension for global communication. It had its origins in the 1950s as a response to a single crucial military question: namely, how could the United States send strategic information across long distances electronically with a maximum guarantee of accuracy and the likelihood of reaching its ultimate destination? This occurred during the early stages of the Cold War, and the fear of communist activities drove even scientific activities. A team of leading scientists was assembled from leading universities across America. They set in motion research that established the foundation for the electronic transfer of information over vast distances. It was to become a marriage of computer technology and telecommunications which evolved into the internet.

Before describing in detail the series of activities and decisions that collectively formed the foundation for the modern-day internet, one needs to note that only a few major innovations have affected international communications. The inventions started slowly. The printing press, the telegraph and telephone in the nineteenth century, but following World War II the infrastructure of global communications finally had been put in place.

In the nineteenth century there were newspapers, which traveled by rail or private mail, and writing, which traveled as letters via the international postal services. Electronic message systems primarily consisted of the telegraph, which tended to expand in tandem with railway systems. Following the telegraph, came the telephone, which saw a rapid expansion along with a telecommunications infrastructure during the twentieth century. Wireless signals started as ship to shore devices and morphed into radio. Radio broadcasting and the creation of networks emerged in the early part of the last century. At the same time, the movie industry was taking shape in both Europe and the United States. The laying of submarine telephone cable under the Atlantic and then the Pacific Oceans further expanded international communications capacity. Later, satellite services and cable broadcasting were introduced to further expand the telephone, radio, television, data, and other forms of telephony. Now, the introduction of digital technologies, bringing convergence, and the Internet represent the next new wave of global mass communication. The internet relies extensively on the interconnection of widely dispersed, global, and interconnected personal computer systems.[1]

Background

The internet system began in the Cold-War era of the 1950s. With a high level of anxiety over issues such as national security, the spread of communism, the Russians' successful launch on October 4, 1957, of Sputnik,[2] and the potential for nuclear destruction created the public will to undertake research on a massive scale. When one combines these fears with the military background of President Eisenhower, in retrospect it is easy to understand how funding and the intellectual critical mass needed for the creation of a system that would eventually become the internet were established during the 1950s. For example, during this era it was widely discussed that the United States was vulnerable to a potential nuclear attack and that such an attack could disrupt nationwide communication systems. Both commercial and military systems were vulnerable. The other concern was the high cost of computing, along with the physical size and awkwardness of mainframe systems, which used punch cards and bulky tapes As a result, in 1958 the US government, established the Advanced Research Projects Agency (ARPA) to promote advanced research in computing and investigate related telecommunication matters. ARPA had the task of determining how computer technology could be successfully applied to military activities. About the same time, the Rand Corporation produced a national security report that documented the extreme vulnerability of the US national communication infrastructure in the event of a catastrophic event. Basically, Rand proved that national communication systems between the East Coast and the West Coast could be interrupted or severed by a nuclear attack. This, of course, had tremendous ramifications for a coordinated military and civilian response. The collective outcome of these concerns was to build what is described as a distributed network, internet's precursor, called ARPANET (American Research Projects Agency).

ARPANET was constructed in 1969 as a distributed national network basically consisting of a number of stand-alone, remote systems. Each system controlled all necessary data, like a number of backup systems. These systems collectively moved data from one system to another. This distributive network allowed for different possible routes, so if one system was down, the message or data would be relayed through an alternative telecommunication route that was part of ARPANET. For example, if the network in Chicago was down, the system would reroute the data through St. Louis or Houston until it reached its final destination, say Los Angeles. Eventually the entire message would be reconstructed as the data communication, arriving via several different networks, reached its final destination. The military thinking was that given a catastrophic nuclear attack in one part of the country, there would be enough ARPANET systems to bypass affected regions so that the Pentagon could communicate with military bases located strategically in the Midwest or on the West Coast, for example. Today the ARPANET system might appear archaic, but it did generate a large number of high-end host computers that had clear commercial applications for the technology and software being developed and supported by extensive federal research funds available through military and national security initiatives.

A second major outcome of the early computer activities that eventually led to the internet was the extensive utilization of university talent. ARPANET was a project to interconnect the technical workings of four academic research groups based at the University of California Los Angeles, the University of California Santa Barbara, the University of Utah, and Stanford University. These groups were selected because they were working on technical design issues and signal protocols for computers in different locations in an effort to communicate with each other and share resources. These academics were the first generation of computer scientists. At the same time, the US Department of Defense was supporting networking and engineering projects at Harvard University and the Massachusetts Institute of Technology that would serve as the nucleus for East Coast high technology research initiatives. Similarly, ARPANET provided the intellectual critical mass on the West Coast that was necessary for the application of communication technologies to various military initiatives. Over time, universities and technical think tanks such as the Rand Corporation began to promote other non-defense uses of the networks. In the early days, newsgroups expanded based on academic disciplines. For example, physicists began to communicate with other physicists electronically, mathematicians with other mathematicians, economists with other economists, and so on. This produced an expanding universe of electronic mail users who were using personal computers or laboratory computers to communicate across a publicly switched network, which initially was under the control of the Department of Defense. ARPANET had become a packet (data) switching network that allowed researchers, via different computers in different regions, to communicate using computer machines. By 1972 the initial four sites had grown to 23, all networked together and pushing the frontiers of new hardware and software design. By 1987 the Department of Defense had transferred responsibility to the National Science Foundation (NSF), in part recognizing the substantial expansion of the internet system that had replaced ARPANET by this time. The NSF was a logical choice because a large number of non-military applications and protocols were being pursued, and NSF wanted to create a university-based network for a wide variety of academics. Also, a number of commercial computer manufacturers were supporting research to create compatibility and open architectural features to assist an expanding market.

By 1990 the internet was seeing substantial use by people who had significant computer programming experience. It was completely text-based, and people had to learn computer operating systems in order to send or receive e-mail or participate in discussion groups. During the 1990s, the creation of the World Wide Web, the mouse, icons, browsers, and search engines that were user-friendly enabled the internet to expand globally and rapidly. During the same period, the rapid decline in the cost of personal computers also enabled widespread applications in homes, schools, and businesses, which had not been foreseen by the developers of the ARPANET system. In order to encourage the widest possible use of the internet, in 1995 the NSF turned over control of the internet to a number of commercial organizations and networks. Thus, today no one organization, government, or corporation owns the internet. Rather, it is a global interconnection of telecommunications systems controlled by protocols and rule-making on a voluntary basis.

Although the internet system was initially a technical medium for scientists and engineers, it has evolved into a mass medium. It has now become a network of networks. The internet consists of four major elements or electronic services: e-mail, FTP (File Transfer Protocol), newsgroups, and two chat areas-IRC (internet Relay Chat) and collaboration. Each of these elements has international communication potential.

The Department of Defense provided the initial funding, but since that time the internet has become a global network with major commercial applications. The internet economy now is growing faster than other sectors of the economy. For example, according to a 2000 University of Texas study, e-commerce now employs more workers than insurance, public utilities, or the airlines. The same study forecasts an additional 62 percent annual growth rate for e-commerce companies.[3] The internet did not become a global network overnight, but certain events have focused its ability to bring together millions of geographically separated individuals. For example, following the deaths of international icons such as Princess Diana or Michael Jackson, cyberspace became a popular meeting place for mourners. Other examples include the publication of NASA's Path Finder pictures from Mars, or the popularity of stock market information. On certain days, thousands of investors switch to internet financial web pages provided by internet sites, broadcasting networks, cable systems, or investment houses.

Initially, the web was viewed as an alternative news source, but now it is a mainstream news source. The web is a mixture of special interest information providers, ranging from governments, to commercial systems, to global broadcasters such as CNN, the BBC, or Time Warner.

The World Wide Web

The World Wide Web (WWW) is an internet-based process that came about through the convergence of advancing technologies and increased sophistication in programming languages. The rapid development of the WWW is a result of distributed processing, which includes storing, displaying, searching, and formatting computer-based information; the global interconnection of PCs; the development of hypertext and a coding standard, HTML; and browsers. Browsers are a key component and basically represent client application software that knows how to communicate through the internet and capture appropriate documents. Browsers also include built-in tools for searches, e-mail, organizing information, and so on.

During the 1990s, there were two major browsers in competition with each other: Netscape Navigator, which was acquired by AOL, and Microsoft's Internet Explorer. Netscape dominated the browser market during the early years, but Microsoft overtook the browser market in the late 1990s. This domination of the browser market came to the attention of the US Department of Justice. In 1999 the Department of Justice found that Microsoft engaged in monopolistic tactics through its marketing and by embedding its browser within Microsoft's operating systems, Windows, to the detriment of competition. Microsoft appealed the decision in the US successfully, but the EU continues to seek some remedies from the firm.

History of the WWW

As a physicist at CERN Laboratories in Geneva, Switzerland, Tim Berners-Lee wrote a seminal paper in 1980 entitled "Enquire-Within-Upon-Everything." It contained a program that linked arbitrary computers but had the additional capacity to sort information by certain categories. The computers could be located anywhere and search for select information, perhaps on particle physics. By 1990 Berners-Lee and others had progressed to the stage of writing papers and software using hypertext for the purpose of allowing European physicists to communicate with each other by computer. Berners-Lee proposed using a single simple interface to search various information sites spread about the internet system without regard to location. He captured the concept of using Hypertext Markup Language (HTML) to select certain words and then search a vast range of documents to discover similar words, listing them as a result of a computer search. The list also contained the remote computer's address (a URL) to obtain the referenced document. This became the basis of the modern World Wide Web. Initially the WWW was limited to professional and academic organization users, but in 1993 the National Center for Supercomputing Applications (NCSA) at the University of Illinois developed user-friendly client browsers called Mosaic. Prior to this development there were about 50 web servers worldwide. By 1994, with the introduction of Mosaic, there were over 1,500. By 1995 the web became the dominant mode for accessing information from remote personal computers over the internet.

In 1994 Mosaic guru Marc Andreessen left NCSA to form the Mosaic Communication Corporation which in turn changed its name to Netscape Communications Corporation. Netscape produced the first version of Netscape Navigator, the early dominant browser for web users. In the 1990s Microsoft released the Internet Explorer 9.0 version, which was to provide overwhelming browser competition for Netscape. The Microsoft browser was able to retrieve remote documents and provide greater speed and display capacity than its competitors. Each generation of browsers added several unique features, which further expanded the utilization of the web for home, business, school, and a plethora of other users.

With the advent of the fifth generation of browsers, the differences between Microsoft and other browsers are now so pronounced that each system inter-faces with external pages that are dependent on the programming language of a specific browser. Thus, users who want the complete universe of pages or sites for any particular subject area have to load both browser programs in order to retrieve web pages that are systematically linked with one or the other of the browser architectural protocols. In part, it was this phenomenon that attracted the Department of Justice's attention, because the dominance of Microsoft's Internet Explorer browser was inclining new website developers to develop soft-ware that could interface with Microsoft's Windows but not necessarily with the Netscape browser, or others. Because Microsoft has popular Windows products preloaded on almost every new PC, this permits Internet Explorer to be embed-ded within Microsoft's product lines. PCs arrive with preinstalled Explorer browsers for users who then either have little need or the sophistication to seek out the competing browsers. Microsoft's browser claims to be faster, smaller, and offering more features. However, owing in large part to the rapid growth of mobile devices and competing browsers such as safari, Firefox, and opera, Explorer is no longer the clear cut head to the class.

Video Games

Any history of the internet would not be complete without acknowledging the role of video games. Whether speaking of Atari, Nintendo, Sega, PlayStation, or Xbox these video game systems have created a generation of computer users who appreciated high speed, enhanced graphics, and interactivity. Successful video games have served as a backdrop against which computer manufacturers must judge each new generation of PC. As a result, video games continue to set new and higher standards for graphics, speed, and sophistication that each gen-eration of PC has to at least match, if not exceed. The other related phenomenon is that video games are a global enthusiasm. Early on, much of the software origi-nated from Japan, but North American, European, and other affluent cultures quickly became willing markets for and manufacturers of these increasingly sophisticated video games. Games became common property of teenagers in core nations.

Currently, video games are either preprogrammed within a cafeteria of software that is preloaded on PCs, or else they are available externally through the internet to be downloaded for personal use. A major point is that video games, although a separate technology using either a modem and a standard TV monitor or a hand-held device, had an impact not only on the technology of the internet, but also on software development, particularly graphics capabilities. Games set the visual benchmark for PC graphics. It turns out that moving from a controller to a mouse is a small step for game users. The global interconnectedness has allowed for gamers in different regions of the world to participate simultaneously through the latest console technology like never before.

Internet Timeline

The following timeline represents the major historical events that cumulatively aided the global system called the internet.

1955 US President Eisenhower approves funding for US satellite development.
1957 USSR launches first the satellite program, Sputnik, which consisted of four satellites.
1958 US Department of Defense establishes the Advanced Research Projects Agency (ARPA).
1960s A series of isolated academic papers in Europe and North America appear detailing packet switching, batch processing, spooling systems, time sharing computers, and network alternatives.
1961 April – Soviets put first man in space.
      May – United States puts man in space.
      President Kennedy calls for massive funding for research and space exploration.
1965 Ted Nelson describes hypertext, a concept using word association to find similar words electronically.
1969 ARPANET created with four university host sites.
      CompuServe established for home and business customers.
      United States succeeds with moon landing and walk on lunar surface.
1970s Several new ARPANET host sites established, including European sites.
1971 USSR establishes first orbital space station.
1972 First e-mail program written.
      Magnavox releases first home video game system named Odyssey.
1973 United States establishes first US space station, Skylab.
1975 Microcomputers introduced.
      Paul Allen and Bill Gates found Microsoft to develop programming languages.

1976   Apple Computers reach market.

1977   Owners of Apple, Radio Shack, Atari, Commodore 64, Texas Instruments, and others begin marketing personal computers designed for schools and home.

University of Wisconsin supports research to interconnect over 100 computer scientists via e-mail.

1980   Apple issues public stock to raise capital for extensive research and development infrastructure. Leads to 1984 introduction of Apple Macintosh desktop computers

Physicist Tim Berners-Lee of CERN Laboratories (Switzerland) writes program to link colleagues' PCs.

1981   IBM enters personal computer market with two key partners, Intel and Microsoft. Because of size and market penetration, IBM sets new PC architect standards. Smaller, lighter, and cheaper clones begin to appear as well, using Intel and Microsoft products and protocols

Bitnet for e-mail and file transfers established between Yale and City University of New York; IBM adopts Bitnet protocol to link IBM university computers.

Several Big 10 universities begin to establish protocols for networking services, e-mail, and list server activities among campuses.

1983   Desktop workstations established by scientists through grants from NSF.

1984   Newsgroups are organized by researchers at universities, research institutes, and computer manufacturers

1985   America Online (AOL) founded.

1986   Microsoft issues public stock and introduces Windows. Screen icons become the industry model.

1989   Steve Jobs creates new computer company, NeXT. This system introduces many innovations for desktop systems. Berners-Lee and others create web browser for NeXT workstations.

Commercial e-mail offered in limited markets by MCI and CompuServe.

Berners-Lee writes a paper detailing a system using hypertext (HTML) that would become the programming basis for the www.

1990   ARPANET is disbanded.

1994   Netscape developed as internet browser and establishes early lead.
Amazon.com launched.

1995   Real Audio is developed for PC's audio use.

Microsoft introduces browser, Internet Explorer 4.0, to challenge Netscape.

Yahoo! and eBay founded. Beginning of online auctions

1998   More PCs sold than televisions.

CompuServe and Netscape acquired by AOL.

Google search engine launched.

1999   Microsoft is charged by US Department of Justice with engaging in anti-trust activities. Wins in US but similar suit still in play with EU.

   Melissa virus swamps e-mail systems.

   Napster, a music file-sharing program, is released.

2000   AOL and Time Warner announce merger to create the largest global communications conglomerate; synergy fails to materialize.

   Love Letter virus originating in Philippines attaches to e-mail addresses and infects hard drives around the globe.

   Globally, old media companies begin to look for potential new media (internet) companies for mergers, acquisitions, or partnership.

2001   Microsoft enters the video game market with Xbox.

2002   Verizon introduces high-speed 3G cell networks.

   Blackberry "Smartphone" is released in the United States.

2003   Digital cameras outsell film units.

   Lawyers for Recording Industry Association of America (RIAA) representing recording artists and studios go after file-sharing and music-downloading

   MySpace launched: owned by FOX Interactive Media/News Corp.

2004   Google goes public with share offering.

   Online advertising exceeds $10 billion; most coming from newspaper advertising.

   Facebook premieres.

2005   Spyware and adware are introduced owing to problems of junk e-mail. MPAA lawyers sue movie down-loaders.

   Apple's iPod sales set record.

   YouTube founded: owned by Google.

2006   Twitter is launched.

2007   Apple and AT & T release iPhone.

2009   Pirate Bay (Sweden) is a bit torrent firm which allows file-sharing of audio and video productions. It was sued by the MPAA and others over internet piracy. Pirate Bay lost the court case but later elected members to the European Parliament and continues to offer free access to movies, music, and television shows.

   European Commission files suit against Google over its scanning of millions of books to create an electronic database of primarily English language books. Google's compensation of authors is an issue in both the US and Europe.

   The RIAA takes two different students to US federal court over music downloading and file-sharing. The RIAA won both cases. The one was fined $675,000, and the other $222,000. But the latter opted for a second trial and the verdict was raised to $1,920,000. She should have quit while she was behind.

2010   Google releases PC operating system called Chrome, which competes with Microsoft's Windows operating system. Netbooks are primary marketing targets for both companies.

   EU continues to investigate American communication conglomerates.

Impact of the Internet

The internet has had a major impact on many areas of life, from e-commerce to distance education. The following paragraphs highlight a single narrow yet important area: government reports. This example illustrates some of the many unexpected influences of the internet.

The availability of government documents on the internet has changed not only the access issue, but also the way information is now provided in an unfiltered fashion. Political pundits no longer have free rein to put their own personal spin, whether of the Left or the Right, on issues in order to direct viewers, listeners, or readers to an "appropriate" point of view. Because of the internet, individuals can apply their own thoughts, ideas, and background to the interpretation of new information.

The internet phenomenon began to expand rapidly in the 1990s. The system has grown enormously, much of the fuel for growth generated by the creation of widely advertised commercial services. The original internet system was designed as a narrow-casting system in which selected users would access select and unique data, or share specialized information. Now it has become a 24-hour system, a mass medium in effect, ranging from full-service web information, to portals,[4] to news websites such as MSNBC or CNN, in addition to services aimed at the more limited high-tech users. Many utilize the internet's search engine feature (see Figure 6.1).

One of the internet's largest users to date was September 11, 2001. News websites were flooded with hits. A separate traffic phenomenon occurred with the 9/11 Commission in 2004. Televised hearings, numerous press appearances and finally a bestselling government report all watched by internet users led to significant pressure on the US Federal Government to act. Demand for copies of *The 9/11 Commission Report: Final Report of the National Commission on Terrorist Attacks upon the United States* swamped Amazon.com and other sales sites.

The important communication point to be made in all of this is that no longer were news editors, pundits, politicians, the US president, or others able to act as gatekeepers to restrict, alter, spin, or limit the information in the report. Rather, millions of average people around the world now have access to the full, unedited government reports at the same time they are presented to the national legislatures.

The Starr Report and summaries of the 9/11 report on the internet changed in a fundamental way the potential for mass dissemination of information to a global audience. The reports represented unprecedented and unique examples of the pervasiveness of the internet as a mass communication system. It represented the democratization of the mass media in that politicians or media elites were no longer able to control, filter, or interject their editorial viewpoints about a significant government document.[5] Average individuals in the United States and elsewhere with access to the internet were able to download the entire report, consume it

1	Google	(74%)
2	Yahoo!	(16.19%)
3	Bing	(4.99%)
4	Ask	(3.15%)

Figure 6.1   Top four search engines in the US, 2009
Source: SEO Consultants

themselves, and draw their own conclusions. They did not have to rely on the door-to-door newspaper the next day, or condensed sound bites on national newscasts to inform them about a major government document. Even the President of the United States, along with his substantial staff of spin doctors and press spokespersons, was left to consume these and other reports from their computers at the same time that millions of people around the globe were doing exactly the same thing.

As a result of the internet, the global public is better informed. They can act as a more informed public jury concerning major political events, such as the invasion of Iraq. But the changes are not by any means limited to politics. The internet is changing the nature and perception of the human environment. Users are creating a third culture, like Featherstone referred to in an earlier work on the origins and growth of a global culture.[6] There is a difference between users and non-users of the internet. And this phenomenon is more pronounced among heavy users. To some extent Marshall McLuhan foresaw this as early as the 1960s when he was theorizing about the mass media being so pervasive as to totally consume all aspects of a person's being – and leaving no aspect of one's being untouched.[7] Finally, along similar lines, electronic colonialism is about the mind being shaped more and more by external media, of which the internet is simply the latest player. The internet does alter, affect, and influence people in psychological ways yet to be foretold or completely understood. The internet is also primarily in English and has a US-centric bias. These two realities have clear cultural consequences for internet users around the globe. From rural villages in India with computer access, to Starbucks internet cafés in almost every major capital of the world, electronic colonialism is on a steady march 24/7.

The internet has an obvious downside. It is capable of relaying, internationally, sordid details about what historically tended to be personal matters. It also can spark erroneous claims that could end a politicians or CEO's career. When an internet site runs a story, the story goes global. It is not restricted to a city, state, or even nation. Rather, it becomes instantaneously available worldwide.

A final note is that the internet's global and instantaneous communication ability, for good or ill, changed public life forever. In the age of the internet there is no privacy. (Just ask the bloggers. They are covered in more detail later in this chapter.) The releases of government reports have made internet history, but they also opened the door for a two-way information superhighway. Various constituents in record numbers e-mailed their elected representatives with their thoughts and ideas about how to vote. Rather than sending a letter by mail, they now quickly – and for free – mail a message to even obscure members of local and national governments. Many representatives are reporting that they have to reassign staff to deal with the flood of e-mail as the public uses the same computers to reply to the contents of government reports as well as to influence the position of their elected representatives. The messages tend to be short and full of typos, but in the final analysis, the sheer volume of e-mail likely has a collective impact. Politicians, or government agencies such as the FCC or the British Oftel, do not have to wait for weeks for the regular mail to arrive to determine where their constituents stand on vital issues.

Internet and Global Television Issues

The story of video on the internet has yet to be written. The video materials available, whether they are television programming or feature movies, have tremendous implications for current producers. With the ability of the internet to broadcast video live, along with worldwide dissemination, current copyright holders could potentially see their materials appear anywhere in the world without their authorization or compensation. The following two examples illustrate the potential problems.

In June 2000 in California, a group of movie studios filed a suit in Los Angeles to close down a website that was allowing viewers to record television shows online. The site was attracting a large number of users and therefore caught the attention of television executives. Applying traditional copyright laws, the movie studios' legal team sought to close down the site immediately for unauthorized taping and redistribution of the video content, which originated from a series of entertainment companies and was available via cable in the Los Angeles area for a cable subscription fee.[8]

A second situation reflecting the convergence of television and the internet is represented by a company based in Toronto, Canada; iCraveTV began in December 1999 with nearly one million customers during its first month of operation and offering 17 online television stations. It provided free internet access for its advertising-supported rebroadcast of Canadian and US television channels.[9] The 24-hour, live streaming service included NBC, CBS, ABC (American Broadcasting Company), FOX, and PBS (Public Broadcasting Service). Within Canada, internet broadcasting services are not regulated under the Canadian Broadcasting Act. What iCraveTV had done was to create 10 Canadian internet super stations for a potential global audience. Providing the integration of television with the internet has not been without its critics. Some claim that the internet site violated copyright laws and constituted trademark infringement. For example, the US-based National Football League was part of a group that took legal action because US internet users are able to access NFL games through stations rebroadcast live on the iCraveTV internet site. Other plaintiffs in the suit were ABC, CBS, FOX, Disney, and Time Warner.

Using internet video streaming or other internet services could place firms in legal difficulties if prosecuted under US law. US law is aimed at protecting the copyright provisions of not only the major broadcasting networks but also major sporting events, which are contracted on an exclusive basis with US-based networks. The internet's role was clearly not anticipated even a few years ago in terms of providing a competing global alternative for the rights holders. Today, rather than confronting streaming video of copyrighted television shows, network and cable companies have developed free sites, such as Hulu, where visitors can watch their favorite shows with commercial breaks from sponsors.

These examples will likely be replicated when some entrepreneurial web provider makes European soccer globally available on the internet. Also, North American professional sports organizations such as MLB (Major League Baseball) and the NHL (National Hockey League), which have developed fanbases worldwide, have developed online portals for people to watch both domestically and internationally for a fee. The International Olympic Committee is also a group that aggressively protects its trademarked products and symbols. To some, this is innovative and a new application for the internet; for others, these users are mere content pirates and rights thieves.

Internet and Hollywood Films

Industries that have been surprisingly slow to change, such as Hollywood and the feature film studios, have been forced to reexamine their global distribution policies because of the internet. Traditionally, Hollywood's major studios would release their films within North America first, and then later, sometimes many months later, would distribute them around the world, primarily to other core nations and then semi-peripheral nations. In a few instances, it could take a year for a major feature film to open in theaters in smaller nations or Eastern Europe. Now Hollywood is confronting the emergence of the global entertainment market. This market is increasingly sophisticated, with potential moviegoers using websites to obtain information about newly released Hollywood films; others are purchasing films through e-commerce businesses that specialize in film distribution, primarily DVD disk technology. A new Hollywood policy of rolling out global distribution of major movies within weeks is a direct response to the changing environment created by the internet. All the major studios are reexamining their global marketing of new films, and the major reason is that Hollywood's hype machine has finally met a force it cannot control – the internet.

Gone are the days when Hollywood could sell its movies in domestic isolation, with little fear that the US marketing message would spread quickly to countries where the films wouldn't be seen for months.[10] An example of this phenomenon was the co-production of Columbia and Universal Pictures, which arranged a global release for Julia Roberts's feature film *Erin Brockovich*. During the opening week, the film became the number one attraction in seven major markets, including the United States, Canada, and five European nations. The global market for films is being approached more as a single market than as a series of isolated markets. Sony is also marketing new releases on an international rather than a national basis.

There are three other interesting facets of this new policy shift, which recognizes the globalization of the Hollywood feature film industry. The first is that the new releases come out only in English; dubbed or translated versions are not available on the initial release date. The second by-product of the change is that the marketing strategy and advertising copy, including photos, for these releases are now all standardized. Identical promotional materials are used across the globe in other core nations. The promos seen in the United States are now the same promos being seen in Europe and other nations promoting Hollywood's latest blockbuster. Hollywood's approach to the global market had to change or face a growth in the pirating of films or alternative purchasing, which would have adversely affected the profitability of the studios' investments in what are in most cases pricey feature films. This is what has led to the third policy shift. In 2005, following the lead of the music industry going after illegal online file-sharing through the courts, the Motion Picture Association of America (MPAA) began a series of law suits to stop illegal online copying of movies. MPAA is seeking to reduce file swapping or peer to peer (P2P) activities involving Hollywood productions. Although the copyright violation and movie sharing is only about 2 percent of online illegal activity (music represents more than 60 percent) the movie industry is really worried about the future. Today things such as .torrent files have made downloading the large video files easier than ever. Many foreign websites create large P2P communities where videos can be found and downloaded within the United States using programs than break down and recreate the files quicker than ever. With each new generation of computers both speed and space will be less of a problem or deterrent. Complicating matters for MPAA is that each new version of file-sharing software is becoming more user-friendly and more difficult to track. Facing these technical realities Hollywood studios are seeking to make some online pirates pay and use these cases to stop others. Even if successful in US courts, the studios still have little hope of legal standing for the enormous threat to their property rights outside the US.

Internet Users

Yet another example of how the internet has caused a reexamination of traditional ways of doing business concerns internet users. According to internetworldstats. com, the top 10 countries with the highest internet usage in 2008 were

1. China: 298 million users;
2. United States: 227.2 million users;
3. Japan: 94 million users;

4. India: 81 million users;
5. Brazil: 67.5 million users;
6. Germany: 55.2 million users;
7. United Kingdom: 43.8 million users;
8. France: 40.9 million users;
9. Russia: 38 million users; and
10. South Korea: 36.8 million users

By 2004, the United States alone accounted for over 50 percent of the global internet usage.[11] At the same time Europe accounted for 25 percent of global usage. It is obvious that core nations were the early inventors and adopters of the internet but today new nations are showing how quickly they are developing technologically. Owing to the exponential increase in users in Eastern Asia the US only accounts for 14.2 percent today. The core nations have all three requirements for internet access: technical expertise, the financial resources to buy the required computers and hookups, and communication infrastructures to deliver interactive internet services. In many cases, peripheral nations lack at least one of these requirements, and in some cases they lack all three.

Not surprisingly, the US is the internet superpower. According to communication scholar George Barnett, "the United States is … the nucleus of internet traffic,"[12] and it is the most central nation on the international networks of both hyperlinks (bandwidth) and infrastructure. In cyberspace, peripheral and semi-peripheral nations rarely communicate directly; almost all internet traffic flows through the US. The nature of the internet today can be partially explained using world system theory, with language, technological, and cultural advantages that help the US remain the most powerful and influential nation in the information age. The US is also home to key stakeholders such as Google, Microsoft, Apple, and social networks.

Another factor that seems to encourage greater internet use is geography. Six nations have geographically isolated populations yet have substantial per capita users. These are the Scandinavian countries of Finland, Sweden, and Norway, as well as Australia, Canada, and New Zealand.

Semiperipheral nations in central and Eastern Europe will likely see the largest per capita gains in new internet users. E-commerce on the internet is now generating significant revenue in all core nations. This will fuel additional demand for internet access as well as growing commercial competition as the market share for electronic purchases of goods and services around the globe expands at a rapid pace.

Computer Viruses

With the advent of the internet came the birth of computer viruses. Some are merely nuisances, while others, such as the Melissa, Love Letter, Trojan horse, Mydoom, and Resume viruses, have affected electronic mail and other files with extremely damaging results. Major corporations have had to shut down their systems owing to some of the more pernicious viruses. These have the potential to erase data, release secure data, change data, or totally freeze or take over computer systems. It is estimated that there are now over 100 new viruses per week. With e-commerce expanding on a daily basis, the impact of viruses can be catastrophic and within a matter of minutes run into the millions of dollars in lost time and business. Although computer viruses first appeared in the early 1980s, macro viruses that spread worldwide with the extensive use of the internet system are a more recent phenomenon. There are also many reports of hoaxes, which are more than major annoyances. Given the recent impact of viruses that embedded themselves in complex and massive ways, even hoaxes have to be taken seriously.

Cyber crime is another new by-product, as well as a legal challenge, of the internet. For example, the I Love You worm code that originated in the Philippines in May 2000 moved via e-mail across Asia to Europe and from there to North and South America. Thousands of individual users were infected, as well as major organizations such as the British House of Commons, Yahoo!, the US Central Intelligence Agency, CNN, and the Ford Motor Company. Although the overall cost of damage from this e-mail worm is difficult to assess, it was well into the millions of dollars.

Basically, computer viruses are uninvited guests that run on your PC. They can attach themselves to other files – mainly e-mail addresses. As computer-programming languages become user-friendlier, and because they are transferable, virus programmers have realized that viruses can now switch from one platform to another without any difficulty. The virus problem is huge because viruses can be initiated by novice programmers, but the consequences can be truly catastrophic as the viruses worm their way globally and in seconds from system to system. Malicious hackers or simply nerdy computer groupies can unleash viruses at any time. Today there is anti-virus software that has helped to reduce the problem. Yet new categories like adware, pop-ups, spyware, and malware continue to infect computers. Removal software is available from several vendors.

Finally, in 2004 in the first felony prosecution of spammers in the US, a jury convicted two spammers of sending vast bulk e-mail messages. Anti spam laws with tougher sanctions are being enacted in several jurisdictions.

Blogging

A new internet driven phenomena called weblogs or web diaries, and popularly cited as bloggers, arrived in the mainstream media by 2004. Historically, some early bloggers, such as engineers or technicians, were adding personal or political comments to their discussion websites as early as the mid-1990s, but a few seminal events occurred in the early 2000s, which moved blogging to a new level.

The first substantial blogger-driven event was a rather focused internet attack in 2002 on the then powerful Republican Senator Trent Lott. Lott had made some inappropriate and racist comments at a party and the mainstream media as usual covered the matter, but only for a few days. But some tenacious bloggers kept the heat on Lott for weeks and called for his resignation. This web-based chorus forced the national media to take another look at the entire episode. Lott did resign. He did so because bloggers were able to build pressure via the internet that put Lott back on the evening newscasts and talk shows in a negative light. A decade earlier he would have avoided such scrutiny and shame.

In 2003 other creative blog users were able to mount a substantial fund-raising drive via the internet for Howard Dean, a candidate for the Democratic presidential nomination. His star rose rapidly as the internet favorite but he and the others lost out to Senator John Kerry. Dean also set the "gold standard" of fund raising by using the internet in creative ways. Barack Obama was to take the matter several steps further by implementing a host of political internet activities which aided his winning the presidency in 2008.

In 2004 bloggers became mini celebrities by being accredited as media representatives at both the Democratic and Republican national conventions.[13] Blogging became a household word much as Google did in record time. Finally, in late 2004 Dan Rather and CBS carried a piece on documents alleging that President Bush was not as solid a National Guard soldier as Bush had claimed. The documents turned out to be false. Again it was the bloggers who that kept the profile and bias of the CBS network alive and forced the mainstream media to again pursue the entire issue. Eventually both Rather and CBS issued apologies for their major ethical lapse. CBS was forced to set up an investigation and as a result other senior CBS personnel were fired. In addition, some websites were calling for Rather to be fired as well. Rather announced his retirement but later sued CBS for wrongful dismissal. The suit has yet to be resolved; CBS was forced to acknowledge that the White House had pressured the network to let Rather go.

A related newer stage of this phenomenon is video blogging. This combines the text-based blog with some appropriate video. The Asian tsunami and amateur video enthusiasts on vacation in the region provided a windfall for vbloggers on several continents in 2005. There are no protocols, permissions obtained, or copyright concerns by the vbloggers. Future dramatic footage, be it a televised confrontation or a natural disaster, will find its way around the world thanks to the growing cadre of vbloggers.

So the debate about the role and eventual fate of bloggers is still to be written. Some claim that they are pretend journalists in t-shirts with a laptop, while others see the new phenomena being the next significant trend in journalism. Bloggers can be rude, crass, and seem to spent a great deal of their time discussing sex, yet they have made the political process more open and clearly have a voice and opinion on high profile issues, whether people or political parties like it or not. Large news corporations cannot ignore their impact, and several now give people to opportunity to weigh in on their own websites or cable television shows.

Another new and booming phenomenon is social networking. Sites such as MySpace, Facebook, Twitter, and LinkedIn have created a new global interface. Although MySpace and Facebook began as social sites, they have developed, both positively and negatively, as ways for professionals to network or for businesses to profile those on the sites. Twitter, a more recent addition to this group, is a way for people to keep fans or friends up to date on their daily activities. It has become so large, that news corporations can now quote people of interest from the site, rather than contacting them personally. LinkedIn, founded in 2002, is a website for professionals to create a web of connections through their peers in their industry. It is business oriented and it gives people the opportunity to provide a miniature résumé to people looking at prospective employees. All of these websites have become incredibly popular, and businesses are trying to find out how to optimize their efficiency using these sites.

ICANN

The Internet Corporation for Assigned Names and Numbers (ICANN) has become both powerful and controversial. It is the outcome of years of recognizing the growth and significance of the internet for the global economy. Domain names and various internet protocols, which carry a unique numerical address, are at the center of the internets' orderly expansion. All computers need an address in order to participate in the internet's growing role in all aspects of modern life. The global internet community "created a need for a new kind of social contract."[14] Milton Müller refers to the various functions that ultimately provide for unique internet names and addresses as "the root."[15] It is clear that ICANN has become powerful because it controls the rights to add top-level domain names, such as .com, .edu, .net, or .org. ICANN is a private company which controls the technical standards of cyberspace. To some extent it controls global information-sharing in the online environment. It raises the bar on the construct of power.

Internet names and related protocols emerged out of and along with the growth of the Advanced Research Projects Agency. Since the funding for ARPANET came from the US military at this early stage, some controversy of who was getting the preferred names was bound to emerge. ARPANET was disbanded in 1990. The US-funded National Science Foundation took over part of the naming function for a period, and then in 1993 the US Federal government gave governance control to Network Solutions, Inc. A rash of "cyber squatting" took place where people would register domain names with the hope of selling them later.[16] By 1998 this and other problems led to the US Department of

Commerce to create a private entity, ICANN, based in California. ICANN was given substantial gatekeeper control over new access to the internet's registries. Challenges to what appeared as a powerful monopoly role emerged.[17] In the US much of the challenge to the functioning ICANN came under the umbrella of antitrust laws, specifically the tough Sherman Anti-trust Act.[18] Even though ICANN is governed by an international Board of Directors, who attempt to insure that technical elements of the internet's infrastructure serve global needs, this over-sight has not kept the global community of users included or content. Currently there are calls for a shift from the US centric coordinating role of ICANN to a mutli-lateral organization and environment.[19] This controversial matter has unexpectedly been taken up with some peripheral nations' zeal within the World Summit of the Information Society (WSIS). It will see a politicized tone for what ICANN and others see as technical rule-making in nature.[20] It also means that the future of internet governance may lead to benefit the ITU or the OECD – as possible new ICANN oversight and structures. Online access in non-Latin letters, such as Arabic or Chinese, for domain names is one step in accommodating the genuine criticism from peripheral nations.

   In closing, the above is not a trivial matter. The future of the internet and how and who governs it internationally is central to the emerging electronic information environment. If fair and equitable access is not spelled out, then it is the peripheral regions that will fall further behind in the digital divide chasm. The core nations to date have controlled the "global village" with its internet connectivity through ICANN and its predecessors. Many civil society groups have been critical of ICANN's closed and tone deaf corporate culture. Some opening up of rule-making and greater access is now being challenged in several fora. A good example is the internet Governance Project which is an alliance of academics seeking to influence internet policy by sponsoring events and publishing position papers about ICANN's policies and procedures. They have a significant following.

Conclusions

Any description of the internet, as well as projecting the future of global communications, deals with history on the run. Given the major technological and software advances being promoted by major corporations and research institutions, there are going to be several additional generations of internet hardware and software. Likewise, the merger phenomenon of old media stakeholders and new internet players, such as Time Warner, is in its infancy. In the future, there are likely to be more mergers of transnational corporations, whether they are based in Europe, North America, or Japan. The internet personifies a dynamic, rather than static, state of affairs. The internet economy is growing at a much faster pace than the Industrial Revolution that began in the eighteenth century. Perhaps more importantly, the potential scope, size and overall economic impact of this economic system is much larger than what we can comprehend today. The key characteristics that distinguish the new economy are information, knowledge, and speed."[21]

Before drawing some general conclusions, a significant point relates to indigenous internet sites. It is true that various linguistic or ethnic groups have created sites that focus on and promote smaller cultural sectors. Many of these are aimed at keeping expatriates informed or aiding children with their ancestral roots. Yet for every page on the internet which is non-English, there are at least 100 pages of English text. The internet is both US centric and English dominated. That is a major reason why the internet is a leading purveyor of electronic colonialism around the globe.

Even so, we can draw six general conclusions. First, although the origins of the internet may be traced back to the 1950s with the sponsorship of the US Defense Department, it is still safe to say that the origin, description, and role of the internet as it has evolved to date occurred within core nations. Innovations and expertise in North America, Europe, and to some extent Japan permitted the development and rise of the hardware and software necessary to establish a global internet system. Semiperipheral nations played only a catch-up role as they attempted to mimic innovations first established and demonstrated within core-nation markets. Semiperipheral nations also tend to face the dual problem of the lack of investment capital to underwrite new internet ventures, and a lack of the high-tech entrepreneurs needed to develop and promote more indigenous internet sites and services. For peripheral regions, the situation is simply exacerbated.

The internet revolution is in progress. Some nations with progressive public policies that encourage foreign capital and reward entrepreneurs will benefit, but other nations may stall or regress over time which weakens their global economic and social positions. Semiperipheral and peripheral nations are distant users of the internet. In those areas where the internet exists, it is primarily available only to elites, whether they are government officials, military, academics, business, or religious leaders. In far too many cases, the average person in peripheral regions is waiting for a first telephone, not preoccupied with browser technologies, e-commerce, Kindle, iPods, or MP3.

Second, the internet represents change. Its impact among information gatherers and providers, whether they are in the media, business, or universities, has been profound. The situation will continue to escalate as e-commerce activities begin to displace traditional mechanisms and modes across the internet. Just as Amazon.com revolutionized the bookselling industry, so virtually every industry will experience similar internet intrusiveness and some global opportunities or competition in the near future.

Third, e-commerce and e-multimedia will take on greater global trappings. The ability to advertise and market on the internet is a global electronic phenomenon.

It has transformed commerce beyond the traditional bounds of the nation-state. The BBC, MTV, CNN, and other media enterprises have long recognized this, but particularly with the merger of AOL and Time Warner, there is a clear demarcation between the old media firms and the new. A firm without an internet presence is destined to a strategic reality of declining market share and influence. The internet represents the globalization of the marketplace in a fashion unprecedented in human history. It brings with it values and economic rituals such as credit cards and advertising that reflect the electronic colonizing of both the mind and the marketplace. Internet global advertising exceeds $10 billion and increases annually. Much of the online ad revenues appear to be coming primarily from newspapers and to a lesser extent from network television. Strategically over time, since the amount of online advertising is going to increase, a fair number of newspapers and magazines will close.

Fourth, capturing the consumer behavior and consumer purchasing power for products and services offered over the internet will become a greater economic force and reality over time. The global success of the Big Five, which are Amazon.com, eBay, Google, Microsoft, and Yahoo! as both viable commercial and electronic leaders, bodes well for not only them but many others as well.

It is not so much an issue of cultural imperialism, as some critics have maintained, as the economic common sense of following the success of various individuals, corporations, and systems that have migrated successfully and quickly to the world of the internet. This phenomenon might more reasonably be called electronic imperialism. The internet is to our future what automobiles and transportation were to our past. Now we are looking at digital nations, virtual spaces, e-commerce, and global systems that link individuals and the internet without regard for time, space, or borders. Whereas time and space were the defining characteristics of the industrial era, so now the internet, where time and space no longer pertain, is the defining medium of the information age.

Fifth, now China will be the largest internet user nation. Also the greatest growth will be across all semiperipheral nations since many core nations represent mature markets in terms of computer sales. Nations such as India and Brazil represent huge untapped markets.

Sixth, internet technologies are not neutral. They impact a broad range of behaviors from information processing, to research strategies, to e-commerce, and e-living. Just as the invention of the printing press had widespread consequences for the Industrial Revolution over the course of the last two centuries, so too, the internet will impact on this and future centuries in profound ways. Marshall McLuhan (1911–80) detailed the printing press's impact on society and individuals in his seminal work, *The Gutenberg Galaxy* (1962). A similar classic has yet to be written about the impact of the internet, but there are early indications that this impact will be substantial. For example, with reference to the internet and information technologies, Alan Hedley states "what is at stake are the very thought processes of those dominated. Only powerful nations currently have the ability to choose the type of information society most compatible with their cultural institutions.[22] This viewpoint is fully consistent with the theory of electronic colonialism. Basically, the internet, whether it is in China, the United States, or some remote part of India, will have parallel consequences for social systems (e.g., education, commerce, discussion groups, friends) and the mind-sets of individual users. Internet users, regardless of time or space, will mentally converge over time with other widely dispersed users. They will come to have more in common with individuals scattered around the planet than with non-users in their neighborhoods, schools, or work.

Notes

1. This chapter seeks to highlight salient aspects of the history and current role of the internet. There is a vast literature on the subject; a few sample pieces include: J. Levine, C. Barondi, and M. Young, *The Internet for Dummies*, Foster City, CA: IDG Hooks Worldwide, 1999; K. Hafner and M. Lyon, *Where Wizards Stay Up Late: The Origins of the Internet*, New York: Touchstone Books, 1998; and Paul Ceruzzi, *A History of Modern Computing*, Boston: MIT Press, 1998.

2. The symbolic role of the Russian series of four Sputnik satellites cannot be underesti-mated. These relatively unsophisticated satellites successfully launched by the Soviet Union demonstrated to US military, political, and industrial leaders that Soviet tech-nology was much more advanced than many had believed. The same rocketry that could propel a Russian satellite into orbit could also be easily modified to launch a nuclear payload aimed at North America. In response, in 1961 US President John Kennedy committed the nation to putting a man on the moon by the end of the decade. Thus began the space race, along with the necessary rocketry to propel not only satellites into space but also manned orbital missions. In July 1969, the Apollo 11 module landed on the moon with Neil Armstrong and Buzz Aldrin.

    Although Sputnik's signal lasted only 18 days, it was sufficient to galvanize the United States to engage in a space race with the Soviet Union. The space race would provide substantial funding for the development of satellites for broadcasting as well as military uses, and the development of manned space vehicles led to the miniaturiza-tion and increased sophistication of computer systems. Although it is highly possible that US academics and scientists would have eventually developed much of the communication technology of today even without Sputnik, Sputnik provided the impetus, focus, and substantial federal funding required to propel the US into the global leadership role it currently holds in computers, satellites, digital devices, mobile telephony, and telecommunications.

3. *USA Today* (June 6, 2000): 1A.

4. Portals are essential navigating tools for searching the internet. They fall into two cat-egories. The first type of portal, available through AOL, Yahoo, MSN Worldwide, Excite, Lycos, and others, helps users search for general interest and broad categories of con-tent. The audience for these major portals has given rise to a second category called niche portals, which specialize in more narrow areas and condensed searches. Good examples are portal sites for graphic artists, gardening, golf, sports, gambling, or

health, or sites in Spanish such as quepasa.com for the global Latino market. These specialty portals have unique features that appeal to specific segments or niches of the broader internet audience. Over time, as new niche segments are identified, these types of portals will expand significantly and ultimately draw users from the general portal sites.

5. The internet has changed the nature and role of the mass media. Just how much is a story yet to be told. At this point, some may argue, with good reason, that the traditional media still set the agenda of public discourse and that the internet traffic is a function of the old media, which still retain elite power. But we are rapidly reaching the point in core nations where the internet will set the agenda and traditional media will be forced to follow. Blogging and twittering are contributing to this shift in agenda setting.

6. Michael Featherstone (ed.), *Global Culture: Nationalism, Globalization and Modernity*, London: Sage, 1990.

7. Marshall McLuhan and Quentin Fiore, *The Medium Is the Message*, New York: Bantam Books, 1967.

8. *Wall Street Journal* (June 16, 2000): B8.

9. In the early 1990s, Mark Cuban, now an owner of the Dallas Mavericks and chair of HDNet, married a PC with a high-speed telephone line to get a distant college basketball game. He subsequently created an internet site using similar connections for distant events that became so popular that he sold it to Yahoo! in 1999 and became a billionaire. Yahoo! now offers its users hundreds of radio and television stations. Yahoo! pays all necessary fees up front for audio and video programming that appears on the internet by way of Yahoo!'s portal.

10. *Wall Street Journal* (June 12, 2000): A1.

11. Ken Cukier of *Communications Week International* (France), in a 1999 paper titled "Bandwidth Colonialism? The Implications of Internet on International E-Commerce," makes the case that the internet is US-centric. The global topology of the internet is US dominated because bandwidth, cost, and technology favor the United States. Cukier cites as an example the fact that Paris-based FranceNet's most powerful server was based in California.

12. George A. Barnett, "The Role of the Internet in Cultural Identity," in L. Leung, A. Fung and P. Lee (eds.) *Embedding into Our Lives: New Opportunities and Challenges of the Internet*. Hong Kong: The Chinese University Press, 2009, p. 354.

13. Matthew Klam, "Fear and Laptops on the Campaign Trail," *The New York Times Magazine* (September 26, 2004).

14. Milton Müller, *Ruling the Root: Internet Governance and the Taming of Cyberspace*, Cambridge, MA: MIT Press, 2002, p. 5. (Müller is an expert on internet matters and a key force in the internet Governance Project).

15. Ibid., p. 6.

16. Lily Blue, "Internet and Domain Name Governance: Antitrust Litigation and ICANN," *Berkeley Technology Law Journal*, 19 (2004): 387–403.

17. Susan Schiavetta and Konstantinos Komaitis, "ICANN's Role in Controlling Information on the Internet," *International Review of Law, Computers and Technology* 17(3): 267–84.

18. Blue, 2004, p. 393.

19. Wolfgang Kleinwachter, "Beyond ICANN vs ITU?" *Gazette*, 66 (2004): 233–51.
20. Milton Mueller and Lee McKnight, "The Post-.com Internet: Toward Regular and Objective Procedures for Internet Governance," *Telecommunications Policy*, 28 (2004): 487–502.
21. Anitesh Barua and Andrew Whinston, *The Internet Economy Indicators*, Austin: University of Texas, June 8, 2000, p. 2.
22. Alan Hedley "Technological diffusion or cultural imperialism? Measuring the information revolution." *International Journal of Comparative Sociology*, 39(2) (June, 1998): 210.

7

American Multimedia Conglomerates

Introduction

Not long ago, US productions, particularly feature films and television shows, dominated theater screens and television sets around the globe.[1] Foreign productions provided relatively little competition. Today, other major global firms either own US production houses, share co-productions, or they produce elsewhere world-class competitive products for a global media market. Sony of Japan, the BBC of Britain, and Bertelsmann of Germany are good examples of foreign multimedia firms which compete daily with US media companies. Yet US firms still control a majority of foreign sales in the global communication market. They are also expanding through regional partnerships, international joint ventures, or outright takeovers. Time Warner, Disney, Viacom, News Corporation, and General Electric, owners of NBC Universal, represent the major US media owners that dominate many global media, global communication, and global media-related markets (Figure 7.1).

Time Warner controls CNN, HBO, Warner Music Group, AOL, and several other media properties. Disney controls ABC, ESPN, Miramax and Touchstone Pictures and more. Viacom owns MTV, CBS, BET, and Showtime. News Corp. owns the FOX properties, Myspace, and the *Wall Street Journal*, and General Electric owns NBC (National Broadcasting Company) television and Universal Pictures. All are headquartered in the United States, the dominant core nation, with extensive semiperipheral and some peripheral market activities. This chapter details origins, assets, and global interests of these major US multimedia firms along with a few others.

It is important to note the profiles of such multimedia firms. First, in terms of revenue, the three largest global media empires are all American. Time Warner,

1	Time Warner (US)
2	Disney (US)
3	News Corporation (US)
4	Viacom + CBS (US)
5	GE-NBC Universal (US)
6	Sony (Japan)
7	Bertelsmann (Germany)
8	VNU (The Netherlands)
9	Activision Blizzard/Vivendi (France)
10	Discovery Communications

Figure 7.1   Global media leaders, 2010

which owns several major properties, is by far the largest; but it does not own a general interest national television network such as ABC, CBS, FOX, or NBC. Disney is second, News Corporation is third, and the fourth largest global media empire is the Viacom.

Second, in terms of electronic colonialism theory, all of the US multimedia empires, along with their extensive advertising networks, project and encourage US tastes, values, mores, history, culture, and language around the world. To a considerable extent, it is this influence that concerns other core,[2] semiperipheral, and peripheral countries because of the impact of US multimedia fare on those countries' domestic media, box office receipts, world view, and their children. In terms of the latter, think Disney, Sponge Bob, Barbie, or Hanna Montana. Foreign nations' concerns cover a vast range of cultural products such as music, movies, television series, magazines, books, and now the internet. In terms of world system theory, the United States' activities in semiperipheral nations, which have large, accessible markets with growing disposable incomes, as well its activities in some peripheral nations, illustrate well the model explaining the broad range of offshore economic activities undertaken by major US communication corporations. Major US global multimedia empires define relations with other nations along several product lines, as well as advertising, on an expanding number of foreign commercial television, radio networks, outlet stores, movie screens, and print publications.

Hollywood- and New York-based communication corporations do well on a global scale because they have four substantial advantages. First, they operate in English, the language of the largest global segment of media outlets with purchasing power. Second, they have access to substantial fiscal resources and capital markets, allowing them to finance multimillion-dollar productions or take-overs. A single Hollywood feature film costs more than most other nations spend annually on all their feature films. Third, US television networks overwhelmingly prefer US made prime-time shows.

ABC, CBS, FOX, and NBC seldom purchase foreign-made programs. Fourth, Hollywood and New York have access to the broadest range of acting talent, producers, writers, and directors. Some of the talent is from other core nations such as Australia, Canada, Britain, France, or Japan. The best global actors and actresses work primarily or exclusively on US productions. Most foreign actors, actress, and musicians dream of the day that they have a contract from an American company. That is their gold standard for defining success in the media sector.

The critics of US cultural imperialism are at a virtual loss about what to do. Some call for media protectionist policies, which emerge from time to time around the globe. Quotas limiting US media imports are a good example. Others simply lament the fact that the business is all about economics and job opportunities and that there are scant opportunities for actors, writers, or producers from semiperiphal and peripheral nations to obtain employment and needed exposure in core nations. Most foreign commercial markets buy US television and movies for their television and theater outlets. For example, across Europe, 60 percent to 80 percent of their purchases of foreign television programming are native to the US. At least 50 percent of the movie screens in Europe show Hollywood productions as well. Across Latin America 60 percent of the movie screens show Hollywood productions. In the future, as the number of channels increases in other core and semiperipheral nations thanks to cable, satellite, and digital technologies, the need for content will only increase the demand for American productions of all genres.

The four largest media conglomerates in the world are all US owned. They are Time Warner, Disney, Viacom (which owns CBS), and News Corporation. They and other significant US multimedia enterprises are detailed as follows.

Time Warner

The merger of America Online and Time Warner created the largest communication organization in the world. It was a $350 billion deal completed in 2000. The merger and anticipated synergies have not gone nearly as well as expected. Initially, the merger faced serious regulatory hurdles in both Europe and the United States, but for different reasons. In Europe the European Commission's antitrust enforcers focused primarily on Time Warner's music holdings in considering whether to approve the deal. For them it was a culturally charged issue. Eventually Time Warner agreed not to pursue the purchase of the major British music empire EMI, and made other concessions, in order to obtain European approval. On the other hand, in the United States the merger had to survive two separate reviews, one by the Federal Trade Commission (FTC) and the other by the Federal Communications Commission (FCC). Their concerns focused primarily on the issue of access, which was a concern on two fronts: access to the vast Time Warner cable systems across the United States, and access to America

Online properties, particularly their e-mail and other e-properties contained in AOL version 9.0.

Essentially, US regulators were concerned about providing a level playing field for competitors who had to deal with the giant merged companies of AOL and Time Warner. Washington power brokers remembered that Time Warner cable division had pulled the cable plug affecting Disney's ABC TV network. This involved millions of subscribers in 1999. The lengthy review process was dominated by negotiations to protect competitors from either of two possible scenarios. First, AOL providing monopolistic preference for Time Warner's vast product lines, and second, Time Warner's cable systems providing clear preference for AOL's internet activities. At the time of writing, Time Warner has nearly 90,000 employees around the globe.

The concern about Time Warner being unfair to a powerful competitor such as Disney's ABC was a defining moment for all other nations. If Time Warner was willing to obstruct a major stakeholder such as Disney, then what chance did the distinctly smaller stakeholders in other core, semiperipheral, and peripheral nations have to withstand the enlarged Time Warner juggernaut? Foreigners perceived the merger as exemplifying the way in which electronic colonialism was reaching not just a new, broader, and more sophisticated level, but moving into a more pervasive phase of global communication, through the internet, where AOL is a major player. Time Warner management and shareholders applauded the marriage, while end users outside the US hardly realized that their domestic or indigenous productions and networks would be fighting for their very survival. The merger also turned out to be a fiscal mess since the synergies failed to appear and the stock took a big dive. In fact, senior management took the "AOL" part of their corporate name off the masthead to improve the image of their core assets so, today, the combined company is known simply as Time Warner. Ted Turner of CNN fame, a major shareholder, quit their board of directors in disgust.

Generally, the analysis of world system theory pits the core nations against the values and interests of the semiperipheral and peripheral nations. But the high-profile merger of AOL and Time Warner clearly presented a situation in which a single core nation – the US – is influencing all other core nations, including Canada, Australia, Japan, the European Union, Latin America, and eventually every other nation on the planet (Figure 7.2).

Before describing the various media assets of Time Warner, it is important to note that the merger is part of the internet revolution. AOL was supposed to bring the technological advances necessary to advance Time Warner to a more sophisticated level of promoting on a global scale its substantial portfolio of communication holdings. AOL had previously merged with other internet companies such as Netscape and CompuServe. The combined company attempted to take advantage of the global growth of advertising that utilizes e-commerce as a major revenue stream. But AOL ran into Google as well as a few others and failed to deliver the riches which AOL management promised. In fact, in 2003 Steve Case the former head of AOL was sacked by Time Warner.

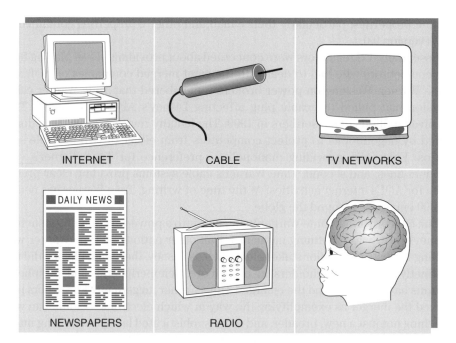

Figure 7.2   Time Warner and AOL's strategic goals, 2002
Source: St. Louis Post-Dispatch editorial cartoon, February 26, 2002.

Finally, an interesting by-product of the merger was that this marriage of old media (Time Warner) and new media (AOL) put all other companies under a microscope, as customers and shareholders alike begin to expect that other old media stakeholders will join with relatively new media enterprise to become more internet savvy. Failure by media firms to adjust to the internet could lead to the same type of fate which the newspaper industry is facing today.

Its major properties include CNN, Warner Bros, HBO, Cinemax, Time Warner Cable, Time Warner Books, Warner Music Group, Time Inc., its publishing arm, and TBS (Figure 7.3). Time Inc. accounts for 15 percent of Time Warner's sales. Warner Bros.' movies and WB television network generate almost 50 percent of Time Warner's sales. They also publish over 30 feature magazines such as *Time*, *People*, and *Sports Illustrated*. The Time Warner video group controls close to 6,000 feature films, including all six Harry Potter films, *The Dark Knight, Gran Torino*, and *Slumdog Millionaire*, 32,000 television shows, and 14,000 animated titles. It operates major book clubs and book publishing through Warner Books and Little, Brown, and promotes print and videos through the Time Life series. Finally, Time Warner controls 50 percent of both Comedy Central and Court TV.

A major Time Warner acquisition was the 1996 takeover of Ted Turner's Turner Broadcasting System (TBS) for $8 billion, which brought all of Turner's properties, including the prestigious global broadcasting news network CNN, as well as TNT and TBS, into the Time Warner family.

```
  1  AOL (+ subsidiaries)
  2  ADTECH/Advertising.com
  3  AIM/ICQ
  4  Atlantic Records
  5  Cartoon Network (+ subsidiaries)
  6  Central European Media Enterprises (31%)
  7  Cinemax (+ subsidiaries)
  8  CNN (+ subsidiaries)
  7  Comedy Central (50%)
  8  CompuServe
  9  Court TV (50%)
 10  DC Comics
 11  Elektra Entertainment Group
 12  Entertainment Weekly
 13  Essence
 14  Fortune
 15  HBO (+ subsidiaries)
 16  HLN (+ subsidiaries and offshoots)
 17  In Style
 18  IPC Group Limited (Europe)
 19  Kids' WB!
 10  Lightningcast
 11  MAD magazine
 12  MapQuest
 13  Money
 14  Moviefone
 15  Mushroom Records
 16  NASCAR.com
 17  Netscape
 18  New Line Cinema
 19  People
 20  Pogo.com
 21  Spinner.com
 22  Sports Illustrated
 23  TACODA
 24  Telepictures Productions
 25  The CW Television Network (50%)
 26  TheSmokingGun.com
 27  Third Screen Media
 28  Time (+ subsidiaries)
 29  Time Warner Books UK
 30  Time Warner Cable
 31  truTV
 32  Truveo
 33  Turner Broadcasting Station
 34  Turner Classic Movies (+ subsidiaries)
 35  Turner Entertainment
```

Figure 7.3 Major Time Warner properties, 2010

---

36   Turner Network Television (+ subsidiaries and offshoots)
37   Warner Bros. Pictures
38   Warner Books
39   Warner Bros. Entertainment(+ subsidiaries and offshoots)
40   Warner Music Group
41   WB Network
42   Winamp

Figure 7.3   *(cont'd)*

Reflecting the growing role of offshore income for all American media conglomerates, Warner films are now making almost twice as much on foreign box-office receipts as compared to domestic ticket sales. More and more movies will be produced for the global audience rather than the declining domestic market.

Time Warner Entertainment History

In 1922, 24-year-old Henry Robinson Luce founded Time Inc.[3] Beginning with *Time* magazine and later *Life, Fortune,* and *Sports Illustrated,* Luce became the leading global magazine publisher. Time Inc. lost its print persona almost overnight when in 1989 it merged with Warner Communications. Warner brought a major video culture to the print culture of Time. The new, combined entity, Time Warner Entertainment (TWE), experienced some merger woes. The two different corporate cultures took time to blend, and senior management experienced turmoil, but eventually Gerald Levin of Time Inc. became chairman and CEO of Time Warner in 1992.

The new focus for TWE was expanded further with the addition of Ted Turner's empire in 1996. Today, journalism and entertainment history coexist at TWE. Gerald Levin recalls Luce's legacy at TWE:

> Luce was adamant that economic progress was inextricably linked to political systems that actively encouraged individual initiative and free enterprise. For me, the advent of a digitally based economy gives Luce's view fresh urgency.
>
> Luce also insisted it wasn't enough for business leaders to pursue efficiency and productivity. Those who entered the executive suites of American business had to have a heightened sense of their responsibility to the common good.
>
> I share this conviction.[4]

Levin also comments on his grasp on the new role for video and cable at Time:

> At the heart of what I envisioned was a world-class news operation in print and electronic media, with the size and resources to immunize it from those who had no regard for its heritage.[5]
>
> I believe that if Luce had entered the media business when Ted Turner did, his instincts as an entrepreneur and journalist would have led him to grasp cable's potential for creating

a new kind of global journalism. In the same way I believe that the 24-year-old Luce who conceived *Time* or the media revolutionary who proclaimed that *Life* was more than a new magazine – that it was a new way of seeing – would have jumped on the internet and been a formative influence on its evolution as a news medium.[6]

Luce was a print man, whereas Levin brought expertise in video, and through the merger with AOL, he also brought internet expertise. Levin was sacked in 2002 and AOL's Steve Case a short time later (Munk, 2004).[7] Also, Time Warner's major competitors – Disney, Viacom, News Corporation, Sony, Bertelsmann, NBC Universal, and others – compete in the same global communication market with many competing brands.

CNN Connection

Although CNN, a Time Warner enterprise, is discussed more thoroughly in Chapter 1, an important issue involving CNN is relevant here. Ted Turner's video empire competed with Time's print focus and culture. Turner's various media properties greatly supplemented Time Warner's strategic moves in the video business. Turner brought with him not only a 24-hour cable news network and other media properties, but also the Goodwill Games, which Turner himself established in 1986 to provide an international platform for amateur athletes while at the same time ignoring Cold-War rhetoric and sanctions. Turner had a global model in mind for both his media properties and his amateur athletics endeavors. He sought to use the games as a way to enrich all humanity, regardless of politics, national boundaries, and historical feuds. Turner thought globally and had a vision of world peace. He was a strong supporter of the United Nations as well. Time Warner dumped the Goodwill Games as well as Turner himself.

In 1990 Turner established the Turner Foundation with a $150 million endowment; it focuses on environmental and global population issues. In 1997 Turner also gave the United Nations Foundation $1 billion to encourage greater global cooperation. He resigned from Time Warner in 2003. Since that time Turner has been giving speeches and media interviews, which are critical of Time Warner's strategic planning as well as the excessive power of media conglomerates (Auletta, 2004).[8]

America Online (AOL)

The AOL side of the merger brings global leadership covering web brands, interactive services, internet connectivity, branded portals, and an expanding range of e-commerce services. The AOL network's handling of over two billion instant messages per day indicates an example of its size. AOL was founded in 1985 and has four major product lines:

1. Interactive Services Group includes AOL's major internet provider activities including CompuServe and Netscape, which are internet portals. This business

group also contains AOL Wireless Services, which is designed to deliver AOL properties to an expanding global group of wireless customers. Whereas most AOL customers today hook up to the internet through a PC, in the future, particularly in Europe and Asia, more and more clients will opt for wireless internet connectivity.

2. Interactive Properties Group contains branded properties such as Digital City; ICQ, a portal; AOL Instant Messenger, which is a popular electronic text message service; as well as Moviefone, Inc., and MapQuest. In 2008, AOL acquired a global social media network Bebo.

3. AOL International Group is responsible for all AOL, CompuServe, and Netscape operations outside the United States. This is a rapidly expanding segment of AOL's overall business. AOL outside the US has more than 10 million subscribers. In many nations, AOL properties are the second leading internet provider. In foreign countries, the main internet provider is generally the domestic telecommunications company, such as France Telecom or Bell Canada.

AOL worldwide (some of the 38 foreign nations):

United Kingdom	Japan
Canada	Germany
France	Puerto Rico
Brazil	Argentina
Latino	Australia
India	France

4. Netscape Enterprise Group included software products, technical support, and consulting and training services. As of May 2008, AOL no longer supports or develops Netscape products.

The number of AOL subscribers around the world was once close to 30 million, approximately 24 million of whom were in the United States. However their subscription numbers have plummeted in recent years and according to the latest numbers, they have only around 6,000,000 subscribers remaining.

AOL competes directly for internet subscription revenues with Microsoft, AT & T, Prodigy, and others. Their web-based search services and portals also face considerable competition from Google, Yahoo!, MSN, Disney's portal and Excite At Home. Even though it functions in a highly competitive environment, AOL has structurally maintained a distinct global lead as the major internet provider. By merging with Time Warner, AOL had hoped to move to a new level in its ability not only to provide connectivity and e-commerce services, but also to deliver around the globe a vast array of content through a mix of free and subscriber services. This major corporate merger is not being universally applauded. A number of key executives have been replaced. The firm still does not have a national television network among its properties. Some major competitors have expressed concern about being excluded or treated as second-class corporate citizens within the vast array of AOL services. In 2008, Time Warner began separating AOL's internet services from its advertising department and in 2009 Time Warner announced that it was restructuring AOL into an independent, publically traded company. Given the amount of decline AOL has seen in the last five years, the company is not likely to last much longer.

Synopsis

Time Warner became the world's largest media company through a long-term strategic plan involving major mergers. In 1989 it merged with Warner Communications; in 1996, it merged with Turner Broadcasting; and in 2000 it merged with America Online. Time Warner now operates in six major communication sectors: cable, publishing, films, music, broadcasting, and the internet. Its cable systems provide some of the most technologically sophisticated digital fiber-optic systems available anywhere. The company has also focused on global markets. This is especially true of its broadcasting undertaking, particularly CNN International, which produces exclusive programming designed for Asia and Europe and reaches over 150 million TV-viewing households in over 212 countries and territories. It is undertaking this without the advantage of a national television network based in the United States such as ABC, CBS, FOX, or NBC.

Finally, it is important to keep in mind that within the US domestic market CNN is number two, behind FOX and sometimes behind MSNBC as well, but globally it is number one and BBC World Television Service is number two.

Disney

Disney is the world's second largest communication empire, after Time Warner, with annual revenues of around $38 billion. Disney started early last century under the leadership of Walter Disney, who had a professional vision of using animated cartoons and feature films as major commercial ventures.[9] His brother, Roy Disney, provided the financial acumen to help build a media giant.[10] The venture produced global icons including widely recognized characters such as Mickey Mouse, Donald Duck, Cinderella, and Snow White. During the 1950s, the major film subsidiary Buena Vista was established, and a number of Disney shows were made for television. Disneyland opened in 1955 in California. In the 1960s, Disney had several successful feature films including *101 Dalmatians, Mary Poppins, The Jungle Book,* and *The Love Bug*. In the 1970s, further theatrical successes included *The Aristocats, Robin Hood,* and *The Rescuers*. Today it still has a strong line-up with movies such as *High School Musical, Toy Story, Hanna Montana,* and *Power Rangers*. Walt Disney World, another major theme park, opened in

```
    1   ABC Television Network
    2   A & E Television Networks (38%)
    3   Biography Channel
    4   Buena Vista International
    5   Citadel Broadcasting
    6   Disney Publishing Worldwide
    7   Disney Stores Worldwide
    8   Disney Channel Worldwide
    9   Disney Consumer Products
   10   Disney Interactive Media Group (PCs, mobile phones, video games)
   11   Disney Live Family Entertainment (ice shows)
   12   Disney Music Group
   13   Disney Stores Retail Chain
   14   Disney Theatrical Productions (Broadway musicals)
   15   ESPN (80%)
   16   Euro Disney (39%)
   17   E! Entertainment (35%)
   18   The History Channel (38%)
   19   Hollywood Pictures
   20   Lifetime Entertainment Services (50%)
   21   Marvel Entertainment
   22   Miramax
   23   Pixar
   24   Radio Disney Network
   25   SOAPnet
   26   Toon Channel
   27   Touchstone
   28   Walt Disney Internet Group
   29   Walt Disney Studios and Pictures
   30   Walt Disney Parks and Resorts
   31   Walt Disney Studios Motion Pictures International
   32   Walt Disney Studios Home Entertainment
   33   Walt Disney Television International
```

Figure 7.4   Major Disney properties, 2010

Orlando, Florida, in 1971. In 1983 Tokyo Disneyland opened, and that same year the Disney Channel began as a cable TV service. In the early 1990s, Disneyland Paris opened and quickly became controversial because of its US cultural orientation. Also, the Disney Corporation purchased Capital Cities/ABC in 1995 and became a major television broadcasting network owner (see Figure 7.4). In the late 1990s, several Disney subsidiaries started websites that include the ability to purchase products directly from Disney anywhere in the world.

Finally, in 2005 Hong Kong Disneyland opened and attracted over five million customers during the first year of operation. The park consists of four themed areas: Main Street, USA, Fantasyland, Adventureland, and Tomorowland. This Disneyland is jointly owned by the Chinese government (57 percent) and Walt Disney Company (43 percent). Plans are already underway to expand the parks size and perhaps add Frontierland to its themes. All themes have a direct connection to electronic colonialism theory since they personify American themes and history. It is difficult to miss when one of the major attractions is called Main Street, USA.

In 2007 Disney joined with GE (General Electric) and News Corp. to start website Hulu. It offers streaming video of movies and television shows. It is funded by commercials and Disney owns 27 percent, like the other two media companies.

Disney currently operates as a global entertainment company with four major business divisions: Media Networks, Parks and Resorts, Studio Entertainment, and Consumer Products.

A major global asset is Disney-ABC-ESPN Television (DAET). Now DAET is available in 240 territories around the globe to over 1300 broadcasters. Part of the media fare is a cartoon channel for children, named Toon Disney. It carries Disney animation shows, movies, and cartoons. Internationally it is offered as part of cable or satellite packages aimed at children's audiences. Given Disney's vast library of video productions, much of it decades old, non-American networks have considerable difficulty competing with DAET and the Toon Channel appeal.

The Disney Interactive Media Group has two main interests: entertainment websites and news websites. These sites include Disney Online, ESPN.com, ABC.com, and ABC news.com. The internet group also offers searches, chatrooms, message boards, and e-mail. As a full-service internet provider, it competes directly with other major portals such as AOL, Microsoft, and Yahoo! Today Disney is a highly diversified communication conglomerate, ranging from broadcasting, to feature films, to the internet, to theme parks and resorts, to Disney stores, which operate in hundreds of locations worldwide.

History

The roots of Disney date back to December 30, 1890, when Walter Disney was born in Chicago, Illinois. Through his early years, Disney held several jobs including volunteering for the American Ambulance Corps, sorting and delivering Christmas mail for the Kansas City Post Office, and eventually forming a company with Ubbe Iwerks called Iwerks-Disney Commercial Artists. By 1920, Disney and Iwerks joined the Kansas City Slide Company, which was renamed the Kansas City Film Ad Service. That same year, Disney produced what he called "Laugh-O-Grams." Essentially, the production of Laugh-O-Grams was Disney's introduction to the world of animated film and the beginning of the Disney Empire. In 1937, *Snow White and the Seven Dwarfs* arrived in cinemas. It represented a new breed of film because it was full-length animation. After Snow White, Disney went on to produce 35 animated feature films. Some of Disney's most famous works include *Cinderella*, *Sleeping Beauty*, *Pinocchio*, *Dumbo*, *Peter Pan*, *Mary Poppins*, *The Jungle Book*, *The Little Mermaid*, *Beauty and the Beast*, *Aladdin*, *The Lion King*, *Toy Story*, and *Hercules*.

To increase exposure and sales, Disney opened several theme parks, which today are the most attended theme parks in the world. The theme parks are Magic Kingdom, Disney-MGM Studios, Epcot, Disneyland, Disney's Animal Kingdom, Tokyo Disneyland, and Euro Disney. Euro Disney is 40 percent owned by Disney and is the largest tourist destination in all of Europe with over 15 million visitors per year. In 2001, Disney opened California Adventure and Tokyo's Disney Sea, and has a theme park in Hong Kong. In all, Disney has 11 theme parks worldwide.

When the Walt Disney Company bought Capital Cities/ABC for 19 billion dollars in the mid-1990s, it entered network broadcasting in a big way. Disney bought Capital Cities/ABC because the Disney Company was having problems getting its programs on television at desirable times. The purchase of Capital Cities/ABC allowed Disney to reach larger prime-time audiences. After all, ABC was the network credited with the highly rated prime-time shows – and audience favorites – *Home Improvement*, *The Drew Carey Show*, and *Monday Night Football*. ABC's Wednesday night lineup was just as popular with one of the network's newest and most watched programs, *Dharma and Greg*. ABC was also popular with Sunday night prime-time audiences, who enjoyed the return of *The Wonderful World of Disney*. Some other solid shows are *Grey's Anatomy*, *Scrubs*, *Lost*, and *Ugly Betty*. Finally, the network picked a winner in *Who Wants to Be a Millionaire?* Winners are defined in the industry as programs which command an advertising rate premium.

News is another important element of ABC Broadcasting. ABC News continues to attract large audiences with *World News with Charles Gibson*, previously known as *World News Tonight*. The news division was enhanced with a second launch of *20/20*, the successful late-evening show *Nightline*, and *PrimeTime Live*. Furthermore, *ABC World News* has always been the leader in foreign news coverage.

In 2002, senior Disney and ABC executives tried to cancel the award-winning *Nightline*. The newsmagazine, which began in the 1980s with coverage of the Iran hostage crisis, has a loyal following and is a credit to moderator Koppel and ABC's News Division. But the senior staffs of Disney and ABC attempted to hire NBC late show star Jay Leno without informing Koppel or his producer. The industry and viewers alike were upset with the crass, secretive move. ABC was perceived to be abandoning its public service mandate in pursuit of a few more dollars. Leno quickly declined the offer, sensing that being part of a plot to end a high-quality news show in a post-9/11 environment would be a career mistake. But in the end, the "bean counters" at Disney are likely to prevail and quality broadcasting will take a hit in the name of profits. Other than NBC's *Today Show* and CBS' *60 Minutes*, news and public affairs programming is not a big commercial success.

ABC Broadcasting also has a vested interest in the following cable networks: A & E (37.5 percent), the History Channel (37.5 percent), Lifetime (50 percent), E! Entertainment (34.4 percent), and Walt Disney Television International. A & E has been the winner of 20 Emmy Awards, and the network has reached more than 70 million subscribers in North America. The History Channel serves more than 42 million subscribers and the History Channel International was launched in 1998 and is available in 51 countries. E! Entertainment has become a leading worldwide provider of entertainment and news information on both television and the internet. In fact, E! Online Entertainment is one of the leaders of the World Wide Web and has a large teenage audience.

ESPN Inc.

Disney-controlled ESPN is the worldwide leader in sports, reaching 77 million homes. All ESPN networks and services are 80 percent owned by ABC. It was founded in 1979. Its main telecast is *SportsCenter* and in 1987 it negotiated with the National Football League to broadcast Sunday night NFL football. ESPN's audience jumped dramatically and now they are a fixture in the global sports culture. ESPN2 was launched in 1992 and has 65 million subscribers and is one of the fastest growing cable networks in the United States. ESPN also reaches households internationally. This 28-year-old network now reaches 150 million households in more than 150 countries and territories and in 20 languages. In 2004 it launched a Spanish network, ESPNU. ESPN.com is one of the most visited websites in the world. In 2003 the US Office of Foreign Assets Control, as part of their anti-Castro preoccupation, fined ESPN for broadcasting sports in Cuba. Finally, Sega is licensing ESPN shows for its video games worldwide. ESPN is a 24-hour sports cable franchise that is a media wonder, much like CNN or HBO.

Theme Parks: Marketing Media Heroes

To further reach audiences internationally through television, radio, cable, and the internet, Disney expanded its theme park business in Europe and Asia. Based on the success of Tokyo Disneyland, which opened in 1983, Disney opened Disneyland Paris in 1992 to further expand international markets. It currently owns 40 percent of the French-based theme park and resort, which has been renamed Euro Disney. Euro Disney operates two parks outside of Paris. They are Disneyland Paris and Walt Disney Studios. The Studios were constructed in 2002 at a cost of over $500 million. Since inception they have welcomed over 150 million visitors. EuroDisney is still losing money and its largest personal shareholder with 16 percent is Saudi Arabian Prince Alwaleed. Euro Disney also contains a McDonald's restaurant.

Disneyland theme parks have been successful and profitable in the United States, Hong Kong, and in Tokyo because the "American" style of doing business worked; however, this was not the case during the early years in Europe. Europeans did not accept or understand the American way of doing business, nor did they like it. Cultural differences created some hostility in France, and the Walt Disney Company did not experience magical success in Europe. Disney executives also failed to do preliminary research, approaching France as though it were a foreign market similar to Japan.

Knowing a country's unique culture is vital to the success of a US company. The Disney training manual is a good example of the problems Disney encountered in France. Before Disneyland Paris opened, the Walt Disney Company built offices and a training center in order to recruit the park's cast members. After passing Disney's pre-hiring procedures, the candidates were then trained. Every employee hired needed to meet and pass Disney's strict personality requirements. Recruits practiced the "Disney smile" and saying "Have a nice day." They also had to follow the 13-page manual outlining Disney's dress code, otherwise known as the "Disney Look." The manual outlines the idealized American appearance: a well scrubbed, happy, all-American look. The manual spells out everything from the appropriate size of earrings, to the appropriate length of fingernails, to the no-tolerance rule on facial hair or dyed hair. The young European employees did not understand or appreciate the "Disney Look." It was difficult for them to adhere to an American look since they were not Americans. They also believed this requirement stripped them of their individualism. As a result of this major culture clash, the French, who contested the strict dress policy, took Disney to court. Ultimately, the Walt Disney Company modified and instituted a new, more relaxed European dress policy.

The Walt Disney Company also failed to research the pros and cons of selling alcohol at Disneyland Paris. Alcoholic beverages are not served in the California, Florida, and Tokyo theme parks, and Disney instituted the same no-alcohol policy at Disneyland Paris, failing to respect the European custom of drinking wine with lunch. Needless to say, the Europeans rebelled against the no-alcohol policy and stayed away in droves. As a result, in 1993 the Walt Disney Company changed its policy to allow the sale of wine and beer at Disneyland Paris. Despite several other examples of Disney's failure to understand local tastes and traditions, it has adjusted to make Disneyland Paris more of a success by adopting other European practices. It also expanded its hotel offerings, and the parks now feature seven hotels, with a total of 8,000 rooms, plus two major convention centers.

Also the Disney expansion into Asia represents a straightforward example of a core-based multinational organization entering a semiperipheral area, in this case China, which has an enormous population of 1.3 billion; thus, China has the potential to become part of Disney's major global network in the twenty-first century. The Hong Kong investment is likely the tip of the iceberg in terms of Disney's future expansion plans across China – and all with the blessing of the communist Chinese government.[11]

Pixar

In 2006 Disney agreed to buy out Pixar Animation Studios. It is a world class computer animation firm that had its origins with filmmaker George Lucas in 1984. In 1986 Steve Jobs, of Apple fame, purchased the computer graphics part of Lucas's firm and named it Pixar. In 1991 Disney signed with Pixar for a series of computer animated feature films and thus began the important relationship from both creative and monetary angles. The first film was *Toy Story* in 1995. It was the first fully computer animated feature film. Before this animated films were hand drawn frames which took enormous amounts of time and talent. The joint venture, Disney and Pixar, film was a huge global success and was the highest grossing movie that year. It was followed by *A Bug's Life* in 1998 and this movie dominated international screens as well. It was followed by *Toy Story 2* which grossed almost a half billion dollars worldwide. Other films were *Monsters Inc.*, *Finding Nemo*, and *Cars*, released in 2006. The Pixar deal has once again made Disney the leading animation studio in the world. It also shifted the revenue stream to one where the global box office receipts exceeded the domestic, US, receipts. And the global revenues only continue to grow and Disney management is well aware of this trend.

Synopsis

The Walt Disney Company began as a small, creative firm established by two brothers: Walter Disney, who was responsible for the animation activities, and his brother Roy Disney, who handled the company's finances and strategic planning. The initial years of the company were extremely successful with the creation of several popular culture icons such as Mickey Mouse and Donald Duck. After World War II, the company began to add theme parks, one in California and later one in Florida. They then expanded internationally with Disneylands in Japan, France, and now China. During the 1980s, the company expanded through Disney stores and greater diversification into related fields. Several highly successful children's and family films were produced during this period, and they ventured into new territory such as the NHL hockey team, the Mighty Ducks, the addition of Disney cable channels, and the addition of Disney Music. In the 1990s, the takeover of the national television network ABC was a major move for the corporation. Currently, Disney's largest unit is its film labels, which include Disney, Touchstone, Buena Vista, Dimension Films, Hollywood Pictures, Pixar, and Miramax Films. These units produce films for the global market, and they market select ABC shows. Finally, the move into Asia with a second theme park in Hong Kong represents a major global move for the Disney Company. Asia represents a vast new market, and Disney appears to be ahead of Viacom and Time Warner in strategically identifying new opportunities in Asia. But not is all well at the Magic Kingdom. In 2004 major shareholders, including Roy Disney, Walt Disney's nephew, were calling for the resignation of the CEO, Michael Eisner.

He simply announced his desire to retire in 2006 (Stewart, 2004).[12] The takeover of Pixar was also a successful venture which has increased Disney's global footprint.

Finally, in the context of ECT, Disney is a classic example. It operates on a global scale with American cultural products across a broad range of media and platforms. It utilizes the latest technology and marketing information to increase market share annually, whether through music, movies or theme parks. More children around the world know Mickey Mouse than any other cultural icon. For other non-American cultures, Mickey and Minnie represent a distinct challenge to indigenous characters, practices, and sales of indigenous goods. For example, in Mexico, children's parties have traditionally featured a piñata, a papier-maché donkey, filled with candy. Now, most piñatas are made in the likeness of either Mickey Mouse or SpongeBob. Another example is Europe. Disney has 45 television channels across Europe which carries their vast library of cartoons and movies. Their sports channel ESPN is offered in 7 countries.[13]

Viacom

History

In May 2000, the Federal Communications Commission (FCC) approved the merger of Viacom with CBS. Viacom, as part of the consolidation in the broadcasting industry, was able to purchase CBS Corp for $30 billion. This immediately gave Viacom control of more than 35 percent of the US broadcasting market. The deal covered all CBS properties, which included at that time 38 television stations, 163 radio stations, and interests in 13 internet companies. Now Viacom is the third largest (after Time Warner and Disney) communication giant in the world. The purchase constitutes an interesting role reversal. Originally CBS, like other networks, produced a great deal of in house programming.[14] But in 1971, the FCC forced CBS to sell all internal production and cable programming units, which it did by creating Viacom.[15] Now 27 years later, Viacom has been so successful that it is in a position to buy its parent, CBS. The FCC dropped the prohibition against networks owning production houses in 1995. As a result, major television networks are now producing more in-house shows in order to contain costs, control the process, and reap the syndication income from successful dramatic series or sitcoms. Viacom is a massive video syndication company with a global reach, which includes properties such as MTV, Paramount Pictures, King World International (*Jeopardy* and *Wheel of Fortune*), United Paramount, Infinity Broadcasting, Simon & Schuster publishing, and hundreds of movie theaters in Canada, Europe, and South America.

Federal regulators' decision to allow the merger reflects a current policy of permitting competition among corporate giants in order to facilitate the efficient and effective use of the market, rather than letting federal regulators rule with a heavy hand. Now several Viacom brands will have to fight it out with the brands of other major conglomerates such as Disney, which owns ABC, News Corporation, which owns FOX, General Electric, which owns NBC, and the even larger giant Time Warner. All of these corporations have major international holdings. They are able to use their North American consumer and studio base to produce videos and movies for domestic and foreign television and theaters, as well as software for their internet sites. Their internet activities are expanding globally as these firms put greater resources and strategic emphasis on internet initiatives, many of which are joint ventures. These North American communication conglomerates almost always cover the costs of production through US revenues, and thus foreign markets, through syndication, represent substantial profits based on two large income streams – the US and global markets.

Viacom is an international stakeholder in major media markets ranging from motion pictures, to television, to publishing, to recreation, to video distribution (Figure 7.5). Viacom owns Paramount Pictures, which began producing feature films in 1912. Viacom controlled Paramount's 2,500-and-growing title library, which contains a number of classic feature films, along with the *Star Trek* and *Indiana Jones* movies, *Braveheart*, and *South Park*. In 2006, Viacom sold Paramount's film library for $900 million. Viacom holds 33 percent of United International Pictures, which manages foreign distribution of Paramount's vast feature film libraries to over 60 countries around the world.

In terms of television, the major products are produced through Paramount Television as well as CBS, MTV, Nickelodeon, VHl, Nick at Nite, BET, and Showtime. Through its holdings, Viacom controls the libraries of major series such as *I Love Lucy*, *The Honeymooners*, *Star Trek*, *Beverly Hills 90210*, and *Cheers*. It also controls Spelling Entertainment, which in turn controls the syndication rights of 16,000 television episodes, including international markets.

Viacom also offers the Paramount channel in Europe, distributed as part of a multichannel package on Rupert Murdoch's satellite system BSkyB. In television broadcasting, Viacom owns 19 TV stations in the United States through its subsidiary Paramount Stations Group. These stations are located primarily in major cities and reach 25 percent of US TV viewing households.

Simon & Schuster, a major publisher, is also a Viacom property, publishing more than 2,400 titles a year. Simon & Schuster is one of the most influential publishing houses for the mass market in the world. It publishes major bestsellers, including books by Stephen King and Frank McCord, and has a strong presence in the children's book market.

In 1993 Viacom and Paramount announced their merger, and Blockbuster Entertainment Corporation announced it would start to invest millions in Viacom. In January 1994, Viacom and Blockbuster announced an $8.4 billion merger. In 2004 Blockbuster was spun off as a separate company. Blockbuster has more than 6,000 video and music stores in 26 foreign nations. Viacom took a majority control of Paramount in 1994, and soon thereafter began assembling the management team for the combined company. At the same time, Viacom announced the

1   BET Networks
2   CBS Enterprises
3   CBS Outdoor
4   CBS Radio
5   CBS Television Network
6   CMT
7   Comedy Central (partial)
8   Famous Players theaters
9   Harmonix (music-oriented video games: Rock Band, Guitar Hero, Karaoke Revolution)
10   Home Entertainment
11   Logo
12   MTV (+ subsidiaries)
13   MTV Films
14   Nickelodeon (+ subsidiaries)
15   Nickelodeon Movies
16   Paramount Pictures
17   Paramount Television
18   Paramount Vantage
19   Rhapsody
20   Shockwave (online and mobile games)
21   Showtime (+ subsidiaries)
22   Simon & Schuster Publishers
23   Spike TV
24   The N
25   TV Land
26   United International Pictures
27   VH1 (+ subsidiaries)
28   www.addictinggames.com
29   www.quizzilla.com
30   Xfire (MMOG social media application used by: World of Warcraft, Call of Duty, etc.)

Figure 7.5   Major Viacom properties, 2010

formation of the Viacom Entertainment Group, comprising the Paramount Motion Picture Group, Paramount Television, and the Paramount Stations Group.

In Latin America, Paramount, MCA, MGM, and FOX have a joint interest in Cinecanal for Spanish-speaking Latin America and in Telecine for Brazil. Combined, these two networks reach approximately two million subscribers.

Viacom is a diversified entertainment and publishing company with operations in four areas: networks and broadcasting, entertainment, video and music/theme parks, and publishing. Through the networks and broadcasting segment, Viacom operates MTV, Showtime, Nickelodeon, Nick at Nite, VH-1, and 111 broadcast television stations. Generally Viacom's networks are offered to customers of cable and direct home-satellite services.

Viacom's future plans are clear. The major changes will be dealing with the growth and expansion of MTV, Nickelodeon, BET, and CBS. Nickelodeon and the Media Group have introduced plans to launch Nickelodeon in Turkey as well as other foreign countries. Viacom hopes to have Nickelodeon spread worldwide so that it can meet the demand for expanding markets with network shows and movies which have proved successful in the United States.

CBS Corporation

In 2005 under the direction of the controlling shareholder and Chairman Sumner Redstone the assets of Viacom were split into two separate companies – CBS and Viacom. CBS took 17 units including all of the CBS television and radio activities, UPN, along with international, outdoor, King World, Simon & Schuster, Showtime, and 50 percent of the CW network. The other 50 percent is owned by Warner Brothers.

In 2006 CBS hired Katie Couric as the first female solo anchor of a network newscast. She came from NBC's *Today Show* and signed a contract making her the highest paid anchor in the world. But to CBS's chagrin the ratings did not follow their bold move. Couric consistently lags behind her two competitors on ABC and NBC. Couric replaced Dan Rather who was the anchor for 24 years and was pushed out by CBS senior management. The major issue at the time was the veracity of a piece Rather did which was critical of President Bush's military service. Rather has a wrongful dismissal law-suit working its way through the US court system, which in part claims that CBS management caved into White House pressure to remove him.

Viacom is managed through two divisions: filmed entertainment and media networks. Viacom kept control of several entertainment brands, including MTV channels, Black Entertainment Television (BET) networks, Paramount Pictures, Comedy Central, and Nickelodeon. BET is distributed globally and can be viewed in Europe, the Caribbean, and Africa.

Synopsis

Viacom has major global interests ranging from Paramount Pictures, BET, and MTV, which are particularly attractive to advertisers because of its global niche market; strong publishing interests with Simon & Schuster; as well as packaged television programming on various global satellite systems. Viacom and CBS International have been active in promoting regional global markets, including Australia, Latin America, and particularly Asia. Viacom is also a major player in international theatrical exhibition operations, with a number of cinemas around the globe. CBC Radio, formerly Infinity Broadcasting Corporation, operates nearly 200 radio stations. Finally, Viacom's profits come from a mix of revenue sources. The primary source is advertising revenue from its media brands, particularly MTV and BET; another source of revenue is sales of books and movie ticket purchases for its Paramount Productions. A clear drag and perhaps a structural issue are the CBS television network problems, including Couric's ratings.

News Corporation

History

In 2004 News Corp., the fourth largest global media company, announced that it was moving its corporate headquarters to the US, confirming the status of the US as the most important multimedia market in the world. It also represented a significant loss to the image and future of Australia as a major player in the Information Age. As one of the largest vertically integrated media conglomerates on the planet, News Corp. gave three major reasons for the move. First, to expand the shareholder base, scope, and demand by becoming an American company. This allows News Corp. to be listed on major US indices which only list US stocks, and to open the company to the many pension funds that are limited to purchasing US stocks. Second, more than 75 percent of their revenue and profits come from US multimedia operations. Only a very small portion of their revenues comes from Australian operations. Third, such a move will provide News Corp. with access to much larger capital markets. These markets may become crucial as News Corp. attempts to create a global satellite sports-entertainment network similar to CNN's all news network. Access to capital is also important in terms of underwriting blockbuster movies for FOX studios.

The largest shareholder of News Corporation is Australian born Rupert Murdoch, a naturalized US citizen who resides in Europe. He is a media mogul unlike any other.[16] With News Corporation, Murdoch has created an international empire of media, technology, and sports franchises. Murdoch himself is conservative and hires senior management of the same persuasion. For example his US FOX network is headed by Roger Alles, a well-known conservative Republican who has worked for and advised Republican presidents. Alles's news divisions have learned how to slant both foreign and domestic news so as to guarantee that it will be aired and that they will not be fired for failing to follow the company's slant. In general, FOX lacks a culture of professionalism and where objectivity does not dominate the handling of news. Rather they prefer to go with an edge and anti-balanced format as personified by Bill O'Reilly and others. They run with the latest rumor or anti-Democratic story.

Murdoch has used sports teams as a vehicle to obtain large audiences for his networks, not only for the sports programming but for other broadcasting initiatives as well. Murdoch tends to be outspoken and come across as unique in the media world. The interconnection of sports and television is simply a growing international phenomenon. Murdoch is also part owner of a new sports channel in Canada, CTV Sportsnet. The growing convergence of sports and television continues with almost monthly announcements of major corporate agreements. Part of the strategy is to control the sports franchise, but these companies also want an advantage in the media rights of the sports league. Murdoch is no stranger to either controversy or sports. His FOX network came out of nowhere to purchase the broadcasting rights of the National Football League. Although the FOX network was initially perceived as a distant fourth national network in the United States, it has become a serious challenge to the Big Three – ABC, CBS, and NBC – with hit shows. Through a separate company Murdoch has a substantial sports cable following that competes directly with Disney's ESPN. In the United Kingdom, Murdoch is a major player with his BSkyB television satellite network, which experienced startup difficulty until it purchased the rights to broadcast Premier League soccer matches. Now BSkyB is a major player with more than seven million subscribers in the United Kingdom. News Corporation's corporate strategy is to use soccer as the engine to sell satellite dishes across Europe. Other European media-related sports and television marriages are easy to find. Italian media giant Silvio Berlusconi owns the AC Milan soccer team, and the international carmaker Fiat controls Juventus. In The Netherlands, Philips Electronics owns AJAX, Amsterdam's soccer team.

News Corporation is a global media firm with significant interests in television, film, books, newspapers, magazines, satellites, cable systems, and sports.[17] It is a diversified global communications corporation with operations and holdings in every core and semiperipheral country as well as most peripheral regions, excluding Africa, owing to the vast range of its satellite networks. For example it has 29 television channels across Europe. Figure 7.6 reflects News Corporation's vast and widespread holdings. In 2007 Murdoch purchased the Dow Jones Company for $5 billion. Dow Jones is the publisher of the *Wall Street Journal* and Murdoch intends to use its staff to aid his FOX business channel with commentaries and business news and stories.

Finally, the Murdoch family, including Rupert's sons, owns about 30 percent of News Corporation. The firm currently makes about 25 percent of its sales from global businesses and 75 percent from US media businesses. This mix may change, perhaps dramatically, with global, particularly Far East, initiatives growing substantially. Murdoch's family situation could easily be confused with the script of one of his soap operas. Rupert Murdoch, now nearly 80 and with a much younger wife, appointed his eldest son, Lachlan, as deputy chief operating officer and heir apparent to become president of News Corporation after Rupert departs. But in 2005 Lachlan abruptly resigned and moved his family back to Australia. Also, his other son, James, stepped down as Chief Executive in 2007 of BSkyB, but continues as Chairman of the Board. Some think that he is now next in line. But Rupert's young wife thinks that she is next in line as well.

1   20th Century FOX (+ subsidiaries)
2   20th Century FOX Home Entertainment
3   American Idol
4   Beliefnet
5   Blue Sky Studios
6   BSkyB
7   Channel [V] Asia Stations America
8   DIRECTV (38%)
9   Dow Jones
10 FOX Broadcasting
11 FOX Family Channel
12 FOX Interactive Media
13 FOX Music
14 FOX News
15 FOXtel
16 FOX Television
17 FOX Searchlight Pictures
18 FOX Sports Latin
19 FOX Sports Net
20 FX
21 HarperCollins (+ subsidiaries)
22 *Herald Sun*
23 Hulu (27%)
24 IGN Entertainment Games
25 MyNetworkTV
26 Myspace
27 National Rugby League
28 NDS
29 *New York Post*
30 *News of the World*
31 Rotten Tomatoes
32 Sky Italia
33 SmartSource
34 STAR TV
35 TATA SKY (20%)
36 *The Australian* (newspaper)
37 *The Courier-Mail*
38 *The Sun*
39 *The Sunday Mail*
40 *The Sunday Telegraph*
41 *The Times* (+ subsidiaries)
42 *The Wall Street Journal*
43 *Times Higher Education*
44 *Times Literary Supplement*
45 *TV Guide*
46 Zondervan

Figure 7.6   News Corporation holdings, 2010

British Sky Broadcasting Group

British Sky Broadcasting Group (BSkyB) is the United Kingdom's leading pay-TV provider. Since 1989 it has distributed television programming to customers in both the United Kingdom and Ireland. It offers 650 radio and television channels via satellite.

BSkyB has over nine million customers. It provides news, sports, and entertainment programs through channels covering nine sectors. They are entertainment, news, children's, movies, sports, music, radio, adult, and specialty offerings. For example, Sky Sports offers over 36,000 hours of sports programming per year over five satellite channels and is seeing a consistent growth in viewership. In August 2003 an episode of US FOX network program *The Simpsons* featuring then UK Prime Minister Tony Blair reached over one million viewers on Sky One. Sky News continues to receive industry awards and now has foreign bureaus in Washington, India, Brussels, Moscow, China, Jerusalem, and South Africa.

BSkyB has pioneered the introduction of digital television to Europe. This service, known as Sky Digital, provides the technically clearest available picture quality, along with CD-quality sound. Sky Digital offers 10 documentary channels, five sports channels, and up to five different movies every hour, along with all BBC television channels.

Finally, a look at BSkyB's multichannel entertainment offerings is informative. Sky One now outdraws the five terrestrial networks with programs such as *Las Vegas, 24, Cold Case, Scrubs, Malcolm in the Middle*, and the globally popular *The Simpsons*. Sky Movies offers 450 movies per week on 11 different pay channels. Some of the movies attracting more than 10 million viewers a week are *Men in Black, Pirates of the Caribbean, My Big Fat Greek Wedding*, and *Bruce Almighty*. Some of the satellite channel offerings are Bravo, Paramount, E!, Hallmark, Hollywood TV, Bloomberg, CNN, Disney, Nickelodeon, MTV (with 5 channels), and VH1 (with 3 channels). As the preceding so amply illustrates, American media fare is embedded in foreign satellite services to a very large extent. Since many of these channels are pay channels, there must be an audience for them. ECT deals with the collective impact of these audiovisual products over time. They are having an effect ranging from British boys preferring to play basketball over soccer to teenagers dancing and dressing like American pop icons. In the case of BSkyB this Americanization phenomenon is further reinforced by Murdoch's ability to direct the placement of his vast US-oriented FOX television and movie studio productions on the UK and Irish satellite systems.

STAR TV (Asia)

In the mid-1990s, Rupert Murdoch's News Corporation acquired control of STAR TV, and in 1998 STAR TV acquired Hutchvision Hong Kong Ltd. Hutchvision Hong Kong was the first Hong Kong-based satellite television licensee; it started broadcasting satellite television services, known as the STAR network, in 1991.

The STAR TV network offers both subscription and free-to-air television services, reaching more than 300 million people across Asia, India, and the Middle East in a multitude of markets, making STAR distinct among broadcasters. STAR TV is the dominant satellite broadcaster in Asia and has viewers in 53 other countries as well. In addition, STAR TV is the only broadcaster to offer such a broad range of programs to all of Asia and the Middle East, with coverage from East Africa to Japan. STAR TV transmits more than 45 programming services in eight languages. It controls more than 10 channels in Hong Kong alone, all of them broadcasting 24 hours a day. Programs feature a mix of movies, news, music, sports, and general entertainment. STAR TV is a commercial network relying on advertising from more than 20 global brands.

The STAR TV channels offer the region's widest television choice, whether in music, news, sporting events, Asian and international dramas and films, or cultural and informational programs. Services carried on the STAR TV network include ESPN, FOX News, and National Geographic. Several other satellite television broadcasters uplink their signals from Hong Kong, including CNN and CNBC.

The National Geographic Channel (NGC) signed a deal to act as a local broadcaster and as STAR TV's representative in India in order to sell ad time on the channel. The tie-in allows NGC to tap into STAR TV's existing marketing resources in the country. The channel reaches millions of subscribes around the globe.

STAR TV launched its pioneering venture into satellite broadcasting by initially transmitting just five analog TV channels. Soon it was experiencing significant household penetration across the continent, increasing connections by tens of millions a year. Today, more than 100 million households across Asia, the Middle East, and India tune into News Corporation's STAR TV. STAR TV's offerings include English-language channels such as MTV, Prime Sports, and the BBC World Service. ZEE TV, which is broadcast in Hindi, was added in 1992.

With a satellite footprint stretching from Turkey to Japan, the STAR TV network was developed to deliver Asian audiences to global businesses and advertisers. But STAR TV has been criticized for airing too much English, violence, and sex. Yet Murdoch is determined to push his STAR TV across Asia.

The countries that have been prime markets for STAR TV have been those ranked among the newly industrialized countries of Asia. This is an example of a core-based multimedia giant offering broadcasting channels in semiperipheral and peripheral nations. Except in India, Singapore, and Malaysia, where the governments have restricted viewer access, STAR TV has been a major success story.[18]

Increasing government deregulation and liberalization as well as technological advances in satellites and receiving dishes ensure a solid future for the broadcasting industry in Asia. In the immediate future, STAR TV plans to consolidate its position as Asia's number one satellite broadcaster. To maximize audience size, there are indications that STAR TV, as well as other foreign satellite channels, will increasingly move to provide local-language fare. Although audiences welcome the local-language programming, the net result is that larger STAR TV audiences are being built at the expense of local and frequently government-owned television networks. Most local stations are still non-commercial and lack the flair and broad scope of STAR TV's multiple channel system. Therefore, the impact of STAR TV, and to a lesser extent other networks such as the BBC and CNN, offer Asia and other nations a new commercial model that is a direct application of electronic colonialism. These advertising-supported networks need audiences to sell to their global brand sponsors in order for both the new networks and the global products to succeed in these new vast markets.

Finally, a subsidiary, Sky Global Networks, incorporates the regional satellite services of BSkyB in Europe and Latin America as well as STAR TV in Asia. News Corporation's Asian focus is now rapidly shifting to concentrate on China. In addition to the STAR TV activities, News Corporation has a minority stake in Phoenix Satellite Television, which is based in Hong Kong and targeted at mainland China. This service carries movies as well as other programming. Minority stakes are also held in Chinese internet portals, Chinese websites, and joint ventures with China's *Peoples Daily Newspaper*. Murdoch's strategic plans involve substantial expansion across China. Coupled with the 2008 Olympics, Wal-Marts, and Disney opening a theme park in Hong Kong, along with other aggressive media and internet activities, according to electronic colonialism theory, it will only be a matter of time before the Chinese population exhibits more Western values, ranging from speaking English, to wearing Western clothing, to Western media consumption, to internet usage, all of which ultimately could lead the nation to achieve core status and leave behind the mostly agrarian and totalitarian society of a few decades ago. This is why News Corporation, Disney, and others are making substantial investments in China.

Dow Jones

This company was acquired by News Corp. in 2006. The Dow Jones Company is widely known for two assets yet it also has significant global activities. Its flagship publication is the *Wall Street Journal*, which was first published in 1889. Also, in 1896, it started the Dow Jones Industrial Average (DJIA) which today consists of 30 blue chip US corporations, one-third of which reside in the information or media sectors. Examples of these companies are IBM, AT & T, Verizon, Microsoft, General Electric, which owns NBC, and The Walt Disney Company. An interesting over-sight is that the largest communication company in the world, Time Warner, is not part of the DJIA; nor is Google.

In terms of international assets, in 1946 Dow Jones started the prestigious *Far East Economic Review* and in 1976 it launched *The Asian Wall Street Journal*, followed in 1983 by *The Wall Street Journal Europe*. In 1994 it established *The Wall Street Journal Americas*, published in Spanish and Portuguese, and in 2004 *The Wall Street Journal India*. Dow Jones is also partnered with the *Financial Times* of London and the *Independent Media* to put out a Russian business daily called *Vedomosti* (*The Record*).

The various *WSJ* editions, both in the US and abroad, have an ultra conservative tone, slant, or bias. One could make the case that the *WSJ* is a development journalism enterprise on behalf of free enterprise. It promotes an editorial mantra of hostility toward social issues or critics of business practices. For example, the *WSJ* has historically campaigned against universal health care, environment legislation, the United Nations, and affirmative action programs. In terms of the Iraq war it provided coverage in unison with the Pentagon. Rather than seeking balance and objectivity in its stories, it stooped to ridicule, much like Bill O'Reilly of FOX News, or Rush Limbaugh's radio rants. As an example, the *WSJ* editorial piece on November 18, 2004 states, "The Al-Zarqawi TV network, also known as Al-Jazeera, has broadcast the tape to the Arab world, and the US media have also played it up."[19] The videotape refers to NBC's Kevin Sites footage of a US Marine shooting a wounded Iraq civilian. Al-Jazeera is an Arab network which provides an Arab perspective that has a wide audience in the Muslim world; it is covered in greater detail in Chapter 13. The *WSJ* in similar fashion had earlier complained about other US and foreign media outlets focusing on the photos of the Abu Ghraib prisoners' abuse. For the *WSJ* this uncritical support for the US's military policy translated into easier access to senior Washington officials for a broad array of future stories during the Bush administration. Since the electon of President Obama there has been substantial negative coverage of his attempt to pass health care legislation. The basic point is that the conservative tone of the *WSJ* properties panders to a global niche, which is an audience defined by wealth.

On the electronic side, in addition to its internet sites for various print properties, since 1997 Dow Jones has had a major global alliance with CNBC. Across both Europe and Asia Dow Jones provides CNBC with business and news programming. With the change in ownership the talent at Dow Jones and the *Wall Street Journal* now have a window on FOX news as well. As the global economy evolves and corporations become more global in scope and talent, the Dow Jones Company is well positioned to expand its business-oriented multimedia properties around the globe.

Synopsis

The elder Murdoch controls all News Corp. properties on a daily basis and he makes sure that they follow his political and corporate leanings. His vast multimedia holdings have always been global in nature. His FOX holdings in the US are increasing in audience share and the decision to move the corporate headquarters from Australia to New York in 2004 further solidify the focus on the FOX sector of the company. With satellite systems in Europe (BSkyB) and Asia (STAR TV), Murdoch may be well on his way to creating a global media infrastructure. His purchase of Dow Jones as well as MySpace illustrate the power of News Corp. to make big deals. The big unknown for the company is who will succeed him. This may be determined by whom his young Chinese wife, and one day widow, supports.

General Electric

General Electric was established in 1892 by Thomas Edison and now has several global product lines such as lighting, appliances, power sources, aircraft, medical systems, financial services, and NBC Universal. It operates in over 100 countries and employs over 150,000 people in the United States and about the same number worldwide.[17] The company has a US annual growth rate of 3 percent and a global growth rate of 6 percent. In 1986, GE purchased RCA (Radio Corporatiion of America), which owned NBC, and in the 1990s, NBC became part of GE's global expansion strategy. In 1996, for example, NBC expanded to offer four overseas channels, two in Europe and two in Asia. CNBC and MSNBC are also available in homes and hotels in Asia and Europe, reaching over 150 million television sets. In 2004 combining French-based Vivendi's Universal properties with NBC's holdings created NBC Universal (Figure 7.7). NBC holds 80 percent ownership, and Vivendi holds the rest.

History

- set industry standards for 70+ years; first to broadcast in color
- first to broadcast in stereo
- first produced made-for-TV movies first to offer early morning news
- first to broadcast online and digitally

---

1   Bravo
2   CNBC
3   CNBC Europe
4   CNBC Asia
5   Focus Features
6   MSNBC (82%)
7   Mun2
8   NBC Television Network
9   NBC Universal Television*
10   Oxygen
12   SyFy
13   Telemundo
14   USA Network
15   Universal Pictures
16   Universal Production Studios
17   Universal Studios Theme Parks

*NBC Universal is 80% owned by GE and 20% by Vivendi

Figure 7.7   Major NBC Universal properties, 2010

Milestones

- 1986 GE became NBC's parent company
- 1993 NBC launched Canal De Noticias
- 1996 prime time's #1 network
- 2000 news division, *Today Show*, *Friends*, and *The West Wing* dominate ratings
  2002 acquired Telemundo and Bravo
- 2004 acquired 80% of Vivendi's Universal properties
- 2007 launches Hulu in partnership with FOX Entertainment and Disney
- 2007–9 NBC Universal pursues overseas ventures with mergers resulting in the ownership of NBC Universal Global Networks, Carnival Films, and Geneon Universal Entertainment Japan
- 2010 broadcasts Vancouver Winter Olympics games
- 2012 broadcasts London Summer Olympic games

Industrial giant GE owns the NBC television network, which serves 15 company-owned and operated stations and more than 200 US affiliates.[18] NBC also operates the 24-hour cable channels CNBC and MSNBC. Although home to such hits as *Law and Order*, *Will and Grace*, *West Wing*, and *ER*, the network, like the others, is losing market share to cable channels and the internet.

NBC is a global media company with broadly diverse holdings that consist of the following elements: NBC television network, NBC-owned and operated stations, NBC Entertainment, NBC News, NBC Sports, CNBC, MSNBC, NBC Cable, NBC International, NBC Interactive, and MSNBC Desktop Video.

NBC has been setting industry standards in technology and programming for more than 70 years. It was the first network to broadcast in color, the first to broadcast in stereo, the first to present a made-for-TV movie, and the first to offer an early morning news program. Also, it was the first television network to broadcast both online and digitally.

NBC's first major organizational change came in 1986 when GE acquired RCA and thereby became NBC's parent company. Then in 1993, NBC launched Canal de Noticias NBC, a 24-hour Spanish language news service, across Latin America. In 1994, Canal de Noticias NBC debuted on cable stations in the United States. In 1996, NBC became prime time's number one network in every category, leading ABC and CBS. In 1999, NBC agreed to acquire a 32 percent stake in West Palm Beach, Florida-based Paxson Communications Corp. for $415 million. The agreement combined NBC's powerful brand name and broadcast group with Paxson, owner of the most television stations in the United States. NBC said the move provided a second national distribution outlet for NBC programming while giving Paxson additional resources to strengthen its broadcast group and PAX TV network. In 2004 GE made a dramatic and significant media move in acquiring an 80 percent stake in Universal television and movies. The renamed NBC Universal is now a much larger global stakeholder in the evolving global multimedia sector.

NBC Universal operates in four divisions: network, production, film, and theme parks. The networks are now extensive and most are carried on cable and satellite channels around the world. NBC Universal television has 14 owned and operated stations along with 200 affiliates. It also controls Telemundo, a large Spanish-language network, with 15 owned and operated stations and 32 affiliates. Telemundo is carried on nearly 450 cable systems. Telemundo Internacional is available in over 20 of the largest markets across Latin America.

The other NBC Universal networks are mun 2, a Latino network aimed at MTV's teenage audience; the SyFy channel; and the USA Network. Offshore, there is NBC Europe, CNBC Europe reaching 85 million households, and CNBC Asia Pacific reaching 30 million. In film, it has a major stakeholder in Universal Pictures. Under this new ownership the corporate strategy is aimed at global expansion. It also controls Focus Feature, which is a worldwide film distribution company. Finally, in addition to Universal Studios theme parks in the US, it also has parks and resorts in Japan and Spain.

NBC also became the main broadcaster for the international Olympic Games. NBC broadcast the Summer Olympics from Atlanta, Georgia, in 1996; from Sydney, Australia, in 2000; and from Athens, Greece, in 2004, marking the fifth straight Summer Olympics broadcast by NBC. NBC Universal Sports also broadcast the 2008 games in China. NBC also had the rights to the 2006 and 2008 Winter Games.

Bravo

Acquired by NBC in 2002, Bravo is an arts and culture network with over 80 million households across North America having access to it. A number of foreign satellite and cable systems also carry the upscale shows, such as the Montreal-based *Cirque du Soleil*.

CNBC

Two of the world's leading media companies, Dow Jones and NBC, came together in December 1997 to create CNBC, the Consumer News and Business Channel. This global alliance created a powerful combination of strengths: Dow Jones produces vital world business and financial news and information; NBC is the leading television network in the United States. This move united the world's most recognized business news brands including the *Wall Street Journal*, CNBC, and Dow Jones. CNBC is available to 175 million households worldwide; it is watched by millions of people around the globe every day. As baby boomers start worrying about retirement, they focus on investing their money, and CNBC has the pertinent information to answer their questions.

Synopsis

General Electric is an enormous global conglomerate with a broad range of products across a wide spectrum of industries. GE's broadcasting interests are fairly recent, having acquired NBC in 1986, but the network has never provided the financial returns of other GE units. For example, GE Financial Services accounts for nearly one-half of GE's revenues. In May 2004 NBC Universal was formed with General Electric (80 percent) and Vivendi (20 percent) combining assets to create a giant global multimedia company. NBC is adding its networks to global cable and satellite channels and is making aggressive moves with internet sites for a greater global profile. Finally, with the various Telemundo networks, they plan to have a major media presence both at home and abroad in the growing Hispanic regions.

Discovery Communications

Discovery Communications is the world's leading non-fiction media company. It reaches more than 1.5 billion viewers in over 170 countries. It has 115 networks and works in 35 languages. Some of its more popular channels are Animal Planet, Discovery Kids, Discovery Channel, Science Channel, TLC, and Planet Green.

It was founded in 1985. In 1987 it began televising live Russian shows to its US subscribers and launched its Discovery Channel in England in 1989 and across Latin America in 1994. The company also owns patents relating to e-books and has three digital media sites, HowStuffWorks, TreeHugger, and Petfinder.

Gannett Co., Inc.

The Gannett Company is an international, diversified news and information company. It is the US's largest newspaper company in terms of circulation, owning 84 dailies, including *USA Today*. *USA Today* has a circulation of over 2.3 million and is available in over 60 nations worldwide. Columnist Peter Johnson provided excellent media coverage but the coverage in this critical area has diminished along with its profitability. In the US Gannett also owns 23 television stations reaching millions of viewers.

Gannett also produces USATODAY.com, one of the major internet newspaper sites in the world. They are also expanding their digital presence on the internet.

Gannett has operations in England, Belgium, Germany, Italy, and China. In the United Kingdom it owns 17 dailies and Newsquest plc, the latter controlling over 200 regional papers, magazines, and trade publications. Newsquest also has over 80 internet sites.

Wal-Mart International

This retail juggernaut now has over 3,720 stores in 15 foreign regions. Wal-Mart International employs over 700,000 workers in Argentina, Brazil, Canada, Chile, China, Costa Rica, El Salvador, the EU, Honduras, India, Japan, Korea, Mexico, and Nicaragua. Annual sales in these foreign nations are close to $100 billion and growing rapidly. They plan to open over 200 new stores in foreign nations annually. The international division is the fastest growing part of the entire company. In time it will be larger than the US number of stores and eventually the top management will come from the international division.

In terms of mutli-media, Wal-Mart has two sectors. First, retail store sales and second, internet sales. It is the fastest growing media seller in both categories. For example, their stores sell DVDs, CDs, gaming systems, and cassettes. They sell more DVDs than any other retailer. They were the largest retailer of new blockbuster films. They are Hollywood's largest customer with 40 percent of all DVD sales.

On Walmart.com they offer three media products. First, DVD rentals via mail in direct competition with Netflix and Blockbuster. Second, music downloads at less than a dollar per song from any genre. Third, sales of DVDs, VHS movies, and other products with an audiovisual connection. Another example of their power is in consumer electronics. Sales of these units are second only to Best Buy, and more than all other combined. When Wal-Mart sells the hardware, like a DVD, games, or CD player, it also sells the software as well. This connection gives it a major advantage over competitors who tend to only sell or rent one or the other.

Now some musicians are signing exclusive contracts with Wal-Mart. A good example is Garth Brooks. He released an exclusive boxed set and on the first day alone sold more than a half million copies. It also set records for pre-orders on Walmart.com. Other artists are lining up to be the next commercial success as a Wal-Mart exclusive.

Wal-Mart is a new global stakeholder in terms of international communication but because of its enormous purchasing power and number of global outlets. It represent a future major player in this sector. It also brings with it market clout, controversy, and a strong US free enterprise orientation. It is a serious and effective promoter of electronic colonialism wherever it goes. Wal-Mart personifies US values and commercial culture. But it is also known for being anti-union and seem to actively promote an adversarial labor-management environment. For example, senior management made a grave error of judgment when they openly campaigned against the election of Barack Obama, since he supported things such as fair wages and non-discrimination, particularly against women. Wal-Mart has faced a large number of class-action lawsuits filed by women over wages and other chauvinistic issues. Finally, the company and the founder's family foundation have provided millions to right-wing extremist groups such as the Heritage Foundation to attack pro-union legislation anywhere.

Virgin Media Inc.

Virgin Media came from the merger of Telewest and NTL in 2006 and the subsequent merger in 2007 with Virgin Mobile. It is an American owned company which operates primarily in the United Kingdom and Ireland, offering digital cable, digital terrestrial television, internet, and telephone service. Its main competitors are BSkyB and Freeview. Virgin Media Television also operates several cable channels in the UK.

Advance Publications Inc.

This is a private company controlled by the Newhouse family. The company has several newspapers, business journals, cable interests, Fairchild and Parade publications, internet and website business, and Condé Nast publications. Condé Nast publishes some of the world's most prestigious magazines – examples are *Vogue, Glamour, Allure, GQ, Brides, Vanity Fair, Wired*, and *The New Yorker*. Conde Nash also oversees several websites. Overall Advance interests employ about 30,000 employees.

The Nielsen Company

The Nielsen Company formed in 2007 as a result of the buyout of the formerly Netherlands-based VNU buyout by six private firms, mainly based in the United States. VNU was founded in 1964 and was a global information and multimedia company with interests in over 100 countries. In 1999, VNU bought Nielsen Media Research and formed the subsidiary, ACNielsen, which lasted until 2007. Nielsen Media Research dates back to 1923, when Arthur C. Nielsen began to form a research company which evolved into the ratings giant. It employs 36,000 people around the world and has its corporate headquarters in New York City.

This firm provides television, radio, and print measurement in over 100 countries. Through Nielsen Monitor Plus, a media-buying and advertising information service, Nielsen measures over 85 percent of the globe's advertising expenditures. Nielsen/NetRating is the leading internet audience measurement and analysis service, including tracking online advertisements. This firm tracks more than 70 percent of the globe's internet traffic.

Finally, Nielsen Media Research provides detailed information of television viewership in the United States for over one million households. But some of its data collection methods and analysis have come under criticism in recent years.

In terms of ECT the Nielsen subsidiaries are prime examples of how core-based firms control much of the data about electronic and print media. The wealth of data, knowledge, and analysis provided by Nielsen to subscribers is enormous, across a vast range of commercial multimedia lines. The advertising giants, for example, are all based in core nations. They have clients in almost all semi-peripheral nations and some peripheral ones as well. Yet the data and research provided to them by Nielsen serves a two-fold purpose: first to strengthen and fine tune what and how they perform for their already existing client base, and second to recruit new clients by impressing them with their arsenal of data and services, of which Nielsen is just one part. For any totally new ad firm to emerge or for any semi-peripheral nation-based firm to become a major ad agency is almost an impossible task. This phenomena and reality of the global role and scope of the existing ad agencies, in partnership with Nielsen, make the quest for more customers for core media products an easier task because the basic research and strategy works relatively well.

Expanding their base to understand in greater detail how the mind works prompted two specific acquisitions. The first was a 2008 move to add IAG Research. This firm deals with advertisement performance and effectiveness research. It measures all ads and product placements on television every night. IAG Research also tracks ad effectiveness on the internet and in movie theaters. The second was another 2008 acquisition of NeuroFocus, a company using cutting-edge neuroscience brainwave monitoring of customers with offices across the US, Europe, Israel, and Asia. They study how the human brain works, particularly as the brain responds to ads and messages. The measurement instrument is the medical procedure called electroencephalogram (EEG). EEG tests the electrical activity of the brain. NeuroFocus offers clients, some of which are the biggest brands in the world, six product lines or services. They are advertising effectiveness, brand and image analysis, competitive advertising intelligence, product pricing analysis, and neuroinformatics database.

These two companies add to the global arsenal of Nielsen as it moves to the next stage of measurement. It does not ask the viewer what they think, rather it looks directly into the brain and record on a monitor what you are thinking. This is at the essence of the theory of electronic colonialism. And Nielsen is not alone in this type of cutting-edge research. Google, Microsoft, Yahoo, Netflix also have confidential algorithms which predict human behavior.

In 2010, a new consortium emerged to attempt to compete with Nielsen Ratings. This group, made up of major media companies as well as advertisers and advertising firms, has a series of complaints concerning the accuracy of Nielsen's ratings. In particular, the group plans to focus on measuring new media such as websites and mobile devices.

Conclusions

Globally there is an expansion of movie theaters, cable systems, satellite distribution systems, personal computers, music, DVDs, CDs, video outlets, and mobile digital devices. This infrastructure is fueling substantial expansion by global communication firms. In particular, US multinational communication corporations such as Disney, News Corp., GE, Time Warner, Dow Jones, Gannett, Viacom, Wal-Mart, and others are strategically repositioning themselves as global corporations rather than simply US communication firms. Their future success and earnings are more and more dependent on international sales. As their internet and other offshore assets grow, they are being propelled into a highly competitive global marketplace. In their corporate annual reports, as well as in other company documents reflecting strategic planning, globalization and their increasing role in that milieu is the dominant theme. In the future continuing global offshore growth for these US-based communication companies will exceed domestic corporate growth.

The growth and impact of US multimedia firms changed considerably. The addition of News Corp. from Australia, and Universal properties to NBC from France's Vivendi, represents an enormous net gain for the US media sector. At the same time it represents a net loss to two other core nations, Australia and France. In Australia's case, the advantage of having the common English language could further propel it to become even more of an electronic communication colony of US popular culture. Some Australian critics of the News Corp. move to New York City cited the cultural and employment issues in their futile opposition to the relocation. Australia and several other nations are likely to continue to lose their bright young talent to Hollywood and New York. The likes of Nicole Kidman, Mel Gibson, Russell Crowe, Crocodile Dundee, Helen Reddy, and Olivia Newton-John represent a talent drain that is only going to increase, as Australia becomes an even greater media outpost and electronic colony of US cultural goods. For most foreign actors and musicians, working in the US represents the epitome of success, both professionally and financially.

Because the United States is the leading core nation, these corporations have become aggressive in other core nations in both Europe[20] and Asia.[21] At the same time, they have expanded into the semiperipheral nations because these nations represent substantial new markets where there is strong demand for US products of all types, ranging from CDs and DVDs, to Ipods, to the internet. These semiperipheral nations also have the greatest number of potential new customers with discretionary disposable income. They represent a new customer base for all the major US communication empires. These emerging markets will grow faster than the more mature markets across core nations.

A good example of global expansion is Disney's new theme park developed in conjunction with Chinese authorities in Hong Kong. Clearly, Disney is positioning itself to use the Hong Kong site as a gateway into the immense Chinese market during the twenty-first century. They are already moving to expand the park. A related expansion into China took place in the 1990s as Rupert Murdoch recognized that his Asian satellite system, STAR TV, could potentially attract a multitude of new customers across China and the entire Pacific Rim. Chapter 14 details more about China and Asian media activities.

US media giants, with their advertising, products, and services have inundated only a few peripheral nations. Most peripheral nations lack the necessary technical infrastructure, ability to provide security, or sufficient disposable income to make it economically worthwhile to establish major activities in these regions. At the same time, some of these peripheral nations are actively seeking to avoid contact with US popular and media culture. They protect and promote an indigenous culture, which is usually low technology, or because of religious beliefs, authoritarian governments, or anti-democratic leaders.

Finally, these global media firms need to continue to grow if they want to remain competitive. Because the potential growth is greater offshore, they will continue to direct greater efforts toward, and place their best corporate executives in, global regions in order to produce the rate of return demanded by senior management and shareholders. This expansion occurs in unison with their advertising agencies. As such, the nations in which they operate in need to have a market-based economy for these firms to thrive, profit, and expand. Obviously, some of this expansion comes at the expense of indigenous production houses, or local advertising agencies. Because these US media conglomerates have enormous libraries of television and feature films that they have already paid for themselves as first-run productions in the large US domestic market, they can compete aggressively internationally with an arsenal of video and audio products that collectively can swamp any foreign network or production house through sheer volume.

Notes

1. The emergence of global television has always had its critics. They focus primarily on the social, cultural, and political aspects of the global dissemination of popular shows. Most of the shows were American, with a few British shows doing well on a global scale. In the 1980s, the global success of Dallas became the rallying symbol for cultural nationalists in several nations. For a broad critique of this phenomena, see Cynthia Schneider and Brian Wallis (eds.), *Global Television*, Cambridge, MA: MIT Press, 1988; and Richard Gershon, *The Transnational Media Corporation*, Mahwah, NJ: Erlbaum, 1997.
2. Europe and most of Europe's former colonies refer to multimedia as audiovisual products. A prime example of this, including a broad, detailed description of the concerns and challenges, is contained in the *European Commissions Economic Implications of New Communications Technologies on the Audio-Visual Markets*, Brussels: European Communities, 1998.
3. W. A. Swanberg, *Luce and His Empire*, New York Scribner, 1972.
4. Gerald Levin, "The Legacy of Henry Luce: Values for the Digital Age," speech to the Aspen Institute, August 7, 1999, Aspen, CO, p. 2.
5. Ibid.
6. Ibid., p. 4.
7. Nina Munk, *Fools Rush In: Steve Case, Jerry Levin, and the Unmasking of AOL Time Warner*, New York: Harper Business, 2004.
8. Ken Auletta, *Media Man*, New York: W. W. Norton, 2004.
9. Steven Watts, *The Magic Kingdom Walt Disney and the American Way of Life*, Boston, Houghton Mifflin, 1998.
10. Bob Thomas, *Building a Company Roy O. Disney and the Creation of an Entertainment Empire*, Boston: Hyperion, 1999.
11. The Chinese government's approval of a major Hollywood-based theme park occurred in the same year that China entered the World Trade Organization (WTO). The two

events are not unrelated. China is attempting to reposition itself as a modern global player in the communication industry. By joining the WTO, it has agreed to open its telecommunications market, allow foreign firms to provide internet services, and increase the number of US feature films imported into China. Beijing, China was the host city for the Summer Olympics in 2008. Clearly, these activities, along with Disney's activities in Hong Kong, reflect the acceptance of US business practices, information technologies, and popular culture. In return, China will no doubt attempt to export more of its goods and services into core nations, particularly the United States. At the same time, however, China has become market sensitive, it wants to participate and follow the rules and regulations, including dispute resolution mechanisms available through the Geneva-based WTO. Although China still cracks down on cyber cafés and is repressive with dissidents, it still aims to move from semiperipheral status to core status by 2020. The European-based Reporters Sans Frontières (Reporters Without Borders) lists China as one of the worst press freedom nations on the planet. Finally, the Disney Corporation, along with other major US corporations, would not be making such major long-term investments in China if it thought these investments would either fail or be confiscated by the Chinese authorities. Although there is no written agreement not to do such things, clearly the Chinese in a broad range of activities are indicating that they want to participate in the global information society of the twenty-first century, eventually on an equal basis as China seeks to become a core nation. But their repressive heritage and practices emerge against progressive media systems far too frequently.

12. James Stewart, *Disneywar: The Battle for the Magic Kingdom*, New York: Simon and Schuster, 2004. Two additional books which trace Disney's influence are Janet Wasko, *Understanding Disney: The Manufacture of Fantasy*, Malden, MA: Blackwell Publishers, 2001; and Janet Wasko, M. Phillips, and E. Meehan (eds.), *Dazzled by Disney?* London: Leicester Press, 2002.

13. In 2007 the European Commission asked the European Audiovisual Observatory (www.obs.coe.int) to collect information on all pan-European television broadcasting channels. The data base on more than 6,000 channels is available through MAVISE (mavise.obs.coe.int). It is the most up-to-date and comprehensive data about the television sector across Europe. It also contains all foreign, mostly American, channels as well. The impact of these American channels and other cultural matters in Europe is detailed in Chapter 9.

14. Robert Slater, *The New GE: How Jack Welch Revived an American Institution*, Highstown, NJ: Irwin, 1992.

15. Tony Chiu, *CBS: The First 50 Years*, New York, NY General Publishing, 1999.

16. Rupert Murdoch's various dealings have come under criticism around the globe. One of the better summaries is contained in Russ Baker's piece in the *Columbia Journalism Review* of May/June 1998.

17. News Corporation's global media ventures have a major strategic asset that other global competitors frequently do not. News Corporation's control of STAR TV in Asia, BSkyB in Europe, as well as several other satellite and cable ventures, allows these networks to draw from the extensive library of software produced by the various FOX production facilities. Through their control of 20th Century FOX studios, FOX Broadcasting, FOX News, FOX Family Channel, FOX Sports Net, and a serves of 22 US-based FOX television stations, News Corporation media and systems managers around the globe have a ready and lucrative arsenal. These FOX shows and channels

provide an enormous competitive advantage to the Murdoch Group compared to the competition, which must attempt to outbid each other in order to purchase syndication game and drama shows, movies, or other programming materials.

18. For a further elaboration on access, cultural imperialism, and the rapidly changing Asian and Indian television environment, see Peter Shields and Sundeep Muppidi, "Integration, the Indian State and STAR TV: Policy and Theory Issues," *Gazette*, 58 (1996): 1–24; KiSung Kwak, "Structural and Cultural Aspects of the Regulation of Television Broadcasting in East Asia," *Gazette*, 59 (1997): 429–33; Amos Oven Thomas, "Regulating Access to Transnational Satellite Television," *Gazette*, 61 (1999): 243–54; and Robert Schmidt, "Murdoch Reaches for the Sky," *Brill's Content* (June 2001): 75–9, 126–9.

19. "Semper Fi," *Wall Street Journal* (November 18, 2004): A18.

20. Reinhold Wagnleitner, "The Empire of the Fun, or Talkin' Soviet Union Blues: The Sound of Freedom and US Cultural Hegemony in Europe," *Diplomatic History*, 23(3) (summer 1999): 499–524.

21. Srinivas Melkote, Peter Shields, and Binod Agrawel (eds.), *International Satellite Broadcasting in South Asia*, Lanham, MD: University Press of America, 1998.

8

Non-US Stakeholders of Multimedia Conglomerates

Introduction

Although some global media systems such as CNN, MTV, BBC, Disney, News Corporation, and the internet come to mind as high profile stakeholders in the global media world, there are clearly other major players. This chapter details the major global media stakeholders outside the US and describes their various communication interests. Although the United States frequently elicits substantial criticism for exporting a Hollywood culture of sex and violence and for dominating television and theater screens around the world, some of the major global enterprises, such as Sony, Vivendi, Bertelsmann, and others, are foreign-owned multimedia corporations.

For example, Japan's Sony Corporation controls Columbia Pictures; properties and brands of Germany's Bertelsmann include Random House, GEO, ArvatoAG, and the RTL Group; France's Lagardère publishes *Elle*, *Car and Driver*, and several other magazines; Nielsen is an important rating firm. These global media conglomerates and others are detailed in this chapter. It should be noted that the British Broadcasting Corporation, frequently called the "gold standard" of public broadcasting, is covered in Chapter 11 as a global competitor to CNN.

Cultural Imperialism

In the 1960s and 1970s, critical scholars produced a body of literature on the subject of cultural imperialism.[1] These scholars condemn the US role in global media expansion. Some of this criticism found its way into the rhetoric of

UNESCO in the 1980s and continues to be repeated by people promoting the MacBride agenda. The agenda seeks to re-ignite the support for NWICO and promote a more equitable and balanced flow of media in the international arena. Without going into detail about the origins of cultural imperialism, it is worth noting that there is simply no monolithic US global media empire. Although there is a global media empire, the media corporations are from various nation-states, but they are all located in core nations. They work in different languages with different interests and strategies, rather than promoting a simplistic New York–Los Angeles plot to capture the minds of unsuspecting foreigners. From records and CDs, to movies, magazines, television, and the internet, there is a great global mix of ownership among the current major multimedia stakeholders. This globalization and consolidation of the communications industry is going to increase and expand over time. About the only common denominator of the several far flung global stakeholders is the desire to make a profit by expanding their audience size or share. They seek more customers to generate greater profits in order to keep their respective senior management, owners, and shareholders happy.

Concerns about the possible effects of the mass media on individuals and cultures have been a preoccupation of academics since World War II. Much of the research focused on the impact of the media on developed core nations, particularly the United States, Canada, and Europe.[2] But a small number of critical scholars began to examine the impact of the media on the less developed peripheral nations and look at issues such as power, domination, economic determinism, and other variables.[3] The "Made in America" label began to take on different meanings to different researchers. But it was Herbert I. Schiller[4] who focused in a theoretical way on issues such as global ownership, one-way flow of information, power, cultural aspects, and the impact of advertising. He studied ways in which core-based media industries were having a deleterious effect on indigenous industries in peripheral countries, as well as how these industries were drawing economic resources, such as box office revenues, from both industrialized and non-industrialized nations around the world for the financial benefit of Hollywood or New York. In the 1970s, the literature on cultural imperialism began to look at other media systems as well, everything from records, tapes, and television, to advertising and children's paraphernalia, particularly Disney products. There was growing criticism and documentation of US media giants by a small cadre of critical scholars. But in 1988, many of these scholars were taken aback when Japan's Sony Corporation paid $5 billion to acquire Columbia Pictures. The Hollywood film landscape began to change dramatically as this merger was rapidly followed by other US industries being bought by foreign corporations as part of the expanding global economy. Many of these transactions and the foreign stakeholders involved are detailed later in this chapter

The significant point here is that although the theory of cultural imperialism was gaining credence as a negative model of global relationships, Sony's deal forced scholars to rethink the question of who owns what and for whom. The problem became a transnational issue rather than a purely Hollywood or "Made in America" issue, as critics had contended for decades. The literature and momentum of critical scholars became stale and lost their spark during the 1990s as major foreign media corporations changed the global media landscape. At one point in the 1970s, the United States dominated the global media system to the greatest extent before or since. Beginning in the 1980s, with the takeover of some Hollywood studios by foreign corporations; the move of German, French, and Canadian companies into global cultural industries; and the entrance of the then Australian-based News Corporation into television and satellite businesses in North America, Europe, and Asia, a highly competitive global media market-place began to develop. It functions to maximize profits from various global profit centers with little regard for nationalistic concerns, culture, language, or academic critics, except when they interfere with the economic goals of these far-flung media empires.

The following sections document the extensive penetration of Europe, Canada, Japan, and other countries into US and global markets by virtue of their invest-ments in a broad range of cultural products that are made and/or consumed in the United States. A model example of this is News Corporation, formerly based and incorporated in Australia. It had 75 percent of its revenues and profits from operations in the US. Reincorporating in the US was a logical move for this cor-poration. All giant foreign media corporations are in direct and daily competition with US giants, such as Time Warner, Viacom, and Disney.

The United States of Europe (USE)

Europe's television, movie, music, cable, and satellite industries are experienc-ing an unprecedented frenzy of consolidation. The 27 European Union nations are working more and more as collective rather than individual nations when it comes to international media. In addition, the EU is constructing trans-European communication policies. Thus, the concept of the United States of Europe (USE) is a valid construct.

Historically, the origins of the USE can be traced to the period immediately after World War II. In 1951 the European Coal and Steel Community was estab-lished under French leadership. The six members were Belgium, West Germany, Luxembourg, France, Italy, and The Netherlands. The agreement reduced barri-ers hindering cooperation and encouraged joint ventures in the two strategic industries, coal and steel. The idea was such a great success that the six coun-tries decided to expand the concept to other sectors. They did so and by the 1957 Treaty of Rome created a "common market" free of trade barriers and tariffs. Institutions, laws, regulations, policies, strategic planning, and in 2002 a new cur-rency, the Euro, were designed to create a single seamless market leading to the USE. This standardization and consolidation also impacted their cultural indus-tries, or as Europeans refer to them, audiovisual industries. Today the USE

1   Bertelsmann (Germany)
2   Vivendi (France)
3   Lagardère (France)
4   BSkyB (Great Britain)
5   Reed Elsevier (The Netherlands/Great Britain)
6   BBC (Great Britain)
7   ARD/Deutsche Welle (Germany)
8   Pearson (Great Britain)
9   Virgin Media (Great Britain)
10   Mediaset (Italy)

Figure 8.1   Top 10 major communication stakeholders by revenue in 2008 according to Nordicom

stands at 27 member nations with more nations seeking admission. In 2004 alone 10 new members, mostly former Soviet-dominated countries, joined the union followed by the admission of Bulgaria and Romania in 2007. One of the possible new entrants is Turkey with a large Muslim population and this will alter the cultural environment across the USE. The current population of the USE is larger than that of the USA.

Considering that prior to 1980 almost all European television and cable systems were either strictly government controlled or government owned; as a result this recent merger mania is new to the European communication's industry. With liberalization and deregulation in the 1980s, there was a substantial wave of privatization of radio, television, and cable systems across Europe as well as the addition of several new commercial channels. Now a third wave of activity is taking place in which transnational communication corporations are becoming larger and larger as they purchase smaller systems across Europe, start entirely new channels or networks, or buy foreign multimedia outlets, prompting some critics to call these countries collectively the "United States of Europe" (Figure 8.1).

The motivation for this activity is straightforward. John Tagliabue puts it this way: "What is causing this frenzy of reorganization? Mainly, the global economy, which is forcing Europe's relatively small players to join forces to cover the costs of switching to digital and pay per view TV and of marketing integrated bundles of television, telephone and internet services."[5] These combined and larger media companies are in a better competitive position because they can offer either larger audience to advertisers, or a larger number of cable subscribers to generate revenues necessary to upgrade cable systems so that they are internet ready. A related phenomenon in the United States of Europe is that more commercial corporations are designing advertising and programs for a pan-European audience. Advertisers want to deal with major trans-European broadcasters for a single package rather than with small individual media outlets on a city-by-city or country-by country basis.

The future media environment of the USE will ultimately resemble the US model of large national entities such as ABC, CBS, FOX, and NBC having a number of major regional affiliates. In Europe there will be major new conglomerates, created through the consolidation of smaller national-based systems that are reaching out to a pan-European audience. Many European communication corporations, which are detailed in the following sections, realize quite clearly that they need to engage in pan-European merger activities or they will be purchased by some other major stakeholder, or be left behind altogether. If they do not expand, they will be left with smaller audiences and reduced revenues in an era when production costs and competition for both European and US television series and movies continue to escalate.

Seen through the lens of world system theory, the following communication corporations are all based in core nations much like the United States. These nations exhibit similar traits that make them highly competitive such as a high gross national product (GNP), heavy deployment of information technologies, and a sophisticated and well educated labor force. These European core nations are also expanding as rapidly as possible into other core as well as semiperipheral nations. Geographically, they have an advantage because many of the semiperipheral nations are adjacent to the European community. Peripheral nations around the globe are in many cases former colonies of European nations. On the one hand, this may give the USE an advantage in marketing their communication products and systems to peripheral nations. On the other hand, deep-seated antagonism and a legacy of hostility between the colonies and their former European masters might prevent some peripheral nations from doing business with their former colonizers.

A final point is that in the US cultural industries and their products are viewed as economic entities, but across Europe and elsewhere these same industries are viewed through a very different prism. They are not solely viewed as economic entities in terms of dollars or euros. The USE views cultural industries, or audiovisual industries, as part of their culture, history, and artistic heritage. Europeans are much more concerned about language, culture, employment opportunities in media industries, and preserving their history than considering media productions as being similar to economic output like corn flakes, apples, lumber, or cars. Proof of this are the many public polices and significant financial subsidies that European entities promote and encourage. The USE is concerned about the cultural homogenization of media industries if they follow a US formula and model. The leadership for the cultural sectors across Europe is assigned to various Ministers' of Culture, which is a high-ranking Cabinet post in almost all nations outside the United States. An example to illustrate this important point follows.

The EU provides specific grants to stimulate the development and distribution of European media productions. The goal is to increase quality and make available trans-European film and television programs across five genres or formats: fiction for television and cinema, movies, documentaries, animation, and new media. The EU also underwrites writing workshops for various media and seminars about new media technologies. Since 2000 this program, entitled MEDIA PLUS, has a budget of over $2.5 billion. Most of the funding goes toward increasing circulation of European films across Europe and the world. In 2006 MEDIA PLUS funded *March of the Penguins* and in 2008 *The Lives of Others* and both won Oscars. Annually about 300 new films are funded by this program. The goal is to push a trans-European perspective onto global screens of all sizes. The hope is to compete with Hollywood for eyeballs as well as revenue.

Bertelsmann

The German-based Bertelsmann group of companies has a strong media presence in over 50 countries worldwide. It is the seventh largest media company globally. Carl Bertelsmann established the company in 1835 as a religious publishing house. Now its revenue is in the billions and it has five major operating units worldwide while remaining a privately held company. Its interests lie in newspapers, magazines, printing, print distribution, broadcasting, music rights management, and various media investments.

Bertelsmann's interests in magazine and newspaper publishing are carried out through its Gruner & Jahr subsidiary, which publishes 285 magazines and newspapers in over 20 countries. Bertelsmann holds a 75 percent stake in Gruner & Jahr. It is also the sole owner of Random House, the world's largest book publishing company. Through its Direct Group division, Bertelsmann markets books to more than 15 million people throughout Europe, North America, Australia, and New Zealand through book clubs and bookstores.

Bertelsmann also has major interests in television, owning 90.5 percent of the RTL Group (formerly CLT-UFA), the largest TV and radio group in Europe. The RTL Group was formed through the 2001 merger of CLT-UFA, Pearson TV, and Audiofina. The company has television stations in Germany, France, Spain, and the Benelux countries, Great Britain, Croatia, Greece, Hungary and Russia. The German RTL Channel alone is the most successful advertising-financed commercial TV station in Europe. In addition to its TV station, RTL Radio targets listeners within a similar geographical market. Finally, the VOX station began airing in 1993, offering nationally informative programs and broadcasting live events, however this proved unsuccessful and in the late 1990s after a series of buyouts, VOX switched its programming towards airing more Western produced series and movies, such as *CSI: New York*, *Gilmore Girls*, and *Six Feet Under*. RTL holds a 99.7 percent stake in the VOX channel. M6 is one of Bertelsmann's television stations in France. Within 10 years, M6 developed into the most profitable advertising-financed private TV station in France. The RTL Group holds a 48.8 percent stake in M6. In addition to the television stations, Bertelsmann owns UFA Film and TV Production. This division is located in Potsdam-Babelsberg and produces 2,000 hours of television each year, making it one of Germany's largest production companies. Finally of Bertelsmann's television interests, UFA Sports in Hamburg is Europe's leading TV sports marketing company.

In 2008, Sony music acquired what was until then known as the Bertelsmann Music Group (BMG), leaving behind only the BMG Rights Management division as a part of the Bertelsmann portfolio. In July of 2009, the American investment firm, Kohlberg, Kravis, Roberts and Co. (KKR), purchased 51 percent of BMG Rights and since then it has expanded on their music catalog.

Internet investments and web-based activities have been uneven and troublesome for the company. In 2000, Bertelsmann ended its five-year partnership with AOL, however it also helped prolong the life of Napster through a series of investments totaling more than $85 million and thus became a target for copyright infringement lawsuits costing the company upwards of $60 million in settlements. Bertelsmann's investment in Lycos ended when the company shareholders decided to liquidate it in 2008. Bertelsmann's online book site was a partnership with Barnes & Noble, and many of its multimedia activities were carried out in conjunction with the Axel Springer publishing house of Germany. In 2004, it sold its interest in Barnes & Noble Online back to Barnes & Noble, Inc., at a substantial loss. In 2008, the company published a hard-copy, condensed edition of the German Wikipedia site with mixed reception. In 2009, Bertelsmann, under the RTL Group, purchased a German social networking site called Wer-Kennt-Wen (Who Knows Whom) which claims over 6.5 million users and has expanded into Austria and Switzerland. Additionally, Bertlesmann has also invested in Qeep, a social network for mobile phones. Both efforts have been touted as an attempt for Bertelsmann to break into the MySpace market and become a direct competitor with the American-based social networking giant.

Vivendi SA

France's Vivendi SA Corporation is a major player in France and across Europe's audiovisual sector. The company was established in the nineteenth century starting with and continuing to have, major interests in public utilities and construction. In 1997 it added communications to its corporate interests by purchasing a 30 percent stake in France's Havas. In 1998 the company changed its name from Generele des Oeaux to Vivendi to reflect its new communications interests. Currently, Vivendi controls 20 percent of GE's NBC Universal; NBC Universal's diverse properties are covered in the preceding chapter.

In 2000, Vivendi acquired the Seagram Company of Canada in a $55 billion merger. Vivendi was after Seagram's three major communication units: Universal Studios and Universal Pictures, as well as the Universal Music Group. It had hoped to create the synergy needed to become a major global player in the rapidly evolving communications sector, but failed badly. Jean-Marie Messier, then the flamboyant president of Vivendi, was not only fired but is now also being sued by his former employer, and he had to pay a substantial fine to the US Securities and Exchange Commission. The proceeding years saw economic trouble and a series of reorganization which resulted in Vivendi selling 80 percent of its Vivendi Universal Entertainment division to GE in 2004 and ending its listings on the New York Stock exchange in 2006.

Vivendi also merged with Canal+ in 2000. Created in 1984, France's Canal+ is the European leader of pay-TV, offering premium programming on several channels. After an initial launch in France, Canal+ is now available across Europe. Currently, it offers 26 channels and has 10.6 million subscribers across Europe. StudioCanal, the company's film division, also offers over 100 films annually and its film library is the third largest in the world. StudioCanal seeks to bring together European film providers for both television and theater distribution in order to encourage the development of a unified, pan-European film industry. As a corporation, it sees itself as the European alternative to Hollywood feature films, yet it is willing to work with US studios and has various co-production deals in Europe with Warner, Paramount, and Vivendi Universal studios. The current cost of producing blockbusters for a global audience is beyond the fiscal reach of most European film studios.

Recent years have seen Vivendi gain new interests in the video game industry. In 2007 Vivendi merged with Activision to form Activision Blizzard with Vivendi owning 54 percent of the company. Activision Blizzard's game portfolio contains such well known titles as: Call of Duty, F.E.A.R., Guitar Hero, Tony Hawk licensed Games, and World of Warcraft. While still ranked third as a global gaming company behind Nintendo and Electronic Arts, Activision Blizzard earned over $5 billion in revenue in 2008.

Universal Music Group (UMG) began as a part of the Universal Pictures film studio and has been owned by various other corporations over the years, however in 2006 it became 100 percent part of Vivendi SA. In 2008, UMG accounted for approximately 18 percent of total revenue brought in by Vivendi and it is the largest record company in the world. UMG is covered in detail in Chapter 10 with the other music companies.

Lagardère Media

Lagardère Media is an extremely diversified French conglomerate with major publishing and media interests as well as military-industrial activities. It produces the Dr. Seuss books, CD-ROM encyclopedias, and several consumer-oriented magazines published internationally, including *Elle, Car and Driver, Woman's Day, Metropolitan Home,* and *Harlequin.* It is now the 10th-largest US magazine publisher overall and the largest foreign magazine publisher in the United States. Globally, Lagardère is the number one magazine publisher. The focus of its various magazines is primarily on advertising and then on circulation. *Elle* has 39 editions around the world. Lagardère also publishes several newspapers in France. Lagardère properties claim close to 40 million readers on a monthly basis. It became one of the first global marketers by promoting the Elle Channel with Parisian cosmetic firm Estée Lauder's Clinique cosmetic brands. The corporation views itself as a global, highly diversified industrial and multimedia group. Lagardère also owns Interdeco Global Advertising, the top advertising agency in France. In 2008, Lagardère acquired Doctissmo, a company that publishes content directed towards women on the internet, as a part of their intentions to expand their magazine enterprise onto the internet.

Reed Elsevier

In 1993, Reed International, a British publisher, merged with Elsevier Scientific Publishers to form Reed Elsevier. Reed Elsevier is based in London and Amsterdam. It is primarily comprised of three divisions: Elsevier, LexisNexis, and Reed Business Information. Elsevier publishes textbooks, journals, and other reference material within the medical and scientific fields. It is the largest such publisher in the world and has a strong presence online. In the last decade, Elsevier has come under fire for its rather expensive subscription fees with entire editorial boards resigning and forming new competing publications. Another controversy arose over the conflict of interest between publishing focusing on medical advancement and scientific enlightenment versus the investment Reed Elsevier had in arms trade, which resulted in the parent company selling its weapons division in 2008. LexisNexis provides online archives of legal documents through www.lexis.com and news stories through www.nexis.com. The company also publishes textbooks, magazines and newspapers in the legal and business fields, as well as offering training courses in the area of taxation law. Reed Business Information publishes over 30 titles, including *Publishers Weekly* and *Variety*. In 2008, Reed Elsevier bought ChoicePoint, an American information aggregator which collects personal and business information and sells it to the US government and private corporations.

Pearson PLC

Pearson, based in the United Kingdom, is a global media company with three main branches: the Penguin Group, the Financial Times Group, and Pearson Education. The Penguin Group is the second largest publisher of books globally. It has branches in North America, Australia, New Zealand, South Africa, India, and China. Authors who the Penguin Group publishes include Tom Clancy, Nora Roberts, Alan Greenspan, Al Gore, Nick Hornby, and the Dalai Lama. Parson also publishes the *Financial Times* (*FT*), which competes directly with the *Wall Street Journal*. The Financial Times is aimed at the global business community and has been a successful newspaper since its introduction in 1888. The Financial Times Group owns 50 percent in shares of the weekly global magazine *The Economist*. Additionally, Pearson has sought a niche in educational and reference publishing. Pearson Education owns Prentice-Hall, Addison Wesley, Pearson Longman, Pearson Higher Education, and Pearson Scott Foresman. As part of its educational niche, Pearson also controls the largest number of websites directly related to major leading textbooks.

Clearly demonstrating the strategic importance of the US marketplace to all non-American communication firms is Pearson's 2008 sales figures on a geographic basis. For their domestic market in Europe the company realized 27.9 percent of their total global sales and by comparison the North American market accounted for 69.7 percent. For all European-based communication companies, they must be successful in the US market in order to be a global stakeholder.

Mediaset

Mediaset is the largest private television or commercial broadcaster in Italy. It controls seven channels in Italy and four in Spain, plus two additional satellite channels. The majority owner is the Italian Prime Minister Silvio Berlusconi; he is also president of the AC Milan soccer club. Mediaset is seeking international expansion for its vast library of soap operas and sitcoms. Beginning in 1997, Mediaset acquired Italian broadcasting rights for all NBC movies and mini-series. In 2004 it began a 24-hour commercial children's channel, named Boing, in partnership with Time Warner. It will also jointly produce major productions for the international market. Mediaset networks are delivered through cable and satellite, which facilitate further global expansion, particularly for the Italian-speaking market. Mediaset also controls the top Italian advertising agency, Publitalia.

Mediaset owns three-quarters of the Dutch television production company Endemol. It produces over 40,000 hours of programming yearly and has some major global hits. Endemol operates across 26 countries globally, including the United States, India, Australia and the Philippines, where it is frequently the largest TV producer. Some of the company's TV success stories are *Big Brother* (on CBS), *Fear Factor* (on NBC), and *Extreme Makeover* (on ABC), which it licenses to major television networks around the globe. From time to time, US multimedia firms seeking a solid television production foothold in the EU have attempted to buy Endemol.

Axel Springer

Germany's Axel Springer group is a major European newspaper and magazine publisher with other media interests including books, video, and internet interests. It has foreign newspaper as well as magazine publications located in Austria, France, Spain, Switzerland, Poland, Hungary, Russia, and the Czech Republic. Axel Springer also has interests in Austrian radio stations and has a 51 percent stake in a Canadian animation studio.

The group has nearly 200 newspapers and magazines and is the largest German publisher in terms of circulation. In 2001 it was adversely affected by an investment loss when the German-based Kirch group went bankrupt. Across Germany media firms that are being sold are being directed to seek out German purchasers rather than outsiders like Murdoch's News Corp. Given the vast amount of consolidation across the media industry, it is becoming more difficult to maintain local ownership and control.

Zodiak Entertainment

Zodiak, formerly of Sweden, is a collection of 30 production companies in 18 nations. It is primarily based across the USE but also has facilities in India, Brazil, and the US. One of its main strengths is a global distribution network. In 2008 Zodiak produced over 200 shows. It is based in London and Paris and owned by Italian De Agostini Group. The group is family owned and private. It operates in four areas: first, publishing, which is the area the company started with over a 100 years ago, with presses in 30 countries and working in 13 languages, second, media, working through Zodiak, third, gaming and lottery services, and fourth, financial raising private equity. It is currently raising capital to underwrite major productions and to acquire additional strategic assets. A primary goal of market expansion is the semiperipheral region.

European Broadcasting Union (EBU)

The EBU is a significant transnational entity for public broadcasters across Europe, the Middle East, and North Africa. Given that almost all nations outside the US have large and successful non-commercial broadcasters, i.e. public service, since 1950, the EBU has been a crucial professional association of national, non-commercial broadcasters. Working in 56 countries, the EBU operates Eurovision and Euroradio networks. It also facilitates the exchange of programming and negotiates broadcasting rights for major sports events, such as soccer and the Olympics, and finally works to facilitate original co-productions among member broadcasters. In 2005 it issued the Madrid Declaration. The five main issues in the Declaration are:

1   the major role played by public service broadcasters to further European integration;
2   a proactive approach on the part of the EBU and its members to support public service;
3   the need for public service broadcasting to be at the forefront of new initiatives regarding digital terrestrial broadcasting;
4   a comprehensive delivery of public service content on the full spectrum of new digital platforms; and
5   the crucial importance of guaranteed stable and long-term funding to allow the full implementation of public service duties.

For the full text of the Declaration see: www.ebu.ch).

Finally, the EBU will be busy monitoring the proposed actions of the World Trade Organization (WTO) as they impact the public broadcasting sectors. The EBU does not view broadcasting as a commercial commodity to be included in WTO's free trade undertakings. (The WTO and its move into the media and cultural sectors are discussed in a later chapter.)

Other Foreign-based Multimedia Corporations

European-based multimedia corporations are by no means the only non-US stakeholders in the global communication industry (Figure 8.2). The following sections detail the primary global communication stakeholders located in nations outside of Europe and the United States.

CanWest Global Communications Corp. (Canada)

One of the largest private broadcasters in Canada, CanWest Global, initially started in the 1970s as a third (behind the CBC and CTV networks) national television network, called Global Television. It has since expanded into cable as well as film and television production activities. It also publishes 12 major Canadian dailies. Beginning in the early 1990s, CanWest bought a 70 percent part interest in New Zealand's only private sector broadcaster, TV3, through the formation of Media Works New Zealand. In the late 1990s, New Zealand began operating a second privately owned network, TV4, and, again, CanWest played a significant role. New Zealand's top-rated commercial radio network, RadioWorks, which includes seven major urban radio stations and other FM stations, was partly owned (70 percent) by Media Works. In 2001 it acquired Radio Works New Zealand, the second largest radio group in that country. In 2006, CanWest sold its 70 percent stake in Media Works New Zealand to Ironbridge Capitol.

During the 1990s, CanWest acquired part ownership of Australia's Ten TV network which it sold in 2009. CanWest has film interests in the United States through its Seven Arts International Division and concluded an internet agreement with Minnesota-based Internet Broadcasting Systems (IBS). This joint venture permitted the expansion of an internet-based network of news and information sites across North America. Los Angeles, Minneapolis, and Cleveland have been targeted for joint venture internet development, along with the expansion of the media outlet Channel 4,000, which is a TV website owned by IBS of

---

1   CanWest Global Communications Corp (Canada)
2   WETV (Canada)
3   Aboriginal People's Television (Canada)
4   Grupo Televisa (Mexico)
5   Globo Communications (Brazil)
6   Cisneros Group (Venezuela)
7   Sony (Japan)
8   Bollywood (India)
9   Zodiac Entertainment (Italy)

Figure 8.2   Non-US and EU major communications stakeholders, 2010

Minneapolis. Currently CanWest suffers from a debt of about $3.9 billion and is trying to sell some assets. It filed for bankruptcy protection in October 2009.

Aboriginal People's Television Network (Canada)

Aboriginal People's Television Network (APTN) was launched in 1999 as a means of promoting positive images and messages about aboriginals and aboriginal lifestyle. The new specialty channel is attempting to reverse the longstanding trend of negative mainstream media coverage of aboriginals. AFTN presents aboriginal programming from Canada, the United States, Australia, and New Zealand. The schedule includes children's, educational, and cultural programming as well as news, current affairs, and political programming. Most programming will be produced, written, and staffed by media professionals of aboriginal ancestry.

Approximately 56 percent of the shows are in English, 16 percent in French, and 28 percent in a variety of aboriginal languages, primarily Inuit. APTN is a clear example of development communication. The goal of the network is to present pro-social and proactive messages on behalf of aboriginal communities as an alternative to the traditional mainstream TV networks, which are staffed almost entirely by non-aboriginal personnel.

Televisa (Mexico)

The roots of the Azcarraga family empire date back to the radio era. Emilio Azcarraga Milmo began his media career with the radio station XEW-AM in Mexico City during the 1940s. The Azcarraga family subsequently owned the station. In 1972 the Azcarraga family formed the giant television network Televisa by combining two other television companies. Emilio Azcarraga Milmo died in Miami in April 1998, leaving Latin America's largest multimedia corporation, Televisa, to his son, Emilio Azcarraga Jean. The Azcarragas now control a sprawling operation that includes four network channels with 260 affiliate stations; a publishing company called Editorial Televisa; two record labels (EMI Televisa Music and EMI Latin); 17 radio stations; several cable channels; one satellite system; a movie company, Estadio Azteca (a massive 120,000-seat stadium); three soccer teams; and an airline. In addition, they have investments in the US-Spanish network Univision; the stateside cable channel Galavision; and a Venezuelan television network. With the rapid growth of Spanish media in both the United States and Europe, the Azcarraga empire is growing, with hopes of competing with the Disney and Sony corporations.

Univision Communications

Univision is the largest Spanish language network in the United States. It was launched in 1961 and currently is experiencing substantial growth. As the US Hispanic population increases rapidly it has become the largest minority in the

United States. Univision features telenovelas, soap operas that last for several months. The Univision network reaches the vast majority of US Hispanic households through 20-owned and operated stations, as well as through 27 broadcast affiliates. Televisa partners with Univision to provide it with a large number of Spanish language programs that appeal to the growing US Hispanic audience. Univision is a major, and sometimes the dominant, channel in US cities such as Miami and Los Angeles, and in several Texas and Arizona cities. Univision is also beginning to attract substantial advertising revenue from major US corporations because reaching the Hispanic audience is becoming more critical to the increasing market share for media and consumer products alike.

Rede Globo (Brazil)

Globo is a multimedia giant with a television network, newspapers, magazines, books, radio, cable systems movies, internet, and records. In addition to owning Rio de Janeiro's largest circulation newspaper, *O Globo*, the company's television interest attract over 60 percent of the Brazilian audience and is the largest television network in Latin America. The company is privately owned by the Marinho family and accumulated enormous debts during the 1990s. They were able to restructure $1.3 billion of their debt in late 2004 and avoid bankruptcy. Historically the Marinho elders have had a close relationship with the political masters of Brazil. In terms of exports Globo has limited sales since they work in Portuguese, with the exception being telenovelas which do well in parts of Europe.

Cisneros Group (Venezuela)

Established in 1929 in Caracas, Venezuela, this is now one of the world's largest multimedia firms in private hands. The chairman and CEO is family member Gustavo Cisneros who directs its vast holding across the Americas. The company seeks to serve the 500 million Spanish and Portuguese markets across Europe and the Americas with high quality audio and video entertainment. The flagship television station is Venevision, the largest in Venezuela. In addition, it has interests in AOL Latin America and DirectTV Latin America, and for the global market, Venevision International. This company, based in Miami, provides Cisneros products across five continents, involving 20 languages in over 100 countries.

Sony (Japan)

Originally established in 1946 under the name Tokyo Telecommunications Engineering Corporation, Sony Corporation got its new name in 1958. Company founders were determined to create new markets with communication technology. The company produced the first Japanese tape recorder in 1950, and by

1955, after receiving a transistor technology license from Western Electric, launched the first transistor radio. The company then produced the first Sony trademark product: a pocket-sized radio.

In 1960, Akio Morita (1921–99), one of Sony's founders, moved to New York to oversee major US expansion. During this time, Sony launched the first home video, a solid-state condenser microphone, and an integrated circuit based radio. Another decade of explosive growth was launched by Sony's 1968 introduction of the Trinitron color television tube. The VCR and the Walkman were other early Sony successes. Competition, especially from other Asian countries, was affecting the Sony Corporation by the 1980s. For this reason, Sony, under Morita's leadership as chairman since 1976, used its technology to diversify beyond consumer electronics. In 1980, Sony introduced Japan's first 32-bit workstation and became a major producer of computer chips and floppy disk drives. Sony expanded its US media empire by acquiring CBS Records from CBS for $2 billion and Columbia Pictures from Coca-Cola for $4.9 billion, both in 1988. Sony was now in the US entertainment industry in a big way. In 1992, Sony allied with Sega to develop CD video games, and with Microsoft to make electronic audio-, video-, and textbooks.

Sony Corporation is headquartered in Tokyo, Japan; the sister company in the United States is called Sony Corporation of America. The company employs 180,500 people worldwide. Sony's major products include audio and video equipment, televisions, information, communications, and electronic components. Some of the products produced for the audio division include CD players, MP3 players, headphone stereos, hi-fi components, radio-cassette tape records, radios, car stereos, and digital audiotape. The video division produces DV-format VCRs, DVD video players, video CD players, digital cameras, and videotapes. The television division produces color TVs, projection TVs, flat display panels, and large color video display systems. Also, computer displays, personal computers, internet terminals, telephones, the Playstation, and car navigation systems are all Sony products.

Sony's music division offers recordings from acts ranging from Britney Spears to Rage Against the Machine. In 2004, Sony merged in a 50/50 venture with Bertelsmann Music Group (BMG) to form Sony BMG Music Entertainment. Then in 2008, Sony bought out the remaining half of the music company and renamed it Sony Music Entertainment which has become the second largest music company in the world. Sony Music includes among its divisions Columbia Records, Epic Records, and RCA Music Group.

Bollywood: India's Film Industry

The cinema of the semiperipheral nation of India rates specific mention. It began in 1896 with a film produced by the French brothers Lumière. Then in 1913 the first Indian-made silent feature film was produced. From these humble origins the film industry in India is now producing over 800 films per year. The vast film industry has been nicknamed "Bollywood" a combination of Hollywood and Bombay. The films are primarily Hindi productions with a number of regional centers producing other films in their own languages.

Bollywood is a major focus of India's popular culture both at home and abroad. The commercial films are shown in the Indian subcontinent, across the Middle East, Africa, Asia, and North America to the large number of Indian expatriates in these regions. The genres of musicals, romance, comedy, and melodramatic themes dominate. A typical budget for a feature length movie with export expectations is still only $2 million as compared with Hollywood stars commanding more than $10 million each for a single movie. Also Indian censors are very active and restrict many plots with a sexual cache. Across India more than six million workers are employed in the cinema sector and leading stars are national heroes. The growth of cable channels and DVDs is providing additional outlets for Bollywood productions and increased revenue growth. Though a niche cinematic industry in terms of global reach it has survived surprisingly well in the face of major core nation competition. *Slumdog Millionaire* is a good example. First it is about a popular US television show, *Who Wants to be a Millionaire?*, hosted by Regis Philbin starting in 1999 on ABC. The network produced 363 episodes. The Bollywood movie, in Hindi and English, was produced in 2008 for $15 million and won eight Oscars, including Best Picture and Best Director. It has grossed over $360 million so far. *Slumdog Millionaire* like most foreign films had global distribution problems and turned to Warner Bros. and FOX for assistance. As a result the two American studios have made millions from the Bollywood production.

Conclusions

This review of global broadcasters illustrates two important points, which will be developed in some detail here. The first is the connection between sports and the mass media. This partnering is particularly common in Europe where many major broadcasting conglomerates also own, in part or in whole, major European soccer teams. US media firms also own several sports teams. The second facet point is the substantial and ever increasing role that non-US media stakeholders are playing in global communication.

The Sports Connection

The connection between sports and the mass media has had a long and checkered career. For example, attempts to link the International Olympic Movement (IOC) and the Summer and Winter Olympic Games with the world television audience were tenuous during the 1950s and 1960s. It was not until the 1970s that the value of media rights for the Olympic Games escalated dramatically because of bidding wars among ABC, NBC, and CBS. In the 1990s, the gray area between amateur and professional sports became even shadier when for the first time professional basketball and hockey players participated in the Olympic Games. Today the Olympics enjoy substantial revenue from a combination of media and marketing funds that were created as part of the selling package for host cities. Host cities incur enormous local expenses but now recoup those expenses, plus tourism dollars, thanks to the huge sums paid almost exclusively by US- television networks. Major US firms purchasing marketing rights supplement these dollars. It should come as no surprise that sponsorship of the Olympics makes sense, and that this sports connection should work for corporations with other sports as well. Even now, the National Football League holds exhibition games in Europe and the National Hockey League holds exhibition games in Asia and Europe as part of their attempts to go global. European football, known in the United States as soccer, has limited exposure in the United States except during the World Cup. The 1999 US women's World Cup victory shown live on television had a dramatic influence on soccer and media exposure in North America. In the future, global sports leagues will emerge, and global broadcasting will parallel that movement. Current media outlets such as News Corporation, Disney, AOL Time Warner, and others may aggressively purchase international sports teams in order to influence or obtain international sports broadcasting rights, primarily for teams that draw enormous global audiences that are ripe for global products such as Coca-Cola, American Express, McDonald's, Kodak, IBM, and UPS.

It appears that Murdoch's News Corporation strategy concerning sports may be changing in Europe. Previously, he had announced large-scale attempts to purchase major media systems which frequently ran into regulatory trouble as the culturally sensitive Europeans looked with disfavor on the Australian born media giant. Also, he has been acquiring part ownership in non-major media outlets across Europe. For example, in 1999 he acquired 35 percent of an Italian digital pay-TV service known as Stream. Murdoch, along with other partners, is now acquiring the rights to broadcast Italian soccer games In Germany, News Corporation bought 66 percent of the niche channel entitled TM3. This relatively obscure channel outbid Germany's number one commercial TV channel for all domestic broadcasting rights to Europe's major soccer league for four years.

Global Stakeholders

These descriptions of transnational media conglomerates reflect a basic point namely, that global communication systems are only partly American in shape, content, and ownership. Many powerful non-US global corporations are extremely active in the global communication marketplace. Even though these non-US firms compete with Hollywood and New York, they do so while sharing the same commercial values. The goal of these global media corporations is to maximize profits for owners and shareholders, much like their US counterparts;

they entered the global arena to increase market share. The global communication stakeholders are all based in core nations. All global media firms rely heavily on foreign customers, whether they are in other core nations, or in semiperipheral, or peripheral zones. These non-US firms need to have a significant presence in the US market to be profitable as well as to be considered major global players. They have taken advantage of the significant structural changes in the 1990s that encouraged privatization and deregulation at the same time that satellite technology, cable systems, DVDs, and the internet were expanding rapidly. In Europe, where government-controlled and government-owned media lost market share and in some cases became a phenomenon of a previous era, aggressive corporations quickly sought either to extend their traditional interests in the mass media, beginning with print products, or move into new areas and make strategic decisions to diversify previously non-media corporations. The outcomes are similar. All major global multimedia corporations are seeking to maximize profits in order to increase or improve the rate of return for their shareholders. They do this through a combination of expanding current markets and adding new market share through acquisitions or joint ventures. Ultimately, they seek the expansion of electronic colonialism just as US global media firms seek foreign customers in Asia and Europe, so Asian and European firms are aggressively pursuing customers in North America. They do so by producing shows and other media products that will attract a substantial customer base along with healthy advertising revenues. Bertelsmann and Sony are prime examples. Sony Pictures Classics spent over $10 million to market a single film, *Crouching Tiger, Hidden Dragon*. But the reality for most foreign firms in the feature film business is that the costs have moved the bar far beyond their reach. One example is that of female movie stars, speaks volumes. Julia Roberts and Cameron Diaz command between $20 to $30 million each per movie. For somewhere between $10 and $20 million producers have their pick of Halle Berry, Drew Barrymore, Nicole Kidman, Reese Witherspoon, Sandra Bullock, Renée Zellweger, or Angelina Jolie. The vast majority of foreign produced feature films do not have total budgets in this league, let alone for a single star.

Clearly, customers with disposable income are free to make choices among a plethora of books and magazines, movies and television channels, records, tapes, internet sites, and other communication products around the globe. Most are unaware of who owns the content, which controls the delivery system, or how important advertising is in terms of revenue for these global empires. Few could identify, or would care, which firm actually owns the product they are viewing, listening to, or reading.

Early in the twenty-first century it is likely that the biggest global communication firms will be conducting most of their business abroad, or capturing more customers in foreign markets, and will have less to do with the nation-state their corporation was established in. A global mind-set, global advertising, and global strategic planning will reflect successful the communication management of tomorrow. Business without borders will be the norm rather than the exception for global multimedia corporations. Like the internet, global communication systems and products will transcend national boundaries.

A new policy issue is looming on the horizon, which could impact the non-American multimedia stakeholders. Namely, the World Trade Organization (WTO) as part of its new round of negotiations is looking to include the audiovisual sector in new multilateral talks (Pauwels and Loisen, 2003).[6] The WTO as part of its broad tariff reduction goal may include government subsidies as well. For many nations, particularly the USE, this could result in the ending of government grants or programs that seek to bolster their film and television industries. More about this important and looming cultural policy issue is discussed in a later chapter.

Notes

1. See, for example, Juan E. Conradi, "Cultural Dependence and the Sociology of Knowledge: The Latin American Case," *International Journal of Contemporary Sociology* 8(1) (1971): 35–55; Kaarle Nordenstreng and Tapio Varis, *Television Traffic: A One-Way Street?* Reports and Papers of Mass Communication no. 70 Paris: UNESCO, 1974; and Thomas Guback, *The International Film Industry*, Bloomington: Indiana University Press, 1969.
2. See, for example, Ben Bagdikian, *The Media Monopoly*, Boston: Beacon Press, 2000; Jeremy Tunstall, *The Media Are American*, New York: Columbia University Press, 1977; Thomas McPhail and Brenda McPhail, *Communication: The Canadian Experience*, Toronto: Copp Clark Pitman, 1990; and Anthony Smith, *The Geopolitics of Information: How Western Culture Dominates World*, New York: Oxford University Press, 1980.
3. See, for example, Andrew A. Moemeka (ed.), *Communicating for Development* (Albany: State University of New York Press, 1994); Oliver Boyd-Barnett, *The International News Agencies* (London: Constable, 1980); Tsan Kuo Chang, "All Countries Not Created Equal to Be News," *Communication Research*, 25(5) (October 1998): 528–63; and Rob Kroes, "American Empire and Cultural Imperialism: A View from the Receiving End," *Diplomatic History*, 23 (1999): 463–78.
4. Herbert I. Schiller, *Communication and Cultural Domination* (White Plains, NY: International Arts and Sciences Press, 1978); and J. Tomlinson, *Cultural Imperialism: A Critical Introduction*, London: Pinter, 199.
5. John Tagliabue, "A Media World to Conquer," *New York Times* (July 7, 1999): 5.
6. Caroline Pauwels and Jan Loisen, "The WTO and the Audiovisual Sector" *European Journal of Communication*, 18 (2003): 291–314.

9

Euromedia

Integration and Cultural Diversity in a Changing Media Landscape

Alexa Robertson

Introduction

Once upon a time, a long time ago (that is to say, before Harry Potter and Gandalf found their way onto the big screen), parents and children across Europe lined up at the cinema and at McDonalds to experience Disney's version of the story of Hercules. This social and cultural ritual occasioned an outburst in what was then Europe's own weekly newspaper, *The European* (Figure 9.1).

The front page cried "Plunder! Disney tears up our cultural heritage" and depicted Hercules tearing apart a book, Mickey Mouse gleefully counting the dollars and Pinocchio, Winnie the Pooh, and Quasimodo looking on in dismay. On the editorial page and in a number of articles inside the paper, *The European* lamented that "the guardians of European culture" were worried about what the paper referred to as the Disney effect. The creative, intellectual, European treasure trove was juxtaposed with a US business empire that was called 'Mauschwitz' because the Disney empire was thought to be something quite other than free. Disney has often said that its strategy is to 'think global, act local' – a virtual paraphrase of Roland Robertson's notion of glocalization. But in the view of *The European*, it was precisely the other way around.

In fact, *The European*, just like Disney, was a commercial interest: a media company that targeted an international audience. But the stance it adopted on its editorial pages bears a striking resemblance to that reflected in European Commission directives such as *Television without Frontiers*, which stipulated that a majority of broadcast time in the ether media of EU member states should be earmarked for European products. It is the same argument that resulted in the founding of Euronews, the channel meant to be Europe's answer to CNN. It is the same argument that underpins such ventures as the European Film Promotion

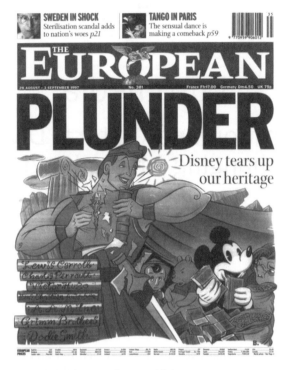

Figure 9.1   Disney tears up our heritage. Reprinted by permission.

network and the MEDIA Mundus audiovisual cooperation program. This argument is that Europeans should be the ones to decide how Europe is seen and understood – not Disney, or CNN, or Hollywood. It resonates with the UNESCO Declaration on Cultural Diversity, which states:

> In the face of current imbalances in flows and exchanges of cultural goods and services at the global level, it is necessary to reinforce international cooperation and solidarity aimed at enabling all countries, especially developing countries and countries in transition, to establish cultural industries that are viable and competitive at national and international level.[1]

In Europe, a continent with 34 official languages, a historically unprecedented project to develop and reinforce international cooperation had been taking place for several decades, and was about to enter a new phase. *Hercules* premiered a few months after the Maastricht Treaty was signed, transforming the European Community into the European Union. As the hero of Mount Olympus was cleaning out stables to the chorus of the muses, the European single market was coming into being, stipulating the free movement of goods and services between EU member states. The number of states swelled, two years after the *Hercules* premiere, to 15, after Austria, Finland and Sweden joined. A decade later it had grown to a Union of 27 members, including eight former Warsaw Pact states – some of them developing countries and all of them certainly countries in transition.

Barely a generation ago, most Europeans had access to one or two state-funded (and, in the case of the former Warsaw Pact countries, state-controlled) radio and television channels. Deregulation started in the early 1980s in the UK under Margaret Thatcher, and spread quickly eastwards, notably to France, where advertising crept into all broadcasting, Italy, where Berlusconi levelled the distinction between media and political empires, and beyond. In Sweden, legislation had to be changed when a renegade channel began broadcasting to the country by satellite from London, and thus circumvented the law against advertising in ether media. By 2008, over 6,500 television channels were available in the European Union (EU) and candidate countries (Croatia and Turkey). While 381 were terrestrial, the majority were accessible through cable, satellite or IPTV. Britons have access to most (883) followed by Germans (300), Italians (284) and French (252). Swedes, who had just two channels at the end of the 1980s, now have access to 136.[2]

The radically altered media landscape in Europe can at times seem a battlefield on which business interests, developers of technology, journalists (often with a strong sense of mission and professional integrity), and policy-makers struggle to gain the higher ground. While often in conflict, they increasingly work in tandem with increasingly active audiences, to transform the European media scene.

This chapter takes a look at the intersection of politics and media globalization in the European context. Most European countries have strong public service traditions, and the ethos remains despite the inroads of commercialization. National governments thus continue to be important players in the European media game. But the focus will be on the European Union, as it has come to play an increasingly central role in communication policy, and because its reactions to technological and economic developments can teach us a lot about globalization in general. It is for good reason that Europe has been called "an exemplary landscape for comprehending globalization."[3] A key question throughout is what has been done to create a communicative space or public sphere that is uniquely European, to counter the impact of US media influence and to forge a common European identity.

The Power of Culture

Shortly before the turn of the millennium, UNESCO launched a fundamental review of cultural policies in light of transformations in the media world. Delegates met in Stockholm to discuss a document entitled *The Power of Culture*, which noted that while technology was yielding a broader range of choices, the increasing concentration of media ownership under globalization was actually limiting access. "How can we ensure," the delegates were asked, "that in every country, the media provide diversified programmes which not only promote a shared national identity but also give pluralistic expression to the variety of social, political and cultural values?"[4] The adaptation of public service broadcasting to the 'enormous' changes in the sphere of communication was thus identified as a key issue. In a variety of documents adopted over the years, UNESCO has sought to protect the 'fruitful diversity of cultures'. In 2009, it called for a renewed discussion, thought necessary not just because of ongoing and deepening globalization, but because of the global financial crisis, the impacts of which "are challenging our very understanding of cultures and identities."[5]

One UNESCO text in particular is often invoked by European institutions and actors, and must thus be considered a starting point for any account of communication and cultural regulation in Europe. It is the UNESCO Convention on the Protection and Promotion of the Diversity of Cultural Expressions, adopted in Paris in October 2005, and usually referred to as "the UNESCO Convention." Its objectives include the creation of conditions in which cultures can "flourish and freely interact," more balanced cultural exchange in the world, and working to make policy-makers in the corridors of power and media consumers in the home aware of the value of diverse cultural expressions. Translated into everyday language, this means that UNESCO thinks it important to resist what some call Americanization, and others refer to as "cultural homogenization" when talking about the results of media globalization.

The UNESCO Convention urges international cooperation and solidarity to enable countries "to create and strengthen their means of cultural expression, including their cultural industries, whether nascent or established, at the local, national and international levels." The aim of the Convention and other UNESCO agreements is to ensure that all societies remain open to the cultural expressions of others. "When States adopt measures to support the diversity of cultural expressions," it is argued, "they should seek to promote openness to other cultures of the world."[6] The idea, in other words, is for states to work together, for the benefit of an internationalised community, rather than go it alone, for the economic gain of individual corporations. This take on the sort of action required of regulators in a globalized world resonates with the aims and language of EU communications policy.

Sans Frontières: EU Communication Policy

As the Berlin Wall was toppling in 1989, and barbed wire throughout Eastern Europe was being penetrated, not by NATO soldiers but by Western media, the European Union agreed on a directive symbolically entitled Television without Frontiers. Its main objective was to create the conditions necessary for the free movement of television broadcasts within the EU, to promote the development of programs with a European dimension, and to stem the deluge of American imports in an era of deregulation.

Television without Frontiers Directive/AMSD

In the view of the European Commission, the single European market that came into being in the early days of globalization applied to television broadcasts as much as anything else. "Just as any of us is free to buy chocolate, wine or a new car in any EU country," it explained to Europeans, "we can also watch TV channels from all over Europe."[7] For the single European television market to function, it was thought that a minimum set of common rules was needed to govern advertising, program production, and the protection of minors. Beginning in 1989, these rules were enshrined in the Television without Frontiers directive, which was a response to the communications revolution of the early 1980s and the growing deficit in audiovisual trade with the US.

The directive was updated over the years, and eventually replaced in 2007 by the Audiovisual Media Services directive. The national governments of EU member states had until December 2009 to apply the new directive, which unlike its precursor covers all digital audiovisual media services. In 1989, the challenge was to regulate media production and distribution in an age when satellite broadcasting showed how porous national borders were. A decade later the issue was less one of top-down developments and "linear" services (with satellite and other broadcasters providing a schedule) as bottom-up and "non-linear" services. The question now was how to respond to consumer behavior: what rules should apply to films supplied at the request of the user, who has control over what and when he or she wants to watch?

According to the European Commission, the new rules are yet another response to yet more technological advancement – which regulators refuse to be outstripped by. They "create a level playing field for Europe" in a new media context and "seek to preserve cultural diversity" and "safeguard media pluralism."[8] It requires no in-depth textual analysis to conclude that language of the EU directive is redolent of UNESCO discourse.

The EU and GATS

European Union policy echoes UNESCO stances in other respects as well. Given the European view that the media play a significant social, cultural and political role, the EU has consistently resisted liberalization of the audiovisual market, an issue that has been hotly debated in the context of GATS (the General Agreement on Trade in Services, a WTO treaty that came into force in 1995). In a number of arguments, the UNESCO Convention has been invoked in support of the view that cultural products are not like other commodities, and must thus be exempt from free trade deals. There has been concern at the growth in the audiovisual trade deficit between the EU and the US. In 1995, the deficit was 4.8 billion USD. By 2000 it had risen to $8.2 billion USD.[9] Another example of a trade imbalance that the EU has identified as a threat is the domination of the internet by US companies. All in all, the view from Europe has been that producers, broadcasters, and distributors from some countries are at a disadvantage, in economic terms, when it comes to competing in audiovisual markets worldwide.

A problem related to the GATS, which has been pointed to by various European actors, is the lack of multinationally-agreed standards on cultural and audiovisual policies. This makes it difficult for individual states to limit their commitments to liberalization (liberalization being the thrust of GATS) to preserve and promote specific cultural identities. In theory, GATS allows flexibility in this respect. In practice, trade panels rather than cultural actors end up deciding on where the limits to liberalization should be set. This tends to be done with economic rather than cultural considerations in mind, and the concern is that they promote uniformity rather than safeguard diversity. EU actors have complained that under GATS, it is impossible to distinguish policy measures that legitimately protect and promote cultural diversity (which the EU favours), and measures which are protectionist (which it is the *raison d'être* of the internal European market to discourage).

Another problem with GATS is that it is seen as conservative, at a time when technological change was instead requiring regulators to be imaginative and willing to adapt to innovations. In various policy documents, EU actors have emphasized that there is huge uncertainty about future developments in digital and interactive audiovisual services. According to one,

> the acceptance, under the GATS, of the mere right to maintain existing measures, or to adopt safeguards with regard to traditional services only (such as cinema, radio and television) would completely fail to conserve the necessary scope for future policy measures.[10]

But the view from Europe is above all that GATS and pressure for liberalization are a threat to the foundations on which the European audiovisual model rests: co-production agreements with other countries, financial support for production and distribution, and the requirement that a certain amount of broadcast time be earmarked for European content.

The EU and Culture

The Maastricht Treaty of 1993 enabled the EU "to take action in the field of culture to safeguard, disseminate and develop culture in Europe."[11] This action comprises, of course, the fields of media and communication.

Since the beginning of the millennium, the EU has had a development plan known as the 'Lisbon Agenda'. Its aim is to make the EU "the world's most dynamic knowledge-based economy."[12] The Lisbon Agenda includes a strategy for culture, said to be a response to globalization. Taking its cue from the UNESCO Convention, the new European strategy is based on the conviction that culture is a vital dimension of international relations.

As should by now be clear, the EU considers the audiovisual industry, including film, to be an important part of the cultural sector. But museums and historical documents and artifacts belong here too; and the European Commission has been promoting the digitisation of "cultural heritage and material" in order to make it accessible online.

The Media Program of the EU

Financial and other support is offered by the EU to the European audiovisual industry under a program called MEDIA. It contributes to the financing of films, television drama, documentaries and animation projects: for the 2007–13 period, the budget is €755 million (approximately 1,400 million US dollars).

US feature films hold shares far above 50 percent in most markets throughout the world, and over 90 percent in the domestic American market. Against this backdrop, European Film Promotion (EFP) was launched in 1997. Although a network of film organisations and institutions, it receives generous support from the EU's MEDIA program. By 2009 it had 30 member organizations representing 31 different European countries.[13] The EFP mandate is to increase opportunities for European film to compete in the international marketplace.

In 2009, the European Commission adopted a new program within this framework, called MEDIA Mundus, for cooperation between Europeans and third countries in the audiovisual sector. The Commission said it hoped to create business opportunities and to increase consumer choice by bringing "more culturally diverse products" to European and other markets. "It's time to go global," said the EU Media Commissioner:

> The international audiovisual landscape has changed significantly over the last two decades, notably through the impact of technological developments like video on demand, internet TV or multichannel digital television. This has created growing demand for more audiovisual content, and we need to "fill" these new technologies with new and exciting content.[14]

The background to the program was the structural weakness in the international audiovisual landscape, which has prevented European producers from taking full advantage of emerging new platforms. The program is also meant to address the paradoxical situation that has arisen under globalization, whereby consumers have increasingly limited choice and access to products of more limited cultural diversity at a time when the number of media outlets is exploding. The soundtrack to this venture could well be the song in which Bruce Springsteen complains: "57 Channels (and Nothin' On)."

The problem identified here is related, but not identical to, that of liberalization and flexibility in the GATS negotiations. Individually, the European Union member states – big countries like the UK, Germany, France and Spain, small countries like Sweden, Denmark and The Netherlands, and countries with rela-tively new capitalist economies like Poland, the Czech Republic and the Baltics – have relatively small markets compared to the US. They lack the critical mass to compete successfully. And viewers are not helping, given their propensity to con-sume US programs and box office blockbusters. While the ideology behind the MEDIA program and MEDIA Mundus is naturally the same, the objectives and mechanisms set out in the latter are said to be radically different.[15]

Protecting Diversity while Encouraging Integration

To sum up, it can be said that while the EU lacked a communication policy for much of its history, the spread of globalization in general, and cultural globalization in particular, and the enduring and even increasing distrust of its citizens, resulted in the EU paying closer attention to communication from the mid-1990s onwards. It now has an audiovisual and media policy that is implemented in four ways. The first is the regulatory framework. The Audiovisual Media Services directive (the sequel to Television without Frontiers) aims to bring about a single European mar-ket for broadcast media and film. The second is comprised of funding programs such as MEDIA and the third of measures to enhance the free flow of online con-tent and to promote media pluralism. The fourth way in which the EU acts is to defend European cultural interests outside Europe – significantly in the context of the WTO. EU policy is thus somewhat reminiscent of Dr. Dolittle's "Pushmi-pullyu," striving as it does to defend cultural specificity, while at the same time investing heavily in bringing Europeans together in a single market and culture.

Apart from the need to protect European cultural products and industries from the onslaught of Hollywood, Bollywood and Australian imports, the EU has been faced with the challenge of consolidating an internal European community as well as the single market. The problem that has plagued the architects of the European project over the years can be summed up in one key phrase – the "dem-ocratic deficit" – and it is on this that many of the steps taken by the EU in the area of communications have been predicated. The most important task currently con-fronting the European Commission – in its own view and in the view of numerous commentators, after the poor turnout in the 2009 elections to the European Parliament – is to restore public confidence in the European Union. The media, both traditional and new, are seen as essential to its accomplishment.[16]

Europeanization and the European Public Sphere

At this point, it might be useful to pause and consider the scholarly debate raging around European integration and communication. Hallin and Mancini (2004) have demonstrated how dangerous it is to generalize about "the media" or even

"European media," as countries in different European regions have profoundly distinct traditions governing the interaction between political systems and media cultures. Their argument is that European media systems fit uneasily in the largely Anglo-Saxon accounts of how media and politics interact, and introduce three media systems models. The "liberal" model is most reminiscent of the US system, characterized by the dominance of market mechanisms. According to Hallin and Mancini, this conforms to the situation in the UK and Ireland. Northern European countries such as Germany, Sweden and Denmark, however, have a different system, in which public and commercial media coexist, but where the state is also more active and civil society more involved. This they refer to as the "Democratic Corporatist" model. The "Polarized Pluralist" model is the third, into which the countries of southern Europe, grouped around the Mediterranean, fit. The media in these countries tends to be integrated more closely into party politics, and there is a different tradition of journalistic professionalism compared to the countries conforming to the two other models.

Given these different traditions, it is perhaps not surprising that many scholars and commentators are more sceptical than the EU about the prospects for Europeanization, the possibility of creating a common European media culture and – what is often thought to be the cure for the democratic deficit – a European public sphere (EPS).

The notion of the public sphere is very influential in European media studies. The concept comes from a book written by Jürgen Habermas in the early 1960s, which only became widely known when it was translated from German into English in 1989. What Habermas had in mind was a hypothetical space between the private realm of the family and the realm of the state, inhabited by citizens who shared ideas and information that mattered to their political choices. The concept is now often used in such a way that the media *become* the public sphere, rather than simply supplying its inhabitants with input. The media are thought to promote the pluralism that is necessary for healthy democracies by offering a place for different actors to be heard.[17] The EU in general, and the European Commission in particular, has indicated that it hopes a European Public Sphere will one day form a place in which feelings of affinity and democratic dependency can be nurtured. It lamented in 2006 that there had been an "inadequate development of a "European Public Sphere" where European debate can unfold," that the public sphere and media in Europe continued to be largely national, and that there are "few meeting places where Europeans from different Member States can get to know each other and address issues of common interest."[18]

A number of scholars have argued that if the same European or EU news is reported on in different media in Europe at the same time, it would be possible to say that an EPS existed.[19] According to this view, the EPS is a "pluralistic ensemble" of issue-oriented publics and the EPS, like Brigadoon in the old musical, comes into being when all of those publics think and talk about the same thing at the same time. Schlesinger – who views the formation of an EPS as an impossible project – claims it would be necessary for the EU to have the same news agenda in all European languages, and for people to think of themselves first and foremost as EU citizens, and only secondarily as members of nations.[20] He is an example of a sceptic who thinks an EPS must fulfil the same conditions as those of a national public sphere. (This view has been criticized by those who point out that if a common language, a common nationwide media system and citizens with a common identity were preconditions for a national public sphere, then few states would qualify for one.) Another way of conceptualizing the EPS is to see it as built from the infrastructures of national public spheres, and filled with reporting and discussion of European issues seen in a European perspective.[21]

Europeanization, in turn, is thought by some to be a bottom-up process through which national public spheres move closer until they final merge in an EPS.[22] Others see it as a top-down process in which the agenda is set by the EU, with the sort of policy measures outlined above. The red thread running through all of these discussions is the lack of European (rather than national) media, and the unsatisfactory nature of the European media that do exist.[23]

The 2009 elections to the European Parliament, mentioned a few pages ago, gave the sceptics ammunition. The election campaigns throughout the continent tended to be matters of domestic rather than European politics, and election coverage in most countries was correspondingly national in focus. Election turnout was more disappointing than usual, and it had never been good. In the wake of the election the refrain of the demise of the European Public Sphere (or indeed, its failure to ever come to life) was sung more loudly.

Just a month before the European Parliament elections, however, more Europeans than ever before followed the Eurovision Song Contest when it was broadcast live on television, and the number of votes cast for the best melody continued its steady climb to unprecedented levels. When the contestants took to the stage in Moscow, an estimated 100 million people watched the same event at the same time in the same communicative space. Voting in the Eurovision Song Contest went further than voting in the European Parliament elections in another way that matters to Europeanization. EU citizens could only vote for politicians from their own states to represent them in the European Parliament: a British Conservative could only vote for a British party, not for a Finnish or Greek Conservative candidate; nor could a Swedish Green vote for a Green candidate from Germany. In their cultural as opposed to civic capacities, however, Europeans could vote for songs and singers from other European countries. Under Eurovision, European enlargement had also gone further than political enlargement: as well as the 27 EU member states, "Europeans" from Russia, Turkey, and other parts of the continent were eligible to vote.

The Eurovision Song Contest is one piece of evidence that Gripsrud (2007) draws on when challenging the EPS sceptics. Citing Eurobarometer opinion surveys as further evidence, he points out that a majority of Europeans are interested in knowing the opinion of citizens in other EU member states on important political and social issues – the sort of behaviour one would expect in a public sphere. Together with Chalaby (2005, 2009), Gripsrud also points to the increasing importance of transnational, pan-Eurovision television. They argue that significant things are afoot when it comes to European broadcasting, and that the traditional connection between national territory and media culture is breaking down.

> The great social, cultural and political differences within the EU make expectations of a uniform, completely integrated European public sphere totally unrealistic. But, importantly, that is not to say that such a public sphere does not exist. [...] Television already contributes to a Europeanization of national public spheres and the minds of citizens.[24]

For Gripsrud, the European Broadcasting Union (EBU) clearly fulfils one criterion for the existence of a European Public Sphere, however defined.

The EBU and Euronews

Thirty years before CNN moved into the global village, the EBU was linking broadcasters throughout the continent in a non-commercial, non-governmental collaborative network. Its nascence coincided with the demise of Pope Pius XII, which prompted the chief editor of Dutch television to famously declare: "I want the dead Pope live!"

The very act of cooperation can be thought to contribute to the emergence of a shared professional culture with common news values. The largest association of national broadcasters in the world, the EBU is larger than the EU, with 75 members from 56 countries in and around Europe. It is for this reason that the Eurovision Song Contest – which is one EBU product – involves participation by non-EU states.[25] Its member broadcasters reach an audience of 650 million each week.

As well as promoting cooperation and exchange between European public service broadcasters, the EBU serves as a lobby organization for them, working to ensure that the role of public service broadcasting is recognized and taken into consideration by decision-makers. It represents its member organizations when the EU deliberates audiovisual policy, and works closely with the UN and UNESCO to ensure that the voice of European broadcasters is heard in the global debate on media policy. In the view of the EBU, "Europe's public service broadcasters are different to other market players; they are committed to public service values."[26] This means that the debate must be about content, and not just delivery mechanisms "or what kind of screen is being viewed," and above all that what is transmitted should be attuned to what is best for society, and not what is best for the market.

The EBU calls itself the "hidden link" in the distribution chain of programs to European households. The Geneva-based office coordinates daily and sometimes hourly transfers of programs, news, sports events, and music between members. This means that relatively poor countries are not at the mercy of expensive commercial operators like Reuters to buy news footage: these broadcasters trade material with each other and together decide which events are most relevant for each "feed." By 2009, more than 30,000 news items were being exchanged each year in this way.

Euronews

The EBU was one of the actors behind the launching of Euronews, the channel widely known as Europe's answer to CNN. It calls itself "the leading international news channel." Launched in 1993, it is now a multilingual, multiplatform service with a mandate to cover world news from a European perspective.

Euronews is based in Lyons, where journalists working the same newsbeat and at the same newsdesk put together bulletins from the same raw material, and broadcast them in English, French, German, Spanish, Italian, Portuguese, Russian, and Arabic. It also differs from most other channels in that there are no anchors, and reporters are rarely seen on camera. In this respect, it is "news from nowhere." On the other hand, many programs are retransmissions of national broadcasts. Through the Euronews portal, viewers in Germany and Greece get to see Portuguese programs about Poland, and so on. Apart from news reports every half-hour, flagship programs such as *Europe*, *Agora*, and *Parlamento* focus on European news.[27] According to its website, "'Euronews' ability to understand and decipher the various political debates and implications of political decisions made within Europe and their effects not only on a global scale but on day to day living make it the only channel best positioned to deliver true 'European' news."[28]

The channel takes in commercial revenues, receives €50 m from the EBU each year, and lists 22 public broadcasters as its shareholders. According to a contract signed by the European Commission in 2005, Euronews was to receive €25 Mio between 2005 and 2010.[29]

Euronews broadcasts to more than 251 million households in 139 countries. It cites statistics which indicate that 171 million households in Europe receive Euronews, compared to 135 million receiving CNN International and 89 million receiving BBC World. The figures are interesting, because while it is common to encounter Europeans who regularly watch CNN and BBC World, it is rare to come across Euronews or who is even aware of its existence.[30] Interviewed in 2008, managing director Michael Peters said (somewhat confusingly) that while Euronews was the most watched international news channel in Europe, no one knew that.[31] This was one factor behind the "extreme makeover" the channel underwent in 2008. It got rid of the blue-and-gold EU colour scheme, toned down the European perspective and toned up the global take on the news, went in for more aggressive marketing and tapped into new delivery modes. Apart from cable, satellite, and terrestrial broadcasts, it distributes news via PDAs, mobile phones, and live video streaming on GPRS, 3G, WAP and i-mode services and links its unedited, raw-news-footage "No Comment" segment straight to YouTube.

Despite its engagement with emerging technology, the channel has a very traditional view of the role of the news provider. This is to keep the well-informed citizen nourished with a regular does of the sort of input thought essential to the health of the public sphere. "At Euronews," says the website www.euronews.net,

> we believe that the growing use of sensationalism in news influences and distorts the viewers' perception of current global events [...] The work of the journalist is not to take sides, but rather to transcribe reality objectively and with complete integrity.[32]

The Euronews philosophy, then, is that the role of a news channel is to supply individuals with "sufficient information to allow the viewer to form his own opinion of the world."[33] And it *does* tend to be 'his' view. Not less than 73 percent of Euronews viewers are men with high salaries and liquid stock investments, opinion-leaders, and frequent-fliers. As such individuals also tend to be staunch supporters of the European Union and a single Euro currency; it is not immediately clear what Euronews can contribute solving the problem of the EU's democratic deficit.

As the EBU pointed out, the global media debate must not just be about delivery systems and screens (or, it could be added, about economics). It must also concern content, if the power of communication is to be understood and if the media's democratic role is to be scrutinized. More than that, attention must be paid to form. Euronews might be popular among busy elites, but it is worth reflecting on whether its short, telegram-like bulletins contribute to engaging Europeans as well as informing them.

In this respect, Euronews – like most other global broadcasters – is under-researched. Among the few studies that have been done, one compared coverage of Europe in Euronews and a national broadcaster.[34] Frydén Bonnier (2007) used a combination of quantitative and qualitative methods to find out which of the two channels could be thought most "Europeanizing." Studying a month of daily reporting, she compared the amount of attention devoted to Europe (a traditional indicator) but also paid attention to communicative style. Was the news reported in a way that made it likely viewers would feel the news had something to do with them, so they could identify with Europe, the EU, or other Europeans? Frydén Bonnier found that Euronews had (perhaps unsurprisingly) a larger proportion of European reports in the sample period and that they comprised a larger part of the total broadcast time than the domestic channel. But after having analysed more than 150 reports, she also concluded that the telegraphic reporting style were much less personalized and engaging than the reports of the domestic broadcasters. "So while Euronews has many more news reports on the EU and European issues, only four percent of them convey to the viewers a feeling of identification with the EU, with Europe, or with other Europeans,"[35] as opposed to a quarter of the reports in the domestic broadcaster. The importance of content and form – and not least narrative tradition – is the focus of the last few pages of this chapter.

Shared Histories, Different Understandings

After two decades of technological revolution, people have abundant opportunities to become informed about what is happening in their world: the explosion of commercial broadcasting and internet resources means that Europeans are no longer reliant on public service channels if they are to be well-informed citizens. But as sceptics about the EPS gleefully point out, they continue to be faithful to their national broadcasters. In a setting with proliferating outlets, television can play a more profound role, and help viewers engage with the world, as well as observe it. Parallel to a "thinning" out of political reporting, there is evidence to suggest a "thickening" of reportage culture. This brings us to an important question: what does cultural diversity mean in practice? Despite all that has been said about "the global newsroom," there is strong evidence that journalists rooted in different media cultures, or speaking to different audiences, are using the semiotic materials circulating in the global mediascape in different ways. This means that members of those different audiences are liable to arrive at different understandings of the way the world works.

In a study that compared how six Europe-based broadcasters reported the world in a six-week period (Robertson, forthcoming), it was found that there was rather less "breaking news" than expected, and that a lot of news was actually "olds," about historical events. A striking example was reporting of the 60th anniversary of the Normandy invasion, known as D-Day. A total of 60 news items about the D-Day commemoration, amounting to 190 minutes of news, was found in the daily reports of six European channels, three of them broadcasting to national audiences, and three of them to international audiences. When looked at more closely, these stories seemed to be making sense of current affairs, and giving viewers messages about how to solve problems that transcend national borders. The findings, which illustrate the diversity that UNESCO and others mentioned here have held to be so important, can be briefly summarized as follows.

The "master" story told by the BBC – i.e. the recurring theme in all its reports – was about the liberation of the oppressed by stalwart heroes. In speeches given significant airtime by the British channel, US President Bush tried to equate the liberation of Europe with the liberation of Iraq. The BBC resisted this frame to some extent. In the days surrounding the commemoration, the fallout from the Iraq invasion and the task of selling a handover plan to the UN was an American mission, fraught with problems. The D-Day invasion, on the other hand – a drama starring British soldiers, with an international supporting cast – was a glorious success and an uncontestedly good cause. The heroes in question are unusual figures in BBC discourse, which other studies have shown tends to privilege elites. Here the focus was on the ordinary men, often with working-class and regional dialects, who were repeatedly celebrated as the most noble and self-effacing of generations. The story told to BBC viewers was about the experiences of these men. It was about something that happened six decades ago, and had little to say about the current state of international relations.

The story told by the public service broadcaster Heute to viewers at home in Germany, on the other hand, was about the present. D-Day had to do with the birth of modern Germany, the importance of having friends, and keeping them. The people in this story were Europeans who had overcome their differences and learned to respect each other. While war veterans featured in this narrative, the main actors were German Chancellor Schröder and French President Chirac, or the Germany and France they symbolized.

In contrast to the profoundly gendered BBC discourse, the Swedish public service broadcaster offered viewers the perspective of women and non-combatants. Instead of revelling in the enthusiasm of the military replay as the BBC had done, nurses gave voice to all those who lived through the carnage, and felt saddened by the thought of so many young lives shed. Also in contrast to its British counterpart, the Swedish newsroom understood the D-Day anniversary to be only ostensibly about the past. What made it interesting was that it provided an occasion for world leaders to have a summit, and sort out their differences over the ongoing US occupation of Iraq.

Rather than painting a different picture from the newsrooms servicing domestic audiences, the European global channels tended to reinforce national tendencies. The stories told by BBC World were strongly reminiscent of those told in the domestic British newsroom, with their "Boy's Own" tone of coverage and the situating of the D-Day story – and by corollary those listening to it – firmly in the past. The BBC World narrative of the Normandy invasion was all about liberation and heroism. By contrast, the global German newsroom, Deutsche Welle, told the story of D-Day in a respectful but not reverent tone of voice. Its master narrative was not one of American and British liberators who had long ago fought shoulder-to-shoulder for a just cause, but one of Europeans who were living in the present, as the best of friends. The metaphor employed was actually stronger: the D-Day anniversary provided the opportunity to reaffirm the marriage vows between a partner who had once been raped and her violator, who had regretted his evil ways and become trustworthy and steadfast.

But of all the channels, it was Euronews that made most of the theme of reconciliation. It made it clear that wars tended to bring out the worst in people – both "now," in Iraq, and "then," in Auschwitz and Paris, where women who had fallen in love with men from the wrong country were made into pariahs. But Euronews acknowledged, like the others, that many had behaved in a human and altruistic fashion as well. As in the BBC, American and British soldiers were among the heroes. But in the Euronews account of the liberation of Europe from barbarity, the heroes also came from the new EU member states. Euronews did more than echo the Deutsche Welle metaphor of mixed marriage. It amplified it. On Euronews, the 60th anniversary of D-Day was celebrated by a Europe that was, as it put it, reconciled with itself. What it said about contemporary international relations was that the world had moved on, and was no longer a place in which differences could be resolved by military conflict. Where both BBC programmes had symbolized D-Day in logos featuring a gun, D-Day was epitimized in Euronews by the passionate embrace of the French and German leaders.

In reports of the D-Day commemoration – as in reports of breaking news and most other events – the six European newsrooms used similar, and sometimes identical, footage. Much of it emanated from the EBU exchange. They talked about the same event at the same time to Europeans across the continent, many of whom shared the same history. For a moment, it was almost as if the revisited Normandy beaches served as a temporary European Public Sphere. Certainly, many of the requirements for an EPS outlined in the past few pages were fulfilled by these reports. But to look at the evidence in this superficial way is to miss an important point, as attention to the master narratives reveals. The facts do *not* always speak for themselves, even if CSI Grissom is fond of saying that they do.

Conclusion

The emphasis in this chapter has been on that which is "European," and support has implicitly been given those who argue that a European Public Sphere *is* taking shape, that media production and use *is* contributing to a European identity, and that European publics *do* have things in common and are apparently aware of it. But the power of national traditions and *Weltanschauung* remain strong – just as UNESCO says it should. Within Europe there are not just different models of media and politics; there are also different historical experiences and narrative traditions which mean that the same event often takes on different meanings in different media.

Different accounts of the world, and messages about the relationship of the intended audience to that world, vary from one media culture to the next. In some European countries, established themes and understandings are reinforced in foreign news coverage rather than worked. At the same time, other outlets are moving away from the very notion of "foreign news," some (like Euronews, BBC World and Deutsche Welle) by their remit; others by the narrative techniques they employ, which invite their audience members to think of themselves as cosmopolitans and members of a transnational community rather than citizens of nations states. They can even make different sense of shared histories.

Even if it predated the actions stipulated in the EC's "Europe for Citizens" program for 2007–13, the Euronews take on D-Day was a good fit with the objectives of this part of the EU cultural plan. Part of the budget allocated to the Europe for Citizens Program was earmarked for projects to preserve "active European remembrance."[36] Although these are mainly projects designed to preserve the places and archives associated with mass deportations and former concentration camps, it could be argued that the media are one of the sites on which collective memories are kept alive.

From the heroes of World War II to those of Mount Olympus: whatever happened to Hercules? In *The European*, Hercules had lost his Greek identity. Pinocchio was no longer Italian; Quasimodo was no longer French and Winnie the Pooh was no longer English. These cultural icons had all become Europeans in the newspaper article which opened this chapter. Some would say that such media discourse is as much a form of cultural imperialism as any commercial strategy devised by a US conglomerate. This is certainly a question to which any student of the media and cultural regulation should give thought.

A decade after Disney cashed in on Hercules, Warner Brothers was making huge profits from the sixth in a series of films about a young man called Harry Potter who saves the world from destruction by an evil wizard called Voldemort, both of whom have impeccable English accents. And *The European* has gone belly-up. A European public sphere may well be taking shape, and Euronews may reach more households than its global competitors, but European audiences remain faithful to their national broadcasters, continue to watch American films, and are rapidly developing global networks of their own, from the keyboards on their computers and cell phones.

Notes

1. http://unesdoc.unesco.org/images/0012/001271/127160m.pdf.
2. European Audiovisual Observatory, www.obs.coe.int.
3. Papathanassopoulos, 2005:46.
4. UNESCO, 1998.
5. UNESCO, *World Report on Cultural Diversity*, 2009.
6. http://unesdoc.unesco.org/images/0012/001271/127160m.pdf.
7. http://ec.europa.eu/avpolicy/reg/tvwf/index_en.htm.
8. European Parliament and Council, 2007.
9. European Audiovisual Observatory, press release, April 9, 2002, www.obs.coe.int.
10. EBU, "Audiovisual services and GATS negotiations," January 17, 2003.
11. http://europa.eu/legislation_summaries/culture/index_en.htm.
12. www.europarl.europa.eu/summits/lis1_en.htm.
13. EFP was officially founded in 1997 during the Berlin International Film Festival. Its founding members were organisations and institutions from Belgium, Germany, France, Greece, the UK, The Netherlands, Austria, Switzerland and the five Scandinavian states as one country grouping. Shortly afterwards, they were joined by Iceland, Portugal and Spain; by Luxembourg and Italy in 1999; the Czech Republic and Hungary in 2002 and Estonia, Latvia and Lithuania in 2003. By 2009 the EFP ranks had swollen to include Slovenia, Bulgaria, Poland, Romania and Serbia.
14. EU Media Commissioner Viviane Reding, press release, January 9, 2009.
15. Proposal for a Decision of the European Parliament and of the Council for establishing an audiovisual cooperation program with professionals from third-worldcountries, MEDIA Mundus, January 2009.

16. COM, 2005, 494 final: 3.
17. Lilleker, 2006; Price, 1995; Dahlgren, 1995.
18. COM, 2006, 35 final: 4–5.
19. See, for example, Trenz, 2004: 292.
20. Schlesinger, 2007a, 2007b.
21. Lingenberg, 2006: 123.
22. See Brüggemann, 2005; Kunelius and Sparks, 2001; Frydén Bonnier, 2007.
23. Axford and Huggins, 2007; Brüggemann, 2005; Frydén Bonnier, 2007; Kleinsteuber, 2001; Machill et al., 2006; Semetko et al., 2000; Splichal, 2006; Schlesinger, 2007a and 2007b.
24. Gripsrud, 2007: 489.
25. In 2009, the competition took place in Moscow as Russia's Dima Bilan had won in 2008; the 2009 winner, Alexander Rybak, represented Norway, which is not a member of the EU.
26. www.ebu.ch/en/about/index.php.
27. See Widholm, 2009 for an analysis of the content and structure of Euronews programming, and a comparison with other global broadcasters.
28. www.euronews.net/the-station/.
29. KOM, 2004, European Commission, 196 slutlig: 20.
30. This, at least, is the experience of someone who lectures at a European university, at two departments who send and receive a significant number of students on exchange to other European countries each year.
31. Rooke, 2009: 94 cites "Euronews Rebrands to Take on Rivals," *The Guardian*, 2008.
32. www.euronews.net/the-station/.
33. Ibid.
34. The national program was *Rapport*, the main evening newscast of Swedish Television, a public service broadcaster.
35. Frydén Bonnier, 2007.
36. http://eacea.ec.europa.eu/citizenship/programme/action4_en.php.

10

Global Issues, Music, and MTV

Introduction

In the twenty-first century, communication, media, and information exports are becoming the primary engine of the global economy for the United States (US). Since the end of World War II, US aerospace industries have provided the primary export product, with sales of both commercial and military aircraft, to various nations around the world. These sales greatly assisted the US balance of payments as well as domestic employment. But with the end of the Cold War, the aftermath of 9/11, and the economic recession the global demand for aircraft has subsided. In addition, the passenger airline manufacturing business has become a global duopoly between Boeing and its European competitor, Airbus. As a result, makers of US cultural products ranging from movies and TV programs to music and computers are overtaking aerospace as the primary US employers and exporters. A good example of this export phenomenon is Viacom's Music Television (MTV) which is available in 168 countries with a potential audience of 400 million households. It has numerous websites, including MTVNHD in 21 countries. The primary demographic is the age group 12 to 34. This is also the prime group sought by advertisers.

According to the US Department of Commerce, the sale of feature films, TV shows, and home video rentals to foreign markets increased significantly during the 1990s. It is projected that global revenues will exceed $35 billion by 2016. The same reports estimate that the US music industry will account for 50 percent of global sales.[1] American films and music are now global commodities and future sales increases have to come from foreign markets. These commodities are the foot-soldiers of electronic colonialism.

When imported products consisted of military aircraft or jumbo jets, there was little widespread concern among foreign populations. But when the imported products began to consist of mass media outpourings with cultural as well as economic implications, animosity began to grow toward the prevalence of core nations' cultural artifacts, video talent, as well as moral and economic values. Clearly, not everyone or every nation welcomes the globalization of the mass media. Many peripheral nations and some industrialized nations, particularly Canada, Ireland, and France, are concerned about the dominance of US global media exports.[2] David Rothkopf explains the issues:

> Globalization has economic roots and political consequences, but it also has brought into focus the power of culture in this global environment – the power to bind and to divide in a time when the tensions between integration and separation tug at every issue that is relevant to international relations.
>
> The impact of globalization on culture and the impact of culture on globalization merit discussion. The homogenizing influences of globalization that are most often condemned by the new nationalists and by cultural romanticists are actually positive; globalization promotes integration and the removal not only of cultural barriers but of many of the negative dimensions of culture. Globalization is a vital step toward both a more stable world and better lives for the people in it. Furthermore, these issues have serious implications for American foreign policy. For the United States, a central objective of an Information Age foreign policy must be to win the battle of the world's information flows, dominating the airwaves as Great Britain once ruled the seas.[3]

The world's information and media flows have been enhanced by the widespread surge in sales of televisions, DVDs, CD players, iPods, satellite dishes, cable, Kindle, and portable personal computers. In addition, there have been infrastructure advancements such as the growth of Blockbuster Entertainment Corporation's video chain with more than 2,600 outlets in 21 foreign countries, or Tower Records, which has over 70 stores in over 15 countries. On the print side, the amount of US content exported around the world is significant. *Reader's Digest* is the largest selling magazine in the world. It is produced in 21 languages with 50 international editions. It has a combined global circulation of 70 million, about 11 million of which is US-based. It also has 15 other international magazines. Even the Hearst-owned *Cosmopolitan*, a niche magazine for women, has global sales of close to five million copies, with 40 foreign editions in 25 languages.

US media companies frequently enjoy an economic advantage denied to almost all of their offshore competitors. The domestic US audience is not only large and wealthy, but it also has a substantial and varied taste for entertainment and media products of all types. This continent-wide market provides the economic resources necessary to support a global culture. In addition, the latest mass media technologies frequently are introduced within the US marketplace, thus allowing US producers to experiment with and refine technical and marketing strategies before moving offshore to an ever-expanding group of global customers.

These customers are in other core nations as well as in all the semiperipheral and some of the peripheral nations.

This chapter reviews communication exports and the globalization of the media marketplace. The export market for US produced television programming and the international music industry is examined in detail. Particular attention is given to MTV, a network that personifies the marriage of global television with leading musicians, and a global youth culture.

As noted earlier, foreign television networks consume large quantities of US television shows via syndication. Particularly attractive are US made situation comedies and dramas with high production values.[4] Major series such as *Dallas*, *Columbo*, *Star Trek*, *Baywatch*, *Seinfeld*, *ER*, *The Simpsons*, *Cosby*, *Friends*, *Sex and the City*, and others dominate many foreign television schedules. For example, it is estimated that an audience in excess of one billion viewers viewed *Baywatch* in 148 nations. *Baywatch* began in 1989 and lasted 10 years with 210 episodes available for syndication. *The Simpsons* is available in over 70 nations and is the longest running animated comedy.

However, in the 1990s an interesting shift occurred. The major networks replaced these expensive dramas and sitcoms with programs based on reality shows or the news magazine format (similar to CBS's *60 Minutes*). Today, the news genre on national television networks is in trouble from the three competing all-news networks, CNN, FOX News, and MSNBC. But reality shows continue to fill the void. One of the consequences of this trend is a steep increase in the prices of the fewer remaining successful sitcoms, such as *The Simpsons*, *Seinfeld*, *Friends*, *Everyone Loves Raymond*, *Scrubs*, or *Frasier*, available for syndication.

Cost Escalations

Among the reasons why networks are cutting back their production of primetime drama is the high cost of such programming. The cost of prime-time episodes now averages about $1.75 million an hour, about double the cost of an equivalent episode a decade ago. Some series are substantially more expensive: each installment of *ER* costs $13 million; Tim Allen of *Home Improvement* personally received $1.25 million per episode; and even the *The X-Files*, which was for a time filmed in Vancouver, Canada, to keep costs down, costs $2.5 million per episode. Each of the six leading actors on *Friends* received $1 million per half-hour episode – and they walked away from that successful show. With high-profile stars demanding larger salaries and with competition for experienced writers and cast, production costs are increasing dramatically. In comparison, news programming costs about $500,000 an hour. Even "reality" shows such as *America's Most Wanted*, *Survivor*, *Cops*, *Candid Camera*, *You're Fired*, or Cosby's *Kids Say the Darndest Things* are relatively inexpensive compared to the costs of leading dramas, comedy, or broadcasting rights for major sports programming.

Audience Fragmentation

As costs escalate, US networks also need to face the reality of a fragmenting audience. CBS, NBC, and ABC dominated the television market from the inception of the medium until the 1980s, when the FOX network joined them. In June 1998, however, these four networks were for the first time outwatched in prime time by audiences viewing cable options. During the 1990s, viewers deserted the major networks to tune into what are often called "narrowcasting" or niche channels. The rapid growth of alternative cable options, including both specialty channels (ESPN, MTV, A & E, CNN, and MSNBC) and super channels, such as WGN of TBS, had a significant cumulative impact on the audiences for the major television networks. The major networks have been reduced to less than 50 percent of the total prime-time audience. They have been forced to scramble to maintain an audience share sufficient to maintain high advertising rates.[5] The addition of time spent on the internet has also taken a toll on broadcasters.

Clearly, one of the factors making the new media offerings so attractive is their ability to target specific or niche audiences. Another is their programming flexibility, which permits them to address unique high-interest events. Take, for example, the infamous white Ford Bronco low-speed chase and the subsequent trial of former football star O. J. Simpson. This case, involving a well-known personality and a lengthy and sordid trial about sex and murder, captivated enormous audiences in North America and abroad. As the dominant news story of its time, it provided audiences with niche news and public affairs networks, with thousands of hours of programming over several months that not only filled their schedules but also attracted a new and larger audience. While the new players focused on the trial, the Big Four networks found themselves in a no-win situation. Leery about abandoning their traditional audiences by preempting afternoon soap operas or prime-time sitcoms, they limited their coverage to the traditional newscasts. Although these networks retained a portion of their audience, many viewers were motivated to tune in Court-TV or other all-news alternatives they had never watched before. All-news networks cover every detail of these major stories, whereas the Big Four networks are forced to select when and how to preempt their schedules. The media's handling of the hearings before the 9/11 Commission is a case in point.

Clearly, technology is responsible for this proliferation of media options and the continued fragmentation of the viewing audience. The number of cable channels is expanding more rapidly than anticipated. With the advent of digital television, viewers will have access to over 100 channels. Even if only a small number of individuals watch these channels, such as the History Channel, the Spanish Channel, or the Golf Channel, the total impact on the networks in the long run will be staggering. In the final analysis, the Big Four networks are not only losing audiences, but they are also losing revenues, thus limiting their ability to experiment with the same number of sitcoms as the early days of television, when they collectively controlled the entire audience base. This reduction in the number of successful sitcoms means that fewer are available for foreign syndication, and thus their price tags have increased substantially. Although this may reduce the US presence on foreign television screens, a simultaneous increase in the viewing of CNN – particularly when global news stories break, such as the Gulf War, the death of Princess Diana, or international terrorism – is likely to ensure that foreign media continue to carry extensive US programming options. (CNN is covered in detail in Chapter 11.)

As costs escalate, audience size shrinks, and advertising revenues decrease, the major US television networks are reengineering their positions and strategies, not only with respect to each other, but also with respect to the myriad cable channels now available. As more broadcast, cable, DVDs, and internet options become available to viewers, General Electric's NBC, CBS Corporation, FOX, and Walt Disney's ABC network are cutting staff. These decisions reflect the reality of escalating programming costs and decreasing viewer ship. Of the original Big Three networks, NBC is well situated, primarily because it responded to the cable challenge by introducing its own specialty channels – MSNBC and CNBC – as a means of competing for the advertising revenue available to these niche markets. NBC also established channels in Europe and Asia. Yet many analysts suggest that these efforts are insufficient and predict that major industry restructuring, including mergers will continue in the future.

New International Realities

Despite the problems, foreign markets are still lucrative for US producers. The proliferation of media options is increasingly an international phenomenon, and this creates new opportunities for US program sales abroad. As technology has led to increased media choices, so also governmental media and regulatory policies have had to adapt. Historically, much of broadcasting, originally radio and then television, in the industrialized countries outside the United States were dominated by public government-supported systems. The British Broadcasting Corporation (BBC) served as the model for many national media networks, particularly in British colonies. For many years, for example, most European viewers had access to only one or two public television channels, which were publicly financed and carried no advertising. Neither private networks, cable, nor satellite services were available or licensed. This situation changed substantially in the late 1980s when privatization, deregulation, liberalization, and commercialization took hold around the globe.

In an era when broadcasting options were limited to one or two public media outlets, regulation was significant. In fact, the rationale for public, as opposed to private, broadcasting relied on the notion that the electronic mass media were social institutions with certain public accountability goals. These media were assigned responsibility for providing educational broadcasting, promoting democracy and human rights, and providing balanced programming. With the introduction of private broadcasting outlets, government regulation was reduced in favor of market forces. Today, this duopoly between public and private broadcasting systems coexists in most industrialized nations. As a result, the viewing and listening public now has substantially more media choices, and US producers have larger markets for their products. Not surprisingly, a growing number of the foreign options have a distinct made-in-America flavor.

Modeling: Creating Indigenous Programs with US Cultural Values

Most foreign nations, with significantly smaller audience bases, are unable to compete with the expensive, high-quality production values of US dramatic television programming. In order to fill the available broadcast schedule and maximize their revenues, they purchase US syndicated programming. Consequently, many nations, industrialized and less developed alike, experience significant erosion of their own cultures. But the issue does not end with the direct importation of US programming.

A more insidious practice has emerged which further threatens national cultures. As mentioned earlier, the US networks have introduced lower-cost reality-based programs or game shows. Although these programs are attractive to US audiences, they do not export well. Because their themes tend to be parochial and time sensitive, their chances for foreign syndication and release are marginal. Instead, foreign producers tend to copy the news magazine or reality show format and insert local content, announcers, or venues. In Australia, for example, which imports significant numbers of US feature films and television productions for domestic consumption, home-grown productions increasingly look very much like US programming. A few examples illustrate the point. Australia has its own version of NBC's *Today Show*; an equivalent of the *Newlywed Game* called *A Current Affair*; a clone of MTV's *Real World* entitled *A House from Hell*; its own *Wheel of Fortune, Funniest Home Videos*, and *60 Minutes*. Thus, even when there is indigenous production capacity, the US influence is visible on foreign television throughout the industrial world, particularly in English-speaking countries. Great Britain, Canada, Ireland, and New Zealand, also major consumers of US television and feature films model many local productions after US counterparts.

The tendency to produce adaptations of US models has both cultural and programmatic implications.[6] Of significant concern is the different manner in which the United States and other nations view cultural industries. The US rationale for promoting television, feature films, DVDs, records, CDs, and other cultural products is based on the notion that the marketplace will determine winners and losers. Sometimes the winners, such as the movie *Titanic, Slum Dog Millionaire*, or *My Big Fat Greek Wedding*, reap enormous rewards for their producers. Other films are duds and force their parent studios into bankruptcy. This is the price investors are willing to pay to ensure that the marketplace rules. This attitude contrasts dramatically with the perception of almost all other nations, which view cultural industries from a non-economic perspective. For them, films, DVDs, radio, music, CDs, and other media products are an expression of their historical roots, current culture, and future destiny. In order to ensure an indigenous media presence, many of these countries subsidize their national radio and television networks, feature film industry, and other cultural sectors.

France provides an outstanding example of the extent to which a country is willing to use tax revenues to subsidize media productions and products to compete directly with US cultural industries. Primarily, although not solely, owing to language constraints, domestic French productions tend to fare poorly in the open global market. The government helped finance the film *Asterix* – at a cost of $50 million, the most expensive French film ever made – in an attempt to recapture part of the French domestic market. Currently, French films garner less than 50 percent of the French market.

The French and other European markets are facing an additional threat – the growth of the US – style multiplex cinema. Although the cineplex has increased the number of screens and cinema attendance, it has failed to create an increase in audiences for European films. Rather, it has promoted the further penetration of US movies in foreign markets, and US box office receipts continue to escalate. Today Hollywood reaps more than half of its profits from offshore audiences, compared with only 25 percent in the early 1980s. Given this shift in profit figures, Hollywood producers are now spending significant sums to market major blockbusters internationally. These multimillion-dollar marketing budgets alone dwarf the amounts available to produce entire films by independent competitors around the globe.[7] Finally, these same Hollywood production houses have added DVDs to their revenue stream with some foreign sales of DVDs exceeding domestic (US) DVD sales.

Global Media Marketplace

The global media marketplace is perceived as being under the control of the United States, which exports its culture through television shows, movies, music, McDonald's, sportswear, and shopping malls. However, Rod Carveth, who agrees that the economy is becoming globally integrated, suggests that the US may be losing its competitive advantage.[8] According to Carveth and others, the US needs to change its strategy if it wants to regain its predominant position in the global media industry. These analysts contend that a number of developments, such as global media mergers and acquisitions; legal and cultural import barriers in the European Union (EU), Canada, and Japan; as well as strategic miscalculations by US media firms, has eroded the country's competitive advantage.[9] In order to reassert itself, strategists suggest that the US must adopt a cooperative rather than a competitive strategy in international media.

For years the United States maintained an international advantage because of its superior talent, technical, marketing, and capital resources. The domestic industry also benefited from the export of its products to foreign markets. In addition foreign talent wanted to work in New York or Hollywood. Throughout this period, US superiority in electronic media was evident, and the US failed to anticipate any competition from foreign markets.

As an early leader in the electronics industry, the US was unprepared when it began to lose its competitive advantage to Japanese and European manufacturers. During the 1980s, major US consumer electronics manufacturers such as RCA abandoned the industry. Although research and development fell off in the US, it blossomed internationally, particularly in Germany, Japan, and France, where substantial strides were made. The US international media presence was further weakened when many countries, including Canada,[10] began to impose restrictions on US media exports as they simultaneously began to subsidize their own media productions, thus creating more programming to compete with US media products. In addition, when twelve European nations joined to form the European Union in the 1950s, they began to open up the former Soviet Union and eastern European countries to freer trade with Europe and Japan. European media companies such as Bertelsmann, Hachette, Canal+, and Pathé began to compete in the global marketplace. Moreover, they were prepared to meet the increasing demand for European-produced programming that reflected the unique identities of Europeans.

Another factor that weakened US domination was a series of mergers or acquisitions through which foreign corporations gained control of US media undertakings. The trend of merger and acquisition activity began when Australian-born media baron Rupert Murdoch and his company News Corporation acquired newspapers such as the *New York Post*, the *Chicago Sun-Times*, and the *Boston Herald*. Another player was Robert Maxwell of the United Kingdom who purchased Macmillan publishing and Saatchi & Saatchi (United Kingdom), the successful international advertising conglomerate. Perhaps the most high-profile acquisition of a media company was that of Columbia Pictures by Japan's Sony Corporation, but others included Hachette's (France) purchase of the Diamond's magazine chain, the sale of A & M Records to Philips (The Netherlands), Bertelsmann's (Germany) acquisition of RCA/Ariolas Records, and VNU's (The Netherlands) take-over of the Neilsen rating company. Non-US companies have consolidated as well, in order to strengthen their combined market share.

In all of these cases, the players were motivated by an appreciation of the manner in which the mergers would permit the companies to combine their strengths to achieve savings in production, distribution, and exhibition of media products on a global scale. They anticipated some type of positive synergy. Moreover, these foreign companies wanted to gain access to the vital US market.

Given the changing global media marketplace and barriers preventing the United States from becoming an international broadcaster, Carveth and others contend that it is important for US firms to merge with and/or acquire international companies if the country wants to regain its international competitive edge. The US needs to jump on the merger and acquisition bandwagon. Virtually every other nation in the world, including those in the European Union, lack sufficient domestic programming to meet their future media goals.[11] The best strategy for ensuring US access to these markets is for domestic companies to form alliances with international players. The resulting co-productions will open new markets. In 1990, for example, NBC and London-based Yorkshire Television formed a joint venture called Tango Productions, which enabled NBC to avoid or at least minimize the import regulations of the EU when selling its media products. Other joint ventures have developed between US and non–US firms. Clear Channel Communications of San Antonio, Texas, now holds interests in several global firms, including a 50 percent stake in the Australian Radio Network (ARN), to go along with approximately 1,200 US radio stations.

The International Music Industry

In the early 2000s, global music sales were over $40 billion. The three leading regions in terms of sales are the United States, Europe, and Japan. English is by far the dominant language for the artists, with one notable exception. The exception is the growing niche market for Spanish music and this is primarily due to one artist: Ricky Martin. The global industry is in a state of flux for two reasons. First, there is a series of potential acquisitions as the industry consolidates on a global basis, and second, how to deal with both legal and illegal downloading of music from the internet.[12]

In examining the music industry, it is important to recognize that most of the relevant information is collected and maintained by Billboard using Soundscan data. SoundScan data collects point-of-sale information on all music formats and configurations sold at about 80 percent of the US retail outlets, and then projects sales for the entire US marketplace. Those data provide a wealth of knowledge about the industry.

Historically the international music industry was dominated by five major global players, all from core nations: Universal Music Group (France), Sony Music (Japan), EMI Group (UK), Warner Music (US) and Bertelsmann (Germany). In 2003, however, Sony Music merged with Bertelsmann's BMG, cutting the number of majors to four. But a new firm, Live Nation Artists, has now taken the fifth spot (Figure 10.1). Of the top five, only two are American owned. Most recording artists need to rely on the US market to recoup their companies' investments in the first album, which now requires the additional expense of video production as part of the initial promotion package. It is estimated that first video album costs now exceed $1 million.

The major players usually control every aspect of the supply chain from copyright on the music through the distribution cycle to the consumer. The corporations have extensive sales outlets in all core nations, all semiperipheral nations, and now some peripheral nations. The dominant artistic language is English, giving a substantial advantage to British and North American artists and bands. Finally, as discussed elsewhere, MTV's global television niche for the teenage market has also served to promote the global expansion of the video music industry.

1   Universal Music Group (France)
2   Sony Music Entertainment (Japan)
3   Warner Music (US)
4   EMI Group (United Kingdom)
5   Live Nation (US)

Figure 10.1   Big five music companies, 2010

Although there are several independent labels, and some occasionally do well with individual records such as Disney soundtracks for movies such as *Pocahontas* or *The Lion King*, the bulk of the global sales, approaching 75 percent, are controlled by the Big Five. Further details concerning their activities and artists are discussed in the following section, along with the role of MTV in the global music scene.

Universal Music Group (France)

The largest global music company is Universal Music Group (UMG). It has two core business units: recorded music and music publishing and is owned by Vivendi of France. UMG has ventures in 77 countries, over 10,000 employees, and more than 25 percent of the world's market for music of all types. It also controls the third largest music-publishing group. UMG also owns the world's leading Latin music company, UM Latin Entertainment. Leading Latin musicians need to sign up with this New York-based, French-owned, company. It is a clear "case study" of electronic colonialism since all Latin countries are in the semiperipheral or peripheral zones.

UMG has 18 record labels, such as Decca and UMG Nashville. Some of UMG's artists include ABBA, Brian Adams, Elton John, Vince Gill, Guns 'N' Roses, Enrique Iglesias, Sheryl Crow, Rolling Stones, Sting, Bon Jovi, Black Eyed Peas, and Shania Twain. It also has almost half of the global sales in the classical music genre.

Until 2000 UMG was a division of Seagram's of Canada. It is also aggressive in providing online music. A major factor in UMG's size and success was the acquisition of PolyGram Records in 1998 by the Seagram group. PolyGram was a major European-based music giant that traced its origin to Siemens Corp., established in 1898. Mergers and acquisitions have been the hallmark of the music recording industry as illustrated by the size and activities of the major record conglomerates. In 2010 it plans to roll out a new online music site, Vevo.

Sony Music Entertainment (Japan)

The second largest music conglomerate is the Sony Music Entertainment Group, the product of a 2004 merger between the music divisions of Sony Corporation of Japan and Bertelsmann of Germany. The newly merged company ran into corporate cultural issues and by 2008 Sony bought out the 50 percent Bertelsmann stake. Sony music controls approximately 25 percent of the global music market.

Sony got into the record business when it acquired CBS Records Group in 1988. Sony's music labels include Columbia, Arista, Epic, RCA Victor, Sony Classical, Legacy, and others. It has major recording artists under contract such as Celine Dion, Mariah Carey, Will Smith, Ice Cube, Barbara Streisand, Charlotte Church, and Bob Dylan. Sony jointly owns the Columbia House record club with Warner Music. Sony has always geared its musical interests to a global, as well as English-language, platform. This global reach reflects its corporate desire to be a Japanese-based corporation with the bulk of its corporate activities carried out in other core nations, as well as semiperipheral and some peripheral nations.

Before its merger with Sony, the Bertelsmann Music Group (BMG) was the fifth-largest music conglomerate. Bertelsmann is an enormous, privately owned, European-based multimedia conglomerate. BMG brought to the merger over 200 record labels including Arista, RCA Victor, and Ariola. Some of BMG's better-known artists were Whitney Houston, Carlos Santana, Elvis Presley, Frank Sinatra, Duke Ellington, David Bowie, the Chieftains, and Barry Manilow.

The Sony music group also provides the music for Playstation 3 and they have a content deal with YouTube.

Warner Music Group (United States)

When Time Inc. took over Warner Bros. in the late 1980s, it also acquired the Warner Music Group. It is the third largest record company, after UMG and Sony. In 2000 Time Warner tried to purchase EMI Music of the United Kingdom, which would have allowed it to control one-third of the global market. The $20 billion deal was dropped because the EU raised antitrust objections.

The record labels controlled by Warner Bros. are Warner Music International, Elektra, Atlantic, Maverick, Reprise, and Rhino. Some of its 1,000 artists are the Red Hot Chili Peppers, Eric Clapton, Faith Hill, and Sammy Davis Jr. In addition to being available at record stores around the globe, Warner Bros.'s artists' music is also available through Warner's online site or through over 150 Warner Bros. stores located in core nations as well as Mexico, the Middle East, and the Pacific Rim. Warner is also a major music publisher. More than half its revenue came from outside the US, but it is still seeking a larger share of the EU market.

In November 2003, Warner Music was sold for $2.6 billion to a group of investors led by Edgar Bronfman Jr. Bronfman, a third-generation Seagram heir, is a native of Canada, but Warner Music remains based in New York. The company had a dispute with Google's YouTube over copyright issues. As a result no Warner musicians were played on YouTube videos until 2009 when it was resolved.

EMI Group (United Kingdom)

The fourth largest music group is EMI, which includes the major labels EMI, Capitol, and Virgin Records. Some of EMI's most popular artists are Diana Ross, Ice Cube, Garth Brooks, the Spice Girls, the Beatles, Norah Jones, Keith Urban, and the Beach Boys. EMI is also the world's largest publisher of sheet music, controlling over one million copyrights. It also has internet interests that offer digital downloads and other e-commerce services.

In October 1999, EMI's merger with Time Warner was abandoned. The $20 billion joint venture would have created the largest music group in the world and provided Warner Music with much greater European sales, which it needs. The European Union's (EU) Merger Task Force opposed the merger. Mario Monti, the former EU competition commissioner, threatened to hold up the merger of AOL and Time Warner unless Time Warner agreed to walk away from the EMI takeover. Some critics speculated that the EU merger officials had an anti-North American agenda in denying the Time Warner deal, considering that the overall music industry is going through a wave of mergers. In 2004 EMI acquired Mute and still continues to add other sheet music properties.

In 2007 EMI was acquired by Terra Firma Capital Partners and since then they have been losing market share and a few artists such as The Rolling Stones and Radiohead. For the first time the company has less than 10 percent of the global media market. It appears that the new owners do not understand the band culture and idiosyncrasies. To complicate matters some former artists have been poisoning the recruiting well with well publicized complaints about the new partners.

Live Nation

This is a distant fifth music and events company formed in 2005. Live Nation's music interests are run by Live Nation Artists. Under contract are Madonna, U2, Jay-Z, Shakira, and Nickelback, a Canadian band. Madonna left Warner Music to join Live Nation. Live Nation owns the House of Blues and promotes several concerts across Europe. In the future it hopes to sign more artists who are dissatisfied with the onerous terms in their current record contracts with other companies.

Synopsis

The five global music groups have extensive corporate activities in many nations. The bulk of the artists, whether contemporary, alternative, rap, classical, country, or rock, are English-speaking artists. The music producers also control as much of the production process as possible, from finding new talent to web-based purchases. The five giant music producers have corporate roots in the United States, Japan, and Europe. They have become industry leaders through a series of mergers and acquisitions, which are likely to continue in the future despite the anti-US bias of the EU's merger commission.

A second significant aspect is that all the major record companies have established significant web-based marketing, retail, and promotion sites for their artists. Yet, as digital distribution systems become available through the internet, some speculate about the long-term consequences for the global recording industry. In response, some recording companies and groups have initiated legal action against the rapidly expanding internet sites that provide non-royalty copies in digital format to internet clients. Future internet online music business is estimated to be worth billions of dollars. The issue is whether consumers will purchase or simply download the necessary software to create audio files, which are technically equivalent to CDs. Several firms are offering MP3 solutions, which permit high-quality digital audio to be recorded and downloaded by home servers. MP3 is the industry term for the new data compression system that allows the pirating of music over the internet, an activity that could clearly undermine and change, perhaps forever, the economics of the global recording industry. The movement toward a free virtual jukebox has been altered, as both UMG and Sony have become shareholders in MP3 format firms. Now they have established a fee structure. Although the internet is discussed elsewhere in this book, it is worth noting here that every single electronic medium is susceptible to change as a result of the internet environment.

Finally, it is worth noting that a number of high profile individual artists have been trying to get out of their lifetime recording contracts. They sign these agreements when they are virtually unknown and the contracts are heavily weighted in favor of the recording studios. Many refer to the terms as servitude.

MTV: The Dominant Global Music Connection

Music recordings are a powerful entertainment medium in their own right. When offered in conjunction with the excitement of video, their appeal is even stronger. Not surprisingly, young people are tuning in to Viacom's Music Television (MTV) channels around the world. MTV reaches over 340 million viewers in 140 countries, particularly in Europe and Asia, and currently is the world's largest television network, broadcast in one-third of the world's TV-viewing households. Viewed primarily by preteens, teens, and young adults, MTV is an impressive global youth television phenomenon. Comprised of 100 affiliated international networks including MTV Latino, MTV Brazil, MTV Europe, MTV Mandarin, MTV Asia, MTV India, MTV Australia, MTV New Zealand, and MTV Africa the MTV network already has the ability to reach a large proportion of the world's youth each day. Moreover, new MTV networks are under consideration. MTV has signed a licensing deal with Russia, anticipating that the country's youth are now ready to tune in to a 24-hour music television network. MTV Russia will likely reach more than 10 million households and feature musicians such as Madonna, U2,

Prince, Nirvana, and the Spice Girls, as well as local Russian groups. Over 80 percent of MTV's total audience is now outside the United States.

MTV was the first 24-hour, 7-day-a-week music video network. It is supported by advertising and constitutes a basic service on most cable networks. Targeted at the 12- to 34-year-old age group, MTV's international satellite-delivered music programming reaches millions daily around the globe. Owned by Viacom, MTV operates several cable television programming services – Music Television, MTV2, VH1, Nickelodeon/Nick at Nite, Country Music Television (CMT), TNN, and TV Land (Figure 10.2). MTV is also experimenting with the internet and its own websites in order to examine the possibilities of providing music in online ventures.

Although there are an estimated 80,000 websites devoted to music, many of which have become digital shrines to major recording artists, MTV.com is the most popular music website in the world. MTV has an internet subsidiary called MTV Group, which controls all MTV websites and the number of websites is enormous. The internet properties are MTV.com, VH1.com, SonicNet.com, various international websites, chatrooms, news, streaming audio, and MTV merchandise.

Because music tastes are highly localized, MTV's global airtime is filled with locally produced programming and American shows. Despite that fact, teens around the world basically are listening to and viewing the same music videos. For example, in 1996, Madonna, Queen, and the Rolling Stones topped the charts of MTV Latino. Although MTV Europe reserves 30 percent of its broadcast hours for indigenous European groups, American artists dominate MTV Europe's top 10 artists. In 2001, MTV Japan went on the air as a 24-hour Japanese-language service. Of course, it goes without saying that musical groups who fail to produce a video to accompany their recording releases are simply excluded from MTV's playtime. Just as CNN has altered the global news business forever, so MTV has altered the global music trade.

Given MTV's popularity, advertising is another issue that bears attention. According to Jay Pettegrew and Roy Shukar,[13] MTV worldwide is one large continuous commercial advertising network. Not only are the music videos "commercials" designed to enhance the sale of albums, but advertising for other products also surrounds them, and many artists openly promote commercial products within the music videos themselves. Many critics assert that MTV is a commercial propaganda outlet specifically aimed at impressionable teenagers.

Clearly, MTV promotes Western popular culture worldwide. Any reciprocal play is limited by the nature of MTV's North American broadcasting schedule. The westernization of global culture is further enhanced by the basic fact that much of MTV programming and most music videos are produced in English. Even MTV Asia's interactive chatline, which requires internet access, functions in English. Concerns about the pervasive commercialism and cultural imperialism of MTV programming worldwide are growing. Jack Banks puts the global influence this way.

> Music video is at its core a type of advertisement for cultural products: films, soundtracks, recorded music, live concerts, fashion apparel depicted in the clip and even the

```
 1   MTV Adria
 2   MTV Africa
 3   MTV Arabia
 4   MTV Asia
 5   MTV Australia
 6   MTV Base UK and Ireland
 7   MTV Brand New Italy
 8   MTV Brazil
 9   MTV Canada
10   MTV China
11   MTV Estonia
12   MTV Europe
13   MTV France
14   MTV Germany
15   MTV Hits Italy
16   MTV Hits UK and Ireland
17   MTV Hungary
18   MTV Idol France
19   MTV India
20   MTV Israel
21   MTV Italy
22   MTV Japan
23   MTV Korea
24   MTV Latin America
25   MTV Latin America Revolution
26   MTV Latvia
27   MTV Lithuania
28   MTV Netherlands
29   MTV Networks Europe
30   MTV New Zealand
31   MTV Nordic: Norway, Sweden, Finland, Denmark
32   MTV Pakistan
33   MTV Philippines
34   MTV Poland
35   MTV Portugal
36   MTV Romania
37   MTV Russia
38   MTV Spain
39   MTV Tawain/Hong Kong
40   MTV Thailand
41   MTV Turkey
42   MTV UK and Ireland
43   MTV Ukraine
44   MTV2 UK
```

Figure 10.2   MTV worldwide, 2010

music clip itself as home video retail product. Omnipresent play of music videos on MTV (and elsewhere) helps shape global demand for this array of products.[14]

Similarly after examining MTV's impact across Asia, Stacey Sowards concludes:

> While MTV Asia has made appropriate, culturally aware marketing decisions that has allowed it to establish a firm base in Asia, the programming is still largely a manifestation of American culture. The differences in comparison to MTV in the United States are surface structural changes at best. There are several programs that are Asia specific; however, many of them are not, but are simply exported from the United States in the same way that *Dallas* and *Baywatch* are. More than 50 percent of MTV Asia's programs are imported directly from MTV in the United States. Additionally, American popular culture is ubiquitous throughout programs; even those that attempt to include Asian cultures. The programs that incorporate Asian cultures reflect American culture, through the way the VJs speak, the music that is aired, and the image that is portrayed. Even the use of Asian VJs fails to avoid the hegemonic nature of MTV Asia, since they also speak English, and attempt to represent American cultures and ideology through fashion and music selection. In fact, the American essence of MTV Asia is probably what attracts such a large Asian viewer ship. Additionally, MTV Asia also has the effect of Americanizing Asian music, as seen by Asian musicians whose key influences are American bands. Furthermore, to be able to watch MTV Asia, one must have access to a satellite dish, excluding most of Southeast Asia, except those that have enough money, usually the elites.[15]

In 2008, the MTV network incorporated political coverage of elections into a segment called *Choose or Lose*, which called on young people to "vote loud." Viewers aged between 18 and 24 accounted for nearly 20 percent of the voters in the US. Presidential contenders and companies such as AT & T and Ford Motor Company now recognize the potential of MTV's campaign coverage to bring their messages into the homes of the 20-somethings. By focusing on the "three Es" – education, economy, and environment – *Choose or Lose* became the primary broker for 30 million young voters who were MTV viewers, while simultaneously providing a venue for candidates and major companies that wanted to target younger audiences for their commercials.

Another example of MTV's social commitment is its AIDS awareness campaign *Staying Alive* which started in 1998. A variety of annual efforts to educate young people about the risks of AIDS and to engage in safe sex practices is the goal of the efforts by MTV assisted by performers Beyonce, Justin Timberlake, Sean Combs, and others.

MTV and Electronic Colonialism

One clear example of the application of the theory of electronic colonialism is found in music television, globally known as MTV. MTV has attempted to colonize not a broad range of viewers and listeners, but rather a select niche, namely the youth culture (Figure 10.3). MTV wants the minds of this global youth culture to follow them and buy the products which surround the music videos as commercials. They also want to influence how these viewers look and think.

1   Music Television
2   MTV2
3   mtvU
4   VH1
5   Nickelodeon/Nick at Nite
6   Country Music Television
7   Comedy Central
8   Spike
9   Logo

Figure 10.3   MTV's global youth culture, 2010

Demographically this is an important group, particularly for advertisers of youth-oriented products, which range from clothes to cultural products such as films, records, PCs, DVDs, and iPods. MTV seeks on a global scale to influence the attitudes, preferences, and purchasing behaviors of teenagers and people in their twenties around the globe. MTV promotes a mainstream diet of primarily British and American artists, plus non-Anglo musicians who usually mimic the format of individual artists or bands that are mainstream in either the US or Europe. They also offer reality shows. MTV does this in order to continue expanding its reach and influence on the attitudes of the younger set in as many nations as possible. MTV is not solely concerned with music or the issues and themes surrounding the music industry; its goal is to positively influence the global teenage audience into accepting commercial habits and products that are predominantly from core nations. In this market-orientated process MTV will produce a handsome profit for its parent, Viacom.

In order to further colonize and capitalize on the global youth culture, MTV has turned to the internet. MTV's own internet service, MTVi Group, seeks young customers with credit cards who can download music materials from the internet for a fee. MTV is banking on the notion that around the globe there are a number of teenagers with sufficient disposable income to purchase music and merchandise over the internet. After years of relentless consumerism on MTV, management hopes it will ultimately pay off through internet-based purchases.

Through electronic colonialism, MTV has managed to marginalize many indigenous artists and indigenous genres of music, from aboriginal music in Australia, to African music, to non-traditional Indian music.[16] MTV gives little time or exposure to these alternative genres. As Jack Banks in his article, "MTV and the Globalization of Popular Culture," notes, MTV has become so influential that both Hollywood film studios and the global record conglomerates now not only use MTV as a major advertising vehicle to reach the teenage audience, but they are also coordinating on a global scale the release of new films or new videos on a preferential basis through MTV's global network.[17]

MTV was one of the first cultural industry giants to recognize the expanding global economy and become a key part of it. Individual artists around the globe will lament their marginalization due to MTV, but, as Banks further notes, "Clearly MTV and music video are influencing the emerging global economy as well as the contours of a global popular culture – what remains uncertain is the role played by MTV in molding a global consensus about the shape of this economy and culture."[18] Given the expanding global strategic plan of Viacom, MTV's parent company, MTV has come to represent the music video juggernaut. That is, if you are a musician who is part of it, you reach a global audience and become rich and world famous virtually overnight; but if you are not part of MTV, your chances of succeeding as a music video artist in any significant way are reduced substantially.

Conclusions

The global media market is in a state of constant change. Much of the change is fueled by new communication companies, technologies, and business practices of core nations. The expansion of cable and satellite delivery systems has provided significant growth internationally for television audiences. These audiences are familiar with US television shows and, as the number of television channels expands through global privatization, liberalization of regulations, and in some cases total deregulation, there will be a host of new customers and viewers for Hollywood sitcoms, TV movies, music videos, and network syndicated shows. Concomitantly, this expanding foreign market has facilitated the growth of cultural industries in the US. It has significantly increased their role and influence within the US economy. Their future role also looks bright, as there is an almost insatiable demand for made-in-America television, music, and movie productions.

One particular medium that has done exceptionally well both domestically and globally is MTV. The marriage of music and video, with most musicians from core nations, has permitted the rapid expansion of this major music television network. The only cloud on the horizon is the emergence of the internet and the strong possibility of digital quality music and shows being pirated from internet sites. This phenomenon could allow listeners to bypass local music outlets, thereby affecting how the product of international music stars is packaged, distributed, and priced in the near future. However, the industry, along with its trade associations, has been fairly successful in recent attempts to protect copyrights (and therefore, to protect profits) against the threat posed by internet file-sharing.

Finally, although the literature and thrust of cultural imperialism has lost its spark, there are still a number of vocal critics. Much of the criticism is aimed at US-based industries, particularly Hollywood, but also to a lesser extent television shows with large global export markets, such as *Baywatch* or *The Simpsons*, or the MTV network. What is interesting is that foreign owned and controlled communication giants such as Bertelsmann and Sony have managed to avoid the storm of criticism directed at Hollywood in general and Disney, Viacom, and

Time Warner, in particular. Yet at the same time, these foreign firms have enjoyed, from a fiscal perspective, the growing market for cultural products around the globe. These foreign firms have recognized the increased importance of US cultural industries, particularly the profitability associated with successful global sales, but they have somehow managed to dodge the hostile criticism that continues to emanate from critical school theorists in Europe, Latin America, and North America. The ubiquity of music and other mass culture products is spread globally but produced by a few core nations, yet the shrill rhetoric of concern and protest is aimed mainly at one core nation: the United States.[19]

Notes

1. *Entertainment and the Electronic Media*, New York and Washington, DC: McGraw-Hill and US Department of Commerce, 1999, pp. 321–9. For a detailed decade-by-decade analysis of US television sales abroad, see Kerry Segrave, *American Television Abroad: Hollywood's Attempt to Dominate World Television*, North Carolina: McFarland, 1998.

2. Some nations have gone to great lengths to thwart the intrusion of Western popular culture. The overthrow of the Shah of Iran was motivated in large part by distaste for the Western values, media, and culture he was promoting in Iran. When the Taliban controlled Afghanistan it took drastic measures, ordering the removal of all televisions, VCRs, and satellite receivers from the country. Canada has taken a less draconian approach. For decades that country has attempted to reduce the influence of US mass media through the promulgation of Canadian content rules that require the media to produce and distribute Canadian material. The French-speaking province of Quebec has gone even further to protect its cultural heritage by instituting a provincial language policy that requires the use of French as the predominant language of business and culture in the province. Language "police" oversee the use of French in all commercial enterprises, going so far as to demand that the French lettering on signs be twice as large as their English counterparts.

3. David Rothkopf, "In Praise of Cultural Imperialism," *Foreign Policy*, 107 (1997): 39.

4. As a general rule, TV sitcoms or dramas need to have at least a three-year run to be successfully syndicated. This provides approximately 66 episodes that can then be sold as a package for either the domestic rerun market or international syndication. Clearly, shows with successful runs of five or more years in syndication enjoy substantial secondary revenue streams in addition to their lucrative initial showings. Now with DVDs, the ownership rights for some shows or movies are a license to print money.

5. Because of high costs, the number of foreign network news bureaus also has been reduced. For example, CBS foreign news bureaus, which once numbered 12; now operate in only four cities – London, Moscow, Tokyo, and Tel Aviv. Yet they continue to hire brilliant foreign journalists, such as Shelia McVicker in Europe.

6. The use of US media models and strategies is not limited to the mimicking of cultural industries but extends even into the field of politics. Britain's former Prime Minister, Tony Blair, hired media consultants to model his political campaign, emulating the successful style of former US President Clinton. Former Chancellor Schroeder of Germany also employed made-in-America campaign techniques including the extensive use of sophisticated polling in order to conduct his successful election campaign.

US political consultants now have branch offices located throughout Europe, Latin America, and elsewhere. They offer assistance to political candidates who wish to utilize the successful media strategies and tactics developed over the last three decades in the United States. This breadth of experience gives these US political media consultants a global market advantage.

This trend is not without its critics. During the 1999 Israeli election campaign, a Washington-based pollster's role became a controversial part of the Labor Party's campaign. In Sweden the Social Democratic Party's hiring of a high-profile US consultant became an issue in the campaign. Clearly, just as there are critics of the Americanization of television and popular culture, so too there are vocal opponents of the Americanization of the political process, particularly during national election campaigns. Much of the US consultants's advice is about how to use and appear on television, as well as how to run negative commercials about their opponents. But in the final analysis this phenomena is just another niche example of the pervasiveness of electronic colonialism theory.

7. Additional details about the plight of the European movie industry are contained in *The Economist* (February 6, 1999): 68. For a more in-depth analysis, see *European Audiovisual Conference, Challenges and Opportunities of the Digital Age*, Brussels: European Commission, 1997.

8. Rod Carveth, "The Reconstruction of the Global Media Marketplace," *Communication Research*, 19(6) (1992): 705.

9. Alison Alexander, James Ovens, and Rod Carveth (eds.), *Media Economics: Theory and Practice*, New Jersey: Lawrence Erlbaum, 1998.

10. Thomas McPhail and Brenda McPhail, *Communication: The Canadian Experience*, Toronto: Copp Clark Pitman, 1990.

11. R. Carvelh, J. Ovens, A. Alexander, and J. Fletcher, "The Economics of International Media," in A. Alexander, J. Ovens, and R. Carveth (eds.), *Media Economics: Theory and Practice*, New Jersey: Lawrence Erlbaum, 1998, pp. 223–45.

12. A look at the turmoil caused by the internet is also detailed in *The Economist* (June 16, 2001): 617.

13. Jay Pettegrew, "A Post-M Moment: Commercial Culture and the Founding of MTV," in G. Dines and J. Hunez (eds.), *Gender, Race, and Class in Media*, Thousand Oaks, CA Sage, 1995, pp. 488–98; and Roy Shukar, *Understanding Popular Music*, London: Routledge, 1994.

14. Jack Banks, "MTV and the Globalization of Popular Culture," *Gazette*, 51(1) (1997): 58.

15. Stacey Sowards, "MTV Asia: Cultural Imperialism in Southeast Asia," paper presented at the National Communication Association Annual Conference, New York, fall 1998.

16. Tony Mitchell, "Treaty Now! Indigenous Music and Music Television in Australia," *Media, Culture and Society*, 15(2) (1993): 299–308.

17. Banks, 1997, p. 51. For a detailed analysis of music videos, see Jack Banks, *Monopoly Television: MTV's Quest to Control the Music*, Colorado: Westview Press, 1996.

18. Banks, 1997, p. 59.

19. To counter this phenomenon, the US needs to focus more attention and funds on the area of public diplomacy; that is why this edition has a chapter on the subject for the first time.

11

CNN

International Role, Impact, and Global Competitors

Introduction

Memories from major global breaking news stories – such as the coverage of China's Tiananman Square protest, both Gulf Wars, the death of Princess Diana in Paris, the Asian tsunami, the fallout following the 2008 Iranian elections, riots, and in the US, the O. J. Simpson, Kobe Bryant, Martha Stewart, Scott Peterson, Robert Blake, and Bernard Madoff legal difficulties – are reminders that the press is on site to bring the viewing public up-to-the-minute news' stories. Newsgathering in the United States is plentiful and apparent on ABC, CBS, FOX, NBC, and other news outlets. In addition, there are now three US all-news channels: CNN, MSNBC, and FOX News. There are two global all-news networks: CNN and the BBC World Television Service.

Major US, European, and Asian television broadcasters have been covering international events since the 1930s. Foreign broadcasters such as the British Broadcasting Corporation (BBC) and Germany's Deutsche Welle, along with many international bureaus of major television networks, have been covering global events on their evening newscasts for decades. What is different now is that the Cable News Network (CNN) changed the global media format in a dramatic way. Viewing went from a format based on 30- or 60-minute prime time newscasts to a 24-hour format that focused on news and public affairs programming from both national and global perspectives. CNN and other all-news networks thrive on controversy, breaking news stories, coups and earthquakes, and stories that go on for days, or even weeks, such as the tsunami response of December 2004. Another example is the 2000 Florida election recount saga which saw CNN's audience rating increase six-fold, while four-year-old MSNBC experienced its highest ratings ever. CNN has attracted competition because it proved there was a niche market for all-news television. CNN is a media property of Time Warner and has been losing market share, particularly to FOX News. More is said about this phenomenon later.

News crosses domestic and international boundaries without regard to time or space. International communication and new technologies have had a profound effect on news institutions, news sources, newsgathering techniques, and audiences almost everywhere. The global media trend grew throughout the twentieth century along with the global economy. This was made possible by radio, wire services, magazines, newspapers, satellites, videophones and the advent of global all-news networks in the 1980s. As more countries opened their borders to imported signals, both news and entertainment took on greater importance as media firms of all varieties sought larger audiences. These larger audiences were often from other core nations, as well as from semiperipheral nations, and occasionally peripheral nations. Media firms sought out these larger audiences in order to increase advertising revenue for the commercial-based global television networks. From the electronic colonialism perspective, the potential impact of the advertising on consumer behavior was frequently a greater cultural concern than the programs themselves. The implications of global advertising and the relationship to world system and electronic colonialism theories are detailed in Chapter 15.

Along with international news coverage comes growing competition. By the 1980s, the world had developed a huge appetite for television programming of all kinds, including news and information. Interestingly, in the early 1980s it was Ted Turner who took the bold initiative to establish the first, 24-hour all-news network. It was based in Atlanta, Georgia. He saw a need and stepped in with his Turner Broadcasting Company. On June 1, 1980, Turner introduced the Cable News Network, otherwise known as CNN. In addition to CNN, in 1981 Turner launched CNN Headline News, and in 1985, the Cable News Network International (CNNI), in reaction to increasing competition. CNNI's goals were to expand internationally oriented programming, upgrade satellite carriage, expand its newsgathering capabilities, and become the primary global television network for news. Ted Turner deserves credit for his tenacity, vision, and deep pockets in terms of realizing that there was a market out there for 24-hour news. He sought to create a better informed public.

Without a doubt, CNN is the godfather of global television news reporting to audiences around the world. Millions in over 200 nations now see the 24-hour all-news format. Historically, the markets for Britain's *The Economist* or the *International Herald Tribune* were early indications that there was a niche market in print for the international news sector. What CNN managed to do was to make the development of the niche television news market a global phenomenon. As the global economy evolves and expands, people are defining themselves in terms of television viewing more as regional, like European or Latin, or as world citizens. They are concerned about world events as well as local, regional, and national events. Turner understood this desire for global information. He had the crucial financial resources to keep CNN on air during its early years. It was not until the mid-1980s that CNN was breaking even, let alone making a profit.

Before CNN, the prestigious French newspaper, *Le Monde* (*The World*), had the definition and concept right. The trouble was it never had the distribution system (or possibly the language factor) to become a world newspaper. Originally, radio faced similar barriers, with one major exception – the BBC World. Although there were other world radio services, none had the network clout, the vast number of colonies, or the international respectability of the BBC World. In terms of television, originally only nation-states, for the most part, developed and licensed television networks. Many were frequently just an extension of their national radio networks. They were delivered by way of limited terrestrial microwave networks or via telephone lines within a nation's borders. No transnational television systems were created until the reality of CNN's success forced other nations, particularly within the European Union, to consider competing services, such as Euronews. Satellites were the major technical force behind CNN's success as well as the creation of other networks, such as France 24 and Al-Jazeera.

CNN was so successful that it attracted competition. Currently, two of CNN's main competitors in Europe and Asia are Rupert Murdoch's satellite channels, including BSkyB, and the BBC. In 1994 the BBC launched a 24-hour television news service, starting in Asia. Although the BBC had previously run a limited European service, the Asian initiative made it a full-fledged competitor of CNN. Another CNN competitor is the EU's Euronews, an effort to present foreign news and analysis from a pan-European perspective.

The French government announced plans for a satellite-based French equivalent of CNN in order to bring a French public policy perspective to international issues. Launched in 2006 it is branded as France 24. The new channel received $40 million in startup funds from the French government and represents the French challenge to the CNN editorial stance on world events, much as Al-Jazeera and Al-Arabiya represent the Arabic challenge and viewpoint to CNN as well as the BBC. France 24 wants the world to understand both the French perspective as well as cultural values. It broadcasts in French and English 24/7, as well as Arabic for 10 hours per day. France 24 is using the internet as its major distribution system as well as being a video broadcaster via cable/satellite. It sees CNN as its major competitor and has put together a staff of over 500 full-time employees complemented by over 1,000 foreign correspondents around the globe.

Because of CNN's national and international successes, in addition to attracting global competition, CNN has managed to attract US-based competition as well. Two new 24-hour all-news networks – MSNBC and FOX News – now provide domestic competition for CNN and its headline news networks (see Figure 11.1).[1]

This chapter details CNN's major international media role from its inception to current activities. It also deals with other major global media organizations such as the BBC, Voice of America, Radio Marti, and Deutsche Welle.

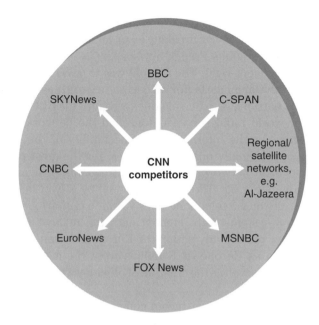

Figure 11.1　CNN's foreign and domestic competitors, 2010

CNN

International news and information gathering changed because of Ted Turner's Cable News Network (CNN). A new era of global reporting was born in 1980 as domestic boundaries became obsolete in an era of satellite and cable. Although several countries and companies were entering the global information market-place, no one news source was to be as successful as Turner Broadcasting and its crown jewel, CNN.

CNN, originally a division of Turner Broadcasting System, is the world's inter-national news leader. In October 1996, Time Warner acquired Turner Broadcasting for $6.54 billion, and Ted Turner became Vice President of Time Warner and its largest shareholder. He has since resigned and lost a fortune, as the later merger with AOL has been a fiscal disaster. The CNN merger created an unparalleled media giant with the ability to bring the most thorough, immediate, and live cov-erage of the world's news to a worldwide audience. In the pursuit of timely, unbi-ased, and in-depth news reporting, CNN pioneered innovative techniques and broke new ground for the television news industry. The high-energy environment at CNN and its sister networks is home to over 4,000 employees worldwide. Currently, CNN has 36 bureaus worldwide. It has also reached several mile-stones. Besides launching CNN Headline News and CNNI, CNN has also branched out into CNN Radio. This division provides all-news programming to nearly 500 radio stations nationwide. In 1988 the division introduced Noticiero CNNI, which produces six hours of Spanish news for distribution on CNNI in the United States and throughout Latin America. And in 1995, CNN was launched into cyberspace. CNN Interactive is the world's leading interactive news service. Its staff of world-class journalists and technologists are dedicated to providing 24-hour-a-day access to accurate and reliable news and information from any location.

As a unit of parent Time Warner CNN has not fared well. A series of senior management changes and missteps at Time Warner have adversely impacted CNN. With budget cuts looming, CNN is stuck in second place, after FOX, and sometimes even slips to third, after MSNBC, in the weekly ratings war.

First Live Broadcast

CNN's first live broadcast involved the high profile black civil rights leader and well-known Democrat Vernon Jordan. On May 29, 1980, Jordan was shot in Fort Wayne, Indiana. President Jimmy Carter visited him in the hospital. CNN distributed the story live during the day before the other major networks had a chance because traditional networks held back such breaking stories for their major evening newscasts. The networks were scooped during the day and were to repeat this lesson frequently as CNN broke stories at any time.

Tiananmen Square

Another major news opportunity in the late 1980s had drastic and unexpected consequences for CNN. In May 1989, President Gorbachev of Russia was making an official visit to China. Because this was the first summit meeting since 1958 between the leaders of the two largest communist nations, all major US networks were provided permission to broadcast from China. CNN, with anchor Bernard Shaw, received permission to establish a temporary outdoor studio in Beijing, close to the Sheraton Hotel. CNN set up a portable satellite earth station in order to transmit its signal to its headquarters in Atlanta, Georgia. After six days, President Gorbachev left China, but CNN still had permission from the Chinese authorities to transmit for another day. By coincidence, the Tiananmen Square confrontation occurred within the next 24 hours. The Chinese authorities were devastated by the global coverage provided by CNN. US President Bush, who was at his vacation home in Kennebunkport, Maine, openly stated that he was watching the events unfold, live on CNN and that all he knew was what CNN was showing – just like the rest of the world. The drama escalated as the Tiananmen Square demonstrators continued to defy Chinese troops and tanks. A separate drama began to emerge as Chinese authorities attempted to cut off the live CNN coverage. The CNN crew refused to disconnect their equipment and the entire incident and confrontation was broadcast live. The Chinese authorities were outraged, but CNN would not cease live coverage until it received an official letter from the Chinese Ministry of Telecommunications revoking the original seven-day transmission agreement. A kind of double coverage ensued when ABC began covering CNN's situation along with its own coverage of the confrontation. During CNN's coverage, Bernard Shaw explained how the network managed to break its live news:

> If you're wondering how CNN has been able to bring you this extraordinary story … we brought in our own flyaway gear, about eighteen oversized suitcases with our satellite gear … We unpacked our transmission equipment and our dish. So whatever you've seen in the way of pictures and, indeed, in the way of words, came from our microwave units at Tiananmen Square bounced right here to the hotel, through our control room on one of the upper floors – I won't mention the floor for protective reasons – back down through cables up on the CNN satellite dish, up on the satellite, and to you across the world … And I have to say this, for those cable stations that want to cut away, and I can't believe that any of you would want to cut away, you're gonna risk the anger and angst of all your viewers if you do … We have about two and a half minutes left on the satellite.[2]

The letter from the Chinese Ministry of Telecommunications finally arrived; it was delivered live and within minutes CNN coverage stopped. The drama and the replays out of Atlanta placed CNN in a new light. It was now truly the global news network it had always claimed to be. But it needed another major global story in order to demonstrate that it had the flexibility, equipment, and personnel to deliver live news coverage that was either comparable or superior to that of the major US and European networks. The Gulf War provided that vindication.

The First Gulf War

CNN was well prepared to be the media outlet for live coverage of the 1991 Gulf crisis. CNN carried not only the bombings but also Saddam Hussein's meeting with British hostages. And when Jordan's King Hussein wanted to deliver a message about the Gulf crisis, he delivered it live on CNN. World leaders began to communicate about the Gulf crisis through CNN; world leaders in North America, Europe, and the Middle East knew the status of the war because they were simultaneously glued to CNN's live coverage. It also created a media superstar in CNN reporter Peter Arnett. Previously, both Ted Turner and CNN executives had courted Middle Eastern governments and television officials and now that groundwork was paying off. CNN was granted permission to broadcast live from Baghdad. The other US networks watched in envy as CNN produced the only global live coverage from the war zone, frequently from behind enemy lines. Bernard Shaw joined the CNN crew in order to provide 24-hour coverage. Despite warnings from the White House to vacate the region, CNN reporters and production crew decided to stay. When the first bombing began on January 16, 1991, all major US and European networks had crews in the Middle East. But four days after the war began, of the hundreds of journalists and crew members, only 17 remained. Nine of these were from CNN. Following Operation Desert Storm, CNN, and particularly Peter Arnett, were criticized for being too lenient by permitting Iraqi officials too much air time during the war. American officials wanted a cheerleading tone. The US military sought propaganda to persuade the

American public that the war was necessary. Given the foibles of live coverage, some mistakes were inevitable, but internationally CNN became the new global medium for breaking world news. It was considered the new "gold standard" because it now had beaten all television networks with its war coverage.

The 1991 Gulf War presented opportunity as well as challenge for CNN. The challenges were twofold. First, was the US public willing to support a military action against a foreign country, particularly after the Vietnam War debacle? Second, would CNN news crews, including production staff, be permitted, as well as technically equipped, to send live signals from Baghdad, the capital of Iraq? The opportunity was straightforward: CNN would be able to broadcast live a major international conflict not only for its vast US audience, but also for a substantial number of viewers around the globe. What made the Gulf War all the more pivotal for CNN's success was the fact that it was not just the first but also one of the few broadcasting outlets permitted by both Iraqi and US military authorities to continue shooting video. European, Canadian, and Asian broadcasting counterparts were denied access to frontline footage.

The Gulf War turned out to be another defining moment in CNN's history. Even the leaders of the two nations engaged in the conflict – the United States and Iraq – openly conceded that they were following the progress of the war on CNN. CNN was interpreting the war for the world. This war was CNN's war. This fact bothered many foreign broadcasters, public policy experts, and politicians in other nations since they were reduced to viewing events and interpreting history in English and at least a step behind CNN. As a result, after the war several governments, particularly European, established competitor or alternative television services so that when major international events occurred, they would have their own broadcasters, analysts, and footage to serve their national interests and present their perspectives, rather than having to rely on a foreign broadcaster, such as CNN. These competitor networks include France 24, Euronews as well as the expansion of the BBC World Television Service, which is covered in greater detail later in this chapter. The Gulf War heightened the context in which the news media covered and defined international news and information stories. Philip Taylor summarizes the significance of CNN's new role as a result of the first Gulf War:

> Throughout the autumn and winter of 1990, thanks to the role which Cable News Network (CNN) had defined for itself as an instant electronic interlocutor between Baghdad and Washington, it became clear that television would play a particularly prominent role in any conflict, with Saddam and Bush frequently exchanging verbal blows via the ten-year-old television network once lampooned by rivals as the "Chicken Noodle News."
>
> But it was already apparent that, by providing a public forum to the traditionally secretive world of diplomacy, CNN was quite simply changing the rules of international politics and that, as a consequence, it was also likely to alter the way in which modern warfare would be projected onto the world's television screens.[3]

The reporter known for his unprecedented coverage of the Gulf War was CNN's Peter Arnett; his war coverage made him one of the world's most visible reporters. Arnett's success in Baghdad is cited as his most significant accomplishment simply because his coverage of the war was broadcast live on television around the globe. CNN positioned Peter Arnett as the archetypal journalist: the reporter who met newly defined professional challenges despite great personal risk and hardship. By staying behind enemy lines to report the story, he exemplified the reporter's responsibilities in an age of live satellite-fed communications.

Although some loved Arnett, he was criticized as well. Some of the criticism focused on Arnett's supposed lack of loyalty to the United States, which is how some people interpreted his insistence on staying behind enemy lines. When Arnett reported that the allies had bombed a plant producing infant formula rather than biological weapons, as the US military insisted, public fears intensified that his dispatches were being used for propaganda purposes. At one point, US lawmakers pressed for control over his broadcasts. The Pentagon wanted him fired.

CNN's news coverage of the first Gulf War again highlighted the network's unprecedented coverage in the international marketplace. But CNN wants to remain the "first choice" provider or "gold standard" of international news and information coverage.

On an average day, CNN has a domestic audience of more than a million households. When major news events break, however, whether in China, Asia, or the Middle East, the ratings go through the roof. CNN captures the vast share of the global television news audience. Interestingly, CNN did not send Peter Arnett to Kosovo, and his fame and position quickly sank at the network. He never recovered from his association with the 1998 Tailwind controversy (discussed later in this chapter) and was dismissed by CNN in 1999.

Cable News Network's presence is felt in every part of the world. CNN has become synonymous with news from every corner of the world. CNN's founder Ted Turner transformed his Atlanta-based company into a creditable international news service with the help of renowned journalists. CNN has launched a new era of global news and information coverage using aggressive strategies ranging from covering news whenever and wherever it happens, breaking the news first, and providing live coverage from the scene. All of these strategies have made Turner's company the leader in shaping international events.[4]

A brief history of CNN is in order here. Turner dedicated the network to around-the-clock news operations in the early 1980s. Satellites were used to deliver CNN to cable operators, but only about 20 percent of US TV viewing households received cable television. Turner needed more viewers if his new venture was to succeed. To increase cable access, he introduced ESPN, HBO, Nickelodeon, Arts & Entertainment (A & E), USA, Disney, Showtime, and CSPAN to attract a larger cable-viewing audience (see Figure 11.2). By 1985, Turner's original news channel was reaching more than 33 million households, four out of five US homes with cable, and nearly 40 percent of all US homes with televisions. Headline News alone had 18 million subscribers. These numbers were vital to CNN's economic success because larger audiences meant greater advertising revenues, and by this time

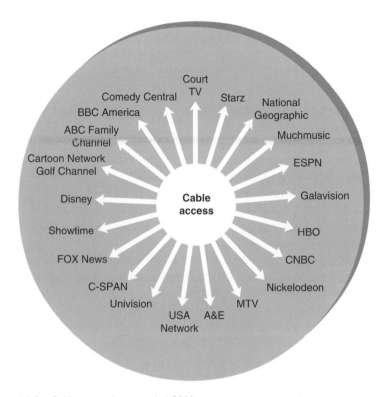

Figure 11.2   Cable networks expanded, 2010

CNN was attracting national advertising accounts. By the mid-1980s, Turner wanted to attract an even larger audience, so he turned to the global market for growth. As international trade and shifts in the world markets became more relevant to the US economy, these activities created demands for more up-to-date global information. CNN also became a model niche cable channel that others began to mimic.

CNN's family of networks has grown to nearly a dozen news channels and a wholesale news service (CNN Newsource) that sells video news to approximately 700 broadcast affiliates worldwide. With Turner's array of 24-hour networks and services, today CNN is a major player in domestic and international programming. Some of CNN's networks consist of the following: CNN, CNN Headline News, CNN Radio, CNN International (CNNI), CNN *World Report* news exchange, CNN Newsource, CNN Airport Network, CNN Interactive, CNN Money, and CNN en Espanol. CNN now has web pages in the following languages: English, Arabic, Spanish, Turkish, Portuguese, and Korean. In 1999, CNN launched a Spanish-language channel in Spain. This service was the first CNN local language news channel completely controlled, staffed, and operated outside of its US corporate headquarters in Atlanta.

In a move that enhanced Turner's presence in global markets, state media monopolies around the world began to allow modest competition. Countries such as India, Japan, Hong Kong, Russia, and South Africa wanted news services in addition to the local coverage that was brought to them by their state (public) broadcasters. Turner moved quickly to reach these new audiences by distributing CNN internationally. CNN now employs a satellite system that covers six continents; it reaches over 200 countries with potential access to half a billion people every day, and has a global team of almost 4,000 people. Even in countries where CNN is unavailable to ordinary people, because of limited cable or satellite systems or because of political censorship, CNN International has become the prevailing choice of viewers in major hotels, government offices, and presidential palaces. CNN's newsgathering has increased its number of international news bureaus to 21 and worldwide news staff to 4,000. A remarkable aspect of CNN's expansion in the 1990s was that it mostly occurred while other US networks were slashing the budgets of their foreign bureaus. Clearly this changed after the Time Warner takeover.

CNN has built much of its reputation as a creditable news source from such news coverage stories as the student protest in Tiananmen Square in Beijing, the bombing of Baghdad, and the burning of the Parliament building in Moscow, and the Indian Ocean tsunami coverage, and 9/11. Because of CNN's extensive coverage of such important international news stories, it is now doing business in China, Baghdad, and Russia. In 1997, CNN opened a bureau in Cuba, even though it was required to obtain US government approval first. To date, no other US network has opened a bureau in Cuba because they refuse to obtain the required US license to report from that nation. One reason CNN has had such a rapid rise is its innovative use of communication technologies to reach larger audiences. Satellites gave CNN a national audience in 1980, and since then satellites have enabled Turner to be the first international broadcaster to link the globe using a mixture of Intelsat, Intersputnik, PanAmSat, and regional satellite signals when existing land-based systems could never have done the job.

The strong relationships CNN has built with networks, news agencies and broadcasting unions worldwide, and with freelancers have enabled CNN to bring news and information coverage to households around the world. Much of its coverage is found in CNN's *World Report* program.

World Report

What has CNN *World Report* brought to the newsgathering table? Beginning in 1987, CNN *World Report* has been an internationally distributed news program consisting of news items contributed by foreign broadcasters. Since its birth in 1987, *World Report* has been an outlet for news organizations of any political persuasion to report news about their countries from their own perspective. As of 2009, over 350 stations representing 150 countries participate in the *World Report*. This suggests that CNN *World Report* continues to serve the needs of world broadcasters. Various news items have been aired from public and private stations such as CCTV in China, Cubavision in Cuba, CyBC Bayrak TV in Cyprus,

MTVMultivision in Mexico, TV Asahi in Japan, RNTV-Radio in The Netherlands Television, SABC in South Africa, and ZBC in Zimbabwe.

World Report has had a considerable effect on CNN and its coverage of high-profile, controversial news and information stories. According to Ted Turner:

> We never would have been allowed to stay in Iraq during the Iraqi war if it hadn't been for the World Report. We've gotten a lot of access as a result of our making a real effort to having people from other countries and other news organizations feel comfortable about us. We've got a lot of access to world leaders and so forth, and then, allowed to be behind the lines and allowed to stay in circumstances where other news organizations weren't allowed to. Partly that was the case that we'd been allowed because so many world leaders were watching us when there's a conflict anywhere in the world, or anything controversial, where people, where leaders need to get their point across. Like Saddam Hussein did. At least we gave him some access that they otherwise wouldn't have gotten if CNN wasn't there, because basically we believe that everyone has a right to be heard.[5]

Turner Broadcasting Company's international success is also its curse. CNN's managers know they are no longer playing in a field of one. Imitators will strive to equal or surpass the US news company's global reach. But CNN's ability to watch its competitors and stay one step ahead will leave little room for a takeover. Competition is healthy for CNN because it keeps forcing the network to reexamine fundamental strategies of global versus niche programming.

Today, executives at CNN state that their goal is to get people around the world to watch CNN. This means being more international in scope and more local from the standpoint of viewers in other parts of the world. To meet the information needs of the global market, CNN generates news programs that are compelling and relevant to a global audience. It also means that CNN reports on important events whenever and wherever they happen. In so doing, the network is trying to expand its role as a global communicator, the channel for diplomats and generals – even angry crowds in streets and town squares – with the potential to shape public life in every corner of the planet.[6] As mentioned, however, CNN's success has attracted competition. Some of its chief competitors, along with one of CNN's less stellar moments, are discussed in the following sections.

CNN's Erroneous Report

In June 1998, CNN, along with *Time* magazine, alleged that the US Department of Defense engaged in damaging activities at one point during the Vietnam War. Specifically, the CNN/TIME allegations concerning Operation Tailwind alleged that the US Army hunted down and killed US defectors, and that as part of this operation, the nerve gas sarin was used. Major wire services and other media outlets picked up the story. A thorough review of Operation Tailwind was undertaken by the US State Department, led by then Secretary of Defense William Cohen, who in July 1998 asserted that investigators had found absolutely no evidence to support the allegations. Shortly thereafter CNN retracted the nerve gas story and dismissed CNN staffers associated with the story. One notable exception was Peter Arnett, who was associated with the false story. He managed to keep his position at CNN, owing in large part to his stature as the most successful reporter for CNN during the Gulf War. But in 1999, he was not assigned to cover the Kosovo conflict, and he was eventually dismissed by CNN for complaining to the press. Many consider that this reporting fiasco will have long-term negative consequences for CNN's credibility as an all-news network, as well as for its investigative reporting standards.

Kosovo and CNN

The Kosovo, Yugoslavia, war in the spring of 1999 was different from the Gulf War in several respects. From a military perspective, there were three major differences in the US position. First, the United States was not involved to protect traditional interests, such as oil in the Middle East, or to stop the advance of communism, as in Vietnam. Rather, it was a humanitarian war fought to stop the ethnic cleansing of Albanians by the Serbian Army.

A second major difference was that Kosovo was NATO's war; the United States participated as only one of 19 NATO countries. Great Britain also participated and became very outspoken during military press briefings carried by the BBC. NATO had its own press spokesperson, Jamie Shea, based at NATO headquarters in Brussels, and US military spokespersons provided daily briefings as well. There were other military briefings by spokespersons from Italy, Greece, Germany, and other NATO nations. CNN was able to give extensive coverage from multiple perspectives. In addition to CNN, all other major US networks and many European networks covered the Kosovo conflict. What became interesting was that no single voice spoke from NATO's perspective. Rather, there were at least three major spokespersons from the United States, the United Kingdom, and NATO. From time to time, they gave different versions or different information about what had happened in the previous 24 hours. The major US and European networks quickly took advantage of any discrepancies. Many US networks had also hired retired military as analysts who provided endless details of the action and commented on what should be happening. Frequently, the commentary put the US State Department on the defensive, or caused the US Secretary of Defense to issue clarification statements. This trend of retired military being commentators became a problem for CNN over its reporting of the Iraq War. It came to light that the retirees were being briefed by the Pentagon and would put a positive spin on the war as well as the interrogation benefits of water-boarding without regard to the facts. Also these same retired generals were working as consultants or lobbyists for military contractors at the same time. CNN either failed to ask or knew and did not tell their audiences of the conflicts of interest that the parade of hawkish military retirees presented.

The third major difference involved NATO's list of legitimate military targets. The traditional targets were power stations, bridges, military barracks, and airfields, but during the Kosovo conflict a new category was added – media outlets. Air raids were directed at Serbian television buildings, radio stations, and press buildings. These attacks on the Serbian media outlets as part of the air war reflected NATO's concerns about winning the public relations war as well as seeking an end to ethnic cleansing.

Following months of air raids, other aspects of the media environment became evident. First, Serbian President Slobodan Milosevic had a stranglehold on the Serbian media and used it as a propaganda machine. At the beginning of the air raids, the Milosevic government expelled all foreign journalists and closed down Belgrade's independent press. As a result, Western journalists, who now had to seek alternative working sites in neighboring countries, began to rely extensively on CNN's broadcast of the Kosovo war because CNN was one of the few Western media companies allowed back into Belgrade. This reliance on CNN escalated with the accidental bombing of the Chinese embassy in Belgrade, and with the accidental bombing of Kosovo refugees by NATO. This allowed CNN to set the media agenda because many reporters miles away from the air raids had to file stories about the daily bombings. Finally, the British press took considerable delight in the acerbic statements of Prime Minister John Major and his Defense Secretary, George Robertson. They began to describe Milosevic in extremely negative terms, ultimately comparing the entire Serbian ethnic cleansing of the Albanians as akin to Hitler's genocide of the Jews during the Holocaust. The British tabloid media played up this excessive rhetoric, causing Major to appear even more hawkish on the Yugoslavian war than US President Clinton. Finally, NATO appeared to lack an overall communication strategy, and during daily press briefings appeared disorganized from time to time and uncertain about what was actually happening. Future NATO-sponsored military activities will likely see a significant improvement in media relations. The Kosovo war presented NATO with many challenges and taught that organization some lessons about media attention and the media's constant demand for up-to-date and accurate information rather than military propaganda.

Lou Dobbs Controversy

In 2009 viewers and media critics began questioning the accuracy of one of CNN's high profile announcer Lou Dobbs. He repeatedly went on anti-immigration tirades and his own negative opinions about Hispanics began to dominate his shows rather than factual reporting. He also picked up on the bizarre fringe attack on President Obama's citizenship status. In response Media Matters began running ads attacking both Dobbs and CNN's bias. The video ad and other items about Dobbs lack of professionalism are found at http://dobbsconspiracy.com/.

The controversy surrounding Dobbs has also become so large that the President of CNN, Jon Klein, has been backed into a corner concerning his support of Dobbs at a time when media analysts are saying that the CNN brand and reputation is being damaged daily by Dobbs. For a network that uses the banner of: "most trusted name in news" the Dobbs matter was a serious issue in terms of protecting the fragile credibility of the news network. Dobbs resigned in November 2009.

Merger Matters

With AOL and Time Warner's merger, CNN faced a new reality and a different set of new bosses. CNN's founder, Ted Turner, left the company in 2003. In 2001 CNN laid off almost 10 percent of its employees when it let 400 employees go. During the same era CNN failed to replace President Rich Kaplan, who was dismissed in 2000. The current president is not well liked by some staff members. CNN has also been losing market share to MSNBC, FOX, internet news sites, and competing international services, such as BBC World TV. John Cook, in his piece "CNN's Free Fall," writes about the lack of strategic planning, downsizing, and new ownership as "the changes have fostered discontent and disillusionment among the rank and file, many of whom were perfectly content with the old CNN."[7] Cook also makes the point about a new, major shift away from the former model of news being the central focus to a personality-centered schedule focused around stars, such as Christiane Amanpour, Wolf Blitzer, Brian Nelson, and Jeff Greenfield.[8] This repositioning of CNN, along with new ownership focusing on the bottom line and ignoring the Dobbs problem means that the Ted Turner honesty, creativity, media acumen, and era have come to an ignominious end.

The CNN Effect

The CNN effect or factor refers to the process by which the coverage of a foreign event by CNN causes that event to be a primary concern for its audience, which in turn forces the federal government to act.[9] What CNN chooses to focus on becomes a major public policy issue, or headache, for the US State Department. CNN has such an impact that it cannot be ignored in Washington. It has the effect of being an outside agenda setting voice for US foreign policy. This factor is extended when other networks begin to match CNN's focus on a foreign news event. When other networks begin to match CNN's coverage then the matter becomes an issue for a series of core governments. Others also argue that what CNN fails to cover, an increasing problem with budget cuts, means that there is no public outcry for action and thus little assistance or policy attention is forthcoming.[10]

For example, the US and British administrations were forced to respond to the Somalia crisis because CNN would not drop their coverage whereas in Sudan a civil war has raged for years with no core nation response since for a time CNN had chosen not to focus on their plight. Even former US Secretaries of State have admitted that they have to keep abreast of what CNN is covering abroad.[11] Finally, in 2005, Florida Governor Jeb Bush, traveling in Asia reviewing the tsunami damage, lamented that as soon as CNN leaves where will be the aid workers and public pressure to assist in the lengthy repairs and costs?

In terms of foreign affairs, if it is not on CNN, it does not exist. It does not matter if it is the US Secretary of State, the British Minister of Foreign Affairs, the head of the United Nations, or a Japanese ambassador; if CNN does not pick up the story it disappears. The ability of CNN to set the global agenda is new to the role of the global media. When it ignores an issue, the issue languishes and fails to make the radar of editors around the world, with few exceptions.

But the phenomena of the CNN effect, agenda setting, or factor may be short lived for CNN as it loses market share. Yet at the same time the media's public policy role will likely even increase as other networks, as well as the internet with its bloggers, pick up the role of focusing greater attention on foreign policy, global issues, and aid. At other times, when CNN focuses on an issue, such as Abu Ghraib and other scandal and torture violations, the governments of the US and Great Britain are forced into a damage control mode. Their spin masters are mere amateurs when taking on the impact and influence of the major media outlets, particularly CNN.

How CNN Was Out-FOXed but Not Out-classed

CNN was the global media king in 1991 with its strong coverage of the first Gulf War but less than a decade later FOX News overtook it in the US market. It did so based on brash personalities like Bill O'Reilly, being in the right place at the right time,[12] and being an unabashed supporter of the wars in Afghanistan and Iraq and all basically all things Republican. Now it is the leading critics of the Obama administration and even the President has acknowledged that fact.

In the early 2000s, CNN was overtaken in the US domestic all news market by News Corp.'s FOX News. CNN continued to attract the largest global news audience (BBC World is second), but in the crucial and enormous home market it was knocked to second place. Quickly this also translated into lower advertising rates and at parent Time Warner, which was bleeding owing to AOL's failure to turn a profit, CNN lost its jewel status. Several management changes at CNN mandated by Time Warner also failed to stop the ratings slide. With FOX News proudly catering successfully to a right of center audience, this has left CNN with an identity crisis as to what and how to attract back its own departed audience. This problem is exacerbated by the high costs of covering the war in Iraq or the tsunami in Asia and the desire of Time Warner to reduce CNN's overall costs.

To put CNN's problem in perspective, consider the results of the 2004 US presidential election. Basically, CNN has tried to be an objective and middle-of-the-road network, and under Ted Turner's leadership this formula worked very well. (It is worth noting that since the merger of AOL and Time Warner in 2001, Turner has lost billions in Time Warner stock and he is no longer with the company.) But the overall US audience shifted as reflected in the federal election breakdown. The right wing of the political spectrum, as represented by the Republicans, won 51 percent of the popular vote, and the liberal wing won 49 percent, most of which were votes going to the Democrats. The problem is that CNN had claimed the center of the electorate – where fewer Americans sit. The media audience either perceived themselves as conservative and viewed FOX News, or as liberal or viewed a range of media outlets, including CNN and the internet. The end result was that CNN was positioned in a declining realm as the middle audience collapsed and moved mainly to the right or to the left for Obama. In essence, the CNN network is now going through a type of identity crisis in terms of what it wants to be and where it wants to place itself with reference to its competitors.[13] The polarizing effect of the elections hit CNN's strategic position hard. Meanwhile Rupert Murdoch's FOX News delighted in its newfound audience niche and increasing ad rates. This has left CNN in an audience quagmire with few repositioning options – unless it makes a direct frontal attack on FOX News by shifting its editorial slant to the right, recalling that Lou Dobbs racist antics are protected by CNN's President Jon Klein, and thus risk losing the audience that it has now.

The Second Gulf War: Embedded Journalists

War coverage took a different track during the second Gulf War in Iraq. The US military, which had a legacy of hostility toward the media, decided to embed journalists in combat units across Iraq and six war ships in the area. Given that the US military had blamed the media for losing the public support for the Vietnam War, that the 1983 invasion of Grenada and the 1989 war in Panama saw heavy control of the press, and that the 1991 first Gulf War was primarily limited to CNN's coverage, it did come as a surprise that the US military would allow hundreds of journalists, photographers, and camera crews to cover the Iraq War in 2003. Embedding affects the tone and nature of the overall coverage. From the boot camp to the front lines, embeds quickly took on an air of camaraderie. They had to follow military guidelines and use military transportation. Overall the tone and slant of the stories and film footage was to the benefit of the US, and to some extent, the British militaries' coverage back home. For example an empirical study of the coverage by embeds revealed "[r]esults revealed that embedded coverage of "Iraqi Freedom" was more favorable in overall tone toward the military and in depiction of individual troops."[14] The authors conclude with a warning concerning the craft of objective journalism when they state:

> However, for the journalism establishment, embedding embodies a 'professionally treacherous' reef. Journalists get to cover combat operations close up, giving them the access to combat operations that they want. But, in the process, they lose perspective and, thus, sacrifice the idealized standard of reporter objectivity.[15]

This response by the embeds was not totally unexpected by the Pentagon, or they would not have done it. Many independent or unilateral journalists, likely to be more critical of the war effort and the lack of weapons of mass destruction, were keep out of Iraq by the US military and were forced to watch the war, likely on CNN, from neighboring Kuwait.

Finally, CNN was treated like any other network and had several embeds along with all competing networks. CNN's virtual monopoly coverage of the first Gulf War had evaporated with the new embed policy. In addition the use of the internet by reporters as well as soldiers also managed to outrun or scoop traditional media. (The new phenomenon of weblogging and twittering is covered in the internet chapter.)

British Broadcasting Corporation (BBC)

The BBC is significant for two major reasons. The first is that it operates a global television service in direct competition with CNN and a host of other regional networks. Second, The BBC as the early public service, non-commercial British radio network was exported around the world as a media model to the vast number of British colonies. As a direct result non-commercial, government controlled broadcasting in the public interest was what millions listened to and then watched with the introduction of television. The commercial model with advertising did not come to many nations outside the US until after World War II. And even then it was introduced slowly and frequently with oppressive regulations, many favoring the public broadcasters.

Radio

The BBC was founded in 1922; it went on the air in 1923 as a private radio corporation but quickly floundered. By early 1927, it had become a public corporation as the British government moved in to save the new medium. Since then, BBC radio has never sought advertising revenue, depending instead on two external sources of income. The first came directly from the British government in the form of an annual grant. The second came from license fees associated with all radio receivers. This licensing fee procedure was replicated with the introduction of television in the United Kingdom and is still in effect today.[16]

From its earliest days, the BBC was committed to public service broadcasting. Lord John Reith, an early general manager of the BBC, describes its mission this way:

> Broadcasting must be conducted, in the future, as it has in the past, as a Public Service with definite standards. The Service must not be used for entertainment purposes alone … To exploit so great and universal an agent in the pursuit of entertainment alone would have been not only an abdication of responsibility and a prostitution of power, but also an insult to the intelligence of the public it serves.[17]

This focus on quality programming became a central tenet of the BBC. Soon the BBC became a model for other nations as radio began to expand around the world. Many of these nations were part of the former extensive network of colonies known as the British Commonwealth. The British not only exported their civil service, English language, and monarchy, but they also exported the public service broadcasting ethic and model of the BBC. As early as 1927, the BBC began experimenting with short-wave radio in order to broadcast to Britain's far-flung and numerous colonies around the globe. By 1932 the BBC started a regular Empire Service by means of short wave. On Christmas Day that year, King George V became the first ruling monarch to broadcast live on radio his greeting to his subjects throughout the world. His speech writer was world famous Rudyard Kipling, author of *The Jungle Book*.

The BBC got a major international boost and acquired an extensive audience through its high-quality reporting during World War II. The BBC became the international voice of World War II and had no global rival. It also amassed substantial political power and influence; for years after World War II, it was able to severely limit the growth of commercial broadcasting and competition in the United Kingdom.

Television

The BBC started the world's first public television service on November 2, 1936. It was transmitted from Alexandra Palace to fewer than 400 television sets. Before World War II, television did not catch on quickly, owing mainly to the lack of programs, the limited range of transmission, and the high cost of television receivers. Because television receivers were expensive, as was the license fee, only wealthy people could afford them. Therefore, programming was aimed at the elite, wealthier audience.

On September 1, 1939, television was shut off – World War II had begun. Without television, the BBC concentrated on radio and quality reporting of war activities. It also started airing a nightly War Report after the regular evening news. By the end of World War II, the BBC had gained a great global reputation as a high quality and objective news broadcaster. And on June 8, 1946, BBC television was started up again to cover the Victory parade. The war was finally over.

From 1936 to 1955, there was only one television channel, BBC TV, later known as BBC One. But on September 22, 1955, for the first time the BBC faced some competition with the introduction of the Independent Television, or ITV. ITV ended the BBC monopoly and introduced a new and completely different style of television. ITV also gave viewers, for the first time, a choice.

One major difference between ITV and BBC TV was that ITV was funded and sponsored by outside advertisers. Also, unlike BBC TV, which used cinema newsreels and still pictures to broadcast the news, ITV used a less formal style of reporting imported from the US evening television newscasts. ITV quickly developed a substantial following.

Further choice in television channels opened up with the arrival of BBC Two in 1964. This allowed the BBC to air popular programs on BBC One, and more specialized, in-depth programs on BBC Two. Another technical move that helped promote BBC Two was the fact that in 1967 it was the first channel to start a color service. Because color televisions were expensive, many British people could not afford them. Also, the first color programs were few and far between. Other early disadvantages of color televisions were that they were bulky, unreliable, and had poor color quality. However after a few years, most of the problems were worked out, and on May 16, 1969, BBC One and ITV were given permission to begin working on their own color services. By the mid-1970s, color televisions were smaller, cheaper, and more reliable, and color programming was now the norm.

In the early 1980s, then Conservative Prime Minister Margaret Thatcher established a committee to investigate the possibility of seeking advertising revenue for the BBC. Despite the investigation and scare to BBC admirers, the commitment to high-quality, non-commercial programming remained intact.

Thanks to the threat during the Thatcher years of being partially privatized or driven by commercial interests, in the 1990s the BBC began to investigate other possible avenues of income. As a result, a new digital broadcasting service was established to compete with Rupert Murdoch's BSkyB. The BBC also began to market a foreign service that is now available on cable in North America and elsewhere. The BBC's online homepage is one of the most frequently accessed websites in the United Kingdom. Currently the United Kingdom also has the BBC equivalent of CNN, shaped in part by the Gulf War when CNN covered the war and the BBC and other European media were forced to play catch-up. The BBC's 24-hour all-news channel – News 24 – has been an early success.

In November 1991, the BBC launched a world service television, otherwise known as BBC World. It is a public service channel funded by the British Foreign Office that uses satellite technology to reach an extensive foreign audience. BBC World is an international news and information television channel broadcast in English 24 hours a day for a global audience. It provides news, business, and weather 24 hours a day, as well as the best of the BBC's current affairs, documentary, and lifestyle programming. The companion BBC World Service Radio has an estimated global audience of over 30 million listeners and is broadcast in 43 languages.

In the late 1990s, the BBC started a second international channel, BBC Prime. This global entertainment channel covers a broad range of programming. BBC Prime is available in most core, semiperipheral, and peripheral regions. Programs dealing with classics, cult comedy, and music do particularly well.

BBC broadcasts have been honed and refined over the years and are now the envy of many of the world's major broadcasters. It has set the world standard by which others are judged. BBC World Services operations are not easily duplicated, because its quality standards are unique. But with the advance of competition, particularly CNN, as well as other satellite and internet services, some are questioning the role and expense of BBC's World services.

The BBC is currently facing a problem related to economics and the future government funding. Because the BBC now attracts less than 50 percent of the domestic audience, there is growing concern that the traditional support for the license fee-funding concept may decline. Although the BBC has a loyal core of supporters, others strongly support the notion that commercial stations, advertising, market share, and ratings should determine the future of broadcasting. Critics claim that the traditions of public support, public service, and subsidizing media are vestiges of a bygone era. Many now want the future of the BBC and other broadcast services to be determined by open market forces rather than by officials behind closed government doors.

Royal Charter 2006–16

Like all major broadcasters the BBC is facing a changing landscape. But since 1927 a unique aspect of the BBC is that it operates under the authority of a British Royal Charter. The charter spells out in detail its public service mandate. There are various UK parliamentary hearings and studies looking at the future of the BBC, including global media services, the internet, and the contentious commercial activities run by BBC Enterprises. A significant part of the BBC Enterprises' services includes BBC America and the selling of Teletubbies paraphernalia. The issue of the balance between resource allocations to national versus international services will also come under close scrutiny.

The BBC is facing the reality, as are other broadcasters, that digital communication has brought convergence and more channels. Today the BBC confronts more commercial competition, both domestic and foreign, the evolution of the internet, and new satellite channels. This will all be open for public discussion and debate since the BBC is a government corporation.

The Royal Charter and Agreement outlines the terms and scope of funding as well as the operational areas in which the BBC provides service, on either a non-commercial or commercial basis. Currently there are three major sources of revenue of the BBC, the license fee, somewhat controversial commercial activities which are growing, and finally government grants. All this is for a radio network capturing about half the total British audience and less than a third of the national television audience.

The critics of the BBC maintain two major complaints about its operations. The first is that the mandated funding through license fees is being used as cross-subsidies for other multimedia activities. Some of these are children's channels, CBBC and Cbeebies, which both Viacom and Disney objected to; various BBC internet sites; and the very successful BBC Enterprises' commercial activities. In conjunction with this complaint, there are two radical solutions offered. First, do away with the license fees altogether and make all services commercial, or second, stick to only non-commercial activities and sell off the profitable commercial ventures.

The second major complaint is about standards and quality. In 2004 the Hutton Report strongly criticized the news and public affairs divisions for lacking proper oversight concerning a controversial story about Iraq. The chairman and chief executive of the BBC resigned over the matter. Others condemn the television side for debasing its shows by chasing high audience ratings as they mimic US networks and go for mindless reality shows. These critics want higher quality shows that reflect world-class production standards, scripts, and on-air talent.

In the midst of the broad range of issues that will form the public debate, including the British House of Commons, is another matter potentially involving all public broadcasters, namely the desire of the World Trade Organization (WTO) to include cultural industries under their tariff concerns. More is outlined about this issue in the chapter discussing the WTO but one example illustrates the possible significance of WTO's plans to the BBC. The current financing of the BBC involves an annual license fee on all radio and television receivers. This is a huge subsidy to the BBC. The WTO does not allow subsidies in its rules, since they distort the commercial, market-based playing field. Thus the BBC could find itself facing a financial crisis if the WTO pushes the matter.

Deutsche Welle

Deutsche Welle is the German online and worldwide radio and television broadcaster. Information is provided 24 hours a day, including up-to-date information on German and European domestic and foreign issues, as well as economic and financial trends focusing on the Frankfurt stock exchange and the new monetary unit, the Euro. Deutsche Welle TV offers 24-hour, commercial-free service, which includes news, sports, and cultural affairs programming. It provides programming in German, Arabic, English, and Spanish.

Deutsche Welle began with short-wave radio transmissions in May 1953, and it is financed mainly with German government funds. In April 1992, Deutsche Welle TV began transmission and was then on the air 14 hours a day. Deutsche Welle TV is now carried by cable systems throughout Europe and is rebroadcast in many parts of the world. Deutsche Welle has also set up internet services in order to compete in the public affairs arena with the BBC, CNN, and Voice of America. Since its inception, Deutsche Welle has received substantial German government support. But with the end of the Cold War and the reunification of Germany, political support and federal government funding could be in jeopardy.

Finally, Deutsche Welle is offering an innovative Master's degree in Media Studies; it will focus on training staff from peripheral regions with a hands-on and inter-cultural approaches.

Euronews

In 1993 the European Union established its own transnational news network, known as Euronews. It is headquartered in France and broadcasts television news in eight languages, which include Russian and Arabic. The impetus to create this trans-European television news network was almost a direct result of

CNN's coverage of the 1991 Gulf War. The European networks were either nowhere to be found in Baghdad at the beginning of the war, or as the war progressed found themselves increasingly relying on CNN's coverage in order to follow the action. US military kept foreign networks away from the battles. In response, 18 European public broadcasters, including France, Italy Germany, Spain, Belgium, and Greece, put up substantial funding to establish Euronews. In addition to government subsidies, EuroNews accepts commercial advertising. A noticeably absent member of Euronews is Great Britain. Like CNN, the BBC is in direct competition for the Euronews audience. (More details were provided about the network in Chapter 9.)

Channel News Asia (CNA)

A new Asian-based news channel, CNA, began service in 2000. Similar to EuroNews, which is attempting to bring a European perspective to European and global events, so CNA is seeking to bring an Asian view to the Asian region, as well as global news events. It is based out of Singapore and has close government ties. CNA is seeking to compete with the major global news services such as CNN International, the BBC, and CNBC Asia. With an all-Asian staff, it has 10 bureaus and about 150 journalists across Asia, more than the three English-language all-news networks combined. Like the BBC, CNA is attempting to serve a market of about 16 million households, whereas CNN International is the clear regional leader, with about 30 million subscribers. CNA is trying to appeal to the Asian demographic in hopes of attracting viewers from across the most populated region in the world by focusing on news by Asians and from an Asian editorial perspective. Some journalists and media critics are concerned about the undetermined role of the Singapore government on the status of CNA independence.

US Department of State and the BBG

The US federal government created the United States Information Agency (USIA) during World War I. Its initial purpose was to coordinate federal international information and counter negative foreign propaganda. USIA became an independent agency in 1953 and expanded its activities to include a broad range of international information, education initiatives, cultural exchanges, and media relations. In 1998, under the Foreign Affairs Reform and Restructuring Act, USIA was essentially divided into two sections. Much of the public diplomacy and foreign exchange activities were relocated in the State Department.

The International Broadcasting Bureau (IBB) became a freestanding, separate agency at the same time to oversee all US, non-military, international broadcasting services. In 1999, the USIA was disbanded altogether.

The activities transferred to the State Department currently include long-standing programs that have an impact on media systems and journalists in other nations. For example, the College and University Affiliations Program (CUAP) seeks to establish relations between US universities and their foreign counterparts. Examples of programs include a Palestinian media center, a grant to a Jordanian university to develop distance learning, and a grant to the University of Chile to establish an environmental science research agenda. The US State Department also funded the Aegean Young Journalists program, which brings together Greek and Turkish journalists. Many of the programs and partnerships funded have similar activities such as workshops, study tours, internships, and a US-based study tour. Another initiative is the Citizen Exchange Program (CEP), which brings both journalism professors and journalists from semiperipheral and peripheral nations to the United States for workshops and information exchanges. A goal of this program is to instill in delegates free-press values so that as their media systems are privatized or created, they will reflect the journalist values and practices of an open and democratic society.

Through the Broadcasting Board of Governors (BBG), the US federal government has substantial involvement in international broadcasting. It is responsible for all US non-military international broadcasting services funded by the federal government. The BBG oversees four major broadcasting outlets (see Figure 11.3).

The latter include Radio Sawa and Al-Hurra, a television network which competes directly with Al-Jazeera. All of these services receive annual grants from the US federal government and policy guidance from the US Secretary of State.

The end of the Cold-War era has seen a noticeable shift in and questioning of the role of these federally funded global broadcasting services. In their initial years, these services were designed as US propaganda voices through which to

---

1   Voice of America
 • World Net
2   Radio Free Europe/ Radio Liberty/ Radio Free Asia
3   Radio and TV Marti
4   Middle East Broadcasting Networks Inc.
 • Radio Sawa
 • Al-Hurra TV

Figure 11.3   Broadcasting Board of Governor's activities, 2010

present, in local languages around the world, the US foreign policy position, the ideology of fighting communism, and US political and free market economic values. Now there is a greater emphasis on promoting US commercial and export interests abroad instead of the hard-line political rhetoric of the Cold-War era. There is also a movement to focus on public diplomacy issues as outlined in Chapter 4.

Voice of America (VOA)

The VOA was founded in 1942 and was heavily funded by Congress during the Cold War. The first three decades focused on fighting communism and combating the global spread of Marxism. Now, in the absence of a global Cold-War environment, the VOA is attempting to reposition itself. It is the international radio and television service and has a weekly global audience of about 100 million people. It broadcasts on short wave, medium wave, and satellite transmissions in English and in 43 foreign languages. VOA programs over 1,000 hours a week and uses its own VOA correspondents at 23 news bureaus around the world, as well as using freelance reporters. VOA provides news, information, and cultural programming around the globe. Some of the programs promote the benefits of democracy, the free press and free markets, human rights, and the American way of life, politics, and business. All programming originates from Washington, DC, headquarters, but under the 1948 Smith-Mundt Act, VOA is prohibited from broadcasting inside the United States.

In the fall of 1994, VOA began television programming. Shortly thereafter it experienced a 20 percent budget cut and began accepting corporate underwriting to improve its budget. VOA TV simulcasts in six foreign languages, including Spanish and Chinese.

A noticeable distinction between the VOA and the BBC is that the former emphasizes a US orientation and a White House viewpoint, whereas the latter focuses on world news and global trends, with minimum attention to solely British news or to the prime minister's agenda. Internationally, the VOA is viewed as a propaganda arm of the US government, whereas BBC programming is perceived as independent, objective, and more credible.

Radio Free Europe, Radio Liberty, and Radio Free Asia

RFE/RL/RFA are private, non-profit corporations funded by the BBG. RFE/RL reach 20 nations across Europe and Central Asia. They have 19 bureaus and broadcast in 28 languages. Their programming is pro-American and promotes free enterprise economies. To some extent they are still caught up in the old Cold-War mentality and duplicate VOA's mission and programming.

RFA seeks to provide American news and views to Asian nations lacking a free press. They broadcast in 10 languages, mostly Chinese related. They also have a website for those with internet access in the region.

Worldnet Television and Film Service

Worldnet was launched in 1983 and is transmitted by satellite from television studios in Washington, DC. The programming is directed to US embassies and other broadcasters around the world. It programs 24 hours a day in English, but other programs are available in a number of world languages such as Arabic, Russian, French, Spanish, and Chinese. Worldnet programs range from public affairs forums, to science discussion, to international call-in programs. Worldnet also transmits some public broadcasting programs, such as PBS's *The NewsHour* with Jim Lehrer.

Office of Cuba Broadcasting

In 1983 the US Congress approved the establishment of Radio Marti under the provision that it would adhere to the Voice of America's regulations In addition, the Reagan administration and the Cuban American National Foundation agreed that the station would be based in Washington, DC, to make clear that this was the official voice of the US government, not an outlet of Cuban exile organizations. Given these provisions, Radio Marti went on the air in May 1985. TV Marti first broadcast in March 1990. In 1998, under legislation passed by Congress, Radio and TV Marti headquarters and operations completed a move from Washington, DC, to Miami, Florida. Since that time Cuban exile extremists have dominated the staffing of both the radio and television studios. The only constant since the move has been large staffing turnover. The tone, professionalism, and vitriolic anti-Castro rants are all likely to change with President Obama's more conciliatory approach.

Under the VOA, Radio Marti's programs are to be produced in accordance with the following VOA regulations (US Public Law 94.30). The VOA charter states:

> The long-range interests of the United States are served by communicating directly with the people of the world by radio. To be effective, the Voice of America (the broadcasting Service of the United States Information Agency) must win the attention and respect of listeners. These principles will therefore Govern Voice of America (VOA) Broadcasts.

> Following are the three policies stated:

> 1. VOA will service as a consistently reliable and authoritative source of news. VOA news will be accurate, objective and comprehensive.

2. VOA will represent America, not any single segment of American society, and will therefore present a balanced and comprehensive projection of significant American thought and institutions.
3. VOA will present the policies of the United States clearly and effectively, and will also present responsible discussion and opinion on those policies."[18]

The provisions stated by Voice of America are designed to ensure accuracy, objectivity, and balance in their content.

Radio Marti broadcasts seven days a week, 24 hours a day, on medium wave (AM) and short wave. Its broadcast includes news, music, and a variety of feature and news analysis programs. With a staff of over 100 employees, Radio Marti's annual budget provides news, talk radio, and information programs. News and news-related programming make up half of Radio Marti's daily schedule. Radio Marti's goal is to fill the information gap caused by more than three decades of Cuban government censorship, There is a one-hour noon newscast, which includes a live interview/discussion segment with experts or individuals in Cuba and correspondents around the world. In addition, there is a half-hour newscast at 4:00 pm, as well as live coverage of special events in the United States and around the world that stress the importance of Cuba. Topics covered with relevance to Cuba include congressional hearings and speeches by Latin American heads of state at major regional and hemispheric events. Despite complaints from the Cuban media, Radio Marti's programs offer listeners a Cuban American perspective on current events. In addition, the broadcasts offer feature and special programs with a wide range of information and entertainment. Some of the programs include roundtable discussions; commentaries by experts on political, economic, social, religious, and human rights issues; testimonies from former political prisoners and from human rights and labor sectors.

Despite efforts by Cuban President Castro to jam the transmission of Radio Marti, Cubans listen in significant numbers. It was for this reason that TV Marti was established: to provide Cuban viewers with programming available in other countries and in the western hemisphere. In addition, TV Marti provides in Spanish news features on life in the United States and other nations, entertainment, and sports. It also provides commentary and other information about events in Cuba and elsewhere in order to promote the cause of freedom in and for Cuba. TV Marti is on the air only for about five hours a day.

Its technical operations are mounted aboard a balloon tethered 10,000 feet above Cudjoe Key, Florida. The signal is then relayed to a transmitter and a highly directional antenna mounted aboard an aerostat for broadcast to Cuba TV Marti's transmission system delivers a clear television signal to the Havana area. Although jamming efforts by the Cuban government make it difficult to receive the signal in the center city of Havana, mobile monitoring indicates that international reception is possible in some outlying areas of the city and other more remote parts of the Havana province.

There is a downside to the unique manner in which TV Marti is transmitted. As mentioned, TV Marti's signals are transmitted from a balloon tethered above the Florida Keys. Also aboard is radar to track drug flights and high speed boats from Latin America. When TV Marti goes on, the radar goes off. Some critics contend that drug smugglers know the transmitting schedule and thus the best time to avoid detection. Finally, Radio and TV Marti have experienced internal management problems. Ultraconservative Cuban exiles dominate management, and the staff consists of fanatical Cuban exiles living in the Miami area. Several journalists have complained and ultimately left because of editorial interference with their stories and assignments. Some claim that they have declining audiences in Cuba and that both propaganda-driven networks are relics of a bygone era and should be closed altogether.

Postscript

In the 1990s, the US Department of the Treasury issued a ruling requiring US media companies and journalists to obtain a license to broadcast, report, or open a bureau in Cuba. For the most part, major US media enterprises objected strenuously and refused to apply for a bureau license. Notable exceptions were CNN and the Associated Press. They and a few others are the only major US broadcasters with licenses and bureaus in Cuba. Others are applying. Failure to obtain a license from the Treasury can result in substantial fines for both the news network as well as individual journalists. Ten years in jail and fines up to $1 million are possible. *Harper's Bazaar* has been fined for a photo shoot.

What is interesting is that the formal position of the US government in international communication debates was to strongly oppose any licensing requirement by any government affecting the media. During the NWICO debates of the 1980s, the US government took the strongest position in opposition to licensing. It denounced calls for government responsibility for, influence over, or control of the mass media. Clearly, however, in the cases of CNN and AP, as well as in its various activities with Radio and TV Marti, the US government is deeply involved in practices that it rhetorically and administratively abhorred during the intense NWICO debates. To foreign critics it makes the US Federal government look duplicitous when calling for a free press. Finally, in 2005 the outing of conservative media commentator Armstrong Williams as a well-paid covert propagandist for the US government did not help America's global media image.

Middle East Broadcasting Networks, Inc.

This unit operates two main networks, Al-Hurra (the free one) television and Radio Sawa (together), on a budget of over $100 million from the BBG. They both broadcast in Arabic across 22 countries in the Middle East. Radio Sawa began in 2003 and television in 2004. The radio provides a mix of Western and

Arabic popular music and has large audiences among teenagers and people in their 20s. The television audience situation has not been as great. Their statistics are minimal compared to competitor Al-Jazeera. It does not help that their news division is located outside the region, in Springfield, Virginia which is not a hot-bed of Arabic life or news stories. The Arab media has heaped scorn on the efforts of the BBG by claiming that they were propaganda tools and avoided reporting on civilian casualties caused by either American or NATO bombings.

Conclusions

The first decade of the twentieth-first century is witnessing significant and long-term changes in global communication. The first was the rise of CNN, which began as a small UHF station in Atlanta, Georgia, and became the predominant global network for breaking news. CNN's effectiveness and expansion were aided substantially by the introduction of small satellite earth stations capable of linking virtually instantaneously CNN's corporate broadcasting center with journalists in any part of the world. Whether the breaking news was occurring in a major urban center such as Paris or Beijing, or in remote deserts or isolated rural areas such as the rural Afghanistan, Iraq, or Kosovo, with a technician and a single reporter, CNN was able to broadcast live many breaking stories.

CNN's success also created a problem. As its role, model, influence, and ability to broadcast major events increased, other nations became concerned that their own governments' policies, including foreign policy, were being ignored or marginalized while CNN broadcast a primarily US perspective on international events. As a result, some nations started to develop alternatives to CNN. One of the most notable is the BBC. Although currently limited in reach, over time the BBC could become a major global broadcaster in the international television news arena as it once dominated the global radio networks. EuroNews is another good example of a network created to present a European perspective on European and world news for Europeans. That is also the expectation of the French as they launch France 24.

Other interesting changes are the substantial growth of Arabic services by major stakeholders. These services have been developed for radio, television, and the internet. Along with this is the shifting focus and funds from former communist countries to semiperipheral regions.

Initially many radio services, particularly those offshore, were based on short-wave radio technology, which, thanks in particular to the internet, is becoming obsolete. A more pressing issue is that of continuing financial support for these primarily government-funded global media services. With the end of the Cold War and the lessening of the fear of nuclear attack, there is a corresponding reduction in governments' desire to fund global radio networks. All short-wave global networks are feeling the stress of decreasing support, both politically and financially. For example, the Canadian Broadcasting Corporation's excellent foreign short-wave service, Radio Canada International (RCI), was eliminated during the 1990s as part of budget cuts. Part of RCI's budget was redirected to promote Canadian exports abroad. Other services have not fared as badly, but all are experiencing declining rather than expanding budgets. Some of these services, particularly the BBC and Voice of America, are shifting attention to the possibility of using the internet as a way of extending their audience reach and justifying government funding. Many are also soliciting external corporate advertising or corporate underwriting for select programming.

A final point is that the major global news networks are based in core nations – CNN in the United States, the BBC in the United Kingdom, Deutsche Welle in Germany, and France 24. These core-based global television news systems are designed for major export markets around the world because the majority of the services are commercially based and seek to extend their commercial viability by attracting larger audiences with the appropriate demographics for their advertisers. So these global systems have two basic audiences, one within the nations where the corporations are based and the other literally scattered around the world. Some are in remote villages and others are in major urban centers with potential audiences in the millions. With the expansion of cable systems and satellite technology, the potential for niche, particularly news or expat networks was recognized early by major innovators and is now being mimicked by broadcasters on a global scale. But all global news networks present a core-nation perspective on the news they cover, and they all cover news in peripheral regions only rarely and even then with a bad news, coup, disaster, or earthquake focus.

Given the end of the Cold War, media relics such as Radio Free Europe and Radio Liberty should be taken apart much like the Berlin Wall. The funds could be used to purchase OLPC (one laptop per child) computers for children in the poorer nations of the European region. Also, the Pentagon has begun a deceptive practice of creating foreign language websites which present only favorable "news" about what the US is doing and leaving out the military's civilian casualties' statistics. Manufactured stories and false military public relations are to the benefit of neither American journalism nor foreign audiences.[19]

On a positive note the US State Department is establishing a new counter-propaganda unit to create FM stations, expanding cellphone services, and training local journalists across Pakistan and Afghanistan. The unit is to push back on the Taliban militants' ability to win the war of words and images. Winning the foreign war of capturing the hearts and minds is as important as the war on the ground. As reported in a *New York Times* piece, "US Turns to Radio Stations and Cellphones to Counter Taliban's Propaganda": "'Concurrent with the insurgency is an information war,' said Richard C. Holbrooke, the special representative for Afghanistan and Pakistan, who will direct the effort. 'We are losing that war.'"[20]

Why it took the Pentagon years to recognize this problem illustrates the outdated thinking of the US military leaders. The same *New York Times* piece points out that in the Taliban regions of Pakistan there are only four legal FM stations while the militants run over 150 illegal stations. Making this new counterpropaganda unit at the State Department a success will require not only substantial funds but also that the CIA, Pentagon, and on the ground military do not undercut State's new media efforts.

Notes

1. Although the focus of this book is on global media, MSNBC and FOX News are relevant models for potential global expansion. They also provide considerable international coverage of leading stories, many connected with the global war on terrorism.

    MSNBC, launched in July 1996, combines three technologies – broadcast, cable, and the internet – in order to provide 24-hour news from around the world. It is jointly owned by Microsoft and General Electric's NBC Universal and primarily combines the national and international news resources of the NBC system along with the financial, business, and technology resources of Microsoft.

    Rupert Murdoch's News Corporation, on the other hand, owns FOX News Channel. It went on the air in October 1996 and provides 24-hour, all-news global coverage, in direct competition with both MSNBC as well as Time Warner's CNN.

    An interesting phenomenon emerged during the NATO bombing of Yugoslavia in 1999. These three all-news networks clearly have an insatiable appetite for news coverage 24 hours a day. This now also includes extensive commentary on global events themselves, in addition to broad coverage of news conferences, video of bombing attacks, interviews with refugees, and so on. A new phenomenon during the Kosovo air strikes by NATO involved the significant new dimension of retired military personnel appearing again and again on all three networks to comment, mostly negatively, about NATO's actions and strategies. As a result, not only did President Clinton have to contend with political opposition to his military strategy in Washington, but also now he had a new wave of critics – that is, an endless cadre of retired generals who were, from time to time, reaching substantial audiences through the all-news networks. This translated, in terms of public opinion, into a larger and more skeptical US public concerning the United States' role in NATO, as well as its military interests in Yugoslavia.

    In general, CNN has been able to attract more domestic viewers than either of its competitors, but there is one notable exception. In June 1999, MSNBC opted to pay the BBC for three hours of live coverage of the British royal wedding of Prince Edward and Sophie Rhys-Jones. For the first time in its brief broadcasting history, MSNBC beat CNN in total households that single day by featuring live a British royal wedding.
2. Hank Whittemore, *CNN: The Inside Story*, Toronto, Canada: Little, Brown, 1990, pp. 295–6.
3. Philip Taylor, *War and the Media: Propaganda and Persuasion in the Gulf War*, Manchester, UK: Manchester University Press, 1998, p. 7.
4. Don M. Flournoy and Robert K. Stewart, *CNN: Making News in the Global Market*, Bedfordshire, UK: John Libbey Media, 1997, p. ix.
5. Flournoy and Stewart, 1997, p. 34.
6. Flournoy and Stewart, pp. 208–9. Additional details about CNN may be found in Piers Robinson, *The CNN Effect: The Myth of News Media, Foreign Policy and Intervention*, London: Routledge, 2002; Royce Ammon, *Global Television and the Shaping of World*

Politics, North Carolina: McFarland and Company, 2001; and S. Kull, C. Ramsay, and E. Lewis, "Misperceptions, the Media, and the Iraq War" *Political Science Quarterly*, 118(4) (December 2003): 569–98.

7. John Cook, "CNN's Free Fall," *Brill's Content* (April 2001): 68.

8. Cook, 2001, p. 122.

9. Piers Robinson, 2002.

10. V. Hawkins, "The Other Side of the CNN Factor: the media and conflict" *Journalism Studies*, 3(2) (May 2002): 225–40.

11. Margaret Belknap, "The CNN Effect: Strategic Enabler or Operational Risk?" Pennsylvania: US Army War College, 2001.

12. Scott Collins, *Crazy Like a FOX: The Inside Story of How FOX News Beat CNN*, New York: Portfolio Press, 2004.

13. Jason Zengerle, "Fiddling with the Reception." *The New York Times Magazine* (August 17, 2003).

14. Michael Pfau et al., "Embedding Journalists in Military Combat Units: Impact on Newspaper Story Frames and Tone," *Journalism and Mass Communication Quarterly*, 81(1) (spring 2004): 83.

15. Ibid., p. 84.

16. Asa Briggs, *The BBC: The First Fifty Years*, New York: Oxford University Press, 1985.

17. R. H. Coase, *British Broadcasting*, London: University of London, 1950, p. 46.

18. www.voa.gov

19. Peter Eisler, "Pentagon Starts Foreign News Sites: Journalism Groups Call Sites Deceptive Effort to Control Message Abroad," *USA Today* (May 1, 2008): 6A.

20. Thom Shanker, "US Turns to Radio Stations and Cellphones to Counter Taliban's Propaganda," *The New York Times* (August 16, 2009): 6.

12

The Roles of Global News Agencies

Introduction

This chapter covers global wire services, which are major components of the global communication system. These wire services bring to international communication different sets of stakeholders, yet each service has a significant role in the daily activities of multinational media enterprises. They are also being driven to expand globally by industry pressure to achieve broader scale and scope. As the global economy unfolds so also the wire services follow. Since World War II, the debate surrounding international communication has in large part focused on the international wire services. During the 1960s, the global wire services became the first and frequent targets of peripheral nations and other critics. During the NWICO debates of the 1970s, most of the issues involved some aspect of wire-service behavior, location (they are all based in core nations), or corporate structure.[1]

Frequently, two general problem areas were cited in discussions of core-based global wire services. First, the wire services focused on covering news that was mainly relevant to colonial powers or dealt with regions where core-headquartered corporations had branch plants. The three major global services, Thomson Reuters, Associated Press, and Agence France Presse, are based in London, New York, and Paris respectively.

The second major issue was that coverage of peripheral nations focused on negative news such as civil strife, natural disasters, or sensational and bizarre events. The wire services reported little if any good news about the poorest regions in Africa, Latin America, or Asia. For most people their view of the world is mediated by what the media covers, or does not cover, in terms of foreign lands. The world is defined in large part by what and how these wire-services cover breaking news abroad.

1   Thomson Reuters
2   The Associated Press (AP)
3   Agence France Presse (AFP)
4   Bloomberg
5   Dow Jones & Company
6   Xinhua News Agency
7   Inter Press Services (IPS)

Figure 12.1   Global news agencies, 2010

Two general groups of researchers attempted to document the wire services's one-way news flow and the imbalance in both East–West and North–South coverage. One group sought funding and a voice from UNESCO, and by the late 1970s its rhetoric and demands had become shrill. The other group consisted of various pockets of scholars in the United States, Europe, the Nordic countries, Latin America, and elsewhere who conducted separate research, frequently using content analysis of a specific medium, usually print. In the final analysis, almost all of the research was critical of the wire services. Researchers frequently studied the print press to document what were perceived as structural problems in the core-based and controlled wire services. With the demise of the Cold War, East–West tensions have evaporated for the most part, but certain structural criticisms remain concerning North–South news coverage.

The major global news agencies (Figure 12.1) are detailed in this chapter. Reuters and the Associated Press are not only the giants but they also control vast television news reporting and internet interests around the globe, in addition to their historical interest in print-based journalism.

Reuters

The earliest is Reuters' wire service which dates back to October 1851; this is when Paul Julius Reuter, a German immigrant, opened an office in London. Reuters transmitted stock market quotations between London and Paris and in its early era focused on business news. The agency soon became known as a news source and started covering wars and elections since they impacted the business environment as well. Eventually it extended its services to the entire British press, British colonies, as well as press in other European countries. Reuters expanded its services and began transmitting general and economic news from all around the world. Reuters' successful news service was booming. In 1865, Reuters was the first wire-service company in Europe to transmit the news about President Lincoln's assassination in the United States.

Through technological advances such as the telegraph and undersea cable facilities, Reuters news services expanded beyond Europe to include the Far East by 1872 and South America by 1874. In 1883, Reuters began to use a "column printer" to transmit messages electronically to London newspapers. This format allowed editors to simply cut and paste stories from the Reuters feed. The use of radio further expanded the wire service in the 1920s, allowing Reuters to transmit news internationally. In 1927, Reuters introduced the teleprinter to distribute news to London newspapers. And in 1939, the company moved its corporate headquarters to its current location at 85 Fleet Street, London.[2]

Reuters's continued success and modernizing of services continued into the latter half of the twentieth century. It expanded in 1964 with the Stockmaster service, which transmitted financial data internationally. In 1973, the company launched the Reuters Monitor, which transmitted news and foreign exchange prices. Following a dramatic increase in profitability, Reuters was floated as a public company in 1984 on the London Stock Exchange and on NASDAQ (National Association of Securities Dealers Automated Quotations) in the United States.

In 1960, Reuters began to buy shares in Visnews, a global television news film agency. Reuters continued buying shares of Visnews until 1992, when Reuters bought out Visnews completely and renamed the company Reuters Television (RTV). RTV is the world's leading supplier of international news material for television, reaching 1.5 billion people daily and delivering material directly to media customers by satellites or terrestrial land-based systems. Customers include broadcasters and newspapers around the world, but the news is tailored specially for financial markets. Broadcasters are supplied with fast, reliable news video ranging from big breaking stories to human interest, from sports to business. RTV service is the oldest comprehensive real-time news and information service that covers breaking news around the globe. It is ideal for those who want to know what is happening around the world because it often includes secondary stories not widely reported in the United States; these stories are broadcast extensively in other nations, however. Reuters's only major competition in supplying news to broadcasters started in 1994 with The Associated Press Television News (APTN), which was established when AP bought out World Television News.

Reuters's corporate position as an international market leader is based on its four strengths

1. a worldwide information and news reporting network known for speed, accuracy, integrity, and impartiality;
2. a constantly developing communications network and a product line distinguishable by its breadth and quality;
3. comprehensive financial databases for both real-time and historical information; and
4. a proven reputation for reliability and continuous technological innovation.

Reuters offers its clients financial, media, and professional products and services. The financial products consist of datafeeds to financial markets and the software tools to analyze data. Under the financial umbrella are transaction products, which enable traders to deal in the foreign exchange, futures, options, and securities markets. The media division delivers news in all facets of multimedia, which include television images, still pictures, sound, and graphics. Reuters's professional product division packages the news in electronic briefings for corporate executives in insurance, advertising, transportation, health care, and other corporate and professional sectors.

In 2008 Reuters was purchased by Thomson Corporation, a Toronto, Canada, communication conglomerate with strong financial data services. The new combined company was restructured into two divisions: professional and markets. The professional division contains the news and information unit that was Reuters. The markets divisions focus on law, tax, and healthcare. Some concerns were raised about the history of Thomson and their historical focus on financial and business news rather than general news or public interest stories. The new owners agreed to follow the Reuters Trust Principles which were establish in 1941. This was at the height of World War II and Reuters reaffirmed its commitment to objective journalism practices along with integrity and freedom from bias or intimidation. The Reuters Trust Principles are five-fold:

1. that Thomson Reuters shall at no time pass into the hands of any one interest, group or faction;
2. that the integrity, independence and freedom from bias of Thomson Reuters shall at all times be fully preserved;
3. that Thomson Reuters shall supply unbiased and reliable news services to newspapers, news agencies, broadcasters and other media subscribers and to businesses governments, institutions, individuals and others with whom Thomson Reuters has or may have contracts;
4. that Thomson Reuters shall pay due regard to the many interests which it serves in addition to those of the media; and
5. that no effort shall be spared to expand, develop and adapt the news and other services and products of Thomson Reuters so as to maintain its leading position in the international news and information business.[3]

Today, Thomson Reuters supplies the global financial markets and the news media with the widest range of information and news products including real-time financial data; collective investment data; numerical, textual, historical, and graphical databases; and news, graphics, news video and news pictures. Approximately half a million users located in close to 60,000 organizations access Reuters information and news worldwide.

The Thomson Reuters editorial reference service unit from London and the daily news diary unit from Washington were relocated to India to save money. Senior journalists are concerned that outsourcing will move up the "food-chain" over time and that the quality of editing as well as reporting on businesses will falter. Several current Thomson Reuters journalists are concerned about the future impact of the outsourcing practice as well as the dominance of financial news.

Synopsis

Reuters established the first international wire-service business. It had the major advantage of following the growth and spread of the British Empire around the world. It has continued to be the preeminent financial- and business-oriented global wire service, but when new markets emerge, Reuters also covers general or breaking news stories around the world thanks to its enormous staff. Today it is a global media and financial conglomerate. Reuters was one of the first media firms to recognize the significance of the internet and to develop a broad range of internet services and sites. Finally, RTV is one of the two major global television news feeds, serving almost all major networks in Europe, North America, and elsewhere. Along with the Associated Press, Reuters is the dominant global wire and video provider for almost all broadcasters and publishers.

The Associated Press (AP)

The Associated Press (AP) is another wire service with roots that date back to the mid-1800s. In May 1848, officials representing six New York City newspapers sat around a table at the *New York Sun's* office discussing the high cost of collecting news, particularly from Europe, by telegraph. The newly invented telegraph made transmission of news possible by wire, but costs were so high that they strained the resources of any single paper. They were all worried about the high costs of covering the Mexican-American War. David Hale of the Journal of Commerce argued that only a joint effort among New York's papers could make the telegraph affordable and effectively prevent telegraph companies from economically constraining newsgathering. Although reluctant at first, the six highly competitive newspapers agreed to a historic cooperative plan, and AP was born.[4] AP was from the start a news cooperative and continues that unique ownership structure today. Over 1,700 member newspapers now own and control the not-for-profit cooperative. They elect an 18 member board which sets policies and rates; Rupert Murdoch is on the board. In addition over 5,000 radio and television stations are clients of AP services.

One year after AP was established, Boston newspapers joined the New York founders of AP Regional. Newspaper groups soon followed – Western Associated Press, Southern Associated Press, Philadelphia Press, and several others. Washington and foreign news were staples from the start. In 1849, Daniel Craig established the Associated Press's foreign bureau in Halifax, Nova Scotia, the first North American port of call for Cunard's ocean liners. Headline news arrived from Europe with each incoming vessel and was telegraphed to New York. This was the practice until the establishment of the transatlantic cable in 1856, which made the Halifax port outmoded for news.

Today, AP's World Service distributes news and photos to 8,500 international subscribers and translates the report into several languages. It offers news directly in only five languages; they are English, French, Spanish, German, and Dutch. For a news-gathering agency it is surprising that it does not offer original coverage in Arabic or Chinese. It has clients in 121 countries and has a full time news and photo staff of about 1,100 domestically and 500 abroad. The journalists abroad work out of 243 bureaus. AP has won 28 Pulitzer Prizes for photography, the most for any news company. With the demise of competitor United Press International in 1993, AP became the major US wire-service.

To meet the growing demand for sports coverage, in 1946 AP established the first news agency wire service dedicated entirely to sports. AP also published and circulated an annual AP sports almanac. Today, the sports wire and all other AP wires move at 9,600 words a minute.

In 1941 radio had become one of the most important means of communication in the United States, and AP was the broadcast pioneer. Between 1933 and 1941, AP's broadcast division had supplied news to radio stations owned by newspaper members only when the news was of major importance. But AP changed that by launching a separate radio broadcast wire called Circuit 7760, the first news organization to operate a broadcast news circuit 24 hours a day, seven days a week. Just one year after Circuit 7760 was launched, AP's broadcast wire was serving more than 200 stations in 120 cities. AP continued to gain broadcast members, and in the 1940s, the AP Radio network was launched. It provided hourly newscasts, sportscasts, and business programs to member radio stations and eventually became the first radio network in the world to be delivered by way of satellite. By 1979 the first news wire designed specifically for television stations was introduced.

AP's global video news was called APTN. It is currently Reuters's only major competitor. APTN has full-time video newsgathering facilities in 70 bureaus and has more than 300 clients, including ABC, NBC, CNN, CBS, FOX News channels, and Univision. APTN's primary service provides top international news stories as well as regional coverage in North America, Latin America, Asia, and Europe. By the mid-1990s, APTN provided video footage of the day's top news stories by satellite to broadcast organizations worldwide. APTN emphasizes enterprise journalism and the practice of telling the entire story in narrative form at critical moments in different international time zones.

Also by 1994, AP had launched AP All News Radio (ANR), a 24-hour-a-day radio newscast. ANR makes it possible for stations in all market sizes to carry the popular and profitable all-news format. Today, more than 50 radio stations are ANR affiliates, and they can easily insert local news and advertising into the ANR format. And finally APTN joined with Trans World International (TWI) in 1996 to launch SNTV, a sports news video agency. The partnership has claimed market leadership, drawing on the strengths of the world's largest newsgathering organization and the world's largest independent supplier of sports programming. SNTV currently serves over 300 broadcasters worldwide.

Because of the ever-changing newspaper and broadcast industry, AP remains a leader because of its new businesses and technological developments. Several new initiatives have enabled AP to support and enhance its worldwide newsgathering. For example, the agency sells packaged news to non-members such as governments and corporations. AP's Information Services Department sells AP Online – a group of subject-specific news wires tailored to each client's industry, public policy, or news needs – to these clients. AP also sells photos to nonmembers through AP's Wide World subsidiary. AP Telecommunication is another subsidiary, which provides members and non-members data and network communication technologies. AP's AdSEND group speeds advertisements from agencies and retailers to newspapers as needed. In response to the widespread use of the internet, AP formed the Multimedia Services Department for AP members to use on their homepages. In 1991, AP developed the AP Leaf Picture Desk so that nearly every newspaper in the United States could receive photos into a personal computer for editing and production. Also in 1991, AP's Graphics Bank became the first online graphics archive for television, using standard telephone lines. In 1994, AP introduced the first digital camera for photojournalists, called the AP News Camera 200. The Associated Press's news business developments are proving successful, and so is the agency's application of technological advances.

DataStream is AP's premier news service, which delivers an entire report of world, national, state, and sports news. Limited DataStream is tailored for midsize dailies that desire a complete news report but may have fewer resources on copy and wire desks. Limited DataStream with expanded sports provides enhanced sports content. AP Basic is tailored for smaller newspapers that emphasize local coverage but still need a high-speed wire with AP's depth and breadth of world, national, and state news. Dial-in Report is for very small newspapers that need a minimum of copy. Latin coverage, or the LatAm wire, provides coverage in Spanish of Mexico and other Latin American countries. AP's western regional service, or West Wire, has a staff in 13 western states that focuses on stories of high interest in the West.

AP's broadcast services include radio programming. *Newsweek On Air* and ENPS *Newsweek On Air* is a weekly one-hour syndicated radio program co-produced by The Associated Press and *Newsweek*. The program features the week's biggest news stories through interviews with newsmakers and *Newsweek* correspondents. ENPS (Essential News Production System) is an electronic news production system, which will soon be the largest broadcast newsroom computer system in the world, linking radio and television journalists, production areas, and archives in more than 100 locations.

AP has been involved with two major controversies. The first is over copyright issues involving unauthorized use of AP products. This is primarily an internet phenomenon. Google, bloggers, websites, and assorted news aggregators are using AP copy without attribution or payment in most instances. AP is seeking syndication fees from violators but it is a daunting challenge because the problem is so widespread.

The second issue is more serious and could threaten the long-run viability of the company. This issue deals with the various fees member company's need to pay for the AP product lines. Almost every newspaper is losing money and circulation so they want AP to reduce fees. Some are threatening to quit AP altogether. AP in response is offering discounts and adjustments to keep subscribers. Sam Zell, the owner of the *Chicago Tribune* and *LA Times* has been particularly vocal about this issue. But as a result AP's revenues will continue to fall at a rate of about 10 percent per year. Layoffs and less news are a likely result; and with less news, more papers and broadcasters will demand lower syndication fees thus precipitating another round of layoffs, etc. With declining newspaper sales AP is becoming collateral damage.

Synopsis

AP has integrated several major technical innovations into its various services, along with a broad array of wire-service-based news, photos, audio, and video feeds, including internet online services to clients around the globe. It is estimated that more than a billion people each day read, hear, see, or watch AP news or photos. AP has become North America's premier wire-service corporation. Its rise was accentuated by the financial problems faced by its one-time competitor, United Press International (UPI). AP's main global rival is Reuters, which offers competing services for almost every AP line from news to the internet. An issue of importance for the future of AP is that some of the 1,550 US member newspaper owners are facing competition from other external media outlets, which are now purchasing some of AP's internet products. This strain on the cooperative may over time lead to changes. Other problems are copyright issues and rebellion about fees from print and electronic media.

United Press International (UPI)

The history of United Press International goes back over 90 years. E. W. Scripps founded the United Press in 1907 to cover news from around the world. In 1935, United Press became the first major US news service to supply news to radio stations. In 1958, United Press merged with William Randolph Hearst's International News Service to become United Press International, or UPI. At that time, UPI was an aggressive and prestigious news service competing directly with AP. During the 1960s UPI had over 6,000 employees and more than 5,000 news subscribers. UPI began the first global wire-service radio network, providing radio stations with voice reports from correspondents around the globe. Several years later in the 1980s, the news service was the first in the industry to let subscribers choose and receive copy by topic and subtopic, rather than by a broad category only. At one point, UPI had over 1,200 radio clients. By 1995 the company completed a system for global satellite transmission that virtually eliminated the need to send news over telephone landlines. But management, ownership, and client problems forced UPI to cut back services. UPI's domestic news bureaus closed offices across the United States. In 1999, UPI sold its broadcast news business to its one time rival, AP, which picked up all US-based UPI radio and television clients.

UPI was privately owned by a group of Saudi Arabian investors, but in 2000 it was sold to News World Communications (NWC), which is operated by the ultraconservative Unification Church. The sale prompted Helen Thomas to resign from UPI after 57 years. The Unification Church, NWC's parent, was founded and is still run by the Reverend Sun Myung Moon. Rev. Moon specializes in sensational journalism with an extremely conservative slant. NWC publishes 20 newspapers worldwide, including *The Washington Times*. Rev. Moon is a wildly grandiose figure who for several decades has publicly proclaimed that he is the second coming of the Christian messiah. He also enjoys conducting mass marriages of his "moonie" followers. UPI is history.

Agence France Presse (AFP)

AFP is the world's third largest wire service, after Reuters and AP. AFP is the world's oldest news agency, dating from 1835, and is one of the world's largest wire services providing full-text articles to its clients around the world. AFP covers politics, economic affairs, diplomacy, culture, science, international, national, business, and sports news written by journalists and correspondents in Europe, the Middle East, North America, South America, and Africa.[5] Many of the bureaus are still based in former colonies of France or in major cities where Reuters and AP have competing bureaus.

AFP has bureaus in 110 countries and operates in 165, and it employs 1,200 staff journalists and photographers, along with 2,000 stringers, reporting out of almost every country in the world. Of these correspondents, 102 are stationed in peripheral nations (22 in Latin America and Mexico and 80 in Africa and Asia). AFP's coverage is not a lucrative proposition, but the agency's operations are subsidized by the income from the many official French government and embassy subscriptions. The English-language service is distributed worldwide and includes reports, roundups, analyses, and news. Subscribers to AFP include 7,000 newspapers and 2,500 radio and television stations. Their largest single customer is the French Government.

Starting in January 1997, the AFP news feed was integrated into Bloomberg's multipanel information screen, produced in London on the European Canal Satellite. The Canal Satellite is an all-digital French direct broadcast channel on several different cable services. The agency also distributes selected news stories from AP. AFP runs the farthest-reaching network of any other news service, providing unmatched depth and breadth of coverage from regions where the other services are weak or absent. AFP is recognized as the premier supplier of information from Asia, Africa, and Arab-speaking nations.

Over the years, AFP has proved itself a leader in journalistic enterprise. For example, it was the first to announce the deaths of Stalin, Pope John Paul I, and Indira Gandhi. AFP has earned many compliments and awards for its continued coverage of some of the world's biggest stories including the 1999 war in the former Yugoslavia and the conflict in Chechnya. Prior to the second Gulf War, AFP was openly skeptical of the Bush administrations' claims about weapons of mass destruction. Unlike the American press, particularly the all news channels, which were all too willing to become part of the war propaganda machine, AFP stood its ground about its objective analysis of the build up to the invasion of Iraq. As a result it was shunned by the White House and excluded from select press briefings. Over time its professionalism and coverage was vindicated.

Today, the agency continues to expand worldwide, reaching thousands of subscribers (radio, television, newspapers, companies) from its main headquarters in Paris and regional centers in Washington, DC, Hong Kong, Nicosia, and Montevideo. All share the same goal – to guarantee a top-quality international service tailored to the specific needs of clients in each region. It also does more reporting from peripheral nations than any other global service.

Bloomberg

Bloomberg was established in New York in October 1981 by Michael Bloomberg when he formed Innovative Market Systems, which in 1986 became known as Bloomberg LP.[6] After 15 years with the investment firm Salomon Brothers, Bloomberg identified the need for a business press suited to around-the-clock global financial information. He started from New York, but by 1987 was opening world offices, first in London, then in Australia in 1989, and the business has continued to grow worldwide since then. Bloomberg news is available in five languages: English, French, Spanish, German, and Japanese; it provides services to over 260,000 users in over 125 countries. The focus of its coverage is in economics, business, financial markets, technology, and global stock markets and trends. Its main source of income is leasing Bloomberg terminals to business clients.

The first Bloomberg television product, launched in 1994, was called Bloomberg Business News, followed by Bloomberg Information TV, and finally European Bloomberg Information TV. Bloomberg Television is a 24-hour financial news channel that reports the economic and political news that affects markets. Its unique TV Data Screen provides financial data and breaking news headlines at all times, even during commercials. It draws on the vast resources of the global Bloomberg organization, including more than 1,600 reporters and editors in 94 bureaus around the world. Bloomberg Television reaches over 100 million TV-watching households through national cable distribution, the USA Network, DIRECTV, and the Bloomberg service, and it airs three half-hour television shows: Bloomberg Business News, Bloomberg Personal, and Bloomberg Small Business. Bloomberg Television offers the top 50 major news stories each half-hour, 24 hours a day.

As mentioned earlier, since 1997 Bloomberg has integrated a major news feed from AFP into its multipanel information screen. The news-feed is produced in London and aired on Canal Satellite, the all – digital French direct broadcast system. CEO Bloomberg, who is also the mayor of New York City, owns 72 percent of the firm, Merrill Lynch owns 20 percent, and Bloomberg employees hold 8 percent.

Bloomberg is a latecomer to the global wire and video service business. Yet it came into the business at a fortuitous time and has an entrepreneurial leader in Michael Bloomberg. With the expansion of cable channels, particularly all-news, and the internet, Bloomberg has found a ready market and a viable niche. The company's various services, with a clear economic focus, are available to clients who reside nearly exclusively in core and semiperipheral nations. As peripheral nations become economically viable and interact with greater frequency with core-based enterprises, subscribing to Bloomberg will make sense, particularly for government and business leaders.

Dow Jones & Company

Founded in 1882, Dow Jones & Company (DJC) has been publishing the major global newspaper of business, *The Wall Street Journal*, since 1889. Since 2007 it has become part of News Corp. In 1976 the company began the *Asian Wall Street Journal* and in 1983, *Wall Street Journal Europe*. DJC also publishes major financial magazines such as *Barron's*, since 1921, and the *Far Eastern Economic Review*, since 1946. In the 1990s, DJC started a joint venture in Russia, where it publishes *Hedomosti*. DJC also controls the Ottaway newspaper chain with 19 dailies and 15 weekly newspapers in the United States. With its financial orientation, Dow Jones competes directly with Bloomberg and Thomson Reuters for the corporate and government clientele. On the electronic side, the Dow Jones news wires have over a million subscribers globally. Dow Jones also owns half of CNBC Europe and CNBC Asia. In 1999 DJC joined with Reuters to establish a new interactive electronic global service to provide business information for corporate and professional clients.

In late 2004, DJC won a fierce bidding war to acquire MarketWatch, Inc., a highly profitable online financial news and information provider, for $519 million. MarketWatch's two sites are the popular CBS MarketWatch and BigCharts.com, and combined they attract eight million unique visitors per month.

Finally, DJC is known for its Dow Jones Industrial Average (DJIA), which was established in 1896 and consists of a pool of 30 blue chip US stocks. DJIA appears globally in newspapers and magazines, and on radio and television business programs. Also in 1999, DJIA made one of its biggest changes in its 103-year history. Originally, only New York Stock Exchange stocks were included in the 30 stocks that make up the DJIA barometer. Now the Chicago-based NASDAQ Stock Market has some companies on the DJIA. Also added were Home Depot and SBC. The four stocks dropped to make room for the newcomers were Chevron, Sears, Union Carbide, and Goodyear. All four had been in the DJIA since at least 1930. Even Woolworth Corp. was dropped in 1997 to make room for Wal-Mart Stores. In 1991, Walt Disney joined the index as US Steel was dropped. General Electric joined the index in 1928. News Corp., Viacom, Google, and Time Warner are not on the index, nor is any advertising agency.

Currently, the 2009 DJIA consists of the following major US blue-chip stocks: 3M, Alcoa, American Express, AT & T, Bank of America, Boeing, Caterpillar, Chevron Corporation, Cisco Systems, Coca-Cola, Disney, DuPont, Exxon Mobil, General Electric (parent of NBC Universal), Hewlett-Packard, Home Depot, IBM, Intel, J. P. Morgan Chase, Johnson & Johnson, Kraft Foods, McDonald's, Merck, Microsoft, Pfizer, Procter & Gamble, United Technologies, Verizon, Wal-Mart, and Walt Disney. The DJIA reflects the evolution in the US economy from industrial society to an information, media, and high-technology society. All 30 firms have significant global activities and all are major stakeholders in the global economy. Each new round of changes will likely see additional information-based corporations, such as Google, being added.

Xinhua News Agency

This is China's leading integrated news company. It is striving for a global role by delivering media services to the regions of China through print and the internet, as well as online advertising and web solutions throughout Asia. Xinhua was established in 1931 and is the state news agency of the People's Republic of China. It is headquartered in Beijing and operates a large number of bureaus in China and globally Xinhua employs more than 7,000 journalists who report on Chinese and world affairs. It publishes several periodicals, has a public relations group, and runs a journalism school. Xinhua is tightly controlled and watched by senior Chinese government officials, particularly in the wake of the violent suppression of protesters in Tiananmen Square. Xinhua is known for its long, dull articles that avoid any criticism of Chinese government officials or actions, and "all foreign news made available to Chinese publications and broadcasters is first processed by Xinhua translators and editors."[7] In addition to its print products, Xinhua is moving into internet activities, but its content is still dull and heavily censored.

Inter Press Services

Inter Press Services (IPS) was started in 1964 by Roberto Savio in Rome. IPS has become a major news agency and has developed into an innovative system for intercultural communication. The agency operates in a manner different from other global news services by promoting a horizontal flow of news on a cooperative basis among developing countries. It also distributes information about developing nation clients to industrialized countries. IPS is a worldwide, nonprofit association of journalists and others in the field of journalism that aims to promote a global communication strategy. That strategy is to bring together civil societies, policymakers, and national and international media.[8]

IPS operations consist of IPS News, IPS Telecommunications, and IPS Projects. IPS News service is an independent global news wire. IPS Telecommunications offers technical expertise for the upgrading of developing nations' communication and information infrastructures. IPS Projects was established to design, manage, and report on projects in the fields of training, information and exchange, and increasing public and media awareness of the importance of global issues.

IPS also has connections with non-governmental organizations (NGOs). For the most part, NGOs have gained widespread recognition for their work with the poor and the oppressed. NGOs have developed as important and increasingly major actors within certain societies, which are mainly in peripheral nations. IPS and NGOs have developed a strategy for cooperation in the twenty-first century. The strategy consists of five major objectives:

1. to be active and useful instruments for linking NGOs from the south (mostly peripheral nations) and from the north;
2. to identify suitable partners among development NGOs in the south and their counterparts in the north, which can help strengthen IPS's reporting on self-reliant, grassroots development;
3. to use NGOs in the south as privileged sources of news for the media of the north, and to disseminate news of relevance to NGOs from the north to the south;
4. to cooperate with NGOs of the south in offering services that can improve their presence in the north and in the media of the north;
5. to offer a forum for joint discussion between NGOs and IPS management staff and journalists on innovative ways to report development action from a grassroots perspective.

A network of journalists in more than 100 countries backs IPS, with satellite communication links to 1,000 outlets. In addition, IPS has regional editorial centers that operate in Africa, Asia, the Caribbean, Europe, Latin America, and North America. More than 250 journalists cover more than 100 countries and provide news and information services for more than 1,000 clients. To date, IPS has two-thirds of its correspondents in peripheral nations who are natives of the countries in which they work. IPS focuses its news coverage on events and the global processes affecting the economic, social, and political development of peoples and nations. IPS reports more than news that is considered "emergency" or negative news; its stories concentrate on issues such as the gap between rich and poor, international trade negotiations, human rights, refugees and international migration patterns, conflict and peacekeeping, environmental protection and sustainable development, population issues, and international debt crises. The IPS World Service news report is delivered via satellite to subscribers. These services are available through online computer facilities, electronic databases, and printed bulletins. An Asian television station also uses IPS feature stories as pegs for documentaries.

IPS products include printed publications, bulletins, columns, and telecommunications. It operates five newspapers under its printed publications division. *Terra Viva Conference Daily* is an independent tabloid newspaper published during major UN conferences such as the 1996 World Food Summit in Rome. *Terra Viva Europe Daily Journal* is produced at the United Nations in New York. Contents include a daily faxed selection of highlights from the IPS wire aimed at policymakers and decision-makers. The *G-77 Journal* is published for the 77 developing countries within the UN system. *IPS Features* is a package of 10 IPS features, special reports, and columns mailed to media clients in the Pacific Rim region. *Rural Development* is a monthly bulleting produced by IPS Africa and the weekly *Africa Bulletin*. News and information covered in the bulletins includes developments, drugs, human rights, religious affairs, environment, investment, energy, population, arts and entertainment, technology, and Latin American integration. The IPS Columnist Service provides a series of exclusive columns written by statesmen and stateswomen, officials, opposition leaders, opinion makers, leading cultural figures, and experts offering insight on major issues. The last product offered by IPS is a telecommunications carrier service, an international information carrier for a variety of organizations.

In conclusion, IPS represents a model of development journalism. It seeks out positive development news from and among peripheral nations. IPS has found an ally in NGOs, and they work together to assist peripheral nation causes and activities IPS is seldom used by major core newspapers or broadcasters.

Conclusions

The major global news agencies operate in a highly competitive environment. On a daily basis, The Associated Press competes with Thomson Reuters and to a lesser extent with Bloomberg, Dow Jones, and Agence France Presse. Both AP and Thomson Reuters have added television news services as part of their product lines. Collectively, they also are active in internet services. New services with a financial focus, such as Bloomberg and Dow Jones, appear to be thriving, while historically broad service companies such as UPI and now even AP appear to be in organizational and fiscal crises.

The major services are all based in industrial core nations, with an extensive bureau network in other core nations and nearly all semiperipheral nations. Now the US is home to both the leaders, AP and Thomson Reuters. The peripheral regions lack bureaus, have only stringers, or are inundated with core news crews when a major coup, earthquake, or bizarre event occurs that affects the core nations' interests or catches editors' attention.

The wire services will in all likelihood continue to thrive and even grow in influence as the cost of placing foreign correspondents abroad escalates rapidly. Many managing editors now are willing to accept wire-service copy or news footage from outside organizations such as Reuters TV or APTN rather than have to bear the expense of placing correspondents abroad on a permanent basis. With modern airline transportation, digital equipment, and satellite feeds, major news outlets dispatch reporters abroad on a crisis-by-crisis basis instead of having a large number of foreign bureaus. This practice of sending a plane loaded with media types is frequently referred to as "parachute journalism." Finally, networks and others let CNN set the international agenda, so when CNN covers a foreign news story, the other networks and services simply match the coverage. But if CNN does not cover a foreign event, the event most likely will go unreported by other major media outlets, such as some of the civil wars and famines across Africa.

Electronic colonialism permeates the wire services, which both directly and indirectly promote a core-based focus and emphasis in reporting values. Their journalists, editors, and management are almost all products of elite universities, have a superb command of the English language, and enjoy decent, and in some cases substantial, salaries. This group is not about to promote a revolution or seriously question the economic structure of the global economy that is providing them, their families, and their firms with a sound financial future. They are part of the ruling elite. This in part accounts for the emphasis on financial news and information, rather than on general interest news, detailed pieces on major social problems, or development issues. Although the wire services were major players in the early days of the NWICO debate, they now completely ignore the debate and concerns raised by either peripheral nations or academic critics from core nations. Their philosophy and outlook is straightforward: basically, they do what they do because it works and is profitable. They are encouraging their own lifestyle and outlook in other nations, particularly in semiperipheral and peripheral regions, so that these areas become future customers for their expanding range of services, which are quickly morphing into internet e-journalism product lines.

By default they are leaving to the emerging blogging world on the internet many stories which the wire services now consider too trivial or controversial. (The blogging phenomena was discussed in Chapter 6 dealing with the internet and related issues.)

Notes

1. Oliver Boyd-Barnett, *The International News Agencies*, London: Constable, 1980; William Hachten and James Scotton, *The World News Prism*, Ames: Iowa State University Press, 2002; Peter Golding and Phil Harris, eds, *Beyond Cultural Imperialism: Globalization, Communication and the New International Order*, London: Sage, 1997; "How News Is Shaped," *Journalism and Mass Communication Quarterly*, 77(?) (summer 2000): 223–72.

2. Donald Read, *The Power of News: The History of Reuters*, Oxford, UK: Oxford University Press, 1992.

3. www.thomsonreuters.com/about/reuters_trust_principles/.

4. Oliver Gramling, *AP: The Story of News*, New York: Farrar and Rinehart, 1940; Peter Arnet, Vincent Alabiso, Chuck Zoeller, and Kelly Smith-Tunney (eds.), *Flash! Associated Press Covers the World*, New York: Harry N. Abrams Press, 1998.

5. Jean Huteau, *AFP. Une histoire de l'Agence France-Presse: 1944–1990*, Paris: R. Laffont, 1992.

6. Michael Bloomberg and Matthew Winkler, *Bloomberg by Bloomberg*, New York: John Wiley, 1998.

7. Jon Swan, "I Was a 'Polisher' in a Chinese News Factory," *Columbia Journalism Review* (March/April 1996): 34.

8. Much of IPS's coverage focuses on major United Nations conferences dealing with global topics. An examination of amount and kind of coverage provided by IPS, AP, and Reuters is found in C. Anthony Giffard, "The Beijing Conference on Women as Seen by Three International News Agencies," *Gazette*, 61 (July 1999): 327–41. American newspapers do not use IPS stories.

13

Arab Media and the Al-Jazeera Effect

Lawrence Pintak

Introduction

The Arab media is in the midst of a revolution. Call it the Al-Jazeera effect. The launch of the region's first all-news satellite channel in 1996 shook the very foundations of Arab journalism. Since the 1950s, Arab media had largely served as a mouthpiece for the region's regimes. All broadcasting outlets and most newspapers were owned by Arab governments, tame political parties, or regime friends. The term "television journalism" was an oxymoron. Investigative journalism was unknown.

Then the young emir of Qatar, who had recently deposed his father in a bloodless coup, decided to invest $140 million in a new channel with a mandate to freely report the news. The launch of Al-Jazeera changed everything. Suddenly, television shows were discussing issues that ordinary people had only talked about behind closed doors. Political dissidents, militant activists and, most shocking in a region where Israel's name was an epithet, even Israeli officials were being interviewed on television.

It was an inspiration to journalists laboring under the old model of media-as-government-mouthpiece. Within a decade, independent or semi-independent newspapers, magazines and television channels could be found from Morocco to Yemen – and everywhere Arab journalists were pushing the envelope of censorship and control.

History of Arab Media

The Arab media was born of the chaos following the defeat of the Axis in World War I and the collapse of the Ottoman Empire. This nascent Arab media fostered a shared sense of "Arabness" in the face of the now-defeated Ottoman Turks

and helped drive the rising political concept of Arab nationalism. Such politicization would remain the hallmark of Arab journalism. In his classic study, William
Rugh classified the Arab media according to a series of typologies based on the
prevailing journalistic ethos in each group of countries.[1] There were clear divisions among these various styles of media, but each reflected a level of politicization that, to varying degrees, remains today.

Lebanon was always the Arab world's media Tower of Babel. With the out-
break of civil war in the early 1970s, Beirut's streets became the battleground of
the Middle East. A shifting array of militias acted as surrogates for the region's
rival governments: pro-Iraqi militias fought pro-Syrian militias; Saudi-backed
militias battled Libyan-funded militias; Nasserites fought Baathists; Christian
against Muslim, Sunni against Shiite. That chaos was reflected in the media.
A cacophony of newspapers and radio stations represented the spectrum of the
country's – and the region's – political ideologies. But even in the relative freedom of Beirut, there were limits. Control came not in the form of government
sanctions, but in a bullet or remote-controlled bomb. One of the leading papers,
Saudi-backed *Al-Hayat*, was eventually forced to abandon Lebanon for London.
The British capital would emerge as the Arab world's *de facto* media headquarter
as *Al-Hayat* was joined by another Saudi-funded paper, *Asharq Alawsat*, the
Palestinian paper *Al Quds al Arabi*, and a variety of others. These would come
to be known as the "pan-Arab media," produced outside the region but distributed across the Arab world.

While the shift of the pan-Arab press to London brought a modicum of freedom to these largely Saudi-controlled publications, television news remained
firmly in the grip of Arab regimes. All television stations and, with only a few
exceptions, all radio stations were owned by governments. Inevitably, newscasts opened with the head of state and consisted largely of "protocol news,"
a mind-numbing series of (almost exclusively) men shaking hands, cutting
ribbons and drinking tea. For the most part, real news was nowhere to be found.
For international coverage – even events in the country next door – these
government channels relied largely on Western video news agencies based in
the UK or US.

The seeds of modern Arab television news were planted during the 1990–1
Gulf War. If you happened to live in Saudi Arabia in the days after Saddam
Hussein ordered Iraqi forces to invade Kuwait, it is likely that you were bliss-
fully ignorant of the fact that war had broken out on your doorstep. For more
than 48 hours after the invasion, the Saudi media remained silent on the conflict as the panicked House of Saud scrambled to decide how to respond. It was
the equivalent of the French being unaware that Spain had invaded Italy. But
not every Saudi was oblivious. Though still illegal in most Arab countries, satellite dishes had already begun sprouting on rooftops across the region. And
while there were no Arab satellite channels, there were plenty being beamed in
from the West – among them CNN and the BBC, both broadcasting news in
English 24 hours a day. For those with dishes, all eyes turned to these Western
broadcasters.

Arab governments quickly realized that they were losing their stranglehold on information. Egypt immediately began broadcasting the output of its state-run TV channel via satellite; but it was just the same old turgid government newscast, devoid of any reporting from the war-zone, received via satellite dish instead of an antenna. No one was fooled. Once the conflict was over and Saddam Hussein had been neutralized, the House of Saud set about dealing with this other threat to their rule – the loss of their information monopoly. In London, they set up the Middle East Broadcasting Centre, a pan-Arab satellite channel that combined entertainment with newscasts that more closely resembled those produced in the West. MBC was owned by members of the royal family, rather than the government itself, so its reporters were freer than colleagues at other Arab media outlets, but still operated under clear strictures. MBC would eventually evolve into the MBC Group, the largest broadcast organization in the region, with a constellation of entertainment, music, sports and news channels based in Dubai. But that would come later, after the launch of Al-Jazeera, the channel that changed the way Arabs saw the world, and their own region.

Al-Jazeera

Long before Al-Jazeera became the channel the Bush administration loved to hate, it had earned the wrath of Arab officials from Morocco to Yemen. Appearing on Al-Jazeera's air were political dissidents, Islamic militants and all the other voices Arab regimes thought they had silenced. As a result, Al-Jazeera's reporters were banned at various times from 17 of the 22 member countries of the Arab League.

The Saudis were particularly incensed by this upstart channel. Al-Jazeera not only impinged on their near-monopoly of pan-Arab media, but the station also had the temerity to give voice to those who would question the House of Saud. As one Saudi newspaper wrote:

> The poisonous ideas that are conveyed via the Western satellite channels are easy to handle because the viewer knows the thought they are trying to convey in advance. However, when this poisonous thought is conveyed via an Arab satellite channel, it becomes all the more dangerous because it is concealing itself behind our culture.[2]

Ironically, given later accusations of bias and unprofessionalism, Al-Jazeera's original news team were almost all veterans of the BBC's Arabic television service, which had withdrawn from an ill-fated joint venture with Saudi-owned Orbit TV when it became clear that the BBC and the Saudi royal family – not surprisingly – had different ideas about what constituted journalism. The channel's staff saw themselves as agents of democratic change in a region trapped in the grip of autocracies.

"Using the Western style, we have broken many taboos," Ibrahim M. Helal, then Al-Jazeera's chief editor, told *The New York Times*, "of course, we upset most other Arab countries."[3] The staff of Al-Jazeera, and many outside the newsroom, saw that as a very good thing. One official in the Clinton White House called the channel a "beacon of light,"[4] and Israeli cabinet minister Gideon Ezra told the *Jerusalem Post*: "I wish all Arab media were like Al-Jazeera."[5]

Then came 9/11 and Al-Jazeera shifted its focus from the oppression of Arab regimes to the so-called "war on terror" and the US invasions of Afghanistan and Iraq. Just days after the attacks of September 11, Al-Jazeera aired the first of many videotaped pronouncements from Osama bin Laden. Without Al-Jazeera, the Al-Qaeda leader might never have achieved the mythic status he would come to enjoy. As the fireside radio chat was President Franklin Delano Roosevelt's "bully pulpit" – the means through which he reached the American people – during World War II, so too did the Qatar-based satellite channel serve as bin Laden's pipeline to the Arab and Muslim people as he launched his military and propaganda assault on the US.

Al-Jazeera's top editors argued that any Western news organization with exclusive access to a major news figure would do exactly the same thing; and, in fact, the four major American networks all ran the early bin Laden tapes until the White House prevailed on their patriotism and the practice was halted. But it wasn't just the channel's relationship with bin Laden that rankled the Bush administration. Its reporters were inside Kabul showing the impact on civilians of the American bombardment of the Afghan capital; they were in Baghdad broadcasting live from the receiving end of the American "shock and awe" assault; and, later, they were inside Fallujah during the US siege of that Iraqi rebel stronghold. Al-Jazeera's audience saw a grim and bloody side of these conflicts largely absent from American television screens and the images were presented by reporters whose commentary reflected the general Arab sense of outrage.

"Arabic TV does not do our country justice," President Bush complained in early 2006, "they put out some kind – sometimes put out propaganda that just is – just isn't right, it isn't fair, and it doesn't give people the impression of what we're about."[6] What, to many Western eyes, was biased and sensational coverage was, to many Arab journalists, the natural response to events playing out in their front-yard, not dissimilar from the flag-waving of the American media after 9/11.

"We belong to this Arab nation and we are there to cover from our own perspective," said Al-Jazeera's chief editor, Ahmed Sheikh, "sometimes it may prove to be very difficult to be impartial. You find yourself carried away with your sentiments."[7]

It was precisely that sensibility which so resonated with Arab viewers after decades of seeing their own region through the prism of a Western TV camera lens. "The genius of Arab Satellite TV is that it [has] captured a deep-seated common existential pain called Arab sensibility and turned it into a picture narrative that speaks to something very deep in the Arab psyche," according to Abderrahim Foukara, Al-Jazeera's Washington, DC, bureau chief.

Media Wars

The emir of Qatar did not launch Al-Jazeera to salve the Arab psyche or because he wanted a membership card at the local press club. He did it for the same reason he invited the US military to move its Gulf Central Command to Qatar – to make himself a player in the region. Though one of the world's richest countries, thanks to oil and natural gas, Qatar was a tiny peninsula – hence Al-Jazeera's name, which translates as "The Peninsula" – jutting out from Saudi Arabia. Geographically and politically it was hidden in the shadow of its much more powerful neighbor. Until Al-Jazeera, pan-Arab media had been dominated by the Saudis. Al-Jazeera gave the emir the power to drive public opinion in directions the Saudis did not necessarily like. That is why, early on, Saudi Arabia banned Al-Jazeera journalists from within its border and unofficially barred its advertising agencies, which dominated the Gulf, from buying commercials on Al-Jazeera. Then, on the eve of the US invasion of Iraq, the Saudis launched their own all-news satellite channel, Al-Arabiya. Those two channels have, ever since, been at the heart of the media wars that occasionally wrack the region.

The 2008–9 Israeli assault on Gaza was one example. The Arab world split into two camps, with Qatar, Syria, and several Gulf states firmly backing Hamas, while Saudi Arabia and Egypt sought to limit the militant group's political gains at the expense of the more secular Palestinian President Mahmoud Abbas. Al-Jazeera's coverage was vivid and emotional, focusing on close-ups of dead and wounded children. Al-Arabiya took a somewhat more cautious approach, eschewing the most gruesome footage and refusing to label the Palestinian dead as "martyrs." "Our coverage was closer to the people," Al-Jazeera's Ahmed Sheikh told this writer as a ceasefire was put in place. Nabil Khatib, chief editor at Al-Arabiya, shot back: Al-Jazeera, he said, was "satisfying the mob" and leading "a campaign for Hamas."

The degree to which the two channels reflected the politics of their respective patrons underlined the fact that the end of overt government ownership of television in the region did not usher in a period of unbridled media independence. Far from it. The rise of non-government media in the Arab world has been accompanied by the rise of a corporate feudalism, in which members of royal families, would-be politicos and cronies of national leaders have come to dominate the media landscape. The Dubai-based MBC Group was emblematic of this trend. Controlled by a son-in-law of the late King Fahd of Saudi Arabia, it owned the top-rated satellite entertainment channels and Al-Arabiya, along with a major stake in another regional giant, the Lebanon-based LBC channel, as well as the region's largest advertising agency and television ratings agency. Pan-Arab channels based in Egypt were largely in the hands of business interests close to Hosni Mubarak, Muammer Qadaffi's son had the monopoly on TV in Libya, and so the pattern continued across the region.

"I'm competing against countries, not companies!" Mohammed Alayyan, publisher and chairman of the independent newspaper *Al-Gad* and CEO of ATV in Jordan, complained.[8] It was all a natural extension of a similar system of control in the pan-Arab print media. "*Al-Hayat* is not a commercial project," the paper's then number two, Abdulwahab Badrakhan explained in 2005, "it is in the first place a political project, like *Asharq Al-Awsat. Asharq Al-Awsat* and *Al-Hayat* never [make] money, and you can understand that because you can consider us as public relations."

Another manifestation of that competition/control model could be found in the so-called "media cities" that dotted the region. The first, and most successful, was created in Dubai, a city-state in the United Arab Emirates. Essentially, a media duty-free zone, it promised both economic incentives and a "hands-off" political approach. That mix attracted regional channels like the MBC Group and its Al-Arabiya channel, Western news organizations, such as Reuters, and broadcasters from various developing world countries where domestic strictures were constraining. Up the road, Abu Dhabi set up twofour54, a media city named for its geographic coordinates, that attracted, among others, a major regional CNN center; Egypt created a similar project where many of its home-grown satellite channels based; and copy-cat centers sprouted up even in places like Syria, where media was tightly controlled. But the promise of freedom soon proved hollow.

Two private Pakistani channels based in Dubai's Media City, GEO TV and Ary One, discovered the hollowness when Pakistan declared martial law in 2007; after the channels refused a demand from the Musharraf government to sign a new media "code of conduct," Emirati authorities gave them two hours to stop broadcasting. Officials left little doubt that the principles of press freedom on which Media City was supposedly based had taken a back seat to Emirati foreign policy. "As an entity within the UAE, Dubai Media City would also observe the broadcast principals of the country's foreign policy and prevent the telecast of news and material that would undermine those principles," said Amina Al Rustamani, executive director of Dubai Media City.[9]

Media and Change in the Arab World

Media remained a tool of power, whether political, economic or religious. And through media, governments – and the families behind them – were seeking to control the pace of change. That strategy appeared to be paying off. Satellite television, and the newly aggressive form of journalism it inspired among many print journalists, *was* having a decided impact on what people thought about and discussed. But media is a tool of change, not a change agent in and of itself. And 16 years after the launch of Al-Jazeera, not a single Arab head-of-state had been unseated. Leaders had died – King Hussein in Jordan, Syria's Hafez Al-Assad, Morroco's King Hassan – but each had been replaced by the son.

Yet there was anecdotal evidence that Arab journalists were having an influence on policy. That was seen in the Syrian government's decision to withdraw its troops from Lebanon after the 24/7 Arab television coverage of anti-Syrian rallies in Beirut produced widespread opposition across the Arab world. Arab government attitudes toward the Lebanese Shiite militia Hezbollah was another example. Saudi Arabia and other governments in the Gulf were overtly critical of the militia early in the 2006 Israeli war in Lebanon, charging that the group's miscalculation sparked the assault. But within weeks, blanket coverage of the conflict by Arab satellite channels produced widespread backing for Hezbollah and by the end of the conflict the emir of Qatar welcomed Hezbollah's leader to the Gulf as an Arab hero.

Still, such examples remained exceptions to the rule. Al-Jazeera may have set the tone for an aggressive new style of journalism in the Arab world, but at the end of the day it was still owned by a government. Its so-called "red lines" – the limits beyond which reporters venture at their own peril – included stories that might negatively impact on Qatari foreign policy. One of the most overt examples of Qatari government influence on the station came as a Cold War emerged between Shiite Iran and the Sunni Arab regimes in the Gulf, Egypt and Jordan. After years in which Al-Jazeera had taken delight in tweaking the Saudis, word was passed down to the newsroom: realpolitik required that they back off.

Across the region, "media freedom" remained a relative term. Every news organization worked within "red lines" dictated by a variety of factors including the country in which the news organization was located, ownership, and the politics of the outlet. "As long as you don't write about the king, the military, religion or sex you can cover anything you want," a Jordanian journalist said of reporting in that kingdom.[10]

But guessing exactly what was off limits was often the biggest challenge. "Even sunny weather can be censored if it is a bad news for agriculture. Taboo topics are updated by the government on a daily basis," explained Sihem Bensedrine, the editor of the online magazine *Kalima*, a frequent target of Tunisian government repression. "I do not think the political system is developed enough to encompass the truth," said another reporter.[11]

Local Journalism

The newscasts of the pan-Arab satellite news channels were dominated by the big stories of the day: Iraq, Palestine, Lebanon, and the simmering confrontation between the Sunni Muslim Arab states and Shiite Iran. This was not unexpected. This was big power politics playing out on the Arab stage. What was missing was the street-level view of individual countries, cities, and villages. In the obsession with the dramatic issues of life-and-death on a grand scale, the questions of who is fixing the roads or the state of the schools were lost.

"There is huge amount of information that is missing because the local stations will not provide it to the viewer and we do not provide it to the viewer because it is local," Nabil Khatib, news chief at pan-Arab Al-Arabiya explained, "things that would make the Arabs better citizens by knowing more about their own realities they are not getting it from anywhere. So there is a huge portion of important data that is missing from their consciousness and this is negatively affecting any democratization process."

Nor were they getting that from the state-run broadcasters. "On the local level we ignore the local aspects of interest to the people, such as raising children and educating them and leave these national issues for larger issues such as Iraq and Palestine," Abd el-Latif el-Menawy, head of news at Egypt TV, confirmed, "this is one way that some of the state owned channels use to escape, because of their inability to tackle local topics. Most of [my] colleagues working in the local media lack the concept of local news."

The reason those channels wanted to "escape" such stories was that these were the areas that caused trouble. For the most part, Arab governments were happy to have their broadcasters fulminating about Israel or focusing on American military actions in Iraq, but they quickly became uncomfortable if the "red lines" around local politics, human rights, or even the domestic economy were crossed. And while the pan-Arab broadcasters occasionally touched on these stories, it was usually only when they became of major regional interest, as in the case of labor unrest in Egypt or pre-election clashes in Bahrain. Otherwise, they were, by definition, *local* stories of little interest to the satellite channels' broad regional audiences. In the West, the national networks, like America's CBS or the BBC in Britain, focused on the national and international stories while their local affiliates in places like Binghamton or Birmingham reported on the potholes and school board meetings; in the Arab world, there was no equivalent.

Change Agents

In the decade after the launch of Al-Jazeera, the very ethos of Arab journalism was transformed. Even among editors on government-controlled newspapers, there was now a desire to push the envelope. A survey of journalists in 13 Arab countries found that 75 percent of them said the prime mission of Arab journalism was to drive political and social change.[12] The same survey found that, despite accusations of anti-American bias, 62 percent of Arab journalists had a positive view of the American people, though, not surprisingly, their attitude toward Bush administration Middle East policy was almost unanimously negative. Half the journalists surveyed described their political philosophy as "democrat," about one-third said reform must be "radical," and they saw their own governments as posing as great a threat to the region as US policy.

In the face of such sentiments in the newsroom, governments continued to fight a rearguard action against these journalistic insurgents. Those efforts came in the form of laws and regulations, such as the much-criticized 2008 Arab League Satellite Media Charter, a retrogressive Big Brotheresque document that reaffirmed the right of governments to pull the plug on satellite broadcasters for a host of vague reasons that included perceived insults to Arab leaders. More chillingly, the backlash against media also included widespread intimidation, assaults, and jailing of journalists across the region, and, in some cases, their murder. Arab countries regularly landed at the bottom of the Freedom House list of countries where media is free,[13] and their leaders just as regularly were among those named "predators of press freedom" by Reporters Sans Frontières.[14] As Salaheddine El Hafez, secretary general of the Arab Journalists' Association, told a press freedom conference in late 2006. "The margins of freedom for the Arab press are severely limited and we have evidence of that in our daily lives."[15]

Arab governments kept talking about media liberalization but in most parts of the region so-called press "reform" laws failed to strip away regulations under which journalists could be jailed for the slightest perceived transgression – and often *increased* the level of control. Truth was no defense. Many journalists found themselves jailed for libel as the result of stories that were factually correct.

In Egypt, where media regulations adopted in 1995 were referred to by journalists as the "Press Assassination Law," the 2005 election brought a slight loosening of the reins on media, but once the last vote was tallied scores of journalists – including women – were attacked, beaten, threatened or jailed. "Egyptian journalism," said Osama al-Ghazli Harb, chief editor of *Al-Siyasah Al-Dawliyah*, "is developing on a tortured journey owing to political manipulation." In Iraq, the deadliest place in the world for reporters and home to scores of newly created media outlets, journalists were being killed for being perceived as too close to the government, too close to the resistance, or too close to particular political parties. "Sometimes they target journalists just to scare journalists in general," according to Al-Arabiya executive editor Nabil Khatib. Militant groups ran their own pseudo-news agencies and one motive for the attacks was to make it impossible for other news organizations to operate. "They are supplying the media [with information and footage] and they pressure you in a way to impose their agenda on you," Khatib explained, "of course we refuse, because we do not want to be used by any party whoever it is – so we pay the price." The tactics were effective. By the spring of 2007, Al-Arabiya had lost 11 staffers to Iraq's violence, several in targeted assassinations, and was left relying largely on local freelancers. "You feel that you are covering the war as if through glass," Khatib lamented.

Even in Al-Jazeera's home country of Qatar, while the emir took steps like creating a center to defend media freedom around the globe, his advisory council was demanding harsh penalties for journalists who criticized the government. One top Egyptian cleric demanded that journalists who insulted the government be lashed with a whip. Others, often shadowy figures working for governments or extremist groups, went even further. One Tunisian journalist had his fingers cut off before being murdered; female journalists in Egypt were sexually assaulted by police agents and warned there was more to come if they did not avoid certain stories; in countries from Yemen to North Africa other women journalists found themselves the targets of government-sponsored sexual smear campaigns; and in Lebanon, journalists were afraid to turn the ignition key of their cars after a string of bombings left two of the country's best-known journalists dead and a talk show host maimed.

It wasn't only governments that journalists feared. Religious groups sought to frog-march journalists according to their own agendas, whether militant jihadists in places like Iraq, Yemen and Algeria, or more traditional religious institutions. In Saudi Arabia, a religious court ordered journalist Mansour Nogaidan of the daily *Al-Riaydh*, to receive 75 lashes for calling for freedom of speech and criticizing Wahabism, Saudi Arabia's strict interpretation of Islam.

"I am not exaggerating when I say the Arab press is witnessing one of the worst periods of its life," Salaheddine El Hafez, vice editor-in-chief of Egypt's *Al-Ahram* newspaper and secretary general of the Arab Journalists Association, told a press freedom conference in late 2006, "the margins of freedom for the Arab press are severely limited and we have evidence of that in our daily lives."[16]

Bloggers, Citizen Journalism, and New Media Activism

The lack of media freedom in many Arab countries means that bloggers have taken on an importance that rivaled that of their colleagues in the West. By one count in 2009, there were close to 40,000 active Arab blogs. The vast majority of those were personal diaries, but a sizable proportion provided politically-driven reportage on local events within their own countries. Egyptian bloggers, who constituted about one-third of the Arab blogosphere, have been at the forefront of this Arab form of "citizen journalism." They broke numerous stories off-limits to the mainstream Egyptian media, most famously by posting online videos of Egyptian police torturing ordinary citizens. Their influence stemmed not from the number of people who viewed their blogs, in part because internet penetration remained low in Egypt and many parts of the Arab world, but in the ripple effect produced when mainstream reporters picked up and republished their stories. Bloggers represented the cross section of Arab politics. But bloggers were only one manifestation of new media in the Arab world. "Facebook Girl," a young Egyptian political activist, rose to prominence when she started a group on the social networking site aimed at supporting striking workers at a time when Egypt was also suffering from a shortage of bread. The group became the focal point for a national strike and inspired other groups around the region.

While the leaders of the Facebook group were overt activists, the line between bloggers and journalists was much more blurred. Some of the bloggers were journalists seeking an outlet for stories they could not publish in mainstream media.

But a small-but-influential group of Egyptian bloggers who gained notoriety beginning around the time of the 2005 Egyptian presidential elections represented a hybrid of frustrated young activists who sometimes acted as journalists – breaking stories of official torture, sexual harassment and other controversial events – but also writing highly-opinionated, sometimes libelous and often obscene essays, insisting all along that they were not journalists. "Yes, I'm biased and I like it this way," blogger Mahmoud Saber told one interviewer.[17]

Yet, despite fears among US policymakers that online activists were driving anti-American opinion, an exhaustive study by Harvard's Berkman Center for internet and Society found that "bloggers are far more concerned with domestic political issues than with the United States or its wars in the region. Criticism of domestic political leaders is the most frequent political topic ... followed by criticism of terrorism."[18]

The debate over the difference between a blogger and a journalist intersected discussions of the political nature of Arab journalism. The assassinations of journalists in Lebanon, widely assumed to have been the work of operatives controlled by the government of Syria, underscored the overlap between politics and journalism in the Arab world. One of the victims, *An Nahar* publisher Gibran Tueni, was a leader of the anti-Syrian political bloc in the Lebanese parliament, and the other two were outspoken opponents of Syria's military presence in Lebanon.

Many Arab journalists saw no contradiction between political engagement and their role as journalists; they sought to balance their obligations as an Arab citizen and their responsibilities as an Arab journalist. "You have a very big responsibility [as a journalist]," said Ibrahim Hamidi, a Syrian who was *Al-Hayat's* Damascus bureau chief, "but this responsibility has two faces. I do not run after scoops because I know a lot of scoops that may harm the country. I might be not objective, but it is the country that you live in that really matters more than your job. The priority is the safety of your country."

Yet corruption was the norm in many newsrooms. An "envelope culture" prevailed, in which it was accepted practice for cash to change hands for stories. It was a product of the abysmal salaries at all but the top satellite channels.

Beginning reporters at Egypt's government-owned newspapers were paid in the $80-to-$90 a month range and the situation was only slightly better at the private papers, while the monthly salary for a newly-hired journalist at state-run Egypt television and radio was just $35. The official salary for top editors was often measured in the hundreds, rather than thousands, of dollars. Even in Saudi Arabia, with its high cost-of-living, the average starting salary for a reporter is about $920 a month. Journalists there jokingly call it "the beggar's job." "You come up short either way," said *Arab News* executive editor Somayya Jabarti, "low pay and trouble getting serious stories published." One poll found that 40 percent of Arabic-language journalists said they would reprint a press release in return for a gift. "It's the whole structure of the job," Jabarti explained, "if they are well paid and well-trained, they won't need the gifts or envelopes."

Individuals were not alone in being tempted by bribes. According to Abdel Bari Atwan, editor-in-chief of the pan-Arab Palestinian daily *Al-Quds Al-Arabi*, his paper was regularly offered "subsidies" by governments ranging from conservative monarchies to radical nationalists.

In the survey mentioned above, Arab journalists chose the lack of "professionalism" and "ethics" as the greatest challenges to their industry. "There is no comparison, to be honest, between the press in the West and the press in the Arab world," according to Osman Mirghani, deputy editor in chief at the Saudi-owned pan-Arab newspaper *Asharq Alawsat*. He saw Western journalists as far more professional than his Arab colleagues. "Having said that, the press in the Arab region is developing, is evolving and I think is moving forward," Mirghani said.

The predominance of opinion in the Arab media was another issue. Al-Jazeera's *Code of Ethics* stated that its reporters must "[d]istinguish between news material, opinion and analysis to avoid the pitfalls of speculation and propaganda."[19] Yet its airwaves, and the pages of most Arab newspapers, were thick with opinion masquerading as reportage. Such an inter-mingling was rooted in the history of Arab journalism. Constrained from reporting facts, newspapers served as mouthpiece of governments, so readers turned to them as reflections of governmental thinking. Former *Al-Ahram* editor Mohamed Hassainein Heikel is revered as one of the greatest Arab journalists, even though he doubled as advisor and confident to the late Egyptian president Gamal Abdul Nasser.

No incident better illustrated the differences between Western and Arab journalism than the controversy over publication of cartoons seen by Muslims as insulting to the Prophet Muhammad. Originally published in a Danish newspaper, the cartoons eventually sparked outrage across the Arab world, with riots in Beirut and Damascus, where the Danish embassies were attacked and burned. Many Western journalists immediately defended the paper's right to publish the cartoons on the basis of freedom of speech. But Arab journalists responded that media freedom must be tempered with respect and responsibility. "When I insult your religion or your feelings it is crossing the limits of freedom of expression," Salama Ahmed Salama, Egypt's most respected columnist, said during the crisis, "for many Europeans, such things are not so important, but here religion is a daily food and we cannot just accept this." Elements within the Danish Muslim community, and their counterparts in the Arab world, exploited the crisis for their own political ends, but that did not change the fact that it highlighted the sensitivity Arab journalists brought to such issues. "Freedom of expression is only half of the truth," Rashid Khashana, Tunis correspondent for the pan-Arab daily *Al-Hayat*, observed at the height of the debate, "the second part is that we must respect things sacred for Christians, Muslims and Jews."

Restrictions on criticism of figures in power were a constant barrier to Arab journalists, but at the same time, many genuinely subscribed to the view first laid out by pioneering Lebanese publisher Boutros al-Boustani in the late nineteenth century. "In order for newspapers to be beneficial to society," al-Boustani wrote, they must avoid publishing stories that violated "the right principles."[20] To be sure, not everyone agreed. But in the above-mentioned study, 80 percent of Arab journalists surveyed partly or completely agreed with the statement, "Journalists must balance the need to inform the public with the responsibility to show respect."[21]

Emerging Models

The fact that Arab journalists themselves held a nuanced view of their role emphasizes the danger of generalizing about the state of Arab journalism. On some levels, the situation was grim; the reports from press freedom groups like Reporters Sans Frontières and the Committee to Protect Journalists made for grim reading. Yet barely a month went by without the announcement of another satellite channel being formed or a license for a new (semi-) independent newspaper being issued. Indeed, at a time when the news industry in the US and Europe seemed on the brink of collapse, prospects for Arab journalists were bright. While the graduates of Western journalism schools faced the very real prospect of unemployment, Arab news organizations were besieging the few journalism schools in the region with offers to hire their graduates.

In some ways, the balance-of-power in international media was shifting from the West to the Arab world, with its vast wealth and newly emergent media. A decade after launching Al-Jazeera, Qatar created an English-language sister channel, Al-Jazeera English, in the hopes of gaining the same kind of influence in the "global south" that the Arabic channel had given it in the Arab world. While its success vis-à-vis competitors CNN International and BBC World in its first few years of existence remained mixed, it was certainly attracting the attention of television journalists the world over. When the channel advertised for a few dozen openings in 2008, it received more than 8,000 applications, many from Western journalists who couldn't find a job at home – or who read the proverbial handwriting on the newsroom wall.

Much the same was happening just down the coast in Abu Dhabi, where some 200 veterans of major US and European newspapers filled the newsroom of *The National*, a flashily-designed paper modeled on Singapore's *Straits-Times*. Headed by Martin Newland, the former top editor at Britain's *Daily Telegraph*, and Hassan Fattah, a former *New York Times* Middle East correspondent, the paper was ultimately owned by the government of Abu Dhabi via the country's $850 billion investment fund.

"We are part of a broader reform initiative," said Fattah, defending the paper's relatively toothless approach to covering the country, "by definition, we will push boundaries and try to make change, but in the Arab world change does come slowly." The truth of that statement was underscored by a new UAE media law implemented not long after the paper was launched, which included heavy fines for carrying "misleading news" that harmed the economy or for insulting members of the government or royal family.

Conclusion

"Journalism is a part of change," Prince Bandar bin Khaled al Faisal, the owner of Saudi Arabia's *Al-Watan* newspaper and grandson of the late King Faisal, said on the sidelines of an international media conference he had helped fund, "and this conference is an effort to say, 'OK, maybe we should expedite the process a little bit because we really do have a lot to lose.'"

Across the region, governments were struggling with how to cope with that change and how to avoid losing ultimate control. For some, that meant tightening the noose on journalists; for others, establishing their own "tame" media owned directly or via proxies; for many governments, it was a combination of both. No government was just throwing open the doors. Even Qatar, home of Al-Jazeera, tightly-controlled its domestic media.

Such contradictions were common; government responses often reflected a lack of understanding of the new rules of the game. When rumors began circulating in the summer of 2007 that Egyptian President Hosni Mubarak might be ill or even dead, the government remained silent. When newspapers published the rumors on their front pages, the government issued a statement saying he was fine. When the rumors took on a life of their own, the government finally brought out Mrs. Mubarak to deny them, which fed the rumor-mill even more. Only then did the president finally appear at a photo-opportunity, something that would have been the immediate response of a government that understood it was no longer enough just to say something to make it so. The government's other response was also telling: it eventually convicted the editors who published the rumors – only to have the president pardon the editors a year later.

Beyond satellite television and traditional media, blogs, Facebook, SMS, Twitter, and the like were also changing the rules of the game. The information dam had become a leaking sieve. The "democratization of media" meant even the poorest peasant was likely to have a cell phone, giving him or her access to a new world of communications. Egyptian groups had exploited that in organizing a national strike and the success of Iranians in mobilizing the masses via Twitter after the 2009 elections was likely to further inspire Arab activists.

For Arab journalists, meanwhile, it was one step forward, one step back, a half-step forward. They were inspired by the possibilities apparent on the television screen each day. But daily they were also forced to cope with the realities of accessing information in societies built on secrecy.

Ultimately, Arab governments would never be able to completely control the flow of information across their borders. But that didn't mean they would not continue to try. Just as Arab journalists would cling to the conviction that, as

Yemeni editor Hamzi Bokari put it, "Journalism is a weapon of mass destruction for oppressive governments."

Notes

1. William A. Rugh, *The Arab Press: News Media and Political Process in the Arab World*, Syracuse: Syracuse University Press, 1979.
2. Quoted in el-Nawawy and Iskandar, *Al-Jazeera: How the Free Arab News Network Scooped the World and Changed the Middle East*, p. 116.
3. John Kifner, "At Arab All-News Channel, Western Values Prevail," *New York Times* (October 12, 2001).
4. "The World through Their Eyes," *The Economist* (February 24, 2005 [accessed February 26, 2005]), available from www.economist.com/displaystory.cfm?story_id=3690442.
5. Dan Williams, "A Real News Maker," *Jerusalem Post* (July 13, 2001).
6. George H. W. Bush, "President's Remarks at US University Presidents Summit on International Education," ed. The White House (The White House, 2006).
7. Unless cited otherwise, all quotes are based on interviews with the author.
8. Lisa Schnellinger and Mohannad Khatib, *Fighting Words: How Arab and American Journalists Can Break through to Better Coverage*, Washington, DC: International Center for Journalists, 2006, p. 15.
9. "National Media Council clarifies closure of GEO, ARY TV Stations," in Emirates News Agency (WAM), Dubai, November 17, 2007, www.wam.org.ae/servlet/Satellite?c=WamLocEnews&cid=1193028279857&pagename=WAM%2FWamLocEnews%2FW-T-LEN-FullNews.
10. Quoted in John Smock, "Final Report, Knight International Press Fellow," Washington, DC: International Center for Journalists, summer, 2006.
11. Ibid., pp. 57–8 and 61.
12. Lawrence Pintak and Jeremy Ginges, "The Mission of Arab Journalism: Creating Change in a Time of Turmoil," *The International Journal of Press/Politics*, 13(3) (2008).
13. "Freedom of the Press 2008: A Global Survey of Media Independence," Washington, DC: Freedom House, 2008.
14. "Predators of Press Freedom," Paris: Reporters Sans Frontières, 2007.
15. "Media Forum Examines Widespread Press Freedom Abuses," World Association of Newspapers (December 11, 2006 [accessed December 11, 2006]), available from www.wan-press.org/article12549.html.
16. Ibid.
17. Staff, "Culture 101: Beyond the Blog," *Egypt Today* (March 2009).
18. http://cyber.law.harvard.edu/sites/cyber.law.harvard.edu/files/Mapping_the_Arabic_Blogosphere_0.pdf.
19. http://english.aljazeera.net/aboutus/2006/11/2008525185733692771.html
20. Quoted in Ayalon, "*Sihafa*: The Arab Experiment in Journalism," p. 268.
21. www.informaworld.com/smpp/section?content=a904515429&fulltext=713240928.

14

Media Globalization in Asia

Junhao Hong

Introduction

In the last two decades or so, media in Asia, especially in countries such as China, Japan, India, and South Korea, have become more and more globalized. Both imports and exports of cultural products have increased dramatically. Asian countries are experiencing a wave of national media sensations much like the West did decades ago.

China: An Ambitious New Player in the Global Media Arena

From 1949, when the communist China was established, to the middle of 1970s, when the country was still under the control of Mao Zedong, the late Chairman of Chinese Communist Party, and his followers, Chinese media was completely closed to the outside world. The media was used mainly as an ideological tool by the Communist Party for political needs.

Mao's death in 1976 and China's new leaders' "open door" policy that started in the late 1970s and early 1980s have ever since drastically changed the country's all-round course, including the mass media system, which is one of the most enormous and complex media systems in the world. Over the past three decades, media, ranging from newspapers, magazines, books, radio and television broadcasting to film production, have all experienced tremendous changes. After 30 years of reform, they are no longer only a pure propaganda machine of the communist authorities, but are a multifunctioned service. While their fundamental role remains little changed as the mouth piece of the Communist Party and the government, they are now also considered as an information and entertainment provider to the people and a public service of the society. Moreover, media have become an important part of the economy. The government has long time ago terminated subsidies to media organizations, though all media organizations are still considered as government institutions. Now, all media organizations must survive through market competitions for advertising revenues, and media have become a crucial part of the overall economy by making financial contributions to the government. Only in several decades since the 1970s, market-orientation and commercialization have become Chinese media's main blood that supports the everyday's existence and operation of the "communist" media system, at least in the name.

Over the past three decades from 1978 to 2008, all the sectors of China's media industry has had a historic proliferation. Newspapers developed from 186 in 1978 to 1,938 in 2007, and newspapers' advertising revenue developed from 0.96 billion Chinese RMBs in 1978 (about $0.12 billion US dollars at the time) to 34.3 billion Chinese RMBs in 2008 (about $5 billion US dollars at the time). Magazines developed from 930 in 1978 to 9,468 in 2008. Production of television programming developed from 38,100 hours in 1985 to 2.55 million hours in 2007, and TV broadcasting developed from 1,200 hours in 1978 to 279,000 hours in 2007. As for television penetration, it reached 96.24 percent in 2007, whereas it was only 57.3 percent in 1982. Especially, digital cable television has had an astonishing growth in the last several years. The subscribers of digital cable TV increased from a total of 276,000 in 2003 to 27.96 million in 2007, showing a more than 100-fold growth in just four years. Despite the fact that the growth of radio broadcasting was affected by TV's development as well as the emergence of internet-based new media, the advertising revenue from radio broadcasting still had a several-hundred-fold growth from 18 million Chinese RMBs in 1986 (about $2.2 million US dollars at the time) to 6.5 billion Chinese RMBs in 2007 (about $0.95 billion US dollars at the time). As for book publishing, the total number of books published in 1978 was only 15,000, but in 2007 altogether 136,200 books were published (*2009 China Statistics Yearbook*, 2009; *Collections of China Journalism and Publishing Statistics, 1978–2008*, 2009). The most eye-catching change is probably the growth of China's internet users. The internet did not emerge in China until 1997. In 1998, there were just 2.1 million internet users in the country of 1.2 billion people, which was far behind most developed nations. But by June 30, 2009, China's internet users increased to 338 million, surpassing the total internet users of 220 million in the United States and thus making China the country with the most internet users in the world (*CNNIC 24th Survey Report*, 2009).

In 2008, the total revenue from China's media industry reached 422 billion Chinese RMBs (about $62 billion US dollars at the time). This amount reflects an 11.36 percent increase over the media revenue in 2007, a 27.61 percent increase over the media revenue in 2006, a 71.55 percent increase over the media revenue in 2005, and an 100.2 percent increase over the media revenue in 2004.[1] In other words, China's media industry doubled its scale in just five years, moving towards an increasingly sizable and noticeable player in the global media arena.

For a long time, China Radio International (CRI) was the third largest external broadcasting service in the world, following Voice of America (VOA) of the United States as the largest one and Radio Moscow of the former Soviet Union as the second largest one. In the last two decades, CRI has had a rapid expansion. Not only has it now replaced Radio Moscow (its current name is Voice of Russia) to become the world's second largest external broadcasting service, but also in many aspects it has even surpassed VOA in terms of expansion speed and broadcasting languages. Particularly, since the beginning of the 2000s the Chinese Communist Party and government have launched a series of campaign to push Chinese media organizations to "Going out of China" to internationalize themselves. With both the policy support and financial subsidies from the government, in 2008 alone CRI established eight new FM broadcasting stations abroad, making the total number of FM broadcasting stations outside China to 19, a 73 percent expansion in just one year. In the same year, the broadcasting hours of CRI increased by 149 hours, making CRI's total daily broadcasting hours reach to 700, a 27 percent jump in one year (*Report on Development of China's Radio, Film and Television*, 2009). The government claimed these developments and expansions were "an important progress in Chinese media's history."[2]

Meanwhile, the four foreign-audience-oriented channels of China Central Television (CCTV) have also been continually expanding their overseas market. The four channels are now penetrating the audiences in 139 countries all over the world. Their total worldwide subscribers have reached 96.5 million, and the overseas subscribers of certain programs have exceeded 150 million. CCTV's offices in America and Europe were both expanded substantially. Moreover, CCTV has established a joint venture with US's satellite TV to transmit its Great Wall program directly to American audiences through satellite TV. In only several years the subscribers of Great Wall program have reached 100,000, and the Great Wall program is becoming a growing brand name TV program. In the same time, the "open door" practice has also substantially internationalized and globalized China's media market as well. In recent years, on average more than 100 foreign TV dramas of more than 1,000 episodes were imported to the country, comparing to just a nominal number 30 years ago. Now, more than 70 countries have regular trading of television programming with China. Moreover, eight foreign TV channels including some of media tycoon Rupert Murdoch's are now permitted to operate in China's certain areas, and a total of 34 foreign TV channels are allowed to be seen in dozens of thousands of three-star or more hotels across the whole China.[3]

During the last decade or so, China's only privately owned – or the only "non-governmentally owned" – satellite TV organization, Phoenix TV, has had a quick move toward an international TV broadcaster. This Hong Kong-based television broadcaster was launched in 2000, with the undisclosed permission of the

Chinese government and all kinds of support in an attempt to deliver "China's voice" to "all the people of Chinese origin across the world." Now, this TV entity has already become a multifaceted world media conglomerate, owning electronic media such as Phoenix Chinese Channel, Phoenix Movie Channel, Phoenix News Channel, Phoenix Europe Channel, and Phoenix America Channel, print media such as *Phoenix Weekly*, and online media such as Phoenix Online Service. Literally, Phoenix's audiences and readers are now indeed all over the world.[4]

China has become one of the world's main film production nations. In 1978, China produced only 46 feature films (excluding those that were produced in Hong Kong and Taiwan; same for the numbers of film production below). Ten years later, in 1997 the number increased to 88. But after entering the twenty-first century, China's film production has had a proliferate growth. In 2002, a total of 100 feature films were produced, and the number jumped to 140 in 2003, 212 in 2004, 260 in 2005, 330 in 2006, and 402 in 2007. In 2008, 406 feature movies were produced in mainland China, thus making the country with the third largest film production in the world.[5]

The box office revenue of China's movies has increased dramatically as well. In 2004, the box office revenue reached a historical high, 3.7 billion Chinese RMBs (about $450 million US dollars at the time). In less than five years, in 2008 the number became 8.4 billion Chinese RMBs (about $1.2 billion US dollars at the time), demonstrating a 130 percent growth over the amount in 2004 and a 30 percent growth over the amount in 2007. Moreover, 60 percent of the box office was from China-produced movies and only 40 percent was from imported movies, the first time in China's history that box office from domestic movies surpassed the office box from imported movies. Furthermore, Chinese movies have been shown in many countries' theaters and have often become a focal topic of social occasions. In 2008, 45 China-produced movies were imported by 62 countries. Among the 7 billion Chinese RMB office box in 2008 (about $1 billion US dollars at the time), 2.5 billion Chinese RMBs (about 400 million US dollars) were from overseas office box, reflecting a 25 percent increase over the figure in 2007.

Despite the fact that in the last few years the global film market has been shrinking, China's film industry has instead been growing healthily. Its overseas office box revenue was 0.6 billion Chinese RMBs in 2003 (about $72 million US dollars at the time), 1.1 billion in 2004 (about $132 million US dollars at the time), 1.7 billion in 2005 (about $210 million US dollars at the time), 1.9 billion in 2006 (about $232 million US dollars at the time), and 2 billion in 2007 (about $286 million US dollars at the time).[6] These steady increases evidently demonstrate the growth of the export of Chinese movies and the increasing popularity of China-produced movies both among the audiences across the world and among the international filmmakers as well. For instance, in 2008 a total of 249 China-produced movies attended 102 international film festivals, and 39 China-produced movies won a total of 72 awards at 24 international film festivals. In addition, in 2008 China co-produced more than 40 movies with more than 10 countries or areas, including Hong Kong, Korea, Singapore, Malaysia, Britain, The Netherlands, France, United States, and Canada. Almost all the top 20 movies in 2008 on the list of China's domestic box office revenue were co-produced by China and other countries.[7]

Since the beginning of the twenty-first century, China International Television Corporation, which belongs to the Ministry of Radio, Film and Television, has been coordinating a number of China's leading central and regional TV stations and television production companies to attend the TV Fair in Cannes (MIPTV and MIPCOM) to promote Chinese TV programs. China Film Overseas Promotion Corporation has been helping both state movie studios and independent film production companies to exhibit movies at Cannes Film Festival and other international film festivals. Since 2007, China Film Forum has become an official activity of Cannes Film Festival, and it has been receiving growing attention and interest among renowned filmmakers from all over the world.[8]

In the same time, China has also hosted more international TV festivals in various places in the country to promote sales of Chinese television programs to foreign TV companies. Among others, Shanghai International TV Festival, Chendu International TV Festival, Hangzhou International Animation Festival, Beijing International TV Week, Guangzhou International Documentary Convention, China International Film and TV Fair, China Radio Development Forum, China-ASEAN (Association of Southeast Asian Nations) Radio and TV Submit, have become internationally recognized important events. More and more foreign companies regularly attend these events and the sale amount of Chinese TV programs and movies at these festivals and fairs has increased steadily.[9]

As part of the central government's Going Abroad Project, which encourages and helps TV stations and production companies to "deliver more Chinese voices and images" to the world, now many Chinese TV stations and production companies have their business or joint venture business in various countries across the world. China-produced television programs are now available in US, UK, France, Spain, Portugal, Japan, Korea, Singapore, Australia, New Zealand, Russia, Mongolia, Vietnam, Thailand, Laos, Cambodia, and Burma.[10]

Animation production was one of the most successful aspects in the Going Abroad Project. In 2008, a CCTV-produced, 30-million-Chinese RMB-budgeted, 1,026-minute-long, 52-episode animation series, *The Little Carp's Adventures* (*Xiao Li Yu Li Xian Ji*), was imported by 51 countries. This program alone made 11.86 million Chinese RMBs (about $1.7 million US dollars at the time) from the overseas market, setting a new record in the history. *The Story of Three Kingdoms*, China's first HD TV animation program that was co-produced with Japan, was sold to more than 40 foreign TV companies in 20 countries.[11]

The advertising industry in China has grown remarkably in the last few years. In 2008, advertising revenues from radio and television reached 70.2 billion Chinese RMBs (about $10.3 billion US dollars at the time), reflecting a 16.85 percent increase over the figure in 2007. The direct reason for this significant increase was mainly the advertising revenues from foreign companies during the Beijing 2008 Olympic Games. The telecasting of the Beijing 2008 Olympic Games was one of the biggest events not only in China's TV history but also in the history of world television. More than 4 billion people across the world watched the televised games. A new record in the world TV history, this figure surpassed the TV audience number of the Sydney 2000 Olympic Games, 3.4 billion, as well as the TV audience number of the Athens 2004 Olympic Games, 3.9 billion. The Beijing 2008 Olympics opening ceremony was said to hit a record high of the world TV rating: 842 million people in the world watched the event, and 658 million people watched the closing ceremony.[12]

Because of the Beijing 2008 Olympic Games, China's total advertising revenue in 2008 had a 29 percent increase of that in 2007. For CCTV alone, its advertising revenue in 2008 reached 17 billion Chinese RMBs (about $2.5 billion $US dollars at the time). This figure displayed a 46.14 percent increase of CCTV's advertising revenue in 2007 (*2009 Report on Development of China's Radio, Film and Television*, 2009). Particularly, during the 17-day 2008 Beijing Olympic Games, CCTV's advertising revenue reached 2 billion Chinese RMBs (about $300 million $US dollars at the time). Especially, from August 8 to August 16, on average, every day 357 million people visited CCTV's Olympic Games website. During the Beijing Olympic Games, the advertising revenue from CCTV's Olympic Games website alone reached 200 million Chinese RMBs (about $30 million $US dollars at the time). In comparison, before the 2008 Beijing Olympic Games, the annual advertising revenue of CCTV's website was only around 50 million Chinese RMBs (about $7.5 million $US dollars at the time).[13]

The Beijing 2008 Olympics also made many global companies very interested in China's huge media market. The biggest foreign sponsors of the telecasting of Beijing 2008 Olympic Games included Coca-Cola, McDonald's, Adidas, Johnson & Johnson, etc. To take the advantage of the Beijing Olympic Games seeking more market share in the world's most populous country, in 2008 Coca-Cola's advertising expenditure in China increased 24 percent, Visa's increased 30 percent, KFC's increased 39 percent, whereas Adidas doubled its advertising expenditure and Nike's had a dramatic growth of 143 percent.[14]

However, not every transnational media company's globalizing move toward China has had a happy ending. To some foreign companies, China is still a puzzle, and they are not sure how to do business in this half-socialist and half-capitalist country or how to play the "China game." In the trend of numerous transnational media corporations' crusading China's market during the last few years, while some transnational media corporations had their celebrations of success in China, some unfortunately met their Waterloos there. Bertelsmann, the world's number four largest transnational media corporation, entered China as early as in 1995. It used to have China's largest Reader's Club that had more than one million members and therefore had a significant market share of the book sale in the country. Partly owing to the swift development of several of China's domestic book publishing and retailing giants, and more importantly owing to the failure of Bertelsmann's marketing strategies in China, which was also largely owing to the insufficient knowledge of this country, over the 13 years from 1995 to 2008 Bertelsmann's business in China had never become profitable. As a result, in early July of 2008 Bertelsmann sadly announced its decision on completely withdrawing its all business in China.[15] Despite so, this "dream" market, the market with the world's largest population and highest economic growth rate, is still attracting many transnational corporations around the world to come with confidence, ambition, and anticipated success.

Nonetheless, the "open-door" policy has not only allowed China to have opened its market to foreign companies including foreign and transnational media companies, but also the government has vigorously encouraged Chinese media organizations to export media and cultural products to other countries. Despite the fact that many scholars suspect that the government's push for Chinese media's entering the global media arena is more out of a political motivation than an economic motivation, after years of efforts Chinese media has become an active new player in the global media arena and is much more noticeable than a couple of decades ago.

The globalization of Chinese media is a two-fold strategy. For the media organizations, they are no longer only interested in the domestic market; they are also aiming at the much bigger and more profitable international market, especially these markets of Western nations. However, for the Communist Party and government, they are more eager to use the export of Chinese media and cultural products to expand China's soft power in the world, which has been in the process of political and economic restructuring since the late 1980s. In other words, while the Chinese media practitioners are eager to take the globalization as an opportunity to get a share of the global media market, the Chinese authorities are more eager to have more "China's voices" in the world's political, economic, and cultural forums, thus exerting more China's soft power in the world.

Especially during the last two years, China has been further accelerating the pace of internationalizing and globalizing its media. Among a number of new actions, three strategic ones are particularly worth noting. The first action is the establishment of China Satellite News Gathering Alliance (CSNG) in December of 2008. CSNG consists of a total of China's 50 leading television broadcasters with CCTV being the leader of this alliance. The purpose of this action is to change China's television broadcasting from many scattered individual "trees" to a mustered "forest" so that it can have the needed capability to compete with CNN and BBC in the world television arena. The second action is that, also in December 2008, the Xinhua News Agency started a visual news service, thus taking it to the same level of the leading global news agencies such as AP and Routers that have become much more effective and competitive in the world media market by transmitting both print and visual news items to their subscribers.[16] The third action is a billion-dollar decision on internationalization of China's media. Earlier in 2009, the Chinese Communist Party and the central government decided to allocate 45 billion Chinese RMBs (about $7 billion US dollars) for an unprecedented "media project." The project is to build up China's media "aircraft carrier" in an attempt to let China's media have more power to crusade to the world media arena to compete with world media giants, such as Time Warner and AOL, Disney, News Corp., Viacom, Bertelsmann, etc. However, the most important and ultimate purpose of all these actions for China's media internationalization and globalization is still a simple and political one: to give China more "right" to say in the world affairs, to let China's voice be more heard across the world, and to help balance the currently still seriously unbalanced "world information and communication order." As soon as this unprecedented strategic media project was revealed by Western media, it immediately drew great worldwide attention. Despite political considerations, the Chinese government publicly denied this project and many Chinese media organizations have already silently started to work vigorously towards the fulfillment of this ambitious project.

Japan: The Global Success of Japanese Animation

Japan is a major player in some aspects of the media and entertainment industry, and especially it has the strength in the global trading of animation and horror films. The Anime (the term refers to Japanese animation) and horror movies represent a special level of expertise that is not seen in any other countries. In the last several decades, Japan's film and animation industries have been remarkably successful both in their home market and in the overseas market as well. This is one of the reasons why Japanese films and animations are worldwide acceptable is their themes.

Japanese film exports are highly concentrated on animations and horror movies. Figures 14.1 and 14.2 depict the market size of Japanese animation and box office revenues from animations. Animation films accounted for 50 percent of the exports to US, 60 percent to Italy, and 27 percent to South Korea. Horror films were for 44 percent in exports to South Korea. In general, Japanese animation occupies more than 60 percent of the world animation market.[17]

The big-hit films in Japan's domestic market or the awarded films at international film festivals are widely distributed abroad. For example, *Howl's Moving Castle*, which was nominated for Oscar in 2006 and won another 8 awards in 2005–6, broke several records at the Japanese box office and was shown in many foreign countries such as Korea, France, Taiwan, Hong Kong and US.[18] According to statistics published by Japan's Ministry of Economy, Trade and Industry, in November of 2004 the film's big hit raised the total animated-film ticket sales to 16 times greater than in the same month of the previous year.

In order to expand its global reach, Japanese film production companies started joint productions with American or other Asian counterparts. For example, Disney is now buying Japanese Anime with games and other products for

Figure 14.1   The market size of Japanese animations (in billion yen), 2005
Source: based on data from JETRO, 2005

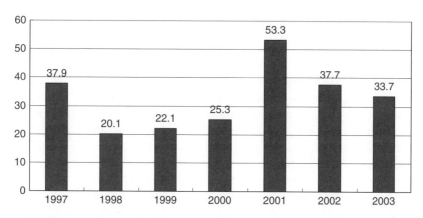

Figure 14.2   Box office revenues for feature-length animations in Japan (in billion yen), 2005
Source: based on data from JETRO, 2005

distribution in other regions. It is also considering joint film and Anime productions in Japan. Disney has established an entertainment content purchasing division within its Japanese subsidiary. Like Disney, many foreign television stations and distribution companies are now investing in animation and film productions in Japan or joint productions with Japanese companies.

IG, an Anime production company whose productions *Ghost in the Shell* and other titles won numerous overseas fans, established a US subsidiary that retains lawyers and accountants familiar with American business practices and legal affairs to help their sales negotiations and joint productions with American distributors. Another major production, *Toei Animation*, also established its US subsidiary in 2004.

Using a new communication technology, Japanese productions and distributors are testing a new global joint venture. Toei Animation is now distributing animation titles via the internet, and its consumers can directly download and watch their programs from its archives. Since the direct sales between production and consumer through the internet allows oversea consumers to access to the contents without any intervention by distributors or exhibitors, consumers can enjoy the content at a more reasonable price and comfortable situation. Hal Film Maker set up a joint venture with a Chinese company for anime production, programming and character merchandising.[19] With these new approaches, Japanese animation and films are aiming to expand business across various regions in the world.

Animation production has increasingly outsourced from other Asian countries. Many Japanese productions are outsourcing to subcontractors in China, Korea, and elsewhere. They send original prints and other digital data to the subcontractors for the stage of animating, coloring and other simple operations. While Japanese productions are more involved in planning, financing, direction and other processes that require high expertise, the subcontractors in other countries are mainly taking part in animating and coloring works. Some market experts estimated that over 90 percent of Japanese animation industry is outsourced. Most market experts agreed that the percentage of Japanese animation production's outsourcing should be at 60 percent. Regardless of whatever the exact percentage is, there is no doubt that only a few animation titles are produced solely in Japan now. For example, Gilbli Studio, a Japanese animation production founded by the world-renowned directors Misyazaki and Takahata, subcontracted part of the work on *Spirited Away* to Korean companies. Some animation productions now even have their own production studios in other countries. For example, Toei Animation has more than 130 employees at its production house in the Philippines.[20]

Since the late 1990s, remaking of Japanese films has become a major trend in Hollywood. After remaking a Japanese horror film *The Ring* turned out to be a big hit in the US market in 2002, many American film productions have bought the remake rights from Japanese films and animations, primarily for Japanese horror films. As shown in Table 14.1, the remade Japanese films include *The Grudge, Dark Water, Pulse, The Ring, The Ring2*, and *Shall We Dance?* Among them, *The Ring* and *The Grudge* were the most profitable in the US market. *The Ring*, remade by Dream Works, has garnered a office box revenue worldwide of more than $230 million, almost six times the remake cost. Dream Works bought the remake from the director Nakata Hideo for only $1.2 million and spent another $40 million to remake the film.[21]

The remakes in recent years have received much more attention than all the previous remakes of Japanese films in terms of its scale and profitability. It is because all the previous remakes were isolated and random events, and therefore the influence could not last too long. But in recent years the marketing strategies were changed. For example, the Americanized *Ring*'s success was followed by other sales of Japanese horror films such as *Ring 2* (purchased by

Table 14.1 Japanese films remade or to be remade by Hollywood, 1977–2004

Remake title	Japanese title	Genre	Japan release
Title undecided	Shiawase No Kirroi Hankachi	Drama	1977
Shall We Dance?	Shall We Dance?	Drama	1996
Title undecided	Joyurei	Horror	1996
The Ring	The Ring	Horror	1998
The Ring 2	The Ring 2	Horror	1999
Title undecided	Chaos	Horror	2000
Pulse	Kairo	Horror	2001
Dark Water	Honogurai Mizu no Soko kara	Horror	2002
The Grudge	Juoun	Horror	2003
Title undecided	Toho J. Horro Theater (6 films)	Horror	2004

Source: based on data from JETRO, 2005

Table 14.2 Domestic spending in Japan's filmed entertainment industry, 2005 (in US millions)

Box office spending	1,799
Home video spending	5,902
Total spending	7,701

Source: based on data from PWC, 2006

Dream Works), *Dark Water* (purchased by Disney), and *Jouon* (purchased by Columbia Pictures).[22]

Horror films account for the majority of films that have been or are planned to be remade. Among the 10 major sales of the remake rights, eight were horror films, while only two were dramas. That is mainly because Japanese horror movies represent a special level of expertise that appeals a wide range of audiences abroad. As Taplin explains, the originality or aura in Japanese horror films comes from solid and well-made storytelling, whereas Hollywood movies heavily rely on special effects and pyrotechnics.[23] Coupled with the uniqueness of Japanese horror films, the demands of audience for exotic cultures and fast action in Hollywood are making the current remaking trend.

A modernized system in production and distribution and the home market effect are some of the main factors for wide acceptance of Japanese films and animations. Given the second largest entertainment market in the world, Japan has a good home market to support the growth of cultural products. The sufficient market size of entertainment and cultural products has helped Japanese films and animations to expand their business abroad. In terms of domestic market size, Japan has the largest film market in Asia, at $7.7 billion, as shown in Table 14.2, which is 47 percent of the total media spending. Domestic films did well at the box office, increasing their ratio of the market to more than 40 percent, but overall box office spending fell in large part because of the low demand for American films. The weakness of US films at box office seriously reduced domestic spending in the film market.

In 2004, Japan's box office revenues were split into 62.5 percent for imported films and 37.5 percent for domestic films, which is relatively quite high among Western nations other than the United States. The ratios of domestic films in box office revenue and number of release have increased at 17.8 percent and 8.01 percent, respectively. According to JETRO, animation films have boosted the market since the mid-1990s. *Spirited Away* set a record of 23.5 million moviegoers.[24] In addition, some other big hits of animations such as Studio Ghibli's *Howl's Moving Castle* and *Sekai no Chushin de Ai wo Sakebu* also helped to boost the domestic share. While domestic films are expanding their market share, imported films are slowly, but steadily losing their dominant position in Japan. For example, the big hit of *Howl's Moving Castle* in 2004 helped the domestic film's market share rise up to 37.5 percent. This implies that domestic films start having competitive advantage over foreign films and this is creating a positive home market effect. Regarding the number of releases, a total of 165 first-run films were released in 2003, showing a big growth from the previous years. The number of domestic film releases has steadily increased during the last few years at 8 percent of annual change. The ratio of domestic films in the market has been increased from 44.6 percent in 2001 to 47.8 percent in 2004.[25]

While Japanese animations are widely accepted all over the world, Japanese TV programs are less accepted by other nations, particularly other Asian countries for political reasons. Korean and Chinese memories of Japanese colonial rule prompted these countries to ban Japanese television programs. However, as Taiwan lifted its ban on Japanese contents in 1993 and South Korea relaxed its ban in the late 1990s, exports of Japanese TV dramas to Taiwan and South Korea have rapidly increased. However, Japanese TV dramas have also met many foreign audiences with widespread acceptance, including those Asian countries. As seen in Figure 14.3, Asia is now the main target market of Japanese television programs with a market share of 46.3 percent, followed by North America of 25.7 percent, Europe of 12.2 percent, South America of 5.5 percent, the Middle East of 1.8 percent, and others of 7.5 percent.

Regarding program genre, as shown in Figure 14.4, 37.5 percent are dramas, and 36.2 percent are variety programs. They are the two most accepted programs imported by countries.

The boom of Japanese TV program export started in the early 1990s when STAR TV began to carry Japanese dramas to other neighboring countries. For example, a Japanese drama, *Oshin*, was aired in 28 countries. Even in Iran that has low cultural proximity, the drama's ratings hit a historic high of 70 percent nationwide. However, there are still some obstacles to Japanese TV dramas from breaking into the US market. For instance, Japanese drama is less attractive to American audiences because it has slow story development and a local theme.[26]

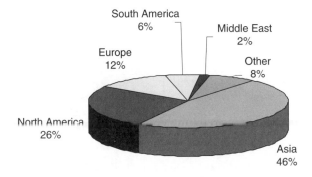

Figure 14.3 Exports of Japanese TV programs by region
Source: based on JETRO, 2005

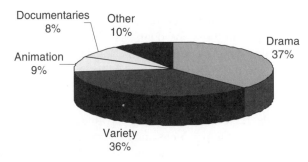

Figure 14.4 Exports of Japanese TV programs by genre, 2005
Source: based on JETRO, 2005

India: The Surge of Bollywood

With the growing impact on the global film industry, India is transforming itself into a new powerhouse of filmed entertainment in the global media market. Although by the end of the 1980s India's film industry was still in a bad shape, India is now becoming the world's largest film producer and an important exporter with the growing Indian diasporas oversea, the entry of satellite television, and the inflow of new financial resources in 1990s. In 2005 India released 1,041 films, which was twice the number of films released by US in that year.[27]

India's film industry is now affectionately nicknamed Bollywood, derived from the combination of Hollywood and Bombay (the former name for Mumbai), the center for India's film production. Bollywood was originally used to refer to India's Hindi film industry in Mumbai, but the term is now becoming a globally recognized brand of Indian film industry. As Mishra describes, "Bollywood has

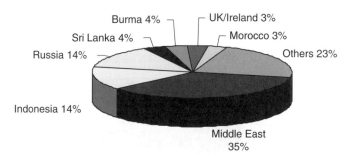

Figure 14.5   Main importers of Indian films in the late 1990s, 2009
Source: based on data from Lorenzen, 2009

become a globally recognized brand; like Darjeeling tea or the Taj Mahal, it has become an emblem of India."[28]

Bollywood exports a massive scale of films to the world, and is creating a major cultural force both in India and overseas.[29] Its films are especially widely accepted in the Middle East, Asia, Africa, East Europe, and now US and UK too, where there are many immigrants from India, Pakistan, or Bangladesh.[30]

Despite the fact that India's film industry has a long history, it has mainly served the national market for a century. However, led by media liberalization and the growing of oversea diasporas, since the 1990s India has been evolving into a hub of film industry that produces and exports hundreds of film across the world. Both India's huge diasporas and the entry of satellite televisions have facilitated the internationalization of Indian films, helping Bollywood to become a powerhouse that produces more than 800 films annually in 15 languages including Hini, Tamil, and Telugu. Bollywood is now producing and exporting its films with a 60 percent growth rate in the last four years, and is integrating into the global media economy.[31]

The Indian filmed entertainment industry is believed to garner its revenue from overseas around $200–360 million annually.[32] In addition, Zee TV, India's biggest Hindi TV channel, has about four million subscribers abroad, collecting 40 percent of its revenue from exports, and Comcas, the leading cable provider in the US, is now offering its VOD (video on demand) services for Bollywood films to its subscribers.[33]

According to the data of 1998, the main importers of Indian films were the Middle East with 35.4 percent of India's total film exports, 14 percent for former Soviet Union nations, and 14 percent for Indonesia. Indian films are consumed in large part by Indian diasporas or the same language groups in the countries (Figure 14.5). For example, countries like Bangladesh that has A 136-million-strong Bengali-speaking population, Sri Lanka that has 3.5 million Tamils, and Malaysia that has 1.5 million Tamil speakers, all have a good potential market for Indian films.[34]

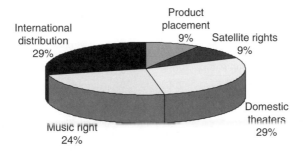

Figure 14.6   The breakdown of Bollywood film revenues, 2005
Source: based on data from Rao, 2005

Since the 1990s, the Indian film industry has grown remarkably in exports to the new Indian diasporas in North America, UK, and Arabic countries, and since the beginning of the twenty-first century it has started entering other Asian countries as well. In the past, the distribution of Indian films abroad was difficult owing to geographical and technological problems. For example, the UK and North American markets were geographically dispersed and therefore were difficult to be covered by small number of screens for Indian films. However, more efficient distribution methods like DVDs and home videos are guaranteeing a better deal for Indian productions, which has enabled the growth of exports at 30–50 percent annually.[35] According to KPMG, now two major Indian film distributors report that the US and UK markets are accounting for more than half of their export revenues.[36] Especially since the beginning of the twenty-first century, India has been taking the largest portion of foreign films screened in the US market, and some Indian films are showing a big hit, earning more than one million US dollars in their first week. In 2005 Bollywood films in US were estimated to make $100 million US dollars.[37] As shown in Figure 14.6, the portion of international distribution is the same as that of domestic theaters.

The new Indian diasporas have played a significant role in making the Indian film industry more stable and profitable. The new diasporas have much higher purchase powers than the Indian home market. The consumers in new diasporas markets may have higher willingness to pay for filmed entertainment and therefore the media market is more potentially profitable. Therefore, the box office revenues in these new diasporas markets are higher than in the home land. The average ticket price in US, UK, and Australia ranges from $6 to $10, whereas in India the average film ticket price is only $35 cents. Thus, the booming exports to these new markets have increased Bollywood's exports earnings at a 30–50 percent annual growth rate in the last five years.[38] As shown in Table 14.3, the average overseas earnings of the top 20 Indian films are around Rs 275 million, equivalent to US $5.7 million.

Table 14.3   Overseas earnings of Indian films, 2001–8 (in Indian Rs. million)

Rank	Film	Year	UK	N. America	Others	Total
1	Kabhi Alvida Na Kehna	2006	175	150	120	445
2	Kabhi Khushi Kabhie Gham	2001	170	147.5	50	367.5
3	Om Shanti Om	2007	105	145	110	360
4	Veer Zaara	2004	152.5	140	65	357.5
5	Singh Is Kinng	2008	115	110	125	350
6	Don	2006	125	100	95	320
7	Dhoom 2	2006	100	117.5	100	317.5
8	Jodhaa Akbar	2008	80	137.5	95	312.5
9	Devdas	2002	120	130	40	290
10	Fanaa	2006	100	97.5	80	277.5
11	Kal Ho Na Ho	2003	127.5	95	45	267.5
12	Kuch Kuch Hota Hai	1998	107.5	90	30	227.5
13	Salaam-E-Ishq	2007	70	90	62.5	222.5
14	Lage Raho Munnabhai	2006	70	102.5	50	222.5
15	Rang De Basanti	2006	65	100	50	215
16	Race	2008	70	57.5	75	202.5
17	Welcome	2007	72.5	45	75	192.5
18	Krrish	2006	60	80	50	190
19	Baabul	2006	82.5	50	55	187.5
20	Main Hoon Na	2004	72.5	82.5	30	185

Source: based on data from India, 2009

Kabhi Alvida Naa Kehna is probably the best example of a Bollywood film's success in the world market, and *Veer-Zaara* was the top-grossing Bollywood film in 2006 at both domestic and international box office, earning over Rs. 445 million (about $11 million US dollars).[39] This film opened strongly in UK and US in 2006 with the first weekend grosses of $1.3 million (Rs. 62.4 million) in US and $1.4 million (Rs. 62.8 million) in UK, making it one of the most successful debuts of a Bollywood film. The success of this film did not wane significantly, so far as it has collected $3.6 million US dollars (Rs. 175 million) in US, $3.1 million US dollars (Rs. 150 million) in the UK, and $2.5 million US dollars (Rs. 120 million) in the rest of the overseas market.

Since Bollywood has been fastest in tapping into global business opportunities, many players in the industry are turning their eyes to the oversea markets and are developing new business strategies. For example, in order to capitalize on the growing global market, Bollywood producers like Yash Chopra and Subhash Ghai have set up distribution offices in the UK and the US. Over the last decade, Yash Raj Films, the top distribution house in the India and 27th in the word, has showed a good performance particularly on export. Through Yash Raj Films's own offices in UK, US, United Arab Emirates, and India, YRF Studios has

Table 14.4   Domestic spending in Indian-filmed entertainment industry, 2002–5

India	2002	2003	2004	2005
Box office spending	1,008	1,023	1,088	1,221
Annual growth		1.49%	6.35%	12.22%
Home video spending	71	80	96	100
Annual growth		12.68%	20.00%	4.17%
Total spending	1,079	1,103	1,184	1,321
Annual growth		2.22%	7.34%	11.57%

Source: based on data from PWC, 2006

also widened its horizons all over the world by marketing and distributing DVDs and VCDs of classic Indian films.[40]

Another significant movement towards internationalization is found in the India China Film Cooperation Commission. India and China joined forces to create the India China Film Cooperation Commission to "strengthen cooperation and promote bilateral exchanges between India and China in the entertainment sector."[41] The commission is considering raising film quotas for each country's films (PWC, 2006). As Rao views,[42] these business strategies can help what Shukla calls "interpenetrating globalism"[43] that nationalities come into direct contact and yet remain highly discrete in the overseas.

The home market effect, oversea diasporas, and the change in government regulation are major factors for Bollywood's continued export growth.[44] As Lorenzen and Taeube analyze,[45] the role of home market boom has served as a facilitator for Bollywood's recent growth of revenues as well as exports. With a high annual growth rate of 25 percent, Bollywood is the fastest growing among other filmmaking industries. In terms of output, it is the most prolific in the world with the commercial film cluster turning out more than 800 films a year.[46]

In details, as shown in Table 14.4, the domestic film market in India rose 11.6 percent in 2005, which led a double-digit growth at the box office. Box office spending rose 12.2 percent, which was the highest ever during the previous five years. The growth of domestic film market was fueled by higher average prices per ticket as more multiplexes entered the market. India is projected to be the fastest growing nation for filmed entertainment industry, with 41.7 percent compound annual increases in the total home video market, contributing to the recent growth of filmed entertainment as a whole.[47]

According to Wildman and Siwek[48] the home market effect is a general tendency that producers in a large home market have a clear advantage in international competition because the large markets provide the producers with more incentive to make larger investment in their productions. Therefore they suggest that the larger investment enables the producers to put more elements that are appealing in the films, and therefore the films can overcome the handicap caused by the cultural differences between home and export markets. As India's GDP is

Table 14.5 Oversea population of Indian diasporas, 2009

Oversea diasporas	Population (000s)	Oversea diasporas	Population (000s)
Nepal	4,000	Fiji	335
Burma	2,900	Oman	310
USA	1,700	Singapore	310
Malaysia	1,655	Kuwait	295
Saudi Arabia	1,500	The Netherlands	220
UK	1,200	Reunion	220
South Africa	1,000	Australia	190
UAE	950	Thailand	150
Sri Lanka	860	Bahrain	130
Canada	850	Kenya	105
Mauritius	715	New Zealand	100
Trinidad and Tobago	500	Yemen	100
Guyana	395	Tanzania	90
Total:			20,790

Source: compiled based on data from Lorenzen, 2009

rapidly rising and a middle class is booming, Bollywood has also taken advantage of the growth in national demand. Aided by the growing home market, Bollywood is doing well in financing, producing, and marketing over 800 films annually. In a Hollywood perspective, most Bollywood firms are small and independent films because their budget is smaller than Hollywood's blockbusters, and the producers rarely have vertical ties with distributors. The average Indian film budget is three million US dollars, as opposed to the average budget of $45 million US dollars per Hollywood movie.[49] However, in the context of Bollywood, these relatively small-budget films are able to be listed up in mainstream box office with high ROI (return on investment), proving the diverse and dynamic characteristic of Bollywood.

The Indian film industry has ethno-geographical advantages because of the large and widely dispersed Indian diasporas. By selling Bollywood films to an audience already familiar with Indian culture and values, the industry can garner additional revenue from them as well as can make larger investment in their productions in the expectation of the future returns from the audience. Therefore, in one sense, the diasporas are potentially another home market for Bollywood films. As shown in Table 14.5, there are more than 20 million Indian diasporas in 26 countries as potential audiences who are familiar with Indian culture and films. These wealthy diasporas function as the most powerful asset for the industry.

Policy-wise, the Indian government provides Bollywood with neither state-subsidies nor any special tax exemption. However, several recent changes in governmental regulation have positively affected the performance and exportability of Bollywood films. For example, the Indian government now allows foreign direct investment (FDI) in film financing, production, distribution, marketing, and associated activities that are related to film industry. Before 1992, the government prohibited foreign investors from directly supporting the domestic film industry. However, after 1992, the government has begun to open its market to the foreign investors. In 2005, the government decided to fully open the industry to the foreign investor, thus allowing Bollywood to attract more finance from the oversea diasporas.[50] Thanks to the inflow of capital into Bollywood, the producers can make blockbuster films that may have more elements appealing to audiences, which enhances the exportability of Bollywood films.

Also, since 2001 the Indian government has classified the film industry as an industry that is able to receive finance from the bank industry. The new policy framework has enabled the film productions or distributors to get the investment from private banks, insurance companies, and other financial institution. The new framework has enhanced the transparency and fair competition in the film industry. At the time of writing, many financial institutions are investing in Bollywood films. After the reclassification of the film industry by the government, the Industrial Development Bank has provided 55 films with financial funds. The Bank of Baroda has invested about Rs. 500 million in *Taj Mahal*, and the Bank of India has invested Rs. 600 million in several film projects.[51] The changes in governmental regulations have modernized the production system of the Indian film industry, which has greatly contributed to the internalization of the film industry.

There are different opinions about Bollywood. As Bollywood is becoming more profitable and expanding its business globally, some scholars raise concerns over the globalization of Indian film industry. Mishra argues that current Bollywood films fail in reflecting Indian's authentic culture and values.[52] He asserts that the influence of oversea diasporas as a finance source is very significant, and therefore Bollywood films are conveying only a "feel good version of our culture."[53] At the time of writing, the foreign market earnings are now responsible for around 30 percent of film budgets, which is equal to or more than the domestic earnings. In this situation, producers cannot but consider the taste of foreign audiences in planning their films and eliminate the elements that may have cultural discounts to audiences. Thus, most Bollywood films targeting foreign audiences would focus on entertainment rather than reality. From this perspective, globalization means westernization or Hollywoodization.

In addition, advertising and the sales of secondary products are increasingly important in film production. In Bollywood film's revenue, product placement and the sales of music rights account for 9 percent and 24 percent, respectively. This situation makies producers focus more on the tastes of middle-class or high-class audiences. During the last few years, most popular Bollywood films such as *Kabhi Kaho Na Pyar Hai* (2000), *Kushi Kabhi Gum* (2001), *Kal Ho Naa Ho* (2003), *Hum Tum* (2004), and *Dus* (2005) featured westernized themes and MTV-style musical aspects. Thus, as Mishra criticizes, Bollywood is becoming a dream world with materially successful Indians who retain "feel good version" of Indian culture.[54]

Korea: the Sweeping Spread of "Korean Wave"

Over the past few years, Korean popular culture, including soap operas, music, and films, has gained a regional popularity in East Asia and is now approaching to other regions of low cultural and geographical proximity as well, such as America, the Middle East, and Europe. According to the Korean Ministry of Culture and Tourism, in 2007 exports of cultural products in Korea accounted for $1.6 billion US dollars, including books, computer games, animation, cartoons, television programs, recorded musical tapes, and characterized products. A report published by PricewaterhouseCoopers (PWC) estimated that in 2005 Korea had the third largest market of entertainment in the Asia-Pacific region, reaching $29.6 billion US dollars and 12 percent of the market shares, respectively.[55] Journalists named the increased circulation of and fandom for Korean popular culture around the world as "Korean Wave" (or *Hallyu* in Korean).[56]

According to some scholars, the Korean Wave started from the big hit of a Korean television drama in China, *What Is Love All About*? The drama was aired on the national China Central Television Station (CCTV) in 1997 and turned out to be an unexpected big hit. Then the television station re-aired the dramas in the next year in a prime-time slot, receiving the second highest rating in China's television history.

Since then, in response to popular demand, several television stations in Hong Kong, Taiwan and Singapore began to fill with imported Korean TV dramas and gained a huge audience. For example, in 1999 another Korean drama serial, *Starts in My Heart*, became a big hit in Taiwan and China, leading other Korean television programs to take up airtime in the region. With the sudden popularity of such Korean dramas, many television stations in Taiwan such as FTV, CTV, and Power TV, began importing and broadcasting Korean TV programs instead of Japanese programs.[57] In 2000, the high demand for Korean programs led a cable channel in Taiwan to specialize in airing Korean TV dramas. For historical and political reasons, Taiwan had been especially receptive to Japanese and Korean TV dramas. But Korean drama *Jewel in the Palace* was watched by half of the population in Taiwan, creating a "han-liu" ("Korean wave" in Taiwanese) that dominate young consumers' taste in entertainment, fashion, and commercial goods. In addition to the huge success in Taiwan, the TV show also became the most watched television drama in the region.[58]

Korean TV dramas have rapidly spread to other neighboring countries such as Japan, Hong Kong, and other East and Southeast Asian countries as well.[59] Korean TV dramas provided a price that was competitive over Japanese ones so that they were commercially profitable. For example, in 2002 Korean TV dramas were only a quarter of the price of Japanese ones, and a tenth of the price of Hong Kong ones.[60] Therefore, the Korean Wave is also a result of conscious industrial strategies of television stations to establish their presence among local and national audiences.[61]

The Korean Wave in music industry began in China too in the late 1990s. A satellite television channel based in Hong Kong, Channel V, regularly aired Korean pop music videos from 1998, which contributed to the huge fandom for Korean pop stars in Asia.[62] Channel V has aided the pop stars to expand their fan base in Singapore, Malaysia, Taiwan, and China. For example, in 1998 a Korean boy band *H.O.T.* reached the top of the pop charts in China and Taiwan. In 2000 its concert tickets were sold out in Beijing, attracting more than 12,000 Chinese youth for each concert. A Korean pop sensation can even be found in Japan, which has the second biggest music industry in the world. In 2002 a Korean female pop idol, Boa, released her debut Japanese album, *Listen to My Heart*. Her debut album reached the top of Oricon Weekly Chart, Japan's equivalent of the Billboard Charts, and became an Recording Industry Association of Japan-certified million-seller album, making it the first album by a Korean artist to reach the top. Following her success, many Korean pop singers have promoted their albums in Japan, and some of them including *Boa* are now expanding into the global market. SM Entertainment, the largest Korean-based agency, producer, and publisher of pop music, expanded its presence by opening subsidiaries in US, Japan, Hong Kong, and China.

In fact, Korea was not a traditional powerhouse of pop music in the world. Just a decade ago, Korean popular culture rarely received much attention from industry and academy. As Kawakami and Fisher comment, Korean popular music did not have anything to match the remarkable contemporary sounds of Indonesia, Okinawa, or Japan. However, the Korean pop music, commonly referred to as K-Pop, is now becoming more mainstream and gaining a global audience.[63]

The Korean Wave was seen in filmed entertainment too. In 1999, a Korean blockbuster, *Shiri*, was released in Japan, Hong Kong, Taiwan and Singapore, attaining critical acclaim as well as large audiences.[64] It became the most popular Korean movie, gaining over six million attendances in Korea and over 1.2 million tickets in Japan. In the view of Joo, *Shiri* heralded a departure from the past by tapping the hitherto ignored commercial viability of Korean films.[65] After *Shiri* and other pioneers, many Korean films have become regular fixtures in cinemas across Asia. For example, *Joint Security Area*, which was released in 2000, became one of the biggest hit films in Japan that was shown on as many as 280 screens.

Korean films are now spreading to North American and Europe with more blockbusters.[66] In response to the increasing demands for Korean film, major US distribution companies such as FOX and Columbia have added Korean films to their global distribution runs.[67] In the meantime, some Hollywood studios are buying the right to remake Korean films. By the end of 2008, more than 25 Korean film's remake rights have been sold at price ranging between $300,000 and one million US dollars.[68] In 2009 DreamWorks remade a Korean horror film, *A Tale of Two Sisters* after buying the right at $2 million US dollars.[69]

With the uprising presence of Korean Wave in regional and international markets, the export of Korean cultural products has grown fast. In 2008, the export

Table 14.6   Exports of cultural products in Korea, 2007 (in US $000)

	Market share (%)
Audiovisual	17%
Book publishing	14%
Advertising	6%
Derivative character licensing	13%
Game	50%
Total	100%

Source: based on data from KOCCA, 2009

Table 14.7   Importers of Korean cultural products by product categories, 2009 (in US $000)

	China	Japan	S. E. Asia	N. America	Europe	Others	Total
Audiovisual	5.8%	39.4%	15.5%	27.6%	7.6%	4.1%	100.0%
Book	10.6%	11.6%	11.5%	42.7%	9.3%	14.4%	100.0%
Cartoon	10.3%	15.4%	12.8%	23.1%	38.5%	0.0%	100.0%
Game	30.9%	31.1%	13.2%	17.7%	5.3%	1.8%	100.0%
Character	15.5%	2.3%	6.7%	33.9%	21.3%	20.4%	100.0%
Edutainment	3.9%	52.9%	3.9%	15.7%	5.9%	17.6%	100.0%
Total share	21.8%	25.3%	12.3%	25.3%	8.6%	6.8%	100.0%

Source: based on data from KOCCA, 2009

of cultural products increased 13.5 percent to surpass $1.55 billion for the first time ever in Korean history.[70] During the past four years, the total exports rose to 27.56 percent compound annual growth rate.[71] In terms of market share, as shown in Table 14.6, game and audiovisual sales accounted for the first and second largest portion of the exports.

Many popular TV dramas are produced by Korea's independent productions and contents providers. However, in most cases terrestrial broadcasters, such as KBS1, KBS2, MBC, SBS and EBS, provide the productions with financial support and buy both television programs and the right to re-distribute the programs. Therefore, they accounted for more than 60 percent in overseas sales of TV programs.

As shown in Table 14.7, both Japan and North America are the top importers of Korean cultural products. The sales to both countries account for more than half of the whole export. China is the third largest market, purchasing 21.8 percent of the total exports of Korean products. In addition, China is the main target market for Korean games, accounting for one third of the export.

For the audiovisual product category, as shown in Figure 14.7, the major importers are Japan, North American and China. Summing up East and South

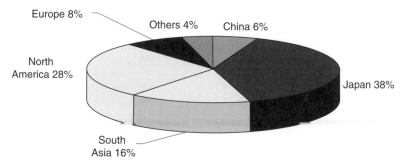

Figure 14.7   Exports of Korean audiovisual products, 2009
Source: based on data from KOCCA, 2009

Asian countries, Asia accounted for 60 percent, being the main target market of Korean audiovisual products. Among the Asian countries, Japan was the most important market for Korea, accounting for 38 percent of the market.

The number of exported Korea films has steadily increased, reflecting the success of the Korean Wave in the international film market. This is a particularly interesting trend, given the dominance of Hollywood films and the overlooked Korean films in the international film market up until several years ago. Since 2001, the sales in the remake right of Korean films has increased when Miramax bought the remake right of a Korean comedy film, *My Wife Is a Gangster*. A list of films that were remade or to be remade includes *Il Mare*, *My Sassy Girl*, *My Wife Is a Gangster*, *A Tale of Two Sisters*, *Seven Days*, and *Ryung*. The most prominent one in this list is a Korean horror film, *A Tale of Two Sisters*. Dream Works purchased it at $2 million US dollars for the remake right. The deal topped one million US dollars that was paid for the right to remake the Japanese film *The Ring*, which was the most successful and profitable remakes in the US market.[72] The list of Korean films being purchased by Hollywood certainly symbolizes a new trend.

Virtually speaking, the Korean Wave is a product of newly liberalized media market. According to Lee and Waterman, countries that have relatively high domestic consumer spending on a given media product should tend to have relatively high exports of that product to other nations.[73] In addition, the deregulation in the film and television market has expanded the growth of domestic market size and thereby has contributed to the exportability of Korean cultures as well.

Led by deregulation and liberalization in the late 1990s, Korea has shown the rapid growth of cultural industries. For example, the domestic film market rose from $1.5 billion in 2001 to $1.8 billion in 2005, and box office spending increased to $890 million US dollars. With the release of popular local films, Korea has had the second largest film market in the region.[74] Coupled with the growth of market size, there has been an increase in production of local films. The market share of domestic films had reached near 60 percent of market share in 2004 while the foreign films' share fell to below 40 percent. These changes have

Table 14.8   Domestic spending in Korea's filmed entertainment industry, 2001–5 (in US $ millions)

	2001	*2002*	*2003*	*2004*	*2005*
Box office spending	510	617	692	815	890
Annual growth		20.98%	12.16%	17.77%	9.20%

Source: based on data from PWC, 2006

contributed to a dramatic transformation of the Korean film market from a rigid, heavily regulated one toward a dynamic, systematic one.

Some scholars believe that the Korean Wave is partially indebted to the government's proactive role in invigorating its cultural industry. The Korean government played an important role in guiding and facilitating the development of cultural industry.[75] One of the former Korean presidents called himself the "President of Culture," and in 1999 established *The Base Law for the Cultural Industry Promotion* by allocating $148.5 million to promote cultural production. In this favorable environment, a number of international film festivals, like Seoul International Film Festival and Pusan International Film Festival, have been held in Korea. These festivals were designed to invite foreign buyers of Korean films. During the administration of the above mentioned President, the budget for cultural sector increased to around $1.3 billion that was mainly for promoting the film industry, which accounted for 1.15% of the total government budget in 2002.[76] Beginning in 2000, the government introduced various programs to support local films. In early 2006, the Ministry of Culture and Tourism introduced a $400 million film development fund to support local films and to provide tax relief for investment in the film industry.[77]

Moreover, coupled with both direct and indirect financial supports from the government, the more lenient censorship and media liberalization has also contributed to the growth of Korean popular cultures. Several scholars claim that the Korean Wave is indebted to the media liberalization in Asia from the late 1990s.[78] They indicate that deregulation and democratization in Korea in the late 1990s has played a significant role in improving the quality of Korean popular culture. As Dator and Seo state, now full-fledged freedom of expression is guaranteed, and previously taboo subjects such as ideological struggles have been allowed, a full degree of freedom is granted without fear of censorship.[79] The more lenient censorship policy for Korean films has allowed the new generation to deal with such sensitive issues as political issues and homosexuality. For example, *Shiri*, a Korean blockbuster dealing with the North–South Korea relations, was released in 1999, and it attracted 6.5 million moviegoers. Two years later, another blockbuster entitled *Joint Security Area* beat the box office record again, reaching 2.5 millions in Seoul alone. Similarly, a gangland saga, *Friend*, again broke the box office record, attracting more than 8.2 million attendances nationwide.

Many researchers have viewed the Korean Wave as the result of a revitalized interest in Asian values among Asian people who share a similar process of modernization. Cultural proximity refers to a tendency that audience members in general have strong preference for film content originating from their own cultural background, which includes language and nationality of actors and actresses.[80] Therefore, some scholars saw that the success of Korean products is due to the blend of good looks and the lack of profanity and sex, as befitting Confucian morals. In respect to cultural proximity, Korean dramas and films are outperforming the upscale Hollywood or Japanese ones in other Asian countries. Korean dramas and films set their emphasis on Confucian-based values, such as family-orientedness, respect for the elderly, and preference for sons, which are highly familiar to Chinese, Vietnamese, and Japanese audiences.

As Kim (2004) explains, the values reflected in Korean dramas and films are very familiar to audiences in other Asian countries. This is especially true in the five most popular Korean dramas in Asian countries, such as *Fireworks*, *All About Eve*, *Autumn in My Heart* and *Winter Sonata*. Popular Korean programs commonly include five values – harmony, tension, compromise, participation, and agreement – which are most appealing to Asian people who have a similar culture frame.[81] Therefore, cultural proximity is a very important factor in explaining the surge of Korean cultural products particularly in East Asia.[82] For example, Singaporean audiences have reinforced local identities aside from the apparent familiarities of Koreans. Shim emphasizes that Korean pop culture skillfully blends Asian and Western values to create its own.[83]

In fact, the Korean popular culture has mixed with the earlier established Japanese, Chinese, and Western pop culture. While some scholars support the theory that the Korean Wave is creating Asian regionalism or cosmopolitanism,[84] some others feel that it is just one of the foreign cultures clearly differentiated from the local culture.[85] For example, some scholars criticize that the Korean cultural products are based on Western modernization, for example, Hollywood-style blockbusters or American-style pop music. The development of Korean media industries and their advance into regional markets are clearly a sign of resilience of the subaltern – and of the "contamination of the imperial," considering the context of decades-long American domination of global cultural industries.[86]

Also, owing to the huge fandom for Korean culture, Korean celebrities have a big impact on consumer culture. It is easy to find Asian youth decorating their appearance just like any Korean celebrities in Vietnam or Taiwan.[87] Given their infatuation with Korean culture, the regional fans are eager to imitate Koreans and the hype has rather provoked a backlash.[88] From this perspective, the huge popularity of Korean cultural products raises concerns for cultural sovereignty issues as same as Western cultures did in the past. As Korean cultural products have been widely spreading across various Asian countries, some have called for a ban on the import of Korean cultural products. From the perspective of cultural imperialism, they defined the Korean Wave as a "cultural invasion" and urged their governments to protect their domestic cultural industries from the invasion. Several governments have indeed introduced protection programs. Among them, in 2006 China's State Administration of Radio, Film and Television decided to cut by half of imports of Korean drama. Also in 2006, Taiwanese government imposed a ban on foreign program's scheduling in prime-time slot and cut almost 80 percent of imports from Korea. In Japan, many blogs began to express antipathy over the Korean Wave's "cultural imperialism" and are urging people to refuse the invasion.[89] But some other scholars feel that although Korean pop culture possibly deteriorates the audience's indigenous identity, cultural imperialism often overlooks that Korean cultural products are contributing to the increase of diversity in Asian cultural industry and are making a cushion to protect Asian cultural industry from the invasion from America or the West.

At any rate, the Korean Wave is now spreading beyond cultural products, driving a substantial increase in sales of every Korean product categories from cars to tourism to electronic products.[90] As Chua states, the fandom for Korean dramas has gone beyond the television screen, spawning consumers's behavioral changes.[91] Lee sees Korean dramas stimulating tourism and raising the number of tourists from China, Taiwan, Hong Kong, Singapore, Malaysia and Thailand who visit the sites where the dramas were shot.[92] Led by the surge of popular cultures in Asia, Korea's media, which had rarely received much attention both from industry and academy in the past, has evolved into one of the most dynamic markets that produce a wide range of cultural products from recorded music to film to computer games.

Conclusion

Media globalization in Asia is still an ongoing process. However, there are several notes to be made. Firstly, Asia is a vast region that not only has the world's highest population, but also the countries in Asia use various political, economic, and media systems and have very different cultural heritages. As a result, the pace, scale, scope, and focus of media globalization in different Asian countries vary from one nation to another. Therefore, the above selected cases cannot be necessarily generalized for the whole of Asia. Secondly, the motivations among different countries for pushing media globalization also vary widely, ranging from being political, economic, to cultural and ideological. Thus, more in-depth studies are needed to fully investigate the overt or covert rational for media globalization. Thirdly, as with many other new trends, media globalization is also a double-edge sword. In different social sittings and at different social phases, media globalization may have either positive or negative, current or potential consequences, or both kinds of consequences together.

Notes

1. B. Cui and K. Zhou, "Seeking Opportunities in Crisis: China's Media in 2009" in B. Cui (ed.), *2009 Report on Development of China's Media Industry*, Beijing, China: Social Sciences Academic Press, pp. 3–35, 2009.
2. *Report on Development of China's Radio, Film and Television* (2009) Beijing, China: Xinhua Publishing House.
3. J. Hong, Y. Lu, and W. Zou, "CCTV in the Reform Years: Setting up a New Model for China's Television?" in Y. Zhu and C. Berry (eds.), *TV China*, Bloomington, IN: Indiana University Press, pp. 40–55, 2008.
4. Ibid.
5. L. Liu and J. Lu, "Overview of the Development of China's Movie Industry" in B. Cui (ed.), *2009 Report on Development of China's Media Industry*, Beijing, China: Social Sciences Academic Press, pp. 247–53, 2009.
6. Ibid.
7. H. Yin, memo on 2008 China's film industry in B. Cui (ed.), *2009 Report on Development of China's Media Industry*. Beijing, China: Social Sciences Academic Press, pp. 254–74, 2009.
8. M. Xu "New Plan of China Film Overseas Promotion Corporation," *Variety China* (May 14, 2007): 9.
9. J. Hong, "Television." In *Berkshire Encyclopedia of China*. Great Barrington, MA: Berkshire Publishing Group, 2009.
10. Hong and Zou, 2008.
11. B. Lu, "China's Animation Products Begin to Enter the International Market." In B. Cui (ed.),*2009 Report on Development of China's Media Industry*. Beijing, China: Social Sciences Academic Press, pp. 298–302, 2009.
12. Cui and Zhou, 2009.
13. Hong, 2008.
14. Ibid.
15. Cui and Zhou, 2009.
16. D. Lu and F. Gao, Competition Analyses of China's Television Industry, 2009 in B. Cui (ed.), *2009 Report on Development of China's Media Industry*. Beijing, China: Social Sciences Academic Press, pp. 228–34, 2009.
17. A. Bynum, "The Problem with Japanese Animation" from www.animationinsider.net/article.php?articleID=1652, 2008.
18. Web Japan, *"Howl's Moving Castle." Trends in Japan*, from http://web-japan.org/trends/arts/art050314.html, 2005.
19. JETRO, "Industrial Report: Japan Animation Industry Trends," *Japan Economic Monthly* (June, 2005).
20. Bynum, 2008.
21. G. Xu "Remaking East Asia, Outsourcing Hollywood" in L. Hunt and L. Wing-Fai (eds.), *East Asian Cinemas: Exploring Transnational Connections on Film*, New York, NY: I. B. Tauris, pp. 192–202, 2008.
22. Bynum, 2008.
23. J. Taplin, "'Crouching Tigers': Emerging Challenges to US Entertainment Supremacy in the Movie Business," *Observatorio*, 2 (2007): 167–90.
24. JETRO, 2005.

25. Ibid.
26. T. Kanayama and T. Kanayama, "Japan." In A. Cooper-Chen (ed.), *Global Entertainment Media-Content, Audiences, Issues*: Routledge, 2005.
27. M. Lorenzen and F. A. Taeube, *Breakout from Bollywood? Internationalization of Indian Film Industry*, Danish Research Unit for Industrial Dynamics, www.3.druid. dk/wp/20070006.pdf, 2009.
28. V. Mishra, *Bollywood Cinema: A Critical Genealogy*. Wellington, NZ: Asian Studies Institute, p. 3, 2006.
29. Lorenzen and Taeube, 2009.
30. Mishra, 2006.
31. Lorenzen and Taeube, 2009.
32. KPMG, and CII (Confederation of Indian Industry), *Indian Entertainment Industry Focus 2010: Dreams to Reality*, New Delhi: Confederation of Indian Industryo, 2005.
33. M. Lorenzen, *Go West: The Growth of Bollywood*, Handelshojskolen: Copenhagen Business School, 2009.
34. KPMG and CII, 2005.
35. Lorenzen and Taeube, 2009.
36. KPMG and CII, 2205.
37. K. Woodman-Maynard, "Bollywood and the Indian Film Industry," *Indian Business*, from www.indianbusiness.com/article/bollywood-the-indian-film-industry, 2006.
38. KPMG and CII, 2005.
39. Box Office India, overseas earnings from www.boxofficeindia.com/cpages.php?pageName=overseas_earners, 2009.
40. Yash Raj Films, "About Us-Company Info" from www.yashrajfilms.com/AboutUs/CompanyInfo.aspx?SectionCode=PRO001, 2009.
41. P. Jayaram, "Chinese Premier in India–India, China to End Border Dispute, Launch Strategic Partnership." *News India Times*, from www.newsindia-times.com/nit/2005/04/22/tow14-top.html, April 22, 2005.
42. S. Rao, "The Globalization of Bollywood: An Ethnography of Non-Elite Audiences in India.," *Communication Review*, 10(1) (2007): 57–76.
43. S. Shukla, *India Abroad: Diasporic Cultures of Postwar America and England*, Princeton, NJ: Princeton University Press, 2003.
44. V. Kohli-Khandekar, *The Indian Media Business* (2 edn.), New Delhi: Response Books, 2006.
45. Lorenzen and Taeube, 2009.
46. S. Rao, "India" in A. Cooper-Chen (ed.), *Global Entertainment Media-Content, Audiences, Issues*: Routledge, 2005.
47. PWC, *Global Entertainment and Media Outlook 2006–2010*, NewYork: PricewaterhouseCoopers LLP, 2006.
48. S. S. Wildman and S. E. Siwek, *International Trade in Films and Television Programs* Cambridge, MA: Ballinger, 1988.
49. Rao, 2005.
50. Lorenzen and Taeube, 2009.
51. R. Bist, "Indian Film Financing Comes of Age." *Online Asia Times*, from www.atimes.com/atimes/South_Asia/FE29Df05.html (May 29, 2004).
52. Mishra, 2006.

53. Ibid.
54. Ibid.
55. PWC, 2006.
56. A. Faiola, "Japanese Women Catch the 'Korean Wave,'" *The Washington Post*, from www.washingtonpost.com/wp-dyn/content/article/2006/08/30/AR2006083002985. html, August 31, 2006.
57. H. M. Kim, "Korean TV Dramas in Taiwan: With an Emphasis on the Localization Process," *Korea Journal* (winter) (2005): 183–205.
58. J. Chan, "Toward Television Regionalization in Greater China and Beyond" in Y. Zhu and C. Berry (Eds.) *TV China*, Bloomington: Indiana University Press, 2009, pp. 15–39.
59. Faiola, 2006.
60. D. Shim, "Hybridigy and the Rise of Korean Popular Culture in Asia." *Media, Culture, and Society*, 28(1) (2009): 25–44.
61. B. H. Chua, *East Asian Pop Culture: Consumer Communities and Politics of the National*, paper presented at the Cultural Space and the Public Sphere: An International Conference, 2006.
62. Shim, 2009.
63. H. Kawakami and P. Fisher, "Eastern Barbarians: The Ancient Sounds of Korea." In S. Broughton and M. Ellingham (eds.), *World Music: The Rough Guide*, pp. 468–72, 1994.
64. S. Kim, "'Renaissance of Korean National Cinema' as a Terrain of Negotiation and Contention between the Global and the Local: Analysing two Korean Blockbusters: Shiri (1999) and JSA (2000)." *The Essex Grad Journal*, 5, 2004.
65. J. Joo, "From Periphery to Center: The Rise of the Korean Film Industry since the Late 1990s," paper presented at the New York conference on Asian Studies. from www.google. com/url?sa=t&source=web&ct=res&cd=1&url=http%3A%2F%2Fwww.newpaltz.edu%2 Fasianstudies%2Fnycas%2F2005%2520GRAD%2520Ryan%2520Prize%2520Jeongsuk%25 20Joo.pdf&ei=RN5WSvmqMMOGtgfHycHdCg&usg=AFQjCNEVwQ7wtF4wrXdYAJU5c Cp1jE-IPg&sig2=Eozs1unUnzYDAJL-eZ5b1g, 2005.
66. P. Frater, "Italy's Eagle Swoops on Its First Korean Title," *Screen Daily*, May 2003.
67. P. Frater, Korea's Jail Breakers Given New Dimension, *Screen Daily* (February 2003); Hancinema, "Korean Films Earn International Critical Acclaim," *HANCINEMA: The Korean Movie and Drama Database*, from www.hancinema.net/korean-films-earn-intl-critical-acclaim-19847.html, June 18, 2009.
68. K. Kim, "Korean Film's Remake Rights Sold to Hollywood," *MaxMovie* (October 18, 2008).
69. P. Clark, "The Uninvited: A Horror/Suspense Movie Review," *eXaminer*, from www. examiner.com/x-14390-Hartford-Movie-Reviews-Examiner~y2009m7d1-The-Uninvited-A-horrorsuspense-movie-review, (July 1, 2009).
70. KOCCA, *Statistics of Cultural Industry*, publication from Korea Creative Content Agency: http://sci.kocca.or.kr/index.jsp, 2009.
71. J. S. Yoon, M. Kang, H. Yoon, S. Choi, Y. D. Kim, Y. S. Kim, et al., *A Research for Promoting a Continous Development of Korean Wave*, Seoul, Korea: KOFICE: Korea Foundation for International Culture Exchange, 2008.
72. S. Lee, E. Kim, and H. Sung, "On the Exportability of Korean Movies., *Review of Development Economics*, 13(1) (2009): 28–38.
73. S. W. Lee and D. Waterman, "Theatrical Feature Film Trade in the United States, Europe, and Japan since the 1950s: An Empirical Study of the Home Market Effect,"

paper presented at the TPRC Conference on Communication, Information, and Internet Policy, 2006.

74. PWC, 2006.
75. Y. Zhu and C. Berry, *TV China*. Bloomington, IN: Indiana University Press, 2009.
76. Shim, 2009.
77. PWC, 2006.
78. J. Dator and Y. Seo, "Korea as the Wave of a Future: The Emerging Dream Society of Icons and Aesthetic Experience," *Journal of Futures Studies*, 9(1) (2004): 31–44.
79. Ibid.
80. Lee, Kim, and Sung, 2009.
81. M. Kim, *Cultural Proximity and the Type of Korean Television Programs in Asian Market*. Paper presented at the 6th World Media Economics Conference, from www.cem.ulaval.ca/pdf/kim.pdf, 2004.
82. K. Yin and K. Liew, "Hallyu in Singapore: Korean Cosmopolitanism or the Consumption of Chineseness?" *Korea Journal*, 2005.
83. Shim, 2009.
84. Dator and Seo, 2004.
85. Yin and Liew, 2005.
86. Shim, 2009.
87. Ibid.
88. R. Maliangkay, "When the Korean Wave Ripples," *IIAS Newsletter*, 2006.
89. Ibid.
90. Yoon, et al., 2008
91. Chua, 2008.
92. S. Lee, "Seoul Survivor," *Straits Times* (April 8, 2003).

15

The Role of Global Advertising

Introduction

Commercial advertising thrives in a free enterprise environment. Market driven economies require advertising in order to succeed in merchandising goods and services both domestically and globally. Today, cultural industries, like others, seek marketing and advertising campaigns in order to create consumer awareness and increase sales. They do this nationally and increasingly internationally. As major multimedia corporations became increasingly global, so their need for global advertising increases. And as the global economy expands, so does the need for global products, global brands, and global services such as advertising. Marketing and advertising globally has cost and brand image advantages. British Airways, Coca-Cola, Ford, GM, BP, GE, Microsoft, Disney, McDonald's, and Procter & Gamble have created persuasive global strategies involving a global corporate vision with a single voice or theme. For example, in 1994, "IBM announced the appointment of one advertising agency with the prime responsibility for executing IBM's strategic voice singularly around the world."[1] Now many multinational corporations seek out a single ad agency with a global reach to provide a broad range of advertising related services. The biggest unresolved issue in global advertising is still focused around a historical debate concerning standardization of all advertising versus adaptation of copy as well as strategies to local markets and tastes.[2] In the future the scales will likely tilt toward the standardization approach as multinational firms seek greater economies of scale and with the huge advertising budgets company headquarters will demand a greater role in the decision-making process.

---

1   WPP Group (United Kingdom)
2   Omnicom Group (United States)
3   Interpublic Group (United States)
4   Publicis Group (France)
5   Dentsu Inc. (Japan)
6   Aegis Group (United Kingdom)
7   Havas Advertising (France)
8   Hakuhodo DY Holdings (Japan)
9   MDC Partners (United States and Canada)
10   Asatsu-DK (Japan)

Figure 15.1   Top 10 advertising companies in 2009 according to *Advertising Age International*

The expansion of major multinational advertising agencies has become a key component in international communication for three major reasons:

1. Corporations themselves are going increasingly global and taking their core-based advertising agencies with them. This includes communication corporations as well as other sectors such as transportation, food and beverages, natural resources, credit cards, etc. As the global economy expands, so does advertising.
2. As multimedia outlets – from privatized radio and television networks in Europe to new media and print outlets in Latin America – expand, they require successful advertising campaigns in order to generate the revenues and attract new customers necessary to succeed as viable commercial enterprises.
3. The growth of satellite-delivered broadcasting channels, along with a rapid expansion of cable systems and networks, have in turn generated demand for increased use of advertising agencies in order to develop a sufficient customer base for either the new services themselves, or the products they advertise.

The following sections highlight the major global advertising agencies that now themselves rank among the biggest firms in the world (Figure 15.1). They are not the advertising agencies of an earlier era that offered a limited menu of services to a few corporations within a single nation. Today, these advertising agencies are truly global in scope. Many are working with global products and offering a vast array of services far beyond print,[3] graphics, and placement advice, services that include everything from accounting practices, to training, to total quality management (TQM) practices, to data collection and analysis, all to assist with the development of corporate strategy plans and to web-based activities.[4] The modern advertising agency is a major partner with its clients in order that both become successful commercial undertakings. It is difficult to conceive of international communication in the current and future global environment without global advertising agencies as a key component.

1   Procter & Gamble
2   Unilever
3   L'Oréal
4   General Motors
5   Toyota
6   Ford Motor Company
7   Johnson & Johnson
8   Nestlé
9   Coca-Cola
10   Honda
11   Sony

Figure 15.2   Top 10 global advertisers by expenditure in 2008 according to *Advertising Age International*

The top 10 advertisers in the world contain only four US-based multinationals, namely Procter & Gamble, General Motors, Ford, and Time Warner. Of the top 10, two are communication corporations: Time Warner and Sony (see Figure 15.2). Collectively they spend over $11 billion annually on competitive advertising globally. This is the basic reason why every major global ad agency has to have a significant corporate presence in the United States. Also, every one of the 10 largest advertisers has major global markets outside the United States, and therefore their ad agencies have to go global in order to keep and properly service these lucrative and prestigious accounts.

These major advertising agencies are based in core nations and carry with them into all semiperipheral nations, and some peripheral nations, values, attitudes, and business practices. For example, these agencies employ the latest in research[5] including surveys, focus groups, knowledge management,[6] and demographic analysis, so that foreign customers look to these agencies rather than to local, frequently small firms, which do not have the arsenal of services, staff resources, or highly educated professionals with MBA or PhD credentials, they would need in order to compete effectively. Finally, the issue of advertising is not restricted to narrow concerns such as the availability of services from major multinational advertising agencies; rather, there is a larger, more conceptual concern of market economies functioning in a free enterprise and democratic environment. Advertising does not fare well or serve any substantial purpose, for example, in totalitarian countries. In such countries, there are frequently only a few products of substantial value to purchase, or when such products are available, few except the ruling elite have the funds to purchase them. Advertising is a necessary ingredient, however, in the expanding market-based global economy, in which nation-states, whether in the periphery or semiperiphery regions, not only have to contend with foreign media, but also with foreign advertising agencies. With deregulation, privatization, and expanding economies, the strategic goal of more and more nations has to take into account as a high priority the consequences of advertising for consumers as well as for their cultures as a whole. Thus, the impact of global advertising has become an important ingredient in an examination of international communication. A good example of the growing role of advertising is the deregulation sweeping western Europe that is resulting in a substantial increase in the number of commercial radio, television, and cable services. This broadly based philosophic and economic movement has consequences for other nations as well, particularly those in eastern Europe:

> Thus, the different East European regimes were confronted not only with the dangers inherent in the importation of programs. They also had to face the more serious dangers inherent in the importation of a mode of organization of the audiovisual sphere inspired by the logic of private enterprise, and of a matrix governed by values in total contradiction with those which they continued to defend "[7]

Today, few defend or call for a return to government-owned and controlled media, a media with no advertising. More media, more choice, along with plenty of advertising, is the accepted environment being promoted by multinational conglomerates clients and ad agencies alike.

The hallmark of global advertising is the trend embracing mergers and acquisitions. For many years the British firm WPP Group held the number one spot. But in 2001, the number three global giant, Interpublic Group, announced the purchase of the fifth largest firm, True North Communications, for $2.1 billion. As a result, Interpublic became the largest advertising firm in the world. Not to be outdone and knocked to second place, WPP in 2004 purchased Grey Global Group of New York for nearly $1.5 billion. But during this time Omnicom Group emerged as number one with other acquisitions and expansion. Then in October of 2008, WPP purchased Taylor Nelson Sofres for £1.6 billon and moved back to the top.

The important question is why are there so many mergers in this industry? The answer is fourfold. First, they hope some type of positive synergy will come about as a result of the expansion. Second, in some cases, the firms want to acquire creative talent not available in house. Third, others seek to acquire a strategic niche to complement current strengths. And fourth, some firms realize they have to be aggressive and expand before a competitor attempts a takeover of either them or a rival they are looking at. Havas of France may be in this position since it failed to win the bidding war with WPP for Grey Global. It is very difficult for midsized advertising firms like Havas to survive in the highly competitive global arena.

Finally, all ad agencies have creative talent but the ability to have one's commercial stand out among the rest is a daunting task. Since there are thousands of commercials seeking our attention, it takes imagination and creativity to get one's message to stand out. Frequently this means being on the cutting edge or pushing the ad or marketing envelope. If an ad goes too far, controversy often results. Two companies known globally for pushing the envelope are Benetton and Nike. For example, Nike ran racy ads during the 2000 Olympics and some media pulled the ads. Also in 2004 Nike had a large media campaign in China featuring Le Bron James of basketball fame. In the commercial he slays a dragon, a symbol of Chinese culture and historic pride. Nike finally pulled that ad. On the other hand, Benetton uses provocative ads to promote social issues. One of their global ads had an oil-drenched duck in a pool of oil. That was it; no clothes or other products in the picture.

WPP

WPP is the largest advertising and communication services group in the world. It consists of over 75 companies with over 2,000 global offices operating in 107 nations. WPP employs more than 135,000 people. The company is largely the creation of English businessman Martin Sorrell, who made his name as financial director of advertising at Saatchi & Saatchi, joining that firm in 1977 and playing a key role in its growth through acquisitions.[8] However, in 1986 Sorrell set out to create his own advertising firm, the WPP Group. In the first half of 1987, WPP turned its attention to the United States market and acquired several US companies. It is the world's largest communication group, providing services to local, multinational, and global clients, including more than 300 of Fortune's Global 500. WPP is engaged in advertising, media planning and buying, market research, consulting, public relations, and specialist communications. More than 50 percent of WPP's sales come from advertising, and it derives more than 88 percent of its sales from outside the United Kingdom. This full-service agency specializes in the planning, production, and placing of advertising for clients in all categories, from radio commercials, to posters and print, to interactive television commercials, to internet and business. Although advertising makes up half its sales, WPP also offers clients media planning and buying, market research and consulting, public relations, and specialty communications. Some of WPP's global clients are IBM, Kraft Foods, Glaxo mithKline, Proctor & Gamble, Johnson & Johnson, Nestle, and Unilever. WPP's most important single territory is the United States, which in 2008 accounted for around 35 percent of its income. The United Kingdom accounted for about 13 percent. The 2008 revenues were over £7.4 billion or about $12.3 billion. This is a significant increase from the early 1990s, when WPP was forced to suspend all dividend payments and refinance its considerable debt.

Some of WPP Group's major subsidiaries are Young & Rubicam, JWT, Ogilvy & Mather Worldwide, Schematic, Mindshare, Hill & Knowlton, Kantar Group, and Research International. Through WPP's subsidiaries, the group is moving into new areas such as the internet, data mining, behavior modeling, and customer retention work. In 2000, WPP purchased Young & Rubicam in a $4.7 billion acquisition to form the world's largest advertising and services group.

In 2008, Young & Rubicam (Y & R) was the fourth largest US ad agency, with 16,000 employees in 186 offices all over the world. Y & R offers a broad range of ad, media, and communication services as well as the controlled public relations giant Burson-Marsteller. Y & R was an employee-owned private company until 1998 when it went public to raise funds for further global expansion. Y & R utilized a number of globally-based videoconferencing sites for both management and clients. Through these sites, Y & R attempts to focus its creative resources, regardless of location, to meet clients' needs. It has a major global marketing subsidiary called Wunderman, which takes a technology focus in order to assist clients with e-commerce and internet-based marketing needs and solutions. Wunderman has over 6,000 employees working in over 50 nations. Overall WPP has as clients over 340 of the Fortune 500 Global companies.

Omnicom Group Inc.

Omnicom Group is the world's second largest advertising organization and is headquartered in the United States. It was formed in 1986 and is a strategic holding company. Its 2008 revenue exceeded $13 billion. It, like other global advertising firms, have been experiencing slower growth since 9/11 but appear to be moving forward with many of the top industry talent. Omnicom employs 68,000 people and has grown recently with the addition of new affiliates. High-profile clients include PepsiCo, McDonald's, GE, and Chrysler. Omnicom provides marketing and consulting services through its Diversified Agency Services unit, which includes Fleishman-Hillard, one of the world's largest public relations firm.

The Omnicom Group operates three global agency networks (BBDO Worldwide, DDB Worldwide, and TBWAWorldwide), plus a range of independent agencies including Cline, Davis & Mann (CDM); Goodby, Silverstein & Partners; and GSD & M Advertising. The three global agency networks all rank in the top 10 global advertising agencies.

BBDO Worldwide, headquartered in New York City, operates nearly 300 offices in 77 countries. From 1994 through 1998, BBDO received 200 broadcast advertising awards in the five major global competitions, substantially more than any other agency. In 2001 it was chosen as the leading global agency of the year by several trade publications. Major global business is from Pepsi, Ikea, FedEx, and General Electric. DDB Worldwide, headquartered in New York City, operates over 200 offices in 90 countries. At the 45th International Advertising Festival in Cannes, DDB agencies won a total of 34 Lions (Oscar's of the advertising world), more than any other advertising agency network, for the third year in a row. Major global accounts are the Sheraton Hotels and FTD. TBWA Worldwide is the last of the three networks of Omnicom and it is also headquartered in New York City. TBWA Worldwide operates 258 offices in 77 countries. In the United States Creativity Magazine named TBWAWorldwide Creative Agency of the Year for four years in a row. Major companies with TBWA Worldwide global accounts are Adidas, Apple, Infiniti, McDonalds, Sony Playstation, and Visa.

Ketchum PR Agency: Ethics Issue

The Omnicom Group owns the public relations firm Ketchum. (It also owns another major public relations firm Fleishman-Hillard, which also got into billing troubles in California.) In 2005 Ketchum received much unwanted media atten tion for laundering a large federal government contract with the Department of Education. It turns out that Ketchum hired a prominent conservative commenta- tor, Armstrong Williams, to covertly hype an education program without disclos- ing that he was on the pay-roll of Ketchum. Nor did he or Ketchum say openly which federal department was paying for Omnicom's PR agency. Another of the commentator's clients for his newspaper columns was the Tribune Company, which immediately fired him for his ethical lapse.

It turns out that Williams did a number of shows on radio and television, as well as print pieces, without divulging that he was being well paid for propa- ganda pieces for the federal government. The PR professional association, Public Relations Society of America, and many others deplored this ethical mess which Ketchum facilitated. After weeks of negative media attention, Ketchum finally admitted its ethical lapse. It will be interesting to see, if over time, other clients, such as Cingular, Home Depot, Kodak, or Pepsi decide to leave this ethically challenged agency – or what the parent conglomerate, Omnicom Group, does about the image nightmare Ketchum has created for it.

Interpublic Group of Companies, Inc.

The world's number three advertising group, The Interpublic Group of Companies (IPC), is headquartered in New York and employs over 45,000 people. It serves a total of more than 4,000 multinational, regional, and local clients. The company's roots trace back to 1930 when two firms merged to create McCann-Erickson. Now IPC has five global operating divisions: Constituency Management Group, FCB Group, Independent Agencies, McCann-Erickson Worldwide, and The Partnership. The various divisions serve the advertising, marketing, and other strategic needs of clients including global companies such as Axe, Johnson & Johnson, Unilever, and General Motors. IPC's revenue in 2008 was over $6 billion. Over the last 20 years, IPC's revenue has increased by more than 1,100 percent and net income has risen 1,800 percent.

IPC has offices in more than 100 countries. Its international public relations unit is one of the largest PR firms in the world. Interpublic is the parent organization of a growing number of leading advertising agencies and marketing communications companies. As the holding company, IPC creates ads through its global networks: McCann-Erickson, Lowe Worldwide, Gotham Inc., Jack Morton Worldwide, MRM

Worldwide, Octagon Worldwide and Draftfcb. The McCann-Erickson World Group was formed in and as a worldwide communications firm, it is dedicated to providing a full spectrum of high-quality marketing, research, and communication services. It is one of the most powerful networks of ad agencies in the world and has a rapidly expanding portfolio of marketing communications companies that operate parallel with the ad agencies.

Publicis Group

Publicis is the largest agency in Europe and was founded in 1926. It has over 45,000 employees in 104 nations. Since 1998 one of its main subsidiaries is San Francisco-based Publicis & Hal Riney. This provided Publicis with a strategic foothold in the lucrative North America market. Its major clients are Sprint and Hewlett-Packard but in 2002 it lost the $300 million Saturn account.

In 2000 Publicis Group purchased Saatchi & Saatchi for $1.9 billion as part of its global expansion. In 1999 Publicis bought 49 percent of Chicago-based Burrell Communications. Burrell is a large ad agency specializing in African American markets. It has several major clients including Coca-Cola, McDonald's, Procter & Gamble, and Sears.

Through a series of major strategic acquisitions, including buying out major rival Saatchi & Saatchi in 2000, Publicis is seeking to become a European and global agency offering a broad range of services. It is trying to move into emerging multinational markets by responding to industry pressure to add foreign subsidiaries. The Saatchi Brothers cofounded Saatchi & Saatchi in 1970. The company used to be part of the advertising giant Cordiant, which in 1997 split into two firms, Cordiant Communications and Saatchi & Saatchi. Since the split of the giant company, business has been good for both parties. Both have a large European focus.

The international holding company Saatchi & Saatchi currently has operations in advertising, marketing, and communications and employs 6,000 workers. Its namesake advertising agency, which generates more than 80 percent of the company's sales, has about 150 offices in more than 90 countries and serves global clients such as Procter & Gamble, Toyota, and General Mills.

The Saatchi brothers made some individuals wealthy when they overpaid for venerable agencies in their misguided strategy to buy their way to the number one spot. For example, when Charles and Maurice Saatchi purchased Bates, then the third largest US ad agency, for $400 million down in 1986 and another $50 million in 1998, it was the highest price paid for an advertising agency. The brothers also paid a premium for two other US agencies that year, Dancer-Fitzgerald-Sample and Backer & Spielvogel. One year later, the brothers attempted to buy J. Walter Thompson, the United States' oldest advertising agency. The ongoing global acquisition frenzy in the ad industry can be traced back to the Saatchi brothers.

In 1994 Maurice Saatchi was dismissed as chairman of the holding company, Charles Saatchi left a short time later. The company continued without them and managed to acquire major accounts such as Toyota and Procter & Gamble. More than one half of its worldwide billings come from North America. Saatchi & Saatchi is key in assisting Publicis in becoming a more dominant global agency.

In 2002 Publicis purchased US-based Bcom3 for $3 billion. Bcom3 was the result of a merger in 2000 among BDM, The Leo Group, and The MacManus Group. Bcom3 was 20 percent owned by Dentsu. The merged firms provides a broad range of communication services such as advertising, public relations, marketing, research, and media buying and planning. One of the partners, Leo Group, has a proud history. Leo Burnett, the founder, has been responsible for creating some of the most successful marketing icons in the United States, including such campaigns as Tony the Tiger, the Marlboro Man, the Pillsbury Doughboy, and the Jolly Green Giant. Founded in 1935, the company provides a full range of advertising, marketing, and communication services to clients such as Coca-Cola, Nintendo, Walt Disney, General Motors, Kellogg's, and Procter & Gamble. Burnett has a 49 percent stake in UK-based Bartle Bogle Hegarty. Burnett's international billings alone were close to $7 billion, and several of its blue-chip clients have been with the firm for decades. Over $4 billion in billings come from non-US-based offices, reflecting Burnett's effective global strategy. Yet the merged firm was still only mid-sized in a land of ad giants and thus to survive it was sold to Publicis. In turn Publicis, which has acquired several key firms, now provides its international clients with seamless and multifaceted ad and marketing advice. For example, it has acquired two of the world's top digital agencies, Digitas and Razorfish. This makes considerable strategic sense since internet-based advertising is increasing while at the same time print and television advertising is declining.

Dentsu Inc.

Dentsu is the fourth largest global ad agency and number one in Japan. The roots of Dentsu date back to 1901 when Hoshiri Mitsunaga founded Japan Advertising and Telegraphic Service Company. By 1946, Dentsu had become a commercial broadcasting, public relations, and advertising entity that modernized its efforts through extensive reliance on market research. In 1951, Dentsu incorporated its radio and television divisions and produced Japan's first television broadcast. By 1959, Dentsu had expanded to the United States by opening an office in New York. Two years later, in 1961, Dentsu joined with Young & Rubicam, the US-based agency, to become a joint venture firm for several major accounts. Dentsu agency continued to expand globally with offices in Chicago, Los Angeles, Honolulu, Paris, Melbourne, and Taiwan. By the mid-1970s, Dentsu was ranked the number one global advertising agency. By the 1980s, it was broadening its efforts with its Total Communication Service and the opening of additional offices in Europe and the Middle East.

The company has over 15,000 employees and is headquartered in Tokyo, Japan. It maintains and operates 32 offices in Japan and has subsidiaries and affiliates in 27 countries around the globe. Dentsu is particularly strong in the United States, Asia, and the Middle East. Dentsu dominates by collecting half of Japan's prime-time billings. Dentsu has over 6,000 clients and some of the major global clients are Canon, Sony, Hitachi, Bell Atlantic, and Toyota. It also has a division that specializes in sports marketing.

Dentsu corporate philosophy was restructured in 1986. Originally developed to define Dentsu's 'srole as a full-service communications company, the corporate philosophy is now composed of corporate objectives, employee qualifications, 10 work guidelines, and the slogan that reflects the company's commitment: "Communications Excellence."

The managers of Dentsu Inc. offer Total Communication Service that include account services, market research and strategic planning, creative development, media services, sales promotion, corporate communications, sports marketing, event promotion, new media and digital advertising, and advertising support systems. Dentsu is committed to making sure each client's message reaches its designated target through its Total Communication Service.

Dentsu has a strategic partnership with Young & Rubicam (acquired by WPP in 2000) as well as a 15 percent stake in the major French advertising conglomerate Publicis.

Aegis Group

The Aegis Group is headquartered in London. It has over 16000 employees in about 80 countries worldwide. The company emerged from the WCRS Group, which dates back to 1979, in 1990. In 2008, the Aegis Group brought in over £1.3 billion or $2 billion. Aegis has two main divisions: Aegis Media and Synovate. Aegis Media concentrates on marketing and accounts for 60 percent of the Aegis Group's revenues while Synovate focuses on market research. Clients of Aegis Media include the Marriot Hotels, Heineken, and Discovery Networks. Synovate works with a number of companies in industries from automotive to agribusiness to entertainment. Vincent Bolloré, a French business man and corporate raider, owns about 30 percent of Aegis, while various other shareholders control the rest.

Havas Advertising

Havas Advertising is a leading pan-European agency. It operates in over 88 countries in addition to Europe, employs around 15,000 people worldwide, and had billings of close to $2 billion in 2005. Europe represents 59 percent of its revenue, with France the major player, and North America providing 30 percent of its revenue. Since 75 percent of all global advertising is by US firms, global advertising agencies that are not US-based require an effective network of subsidiaries in the United States to succeed as global firms. In Latin America, Havas Advertising operates in Mexico, Brazil, and Argentina. It also has a major sports planning and marketing subsidiary. Major clients include Wal-Mart, Kraft, Coca Cola, and BP.

Havas had been aiming to become one of the top five global advertising agencies in the next decade, but in 2005 missed the buy of US-based Grey Global to the British ad conglomerate WPP. As an international agency, Havas should increase its multicultural activities through a global strategy of meeting the needs of clients and their products through a larger network of global brand managers. Havas's global ad agency is known as Euro RSCG Worldwide.

Hakuhodo DY Holdings

Hakuhodo is the second largest advertising conglomerate in Japan and the eighth largest in the world. It is headquartered in Tokyo. The holding company was established in October of 2003. It has over 8,000 employees and two main branches: their advertising companies and their integrated media companies. Their advertising companies include Hakuhodo, Daiko, and Yomiko. Hakuhodo dates back to 1895 and outside of its 22 offices in Japan, it has 68 offices across 18 countries worldwide. Their clients consist of such brands as Sony, Panasonic, Lycra, Dupont, and Toshiba. Daiko was founded in 1945 and focuses more on the Japanese and Asian markets. In 2005 alone, it brought in $1.5 billion and its clients include Nintendo, Matsushita Electric Industrial Co., and Nike Japan. Yomiko was founded in 1929, and like Daiko, it concentrates on the domestic market with some activity in China. These three advertising companies joined together in 2003 primarily to compete better with the rival Dentsu.

MDC Partners

MDC Partners, previously known as Maxxcom, is based out of Toronto and New York City. It was founded in 1980 and is Canada's largest advertising group, however MDC is best known for its American holdings in Crispin Porter & Bogusky and Kirshenbaum Bond. It has almost 6,000 employees and in 2008, it brought in $585 million in revenue. Almost one-fifth of MDC's income is from Sprint alone, with other clients include AOL, Burger King, Xerox, Purina, and Volkswagon.

Asatsu-DK

Founded in 1999 with the merger of Asatsu and Dai Ichi Kikaku, Asatsu-DK or ADK is Japan's third largest advertising firm after Dentsu and Hakuhodo. ADK has 38 offices in 15 countries around the globe and has a good working relationship with one of its main shareholders, the WPP Group, which accounts for 20 percent of ADK stock. ADK also has a 5 percent interest in the WPP Group. While heavily involved in advertising, over half its income is generated by its media and television division. ADK's client list includes Toyota, Fuji, Nissan, Honda, Mercedes, and Ford among others.

Conclusions

The premier global advertising and communication service agencies are in a highly competitive market for creative talent as well as additional customers. The global agencies, all based in core nations, are primarily located in North America and Europe. The European and Japanese agencies need to have a major presence in North American markets because that is where the bulk of the corporations that engage in substantial international advertising are located. All major advertising firms have an extensive network of subsidiaries and offices in core, semiperipheral, and a few peripheral nations. Many of the offices are located in former colonies, particularly those of Britain, Spain, or France. During the past decades, a substantial amount of consolidation has taken place in the industry. The large firms are becoming larger in order to offer a broader range of services to current and prospective clients. Given the continuing global privatization of media outlets as well as the increase in channel capacity owing to technological innovations such as digital systems, there will be a growing demand in industrialized and emerging nations for commercially effective media advertising in the future. The merger mania is also likely to continue once the global economic downturn ends.

Finally, critics of cultural imperialism blame US ad agencies for their global reach on behalf of multinational clients. Yet the actual picture is quite different. The largest ad agency in the world – WPP Group – is British. In fact, most of the top global ad agencies are non-US owned or controlled, with the exception of the Omnicom Group, the Interpublic Group, and MDC Partners. In reality, a set of core nations – the United States, France, Britain, and Japan – collectively are spreading the advertising mantra around the globe for an increasing number of multinational firms. These giant ad firms and their clients have a strong vested corporate interest in expanding the global economy.

The role and impact of global advertising is a key component which helps define and substantiate both world-system and electronic colonialism theories. The following list outlines the key links among global advertising agencies and world-system and electronic-colonialism theories:

- The major global ad agencies are all based in core nations. They act as savvy electronic imperialists on behalf of their global clients.
- All major agencies have to be based in or have major subsidiaries in the United States. US multinational firms purchase the bulk of global ads.

- All major agencies have offices in major cities of other core nations.
- All major agencies have offices in semiperipheral nations and this is the richest region for future growth.
- Owing to the saturation and maturity of core markets, ad agency expansion is available primarily through two routes: through corporate expansion to additional major cities in the semiperipheral zones, particularly in Latin America or Asia, and through acquisition of medium- and small-size ad agencies, or related businesses in core nations. The big will get bigger in this industry.⁹ Interpublic's bid to take over True North, WPP's buying Grey Group, and Publicis's purchase of Bcom3 are excellent examples of this trend.
- Mid-sized ad firms, such as Havas, are poorly positioned or equipped to succeed in an industry of global giants.
- Major ad agencies employ extremely creative personnel plus cutting-edge research techniques to produce effective marketing and media commercials for their clients. As a result, they are major players in the electronic colonialism of the global marketplace. The firm NeuroFocus is focusing on the next generation of research techniques for the advertising industry to find out what is in the minds of consumers.
- There are no major agencies headquartered in peripheral nations. Nations in this least affluent zone consider themselves fortunate to host a branch office of some core-based major agency. The major agencies offer such a plethora of sophisticated services that indigenous ad firms in other zones find it virtually impossible to compete effectively for large international accounts.
- There is a fundamental shift occurring in the advertising business. Basically, traditional media are reducing their advertising expenditures or accounts by about 10 percent. By contrast, the amount of advertising on the internet is increasing by about 10 percent annually. This movement from old media, particularly print including such icons as *Reader's Digest*, to new media will continue to the advantage of internet-based companies.

Finally, the major agencies have branched out to offer full-service, seamless packages ranging from accounting, to management training, to assessment, to strategic planning so that clients in the lesser two zones become ensnared in electronic colonialism practices without fully contemplating the long-run behavior, impact, and attitude shifts required.

In the lesser two zones, those countries with market-driven economies and expanding media outlets will experience more competition from core-based agencies seeking new accounts, including the strong possibility that core-based agencies will invest in local ad agencies as fully or partially owned or controlled subsidiaries. From the perspective of electronic colonialism, advertising has a greater role and impact on foreigners' minds, lives, values, and ultimately purchasing behaviors than the audio or video programming or print copy these ads accompany or surround. The goal of ad agencies is to influence others attitudes, behaviors, and ultimately lifestyles. Their goal is to replace traditional buying habits with new behaviors leading to the consumption of core nations' goods and services. To some extent, global ad agencies are the foot soldiers of electronic colonialism theory. They are promoting core nations' values and products to an ever-increasing number of individuals and nations across the globe on a daily basis.

In the future, with the expansion of the global economy and markets, along with more media technologies, new commercial opportunities will appear for aggressive global ad agencies. This will clearly extend beyond cable, wireless, and satellite channels to include the internet. Major agencies are experiencing industry pressure to achieve broader scale and scope by expanding their services and acquiring subsidiaries as they themselves confront global competition. For all major agencies, more than half of gross revenue now comes from global billing. Domestic billings, even in the United States, are no longer sufficient to sustain a major player among the global agencies. All stakeholders need a plethora of clients in an expanding range of foreign countries, primarily the semi-peripheral regions since the core nations, in general, have mature or saturated markets. Advertising is an industry in which the chief stakeholders need to continue to grow and acquire other firms or they may find themselves being acquired by some other aggressive firm based in Europe, Japan, or the United States.

Notes

1. Wayne McCullough, "Global Advertising Which Acts Locally: The IBM Subtitles Campaign," *Journal of Advertising Research*, 36 (May–June 1996): 12.
2. M. Agrawal, "Review of a 40-year Debate in International Advertising Practitioner and Academician Perspectives to the Standardization/adaptation Issue," *International Marketing Review*, 12 (March 1995): 26–48.
3. Industry overview: "Press: Still the Largest Medium," *International Journal of Advertising*, 18 (August 1999): 405–11.
4. Wossen Kassaye, "Global Advertising and the World Wide Web," *Business Horizons*, 40 (May–June 1997); Kuen-Hee Ju-Pak, "Content Dimensions of Web Advertising: A Cross-National Comparison," *International Journal of Advertising*, 18 (May 1999): 207–232; and David Schumann and Esther Thorson, *Advertising and the World Wide Web*, Mahwah, NJ: Lawrence Erlbaum, 1999.
5. Demetrios Vakratsas and Tim Ambler, "How Advertising Works What Do We Really Know?" *Journal of Marketing*, 63 (January 1999): 26–43; and Marieke Derlooij, *Global Marketing and Advertising*, London: Sage, 1997.
6. Michael Ewing and Doug West, "Advertising Knowledge Management: Strategies and Implications," *International Journal of Advertising*, 19 (May 2000): 225–44.
7. Tristan Mattelart, "Transboundary Flows of Western Entertainment across the Iron Curtain," *Journal of International Communication*, 6(2) (December 1999): 118.
8. WPP is a publicly traded stock on the London and New York exchanges. WPP was incorporated in 1871 in the United Kingdom as Wire and Plastic Products Limited; the WPP of today is far removed from its original focus.
9. Andreas Grein and Robert Ducoffe, "Strategic Responses to Market Globalization among Advertising Agencies," *International Journal of Advertising*, 17 (August 1998): 301–20.

16

Summary and Conclusions

Introduction

This chapter reviews major aspects of the theories and landscape of global communication. Although currently there is relatively little concern about NWICO and the role of specialized UN agencies such as UNESCO, there is still concern about the cultural, social, and economic impact of global communication trends. An unexpected exception is the ITU's role with the World Summit on the Information Society (WSIS). With widespread utilization of the internet, transnational corporate acquisitions and mergers among media, telecommunications, and advertising corporations, and the expanding economic role of cultural industries, the entire issue of global communication has moved to a new stage.

The issue and impact of communications corporations is no longer a trivial or marginal matter for policymakers, researchers, or investors. All core nations rely for their economic health and viability on the success in foreign countries of their communications' corporations. In previous decades, other leading corporations, such as those in the agriculture, automotive, natural resources, or aerospace industries, made major contributions to the creation of new jobs and new wealth; but that is no longer the case. Particularly with the end of the Cold War, the aerospace industry, which includes military aircraft, has seen a substantial reduction in employment, impact, and influence. As a result, the success of cultural industries, domestically and in foreign markets, has become a vital component of successful international trade. Those nations that enjoy successful global communication corporations such as Disney, Time Warner, Viacom, Sony, News Corporation, Bertelsmann, and NBC-Universal, clearly count on these firms having continued success in order to keep domestic employment high, as well as keep their balance of trade ledgers "balanced" in a favorable direction.

Cultural industries are a concern of national and international policymakers as well as major corporations in North America, Europe, and Asia. With the drive to increase market share, coupled with more sophisticated technology and advertising, many new markets are being inundated with media fare created and owned by large foreign stakeholders. Now even more and larger foreign communication stakeholders are competing aggressively with each other in nations and markets on other continents – frequently several time zones and cultures away. This is particularly true in semiperipheral nations, which are the next frontier for multinational communication corporations. Core-based firms are aggressively developing and promoting new media opportunities in semiperipheral nations in order to increase market share. Whether these firms are building new modem multiplex movie theaters or expanding access to the internet, the semiperipheral nations have become the commercial battlefield for core communication stakeholders. Also, sponsored media seminars and workshops dealing with the values and practices of Western free-press traditions are increasingly offered in semiperipheral nations. UNESCO now sponsors many of these seminars. In this collective process, indigenous cultures are at significant risk.

Finally, the proliferation of global music, movies, tapes, advertising, and websites for preteens and teenagers has led to a new generation and culture gap. These groups now experience in common audio and visual materials, activities, language, topics, and in many cases clothing and values that cut across this key demographic segment in North America, Asia, and Europe. These audio and video materials give them similar expressions and worldviews that are increasingly remote or different from those of their parents or even their older siblings For the adolescents (who are particularly heavy media consumers) in this growing global segment, including MTV groupies, Britney Spears look alikes, and Bart Simpson wanna-be's, their attitudes, dress, language, and behavior are increasingly at odds with their parents' or their teachers' generation. Between these kids and their grandparents, particularly those who emigrated from another nation and speak a non-English language, this phenomenon has created an even greater cultural and behavioral divide.

As a result, because of the impact of global communication, many teenagers around the globe have more in common with each other, thanks to MTV and social websites, than they do with any other normative groups with which they interact, including parents, grandparents, relatives, or teachers. The long-run implications of this relatively recent global media phenomenon have yet to be determined, researched, or fully understood.

One attempt to understand the role of media in society and its impact on culture is to view it through the lens of mediatization as well as electronic colonialism theory. This perspective looks at mass media as having profound interrelated effects on institutions, individuals, their culture and society. In "The Mediatization of Society: A theory of the media as agents of social and cultural change," Stig Hjarvard stated:

Mediatization is to be considered a double-sided process of high modernity in which the media on the one hand emerge as an independent institution with logic of its own that other social institutions have to accommodate to. On the other hand, media simultaneously become an integrated part of other institutions like politics, work, family, and religion as more and more of these institutional activities are performed through both interactive and mass media. The logic of the media refers to the institutional and technological modus operandi of the media, including the ways in which media distribute material and symbolic resources and make use of formal and informal rules.[1]

Mediaization takes a broader look at the significance of the mass media, much like ECT.

Peter Weingart talks about the key role the media play in terms of forming public opinion as well as the perception of self.[2]

Summary

As outlined in the beginning chapters, international communication theory is going through a transformation. Earlier attempts at theorizing have failed to develop models or research agendas that match the reality of the contemporary role of global communication. Theories of modernization, dependency, and cultural imperialism have failed to satisfactorily explain global communication. The old theories only explain part of the global picture.

Part of the theoretical failings is a function of three related events. The first is the end of the Cold-War era and the parallel decline in influence of socialist media critics, whose ideas and rhetoric became stale. The second event comprises numerous technical advances such as the creation of a new major global communication phenomenon, convergence, digital environments, the internet, or the reach of the latest satellites. The third event is the emergence of several major global communications stakeholders, many of which are non-US owned and controlled. Europe, Japan, Canada, Mexico, and others have major stakeholders in this important and expanding sector. Collectively, these events have led to the need to reanalyze and reformulate the theoretical underpinnings of the discipline of international communication. That is what this book is all about. It proposes a new theoretical perspective that unites world-system theory (WST) with electronic colonialism theory (ECT). This combination places the discipline on a contemporary theoretical foundation for the purpose of explaining the global communication landscape. Various activities continue to increase the need for understanding the various components that collectively influence international communication. The preceding chapters cover the salient features as well as the expanding globalization of the corporate giants in this field. Even though some of the stakeholders shift, through mergers etc., the underlying core analysis – WST and ECT – as laid out in this book remains viable and credible.

Before reviewing these components, remember that the impact on international communication at the end of the Cold War should not be underestimated.

First, much of the research undertaken in the 1970s and 1980s focused on issues or media content that had a distinct ideological focus and slant that emphasized a dichotomy between capitalist and socialist worldviews. This outmoded dichotomy renders many of the studies and their conclusions marginal or suspect in the new post-Cold-War environment. Second, the volume of international news was higher during the Cold War because many publishers, editors, and journalists set their priorities according to the Cold-War dichotomy and resulting international tensions. It was a great deal simpler for editors when the thrust of US foreign policy could be summed up in two words: stop communism. With that old dichotomy almost invisible, the interest and attention paid to international news has shifted because of terrorism and 9/11. Third, after September 11, 2001 international news came back on the media's radar big time. The global war on terrorism, the Afghanistan war, and the Iraq war – the trifecta of agenda setting – reclaimed the front pages and face time of television news around the globe. Fourth, as the global economy continues to expand through a series of mergers and acquisitions in the communications and other sectors, we would expect global business news coverage to increase in order to monitor the expanding global economy. Finally, the United States is looking for a new role within UNESCO, and for a number of years it has also played precarious roles within the United Nations, including withholding its substantial financial dues for a considerable period in the 1990s.

Rather than promoting global organizations and encouraging greater multilateral cooperation through the UN and specialized UN agencies and organizations, the United States has never appeared as either a team player or a major leader in multilateral organizations. This US attitude is anomalous considering that the vast majority of global corporations are headquartered in the United States. The US corporations have the greatest vested interest in global peace and stability as well as in economic and monetary systems that are functional and stable. Yet with the end of the ideological confrontation and a reduction in serious international threats, the US government seeks only peripheral roles, if any, in almost all global agencies that influence, examine, monitor, or set rules affecting international communication. In some cases, isolationists in Washington adopt a fortress mentality, or support only global communication policies that clearly benefit the United States, frequently at the expense of other nations. More is discussed concerning this aspect under "McPhail's Paradox."

NWICO

The New World Information and Communications Order (NWICO) dominated international communication debates for several decades. A combination of newly independent nations, many of which were former colonies of core nations, plus the ideological interests of communist republics, propelled the issue of news flow and the role of the mass media into a contentious position. Industrialized core countries view the press as independent and non-governmental – that is, as public shareholder-owned broadcasting and communication corporations as well as delivery systems. Although the shrill ideological rhetoric of the supporters of NWICO has faded, when one examines the underlying issue of what determines international news flow more closely, it is clearly not a balanced process. Some of these matters are now playing a role at the WSIS and NWICO, which is on life support, may get an unexpected boost as an outcome of deliberations at the WSIS.

Global mass media do not work in a vacuum; they work in an environment in which certain factors dominate the decision-making process, which virtually guarantees that certain news will be covered extensively whereas other news will be virtually ignored. For example, two broad roles have emerged from global media studies that account for a great deal of what does or does not get covered: gatekeeper roles and logistical roles.[3] Examples of gatekeeper roles include wire-service decision-making, negative news such as the Asian tsunami, or the coups-and-earthquakes syndrome. The logistical roles include economic interconnectedness, cultural affinity, such as being a former colony, speaking the English language, or regionalism. From a straight economic perspective, much of what happens in peripheral nations is of little monetary consequence to core nations. The major exceptions are significant deviances from the norm, such as when there are major earthquakes, coups, tidal waves, or civil war, particularly if the event is covered by CNN. Peripheral, developing nation news reaches the front pages or television sets in major industrialized, core nations when it is bad news. Otherwise, the vast number of nations in the periphery zone receives no media attention at all year after year.

Aspects of NWICO position are supported by empirical research produced in North America and Europe, but NWICO proponents call for solutions involving some type of government control, which clearly falls on deaf ears in boardrooms and newsrooms in industrialized, core nations. Yet the WSIS and aftermath have reignited some of the concerns raised by critics during the NWICO debates at UNESCO over two decades ago. Many of the issues raised by NWICO are placed in a better and more meaningful perspective when viewed through the dual theoretical prisms of electronic colonialism and world-system theories or perspectives as outlined in previous chapters. A brief synopsis follows.

Electronic Colonialism Theory (ECT)

Electronic colonialism theory[4] posits that foreign produced, created, or manufactured cultural products have the ability to influence, or possibly displace, indigenous cultural productions, artifacts, and media to the detriment of receiving nations. On one level, ECT examines economic transactions through which a number of large multinational communication corporations engage in the selling of culturally embedded goods and services abroad. These corporations view the transactions as revenue-producing activities that increase market share and maximize profits for themselves and their shareholders. All of this is accomplished in unison with other firms, particularly advertisers, and multilateral agencies such as the WTO, ITU, or the OECD. Yet ECT also looks at the social and cultural impact of these same economic activities. Effects include attitude formation, particularly among young consumers who seek out foreign cultural products, ranging from comic books, to music, to videos, which represent distant cultures and dreams – products that are produced and manufactured primarily in a totally different environment and culture.

ECT provides the theoretical backdrop for examining the long-run global consequences of core nations' multimedia offerings in semiperipheral and peripheral nations. It provides a means for examining and understanding some of the broader issues, particularly in regard to semiperipheral and peripheral nations, concerning the plethora of cultural products, messages, and industries from a global perspective. The major communication industries tend to be located in a few wealthy core nations, whereas their customers are dispersed around the globe and come from different linguistic, social, economic, religious, and political environments. Yet over time ECT speculates that these differences will shrink in favor of the producing nations, which frequently work in English. This movement toward English as the language of the "global village" even applies to the EU. The only language that most Europeans speak, other than their native tongue, is English. Most meetings including academic conferences across Europe are conducted more and more in English.

As Europe attempts to find a new transnational identity, it still has no major global players in the internet domain. Intel, Microsoft, IBM, Apple, Google, Yahoo, YouTube, MySpace, Twitter, Ask.com, Lycos are all American companies with a global footprint. The EU has established a number of programs to correct this situation but none have managed to get enough traction to be considered a threat to the preceding firms.

Three important factor factors are evident in Figure 16.1. First all these companies are located in a single zone – the core region. Not one is even from the

1   Time Warner
2   Viacom
3   Disney
4   British Broadcasting Corporation
5   Sony
6   News Corporation
7   Bertelsmann
8   Associated Press/Reuters (tie)
9   GE's NBC Universal
10   Omnicom/WPP (tie)

Figure 16.1   The 12 most important communication companies in the world, 2010

semiperipheral zone. Second, the language of the global media is English and over time will continue to even be more so. Third, except for the BBC, all have and need to have a strong presence in the crucial US market.

Over time, most of the corporations described in the preceding chapters will have more customers and make more revenue outside their head offices' nations. They are truly global and not national entities.

Let us look at two examples to illustrate this point. First, in their advertising, more corporations are moving toward a single, global strategy. Firms such as the Ford Motor Company are seeking to consolidate their advertising and marketing expenditures within a single advertising agency that has a global reach and work-force. The Ford advertising budget is over one billion dollars a year. This requires a vast number of employees from Ford's advertising agency – the WPP Group of the United Kingdom[5] to carry out an effective global marketing and advertising campaign. Only a few years ago, large corporations such as Ford would have utilized perhaps half a dozen agencies in various parts of the world to carry out their corporate advertising. Now they view this fragmentation as both too expensive and counterproductive.

The second example is Coca-Cola.[6] This is a $2 billion account for Interpublic Group of New York. Coca-Cola's offshore sales exceed domestic distribution of its global brand. Previously, Coca-Cola had over 30 advertising agencies handling its products around the world. Now it is attempting to focus on a global strategy and a global message in order to increase foreign sales substantially.

The purpose of providing these two examples is to make the point that global activities on behalf of major corporations take place in order to maximize sales and thus profits in more and more foreign nations. These nations and customers are concentrated in other core as well as semiperipheral regions.

Basically ECT explains the phenomena of a dominant Anglo-Saxon paradigm, utilizing the English language, which is spreading globally by two primary forces. The first one spread the base for what would lead to the current domination of media industries by primarily American firms. That was the British Empire. It took literature, culture, the BBC as a model, Reuters, and the English language around the world. The second wave or force is the contemporary global media scene dominated by Hollywood movies, American and British music, text books, CNN, AP, syndicated television series, popular culture, the majority of internet host sites, Google, and more of the English language. That is why non-English speaking nations are at a loss in terms of what to do about the long term implication of ECT, or how they can create a global winner in the media arena.

World-System Theory (WST)

World-system theory[7] is a means of organizing from theoretical perspective global activities in the international communications field. WST basically divides the world into three major sectors: core, semiperipheral, and peripheral.

Core nations, relatively few in number, exercise vast economic influence and dominate relationships and transactions with the other two zones. The United States, the European Union, and Japan are some of the dominant stakeholders in the core group. This group has the power to define the rules, timing, and content of transactions with nations or regions in the other two zones. Some current core nations, such as Australia, Norway, Canada, and New Zealand, are becoming increasingly concerned that they may slip into the semiperipheral zone if they are not able to attract, finance, and keep information industries, entrepreneurs, and educated workers. The loss and impact of News Corp. shifting from Australia to the US is an example of how important the leading core nation, the US, is in terms of centrality to the global economy. Barnett and Salisbury examined WST with reference to communication/information. Looking at data from the international telecommunications network, they conclude "The results indicate that the network is composed of a single group with the United States and the other Western economic powers at the center and the lesser developed countries at the periphery. A nation's centrality in the network is significantly correlated with its GDP per capita".[8]

Semiperipheral nations are substantial in number and are those nations that interact with core nations but currently lack the power and economic institutions to join the elite core group. China, Mexico, Brazil, India, and some of the Middle East nations, which were discussed in chapter 13, are trying to reposition themselves as core nations. Some others are attempting to fast-track their entry into the core region by requesting membership in the European Union. That is why the current EU community will likely grow to 30 or so over time.

Finally, the peripheral zone is made up of developing nations. These nations and regions have relatively little if any power, and their economic dealings with the semiperipheral and core nations benefit these two last zones. Many African, Latin American, and most Asian nations belong to the periphery. They are basically exploited by the other zones; they have few media exports, little connectivity to the internet, little education, little technology, poor health, poor literacy rates, and much poverty.

World-system theory's characterization of global nations does provide a theoretical framework for addressing the question of why communication industries located in core nations have the market and economic advantage in dealing with the other two zones. To some extent, WST is an extension of the one-way flow argument developed decades ago, but when we look at the traffic patterns, whether in music, movies, television series, the internet, or any other cultural product, clearly the core zone dominates, the semiperipheral is next, and the peripheral is at the very bottom of the hierarchy. All major communication corporations, whether advertising, print, wire service, movies, electronics, video, or internet, have their world headquarters in core nations, have extensive dealings with semiperipheral nations, including purchasing subsidiaries to ensure market penetration, and have relatively little corporate presence in the periphery.

The theories of electronic colonialism and world system form a continuum that, together, describes and explains the underlying essential elements in international communication. ECT focuses primarily on the impact on or attitudes of individuals and groups. It deals with what happens to individuals when they are repeatedly exposed to foreign-produced communications with a cultural cachet. These messages convey foreign personalities, foreign dress, foreign history, foreign norms, foreign values, and foreign tastes. Frequently these values are at variance with indigenous cultures and lifestyles, particularly in peripheral nations. Individuals and groups are viewed as customers, and when combined or aggregated, they are equated with market share. To a large and expanding extent, the goal of global communication corporations is to make electronic colonies of large segments of the population around the globe in order to increase market share and maximize profits. ECT utilizes a cultural lens.

WST moves the analysis into the economic territory that underpins the global trading system within which communication industries operate. WST focuses on the substantial activities and power within communication industries located in core nations, and how they utilize this power for systematic advantage in their economic relationships with semiperipheral nations and peripheral nations. WST focuses more on the macroeconomic and policy dimensions of the corporate decision-making process, whereas ECT focuses more on the impact of foreign products, ideologies, and software on individuals, or their minds.

ECT Plus WST

Combining the two theories provides the most powerful explanation of the contemporary phenomenon of global communication that is available to students, policy analysts, corporate planners, and researchers alike. The failures of modernization, development, and cultural imperialism theories, as well as other scattered attempts to explain certain narrow, micro segments of the international communication field, have not moved the discipline much beyond either anecdotal impressions or ideologically laced charges. These charges and lack of data to support them are particularly transparent and obvious in NWICO activities. As the role of international communication continues to expand, these two combined theories represent an opportunity for greater insight and understanding of this most significant global phenomenon.

McPhail's Paradox: The US, Modernity, and Future Actions

There is no doubt that the US has the greatest vested interest in the global economy. As a nation-state it has the largest number of multinational companies, many in the communication sector, which depend on global commerce and transactions as a major source of jobs and income. The US needs global order and rules to keep its industries functioning and growing. They are the prime beneficiaries of global rules and the global economy. They need the UN and its specialized agencies, like the UNESCO, WTO, and ITU, to function effectively. But there is within the US a clear cultural chasm or disconnect between the progressives, concerned, educated and those threatened by change, immigrants, international agencies, and new ideas. But the US needs the global economy and the global economy needs the US.

Yet the US population, in general, and the Federal government, specifically, is among the harshest critics of international agencies. They stand against modernity. They are threatened by transnational agreements and frequently are in violation of them. The loss of faith in the UN is a byproduct of the US continuously circumventing it. They were out of UNESCO for years and withheld funds to the UN for years thanks to Senator Jesse Helms. The US is one of the most frequent violators of WTO's rules promoting free trade. The recent imposition of steel tariffs by the US is a case in point. In other sectors the US simply refuses to participate, ratify, sign, or support global measures even though it is a major stakeholder.[9] The Kyoto environmental Protocol, the Law of the Sea, the Land-mines agreement, the global Convention on the Rights of the Child, the Convention on Elimination of Discrimination against Women, the International Criminal Court, and other international initiatives designed to produce an orderly, safer, and better world are lacking a US signature or support.

Rather than promoting international tolerance, cooperation, and furthering global social justice, they promote a narrow, ethnocentric "America First" mantra. The US casts an image of not wanting to be a global team player. It does not get the larger picture. Although the most powerful nation on earth, it avoids global leadership roles in the UN system and multilateral organization elsewhere. It is as if it fears the consequences, or it desires to shun modernity. Yet it is clearly going to be and currently is the nation, which should be leading and supporting all global rules, laws, practices, and organizations. All the US-based multinational communication conglomerates need all of the preceding global rules to work.[10]

In contrast, Australia, Canada, the Nordic nations, and many others promote social justice through multilateral organizations. Not the US. Canada as the US's largest trading partner is a symbolic "case study'. Canada is in endless trade fights with the US. The US is quick to initiate bi-lateral trade fights across a number of sectors, fish, lumber, steel, beef, and cultural industries. The smaller nation of Canada does not look for magnanimous consideration from the US. Even compromise is outside the rhetoric of the US State Department for its largest trading partner – Canada. It seeks to crush its Canadian trading partner. It plays hardball at every turn. Even though Canada on the world stage is a relatively minor actor in the global economy, the US, as a policy strategy, treats it as an enemy. Never mind that Canada allowed hundreds of US commercial airlines to land in Canada after 9/11. Or those Canadian hydroelectric companies routinely assist US states hit by natural catastrophes. Or that over 130 Canadian soldiers have been killed in Afghanistan fighting against terrorism. Yet the US foreign policy is to protect and maximize American interests. It is ethnocentric. No compromise, no concessions.

In the new environment of the post-Cold-War era, the US business empire rules. It is no longer the hegemony of the British Empire when it ruled the seas, but now it is the US empire which rules the global airwaves and most of the international media.

An example of the above is the US's complaint to the WTO against Canada. The issue is mainstream culture. Canada, where 80 percent of magazine sales are US magazines, had sought a modest relief position. The US objected since it considers any attempt to protect an indigenous cultural industry as unacceptable. The issue was a "split-run" of US-imported magazines where token Canadian advertising and content were required by Canadian regulations but were strongly protested by US publishers. When is 80 percent of a foreign market not enough? – when it is an American media conglomerate in cooperation with the US federal government. The US won the WTO complaint and now enjoys more than 85 percent of Canadian domestic magazine sales.

The global economy is the life-blood of a vast number of American multinational firms; just consider a few such as General Electric, IBM, Microsoft, Time Warner, Disney, News Corp., or Viacom. Yet who is the first to criticize the UN, or UNESCO, or other international agencies and agreements? – the US. And several of the US media, such as the *WSJ*, FOX network, Sinclair Broadcasting, the National Review, and the New York Post champion this paradoxical stand. It is not as if they are discussing small nations such as Greenland, or New Zealand. They would be relatively unscathed if the global trading system collapsed. The US would be devastated. But they and many in the media, like Rush Limbaugh, Brit Hume, Glenn Beck, Sean Hannity, and Bill O'Reilly, are the biggest complainers across a broad range of issues when it comes to the UN, social programs, bilingualism, outsourcing, immigration, global trade, or international agreements. It is clearly a paradox seemingly better understood by foreigners than Americans themselves at all levels of work, government, and the media.

As many core nations move beyond modernity to post-modernity, the position of the US on the world stage stands in stark contrast in terms of its overall response to the possibilities of being a global communication leader.[11] It is more likely to be perceived globally as a rather narrow minded, somewhat vindictive, disliked nation in international fora. In the future, how the US handles the delicate issues of culture, media, diversity, and participate in multilateral agencies and fora will likely determine the outcome of this paradox. US history is not on their side.

Conclusions

It is difficult to formulate conclusions when dealing with international communication. The field is in a state of flux, and global changes affect it on a daily basis. The three major engines driving the change are innovations in communication technologies, the global war on terrorism, and the global economy. The world is a different yet better place because of international communication. Many citizens are better informed and major corporations are able to experience success, including expanding employment opportunities because of the possibilities and potential provided by innovations in international communication. But beyond broad generalizations, there are still a few more specific conclusions that can be drawn from an understanding of the various stakeholders, nations, as well as global communication corporations. The following four conclusions focus on sovereignty, continued globalization, and the internet. Clearly, other conclusions may be drawn, but given the rapid pace of change in this sector, the following are the most likely predictions.

First, the audio and video history of international communication has been dominated and will continue to be by US music, television, feature films, and internet portals. Starting with the likes of Disney cartoons and animation movies, *I Love Lucy, Melrose Place, Dynasty, Dallas, Baywatch, Cheers, Star Trek, Cosby, the Simpsons*, to *Friends, Sopranos, Sex and the City*, and House American television shows have dominated television sets around the world. The same is true for CDs, DVDs, and movie screens as well. In fact DVD sales now represent a major tertiary (following the primary screening on television or in theaters, then syndication rights) source of windfall profits for rights' holders. Some of the leading DVD sales that are once again contributing to the financial health of the studios are *Lord of the Rings, Shrek, Star Wars, Harry Potter, Spider-Man, Seinfeld*, and *The Simpsons*. Networks and studios are scrambling to put out additional releases of old stock at a rapid rate as most US and other core nations homes acquire DVD players.

The important fact about all this is that no one is forced to watch these shows or listen to the music. There is no gun to anyone's head to watch US television, movie productions, or listen to music. They do it because the scripts, production values and sets, acting or singing talent, and budgets create world-class materials. Also foreign buyers from commercial and non-commercial television networks from around the world flock to New York, Hollywood, and Las Vegas trade shows to bid for the syndication rights to US television network or cable shows and series.

This demand by offshore buyers has been increased by the proliferation of new television stations and movie multiplexes, cable systems, satellite channels, and DVD or iPod players. Along with the increase in leisure time, more individuals in core and semiperipheral countries having disposable income and being able to understand English, particularly teenagers, contribute to the escalating global demand. When you couple that with the internet which is American centric, mainly in English, and carries more and more audiovisual content, this tends to assure the continuing influence of American multimedia conglomerates. The influence is also cultural in nature. Since core nations are highly competitive and exhibit mature markets at home, the greatest impact of these latter phenomena is likely to be most prevalent in semiperipheral nations. Over the next decade it will be the semiperipheral nations that are the battle-ground for the stakeholders discussed in this book. Finally, the marketing and advertising budgets of the global media conglomerates are huge. Their sophisticated approach to their customers around the world leaves little to chance.

As a collective result of the above, the electronic colonization of vast numbers of people not only continues but just as the British ruled the globe by controlling the seas, so now the US and a few others rule the air-waves, television and movies screens, and the emerging digital universe. The minds of the many, without regard to time or space, are clearly influenced by the flow and content of a vast range of core nation media products and options. As a result ECT is becoming more powerful as a theory for understanding and organizing the impact of global communication over time.

Second, the plethora of transborder activities among major media, advertising, telecommunications, and internet firms is rendering historical national boundaries, and in some cases policies, obsolete. The ability of US communication firms to transmit information or products globally, as well as for foreign firms to sell their cultural products in the lucrative US market, is making national communication policies and political boundaries an issue of the past rather than the future. For example, CNN, FOX News, MSNBC, the BBC, AP (Associated Press), Reuters, Euronews, and others go wherever there is news. Time Warner, Disney, Sony, Bertelsmann, Viacom, NBC Universal, and even the BBC seek foreign markets or audiences where there is a viable consumer base and a potential for profitability. The internet goes wherever there is a modem, a computer, and some type of internet access, which may be hardwired or wireless. Thus, as global communication companies, along with their advertising agencies, expand markets and merge with more and more foreign firms, the concept of a single head office of a single nation controlling, taxing, or regulating global communication firms is becoming increasingly problematic. This alteration of sovereignty received an unexpected boost with the collapse of the Berlin Wall and the eventual lessening of international tension that was prevalent during the Cold War. There were no longer two dominant superpowers, each with enormous arsenals of propaganda and weapons to protect their nation-states as well as those of their allies. During the 1990s, a vacuum emerged as only a single global power remained – namely, the United States. Into this vacuum moved the major stakeholders in the global economy. Multinational corporations simply usurped economic power and some political power in order to promote their interests across national boundaries. For example, today several multinational corporations are more powerful and have greater reach and greater influence than any nation in the periphery. We now live in a world where a single individual, Bill Gates of Microsoft, is wealthier than the entire group of nation-states in the periphery. It appears that although the concept of the nation-state has lasted about 600 years, policymakers and corporations alike are now questioning it. This phenomenon will push multinational organizations and transnational regional agreements into ever-increasing important roles, because domestic, national control is now clearly a pre-internet phenomenon. Institutions such as the UN, UNESCO, ITU, WTO, and OECD, and the European Union are willingly adopting entirely new regulations, currency, and ways of doing things in the post-sovereignty era. This is the post sovereignty reality. Yet at the same time, many of these same firms and phenomena, such as the internet, are fueling a resurgence of nationalism and localism, and some hope that they are a means of protecting and reinforcing indigenous cultures, groups, and languages.

Third, a fundamental aspect of the global economy will dominate the current and future global landscape of international communication. Specifically, the economies of scale are driving substantial corporate mergers and acquisitions.[12] This is true in every aspect of the cultural industries phenomenon, starting with advertising agencies and moving on to global media, wire services, and internet corporations. Old media in particular, for which print products are the predominant revenue generator, will have to either acquire new media themselves or be bought out by some aggressive new media entrepreneur. There will be no standstill in the global communications sector. Stakeholders will either move aggressively to expand market share through innovation, mergers, and acquisitions, or they themselves will become targets for either friendly or hostile takeovers. The global economy is not user-friendly or cost effective to small players in the communications sector.

The transfer of concepts, philosophies, and practices of liberalization, deregulation, and privatization across all core and semiperipheral nations has meant that the communications sector, which tended to be focused mainly within nation-states, has now taken on truly global dimensions. This is true across all elements of the industry – advertising, media, both audio and video, as well as in technology, particularly the internet. The leading nation in the globalization phenomenon is the United States, but the European Union has also been extremely active in the globalization process. This is particularly true in two ways:

1. the activities and strategic plans of Japan's Sony, Germany's Bertelsmann, France's Publicis advertising, and the United Kingdom's BBC and WPP are informing and influencing others about how to compete in the global economy;
2. all major European communication firms recognize that they must have some type of presence in the United States in order to be an effective global stakeholder.

All major communication industries, regardless of national origin, have identified the North American market as essential for major stakeholder status in the globalization process. Finally, another aspect of globalization is the combination of old media and new media. The merger of AOL and Time Warner, despite their missteps, defines the phenomenon, but it also reinforces and expands the globalized role that all communication industries need to identify, deal with, and ultimately take on.

The globalization of the communications industry has several consequences. First, the original thrust of cultural imperialism was to loudly criticize the Hollywood feature film industry. This is now a uninformed perspective, because Hollywood is no longer totally owned by US interests. Instead, foreign communication conglomerates such as Sony of Japan and Bertelsmann of Germany have substantial global media holdings. The global communication industry is not a monolithic empire, but rather a phenomenon that is now widely dispersed among core nations, with a few semiperipheral nations desperately trying to obtain core-like status through their own expansion via select mergers and acquisitions, particularly in the film industry. Within the communications sector, strategic planning is about global planning, not domestic or national planning.

Fourth, the role of the internet is still evolving. Just a decade ago the internet was a relatively isolated technical phenomenon for which scientists and other experts were still developing key components and applications for scientific or primarily industrial applications A mere 10 years later, the internet has become a major phenomenon affecting global communication and commerce in unheard-of ways. The volume of usage, the depth and breadth of users worldwide, and the dramatic impact on e-commerce, e-learning, and e-public policy are astonishing. Yet, in spite of its significant role across core nations in particular, the internet is still in its infancy. The internet of today is analogous to the invention of the printing press, the early days of the assembly line, or the early applications of the computer chip. We are in the early phase of what will become a mature industry, which will likely be replaced eventually by some other technological invention or by a mix of technologies and other factors.

One other significant aspect of the internet is that it has empowered the individual to make different choices in different ways. Individuals may obtain news directly from the internet without the filtering of publishers, editors, or journalists. Or they can create their own blogs or vblogs and seek an audience for their musings. Individuals anywhere on the planet may also purchase cultural products or view them through their terminals without leaving their home, school, or place of business. This phenomenon is not just available to individuals in a single or a few nation-states; it is a globally dispersed phenomenon in which geography becomes irrelevant, particularly as wireless internet connections pop up around the globe. The prevalence of the internet is related to the sovereignty issue because the information on the internet is as portable as the technology itself. Industrial-era concepts such as space, location, control, bricks and mortar, and monopoly are marginalized in the age of the internet.

Finally, as evidenced by mergers across the stakeholders, the communications industry recognizes that multinational conglomerates will become the model and new benchmark for successful global communication stakeholders. This will involve a blurring of traditional boundaries of all communications sectors, as the global economy forces the application of the internet into every segment of the international communications market. The digital output and world of core nations will speed the internet into homes and villages around the globe in record time. Over time, more semiperipheral nations will mature into core nations, and then the issue will become how and which peripheral nations will evolve into the semiperipheral zone. The cutting edge of innovations influencing the internet, however, will continue to appear first and quickest across core nations.

Connection between Public Diplomacy and ECT

The chapter on public diplomacy marks a new beginning in terms of the potential role of the media on a global scale. The goals and means are fairly clear. The goals are to influence the hearts and minds of others by non-military interventions of all scales, the means are scarce when it comes to the proper funding of initiatives. The lack of funding reveals a blind spot concerning the potential of public diplomacy. The US defense budget for 2010 is about $684 billion, including the wars in Iraq and Afghanistan. The US public diplomacy budget, no matter how you calculate it, is less than 1 percent of the military budget. Yet military force alone cannot win the war against terrorism. Body counts and prisoners are not indexes of success in terms of the hearts and minds debate.

The 9/11 Commission Report stated that: "We have come together with a unity of purpose because our nation demands it. September 11, 2001 was a day of unprecedented shock and suffering in the history of the United States. The nation was unprepared".[13]

Today the US is still unprepared; in fact, it may have more enemies out there than it did on 9/11. The two wars have been a breeding ground for extremist jihad causes and recruitment in the Middle East and elsewhere.

The 9/11 Report continues:"Across the government, there were failures of imagination, policy, capabilities, and management … The most important failure was imagination".[14] The emergence of a new stateless terrorist enemy was both missed by the US military as well as its Cold-War response and rhetoric.

This is a sad commentary on the evolution and outcome of what President, and former decorated General, Eisenhower warned against some five decades ago. In his farewell address after eight years as president, Eisenhower warned against the might and adverse influence of the military-industrial complex.[15]

There is no public diplomacy complex. It is a lose group of NGOs, foundations, and frail government projects that collectively are drowned out by the lobbyists and warrior hawks that Eisenhower warned us about. The prestigious New York Times columnist, Frank Rich, puts it this way:

> You might wonder whether networks could someday cut out the middlemen – anchors – and just put covert lobbyists and publicists on the air to deliver the news. Actually, that has already happened. The most notorious example was the flock of retired military officers who served as television "news analysts" during the Iraq war while clandestinely lobbying for defense contractors eager to sell their costly wares to the Pentagon.[16]

The US amply funds several war colleges but not a single peace or public diplomacy college. If only 10 percent of the military budget was to be redirected to public diplomacy and winning the hearts and minds of those labeled the enemy then some progress may be made. But the imagination of the top US officials has been paralyzed by the post-9/11 environment where military contractors moved swiftly and effectively into the policy vacuum.[17]

What is the Relationship of All This to ECT?

In general communication media carry two sets of values; the one is the impact of the hardware itself (McLuhan, 1964), the other is the software or content. It is the spread and impact of core-manufactured content of all genres that electronic colonialism is about. Technology itself is not neutral (Ellul, 1964, and Heidegger, 1977). For example the use of computers is guided by essential codes which must be followed and alter how users obtain information. But setting aside the hardware phenomena and looking at the software leads to this general statement. Core-based, mostly American, media carry cultural and linguistic (mostly English) values. These values cut across a number of different attitudes and behaviors depending on the receiver, for example, young children being Sponge-Bob fanatics, or teenagers switching from their own native music to the latest hits on MTV.

But there is a deeper meaning conveyed by this entire new media, particularly in peripheral and poorer regions of the world. Over time and with increasing consumption of media fare they want to become like us. They want our clothes, lifestyle, and they see the good life that has escaped them. I realize that there is no mega study confirming this, but there are traces of this phenomenon in some of the empirical studies (Norris and Inglehart, 2010). But we know that with the reunification of Germany, the German West did not want to become like the communist East, rather the East wanted to become like the West. They wanted freedom, choice, better lives, and access to even more media and popular culture. This package also comes with democracy and free enterprise businesses. The East Germans learned all this by watching and listening to British and American shows, movies of all sorts, and music, from jazz to the Beatles. *Dallas* and *Dynasty* did more to undermine communism than all of the US propaganda campaigns. The same overall picture is also true of the other former communist countries which stampeded to become members of the open and democratic European Union after the end of the Shaw. Here is the essential point and connection with ECT. Spreading democracy around the world at the end of a gun simply will not work. Declaring people enemy combatants and putting them in jails like Abu Ghraib or Guantanamo not only does not work but actually increases recruitment of more radical enemies of the US and other core nations. What appears to work is spreading mass media to other nations through a broad range of public diplomacy initiatives. The more foreign nations consume of modern communication, the more they will want to be like us. That is why some foreign nations and some religions ban or shun Western media. They know it contains values and shows people enjoying freedoms. The internet is China's, Iran's, and other authoritarian regimes worst nightmare.

Consider the following scenario. What would be the long term impact of an imaginative program to utilize 1 percent of the current budgets of the US Departments' of Defense, State, Education, and Homeland Security for the purchase and dissemination of enormous numbers of the One Laptop per Child (OLPC) systems across the globe? These children are tomorrow's leaders. They will be either for core nations' values or against them. The more we provide them with access to hardware and software, and not armaments big or small, the more likely they will want to have a say in their future being better than their past. When one uses an iPod or Google you have to make choices and they will too. It becomes a smaller step to then make choices about candidates in open and free elections. To be denied such choices brings about a backlash and open protests, using the latest digital communication devices, like in Iran, with more to come.

In closing, I realize those in the cultural imperialist's camp and cultural purists will lament any increase in American media and culture around the world; but mass media does work in terms of spreading the message and mechanisms of choice. It feeds the image of a better life. But as long as the military-industrial complex which General Eisenhower warned us about continues to high-jack both dollars and policy concerning global matters, then making the world safer is one of the last things the current post-9/11 approach will achieve.[18]

Notes

1. Stig Hjarvard, "The Mediatization of Society: A Theory of the Media as Agents of Social and Cultural Change," *Nordicom Review*, 29(2) (2008): 105.
2. Peter Weingart, 'Science and the Media', *Research Policy*, 27(8) (1998): 869–79.
3. Denis Wu Haoming, "Investigating the Determinance of International News Flow: A Meta-Analysis," *Gazette*, 60 (December 1998): 493–512.
4. Thomas L. McPhail, *Electronic Colonialism*, Newbury, CA: Sage, 1986.
5. "WPP Leads Way in Global Ties to Clients," *Wall Street Journal* (December 1, 2000): B6.
6. "Coke Gives Nod to Interpublic for Ad Contract," *Wall Street Journal* (December 4, 2000): B12.
7. Thomas R. Shannon, *An Introduction to the World System Perspective*, Boulder, CO: Westview Press, 1996. A look at the variables underlying globalization may be found in James Mittelman, *The Globalization Syndrome: Transformation and Resistance*, Princeton, NJ: Princeton University Press, 2000. It is informative concerning the resistance to cultural hegemony.
8. George Barnett and Joseph Salisbury, "Communication and Globalization: A Longitudinal Analysis of the International Telecommunication Network," *Journal of World Systems Research*, 2(16) (1996): 20.
9. The issue of US isolationism is not new. For example, the US has never ratified the 1919 Treaty of Versailles, which formally ended World War I. The Treaty included a League of Nations, which was heavily promoted by US President Woodrow Wilson. Despite extensive efforts by Wilson, including a cross-country speaking tour to get support from radio, magazines, and newspapers, the ethnocentric isolationists in Washington prevailed. Other nations that signed the treaty were France, Germany,

England, Italy, and Japan. Also noted US aviation hero, Charles Lindbergh and other fascists campaigned aggressively against the US entry into World War II, which commenced in1938. They were prevailing and supporting Hitler until the bombing of Pearl Harbor in December 1941. That turned out to be our ancestors's 9/11.

The Bush era also became the "gold standard" for ignoring or flaunting international laws and agreements against torture. It openly ignored the Geneva Convention, which seeks to limit the atrocities of war.

10. Noted media scholar William Hachten has a similar take on the situation. He states, "the fact remains that international society is marked by the absence of collective procedures, by competition rather than cooperation, and by the lack of a commitment to a common goal – in other words, a situation that approaches anarchy" *The World News Prism*, Ames: Iowa State University Press, 2002, p. 12.

11. For a discussion of the failure of the US to do the empire walk well, see Deepak Lal, "An Imperial Denial," *Yale Global Online* (January 6, 2005). It may be found at http://yaleglobal.yale.edu.

12. "Cross-Border Mergers Soared Last Year," *Wall Street Journal* (July 19, 2000): A18. This article traces merger activities, and it notes a 50 percent increase over the 1998 rate. This rate continues today following a lull after 9/11. The United States, United Kingdom, Sweden, Germany, France, and Canada dominate the global buying. One sector, advertising, is particularly active.

13. 9/11 Report "Executive Summary," *The 9/11 Commission Report*, Washington: Replica Book, 2004, p. 1.

14. Ibid., p. 9.

15. www.youtube.com/watch?v=8y06NSBBRtY.

16. Frank Rich, "Is Obama Punking Us?" *The New York Times* (August 9, 2009): 8.

17. You will recall that in chapter 1 we referred to four epochs of colonization: military, Christian, mercantile, and electronic. Most of the theory developed in the book was the last and current phase of electronic colonialism. But the second phase which dealt with the brutal Christian Crusades against the Muslims and other religions has reappeared in two instances. The first was then President Bush's remarks soon after September 11, 2001 when he referred to a "Crusade" against terrorism; then he launched a war in Iraq where the population is mostly Muslim. The second instance is still playing itself out and is directly connected to a military contractor Blackwater/ Xe. This firm acted as a private army in Iraq and it is run by a fundamentalist Christian conservative Erik Prince. He recruits retired military and former CIA agents to go on what he reportedly claims is a religious-based crusade against Muslims in Iraq. The use of deadly force is under investigation by both the US Congress and the Department of State. These two recent examples of the concept of the crusades returning has been picked up by the media, particularly the FOX networks and the *Wall Street Journal*, who have been defending Blackwater/Xe and Erik Prince on their twenty-first-century crusade across Iraq.

A related story details how the CIA in 2004 secretly hired Blackwater to assassinate select Al-Qaeda leaders without notifying the US Congress as required by law, J. Risen and M. Mazzeti, "CIA Said to Use Outsiders to Put Bombs on Drones," *The New York Times*, August 20, 2009, www.nytimes.com/2009/08/21/us/2/intel.html. Finally by 2010 the US Department of Defense had more than 100,000 military contractors, such as Blackwater/Xe and Halliburton, in Afghanistan on various deadly missions, basically acting as private army, at a time when there were about 65,000 US soldiers on the ground.

18. This type of imaginative experiment in public diplomacy is not limited to what the US should do differently and creatively; other core nations have a vested interest in reducing terrorism and extremism as well. And the money is there but it is being misapplied. Consider that the North Atlantic Treaty Organization (NATO) was created in 1949; the purpose was a common defense strategy against the threat of the then powerful Soviet Union and to counter the global spread of communism. The old Soviet Union imploded in 1989 with the fall of the Berlin Wall and thus NATO's rational and purpose imploded as well. Not quite. The military-industrial complex is alive and too well. NATO has just ordered 180 huge military aircrafts at a cost of over $25 billion dollars. Imagine the number of schools, libraries, and OLPC computers that could cover the needs and change the hearts and minds of children in many peripheral nations. NATO's armaments budget now is actually larger than when it actually had clear mission of stopping communism. It and the US Pentagon continue to ignore that the internet ultimately supports the emergence of civil society and promotes a drive toward choice and democratic institutions.

Select Bibliography

2009 China Statistics Yearbook. Beijing, China: State Statistics Bureau, 2009.

2009 Report on Development of China's Radio, Film and Television. Beijing, China: Xinhua Publishing House, 2009.

Albarran, Alan B., and Chan-Olmsted, Sylvia M. *Global Media Economics: Commercialization, Concentration and Integration of World Media Markets.* Ames: Iowa State University Press, 1998.

Alexander, Alison, Owers, James, and Carveth, Rod (ed.). *Media Economics: Theory and Practice.* Mahwah, NJ: Lawrence Erlbaum, 1998.

Artz, B. and Kamalipour, Y. (ed.). *The Globalization of Corporate Media Hegemony.* Albany: State University of New York Press, 2003.

Auletta, Ken, *Media Man*, New York: W. W. Norton, 2004.

Axford, Barrie and Richard Higgins. "The European Information Society: A New Public Sphere?" In Chris Rumford (ed.), *Cosmopolitanism and Europe.* Liverpool: Liverpool University Press, 2007.

Bagdikian, Ben. *The Media Monopoly.* Boston: Beacon Press, 2000.

Banks, Jack. "Music Video Cartel: A Survey of Anti-Competitive Practices by MTV and Major Record Companies." *Popular Music and Society* 20(2) (1996): 173–97.

Banks, Jack. "MTV and the Globalization of Popular Culture." *Gazette* 59(1) (1997): 43–60.

Barber, Benjamin R. "Democracy at Risk: American Culture in a Global Culture." *World Policy Journal* 15(2) (1998): 29–42.

Barnett, G. A.; and Salisbury, J. G. "Communication and Globalization: A Longitudinal Analysis of the International Telecommunication Network." *Journal of World Systems Research* 2(16) (1996): 1–20.

Barnett, George A., Salisbury, Joseph G. T., Kim, Chul Woo, and Langhorne, Anna. "Globalisation and International Communication: An Examination of Monetary, Telecommunications and Trade Networks." *Journal of International Communication* 6(2) (1999): 7–49.

Barnett, Robert. *The Global Jukebox: The International Music Industry*. New York: Routledge, 1996.

Barua, Anitesh, and Whinston, Andrew. *The Internet Economy Indicators*. Austin: University of Texas, 2000.

Beltran, Luis. "Alien Premises, Objects and Methods in Latin American Communication Research." *Communication Research* 3 (1976): 107–34.

Berenger, Ralph. *Global Media Go to War: Role of News and Entertainment Media during the 2003 Iraq War*. Spokane: Marquette Books, 2004.

Bist, R. "Indian Film Financing Comes of Age." *Online Asia Times*, from www.atimes.com/atimes/South_Asia/FE29Df05.html, May 29, 2004.

Bloomberg, Michael, and Winkler, Matthew. *Bloomberg by Bloomberg*. New York: John Wiley, 1998.

Bob, Clifford. *The Marketing of Rebellion: Insurgents, Media, and International Activism*. New York: Cambridge University Press, 2005.

Boyd-Barrett, Oliver. "National and International News Agencies." *Gazette* 62(1) (2000): 5–18.

Brüggemann, Michael. "How the EU Constructs the European Public Sphere." *Javnost: The Public* 12(2) (2005): 57–74.

Bush, George H. W. "President's Remarks at US University Presidents Summit on International Education," edited by The White House. The White House, 2006.

Bynum, A. "The Problem with Japanese Animation" from www.animationinsider.net/article.php?articleID=1652, 2008.

Byun, H. *Analysis and Projection for Korean Industry in 2009*. Seoul, Korea: Korea Film Council, 2009.

Campbell, Robert. *The Golden Years of Broadcasting: A Celebration of the First Fifty Years of Radio and TV on NBC*. New York: Scribner, 1976.

Carveth, Rod. "The Reconstruction of the Global Media Marketplace." *Communication Research* 19(6) (1992): 705–724.

Cave, Martin, and Collins, Richard. "Regulating the BBC." *Telecommunications Policy* 28(3/4) (2004): 249–72.

Chalaby, Jean K. *Transnational Television Worldwide: Towards a New Media Order*. London: I. B. Tauris, 2005.

Chalaby, Jean K. *Transnational Television in Europe: Reconfiguring Global Communications Networks*. London: I. B. Taurus, 2009.

Chang, T. K., and Lee, J. W. "Factors Affecting Gatekeepers' Selection of Foreign News: A National Survey of Newspaper Editors." *Journalism Quarterly* 69 (1992): 559–61.

Chase-Dunn, C. *Global Formation: Structures of the World-Economy*. London: Basil Blackwell, 1989.

Chin, Tony. *CBS: The First 50 Years*. New York: General Publishing, 1999.

Chua, B.-H. "East Asian Pop Culture: Consumer Communities and Politics of the National." Paper presented at the Cultural Space and the Public Sphere: An International Conference, 2006.

Clark, P. "The Uninvited: A Horror/Suspense Movie Review." *eXaminer*, from www.examiner.com/x-14390- Hartford-Movie-Reviews-Examiner~y2009m7d1-The-Uninvited-A-horror suspense-movie-review, July 1, 2009.

CNNIC 24th Survey Report. Beijing, China: China Internet Network Information Center, 2009.

Coase, R. H. *British Broadcasting*. London: University of London, 1950.

Cohen, Y. "Foreign Press Corps as an Indicator of International News Interest." *Gazette* 56 (1995): 89–100.

Collections of China Journalism and Publishing Statistics, 1978–2008. Beijing, China: State Journalism and Publishing Bureau, 2009.

Coombs, Tim. "The Internet as Potential Equalizer." *Public Relations Review* 24 (1998): 289–303.

Corner, John, Schlesinger, Philip, and Silverstone, Roger. *International Media Research: A Critical Survey*. London: Routledge, 1997.

Cowen, Tyler. "French Kiss-off: How Protectionism Has Hurt French Films." *Reason* 30(3) (1998): 40–8.

Crystal, David. *English as a Global Language*. Cambridge: Cambridge University Press, 1997.

Cui, B., and Zhou, K. "Seeking Opportunities in Crisis: China's Media in 2009." In B. Cui (ed.), *2009 Report on Development of China's Media Industry*. Beijing, China: Social Sciences Academic Press, pp. 3–35, 2009.

Cullity, Jocelyn. "The Global Desi: Cultural Nationalism on MTV India." *Journal of Communication Inquiry* 26(4) (2002): 408–25.

Dahlgren, Peter. *Television and the Public Sphere. Citizenship, Democracy and the Media*. London: Sage, 1995.

Danaher, K. *10 Reasons to Abolish the IMF and World Bank*. New York: Seven Stories Press, 2001.

Dator, J., and Seo, Y. "Korea as the Wave of a Future: The Emerging Dream Society of Icons and Aesthetic Experience." *Journal of Futures Studies* 9(1) (2004): 31–44.

De Beer, Arnold, and Merrill, John. *Global Journalism*. Boston: Allyn & Bacon, 2004.

Defleur, Melvin, and Ball-Rokeach, Sandra. *Theories of Mass Communication*. New York: Longman, 1975.

Dieckmann, O. "Cultural Determinants of Economic Growth: Theory and Evidence." *Journal of Cultural Economics* 20(4) (1996): 297–320.

Elasmar, Michael G. "Opportunities and Challenges of Using Meta-Analysis in the Field of International Communication." *Critical Studies in Mass Communication* 16(3) (1999): 379–89.

Ellul, Jacques. *The Technological Society*. New York: Knopf, 1964.

El-Nawawy, Mohammed, and Iskandar, Adel. *Al-Jazeera*. Cambridge, MA: Westview Press, 2002.

European Broadcasting Union. "Audiovisual Services and GATS Negotiations: EUB Contribution to the Public Consultation on Requests for Access to the EU Market." January 17, 2003.

European Commission. "WTO members' requests to the EC and its Member States for Improved Market Access for Services," Consultation Document of November 12, 2002.

European Commission. "Action Plan to Improve Communicating Europe." ec.europa.ed.

European Commission. KOM 196 slutlig, "Om en informations- och kommunikationsstrategi för Europeiska unionen," www.europarl.europa.eu, 2004.

European Commission. "The Commission's Contribution to the Period of Reflection and Beyond: Plan D for Democracy, Dialogue and Debate." COM 494 final. www.ec.europa.eu, 2005.

European Commission. "White Paper on a European Communication Policy," COM 35 final, ec.europa.eu, 2006.

European Parliament and Council. "Directive 2007/65/EC." December 11, 2007. *Official Journal of the European Union* L332/27.

Faiola, A. "Japanese Women Catch the 'Korean Wave.'" *The Washington Post*, from www.washingtonpost.com/wp-dyn/content/article/2006/08/30/AR2006083002985.html, August 31, 2006.

Featherstone, Michael (ed.). *Global Culture: Nationalism, Globalization and Modernity.* London: Sage, 1990.

Fernández-Quijada, David. "Strategies of Transnational Media Corporations in the Spanish Television Industry." Observatorio Journal 3(2) (2009): 85–112.

Fiske, John and John Hartley. *Reading Television.* London and New York: Methuen, 1978/2003.

Flournoy, Don M., and Stewart, Robert K. *CNN: Making News in the Global Market.* Bedfordshire, UK: John Libbey Media, 1977.

FOX, Elizabeth. *Latin American Broadcasting.* Luton: University of Luton Press, 1997.

Frater, P. "Italy's Eagle Swoops on Its First Korean Title." *Screen Daily*, May (2003a).

Frater, P. "Korea's Jail Breakers Given New Dimension." *Screen Daily*, February (2003b).

"Freedom of the Press 2008: A Global Survey of Media Independence." Washington, DC: Freedom House, 2008.

Frydén Bonnier, Minna. "Europeanization in European News Broadcasts? A Comparative Study of Euronews and Rapport." Masters thesis, Department of Political Science, Stockholm University, 2007.

Gershon, Richard A. *The Transnational Media Corporation: Global Messages and Free Market Competition.* Mahwah, NJ: Lawrence Erlbaum, 1997.

Giddens, Anthony. *Modernity and Self-Identity.* Stanford, CA: Stanford University Press, 1991.

Giffard, C. Anthony, and Rivenburgh, Nancy K. "News Agencies, National Images, and Global Media Events." *Journalism and Mass Communication Quarterly* 77(1) (2000): 8–21.

Gilboa, Eytan. "The CNN Effect: The Search for a Communication Theory of International Relations." *Political Communication* 22 (2005): 27–44.

Golding, Peter, and Harris, Phil (eds.). *Beyond Cultural Imperialism: Globalization, Communication, and the New International Order.* London: Sage Publications, 1997.

Grant, Peter and Wood, Chris. *Blockbusters and Trade Wars.* Toronto: Douglas and McInytre, 2004.

Grein, Adreas, and Ducoffe, Robert. "Strategic Responses to Market Globalization among Advertising Agencies." *International Journal of Advertising* 17(3) (1998): 301–20.

Gripsrud, Jostein. "Television and the European Public Sphere." *European Journal of Communication* 22(4) (2007): 479–92.

Habermas, Jürgen. *The Structural Transformation of the Public Sphere.* Oxford and Cambridge: Polity/Blackwell, 1962/1989.

Hachten, William, and Scotton, James. *The World News Prism: Global Media in an Era of Terrorism.* Ames: Iowa State Press, 2002.

Hall, Thomas D. "The World-System Perspective: A Small Sample from a Large Universe." *Sociological Inquiry* 66(4) (1996): 440–54.

Hallin, Daniel C. and Paolo Mancini. *Comparing Media Systems. Three Models of Media and Politics.* Cambridge: Cambridge University Press, 2004.

Hancinema. "Korean Films Earn International Critical Acclaim." *HANCINEMA: The Korean Movie and Drama Database*, from www.hancinema.net/korean-films-earn-intl-critical-acclaim-19847.html, June 18, 2009.

Hanink, D. M. *The International Economy: A Geographic Perspective*. New York: John Wiley, 1994.

Hedley, Alan. "Technological Diffusion or Cultural Imperialism? Measuring the Information Revolution." *International Journal of Comparative Sociology* 39(2) (1998): 198–223.

Heidegger, Martin. *The Question Concerning Technology and Other Essays*. New York: Harper and Row, 1977.

Heikkilä, Heikki and Kunelius, Risto. "Journalists Imagining the Public Sphere." *Javnost: The Public* 13(4) (2006): 63–80.

Heo, J. (2002) "The 'Hanryu' Phenomenon and the Acceptability of Korean TV Dramas in China." *Korean Journal of Broadcasting* 16(1), 496–529.

Hersh, Seymour. *Chain of Command: The Road from 9/11 to Abu Ghraib*. New York: HarperCollins, 2004.

Hills, Jill. *The Struggle for Control of Global Communication*. Urbana, IL: University of Illinois Press, 2002.

Hjarvard, Stig. "The Mediaization of Society: A Theory of the Media as Agents of Social and Cultural Change." *Nordicom Review* 29(2) (2008): 105–34.

Hoggart, Richard. *An Idea and Its Servants. UNESCO from Within*. London: Chatto and Windus, 1978.

Hojman, David. "Economic Policy and Latin American Culture: Is a Virtuous Circle Possible?" *Journal of Latin American Studies* 31 (February 1999): 167–90.

Hong, J. "Television." In *Berkshire Encyclopedia of China*. Great Barrington, MA: Berkshire Publishing Group, 2009.

Hong, J., Lu, Y., and Zou, W. "CCTV in the Reform Years: Setting up a New Model for China's Television?" In Y. Zhu and C. Berry (eds.), *TV China*. Bloomington, IN: Indiana University Press, pp. 40–55, 2008.

Hopkins, Mark. "A Babel of Broadcasts." *Columbia Journalism Review* 38(2) (1999): 447.

Hoskins, Colin, McFadyen, Stuart, and Finn, Adam. *Global Television and Film: An Introduction to the Economics of the Business*. New York: Clarendon, 1997.

Hudson, Heather. *Global Connections: International Telecommunications Infrastructure and Policy*. New York: Van Nostrand Reinhold, 1997.

Hughes, Sallie, and Lawson, Chappell (2005) "The Barriers to Media Opening in Latin America." *Political Communication* 22: 9–25.

Huteau, Jean. *AFP: Une histoire de l'Agence France-Presse, 1944–1990*. Paris: R. Laffont, 1992.

India, B. Overseas earnings from www.boxofficeindia.com/cpages.php?pageName=overseas_earners, 2009.

Iwabuchi, K. "Cultures of Empire: Transnational Media Flows and Cultural Disconnections in East Asia." In P. Chakravartty and Y. Zhao (eds.), *Global Communications: Toward a Transcultural Political Economy*. Lanham, MD: Rowman & Littlefield, pp. 143–61, 2008.

Janus, N. "Transnational Advertising: Some Considerations of the Impact on Peripheral Societies." In R. Atwood and E. McAnany (eds.), *Communication and Latin American Society: Trends in Critical Research, 1960–1985*. Madison: University of Wisconsin Press, 1986.

Jayaram, P. "Chinese Premier in India–India, China to End Border Dispute, Launch Strategic Partnership." *News India Times*, from www.newsindia-times.com/nit/2005/04/22/tow14-top.html, April 22, 2005.

JETRO. "Japanese Film Industry." *Japan Economic Monthly*, May 2005.

Joshi, Lalit, and Malcolm, Derek (ed.). *Bollywood: Popular Indian Cineba*. London: Dakini Books, 2002.

Joo, J. "From Periphery to Center: The Rise of the Korean Film Industry since the Late 1990s." Paper presented at the New York conference on Asian Studies, from www.google.com/url?sa=t&source=web&ct=res&cd=1&url=http%3A%2F%2Fwww.newpaltz.edu%2Fasianstudies%2Fnycas%2F2005%2520GRAD%2520Ryan%2520Prize%2520Jeongsuk%2520Joo.pdf&ei=RN5WSvmqMMOGtgfHycHdCg&usg=AFQjCNEVwQ7wtF4wrXdYAJU5cCp1jE-IPg&sig2=Eozs1unUnzYDAJL-eZ5b1g, 2005.

Kakuchi, S. "Japan's Indie Film Industry Reeling." *Asia Times*, from www.atimes.com/atimes/Japan/EI18Dh03.html, September 18, 2003.

Kanayama, T., and Kanayama, T. "Japan." In A. Cooper-Chen (ed.), *Global Entertainment Media-Content, Audiences, Issues*. London: Routledge, 2005.

Kawakami, H., and Fisher, P. "Eastern Barbarians: The Ancient Sounds of Korea." In S. Broughton and M. Ellingham (eds.), *World Music: The Rough Guide*. London, UK: Rough Guides, pp. 468–72, 1994.

Keeyton, Jeffery. *Not Teflon: MTV Design*. New York: Universal Publishing, 2004.

Kennedy, Paul. *The Rise and Fall of the Great Powers*. New York: Vintage Books, 1989.

Kim, H. M. "Korean TV Dramas in Taiwan: With an Emphasis on the Localization Process." *Korea Journal* (winter) (2005): 183–205.

Kim, Kyungmo, and Barnett, George. "The Determinants of International News Flow: A Network Analysis." *Communication Research* 23(3) (June 1996): 323–52.

Kim, M. "Cultural Proximity and the Type of Korean Television Programs in Asian Market." Paper presented at the 6th World Media Economics Conference, from www.cem.ulaval.ca/pdf/kim.pdf, 2004.

Kim, S. "'Renaissance of Korean National Cinema' as a Terrain of Negotiation and Contention between the Global and the Local: Analysing Two Korean Blockbusters: Shiri (1999) and JSA" (2000) *The Essex Grad Journal* 5 (2004).

Kim, Y. D. *A Comparative Study of Production System for Televisoin Dramas between Korean and Japan*. Seoul, Korea: Korean Broadcasting Institutiono, 2009.

Kleinsteuber, Hans J. "Habermas and the Public Sphere: From a German to a European Perspective." *Javnost: The Public* 8(1) (2001): 95–108.

Knightley, Phillip. *The First Casualty*. New York: Harcourt, Brace and Jovanovich, 1975.

KOCCA. *Statistics of Cultural Industry*. Publication from Korea Creative Content Agency, http://sci.kocca.or.kr/index.jsp, 2009.

Kohli-Khandekar, V. *The Indian Media Business* (2 edn.). New Delhi: Response Books, 2006.

KPMG, C. C. o. I. I. a. *Indian Entertainment Industry Focus 2010: Dreams to Reality*. New Delhi: Confederation of Indian Industry, 2005.

Kraidy, Marwan. "The Global, the Local, and the Hybrid: A Native Ethnography of Globalization." *Critical Studies in Mass Communication* 16 (1999): 456–76.

Kunelius, Risto and Colin Sparks. "Problems with a European Public Sphere: An Introduction." *Javnost: The Public* 8(1) (2001): 5–20.

Kwasi, Amsu-Kyeremeh (ed.). "Indigenous Communication in Africa: A Conceptual Frame-work." *Perspective on Indigenous Communication in Africa*. Legon, Ghana: School of Communication Studies Printing Press, 1998.

Lee, Raymond L. M. "Globalization and Mass Society Theory." *International Review of Sociology/Revue Internationale de Sociologie* 12(1) (March 2002): 45–60.

Lee, S. "Seoul Survivor." *Straits Times* (April 8, 2003).

Lee, S. W., and Waterman, D. "Theatrical Feature Film Trade in the United States, Europe, and Japan since the 1950s: An Empirical Study of the Home Market Effect." Paper presented at the TPRC Conference on Communication, Information, and Internet Policy, 2006.

Lee, S., Kim, E., and Sung, H. "On the Exportability of Korean Movies." *Review of Development Economics*, 13(1) (2009): 28–38.

Lewis, Seth, and Reese, Stephen. "What is the War on Terror? Framing through the Eyes of Journalists." *Journalism and Mass Communication Quarterly* 86 (spring 2009): 85–118.

Lilleker, Darren G. *Key Concepts in Political Communication*. London: Sage, 2006.

Lim, Yon Soo, Barnett George, and Kim, Jang Hyun. "The Structure of International Aid Flows and Global News Media." *Journal of International Communication* 14(2) (2008): 117–42.

Linden, Ank. "Overt Intentions and Covert Agendas." *Gazette* 61(2) (1999): 153–75.

Lingenberg, S. "The Audience's Role in Constituting the European Public Sphere: A Theoretical Approach Based on the Pragmatic Concept of John Dewey." In N. Carpentier et al. (eds.), *Researching Media, Democracy and Participation*. Tartu: Tartu University Press, 2006.

Liu, L., and Lu, J. "Overview of the Development of China's Movie Industry." In B. Cui (ed.), *2009 Report on Development of China's Media Industry*. Beijing, China: Social Sciences Academic Press, pp. 247–53, 2009.

Lorenzen, M. *Go West: The Growth of Bollywood*. Handelshojskolen: Copenhagen Business School, 2009.

Lorenzen, M., and Taeube, F. A. "Breakout from Bollywood? Internationalization of Indian Film Industry." *Journal of International Management* 14 (2008): 286–99.

Lu, B. "China's Animation Products Begin to Enter the International Market." In B. Cui (-2009 Report on Development of China's Media Industry*. Beijing, China: Social Sciences Academic Press, pp. 298–302, 2009.

Lu, D., and Gao, F. "Competition Analyses of China's Television Industry." In B. Cui (ed.), *2009 Report on Development of China's Media Industry*. Beijing, China: Social Sciences Academic Press, pp. 228–34, 2009.

MacBride, Sean. *Many Voices, One World*. New York: Unipub, 1980.

Machill, Marcel. "Euronews: The First European News Channel as a Case Study for Industry Development in Europe and for Spectra of Transnational Journalism Research." *Media, Culture and Society* 20(3) (1998): 427–50.

Machill, Marcel et al. "Europe-Topics in Europe's Media." *European Journal of Communication*, 2(1) (2006): 57–88.

Madden, Normandy. "Cable, Satellite Media Lure Influential Viewers." *Advertising Age International* (October 1999): 36.

Malek, Abbas. "Introduction: News Media and Foreign Policy: A Field Ripe for Research." *Journal of International Communication* 4(1) (1997): 1–10.

Maliangkay, R. "When the Korean Wave Ripples." *IIAS Newsletter*, 2006.

Martinez, Arnando. "The New World Order and What We Make of It." *World Policy Journal* 16(3) (1999): 692.

Mattelart, Tristan. "Transboundary Flows of Western Entertainment across the Iron Curtain." *Journal of International Communication* 6(2) (1999): 106–21.

McChesney, Robert W. "The Internet and US Communication Policy-making in Historical and Critical Perspective." *Journal of Communication* 46(1) (1996): 98–124.

McCullough, Wayne. "Global Advertising Which Acts Locally: The IBM Subtitles Campaign." *Journal of Advertising Research* 36 (May–June 1996): 11–15.

McDonald, Ian R. and Lawrence, Regina G. "Filling the 24 × 7 News Hole: Television News Coverage Following September 11." *American Behavioral Scientist* 48(3) (2004): 327–40.

McKee, Kathy Brittain. "Why I [Still] Want My MTV: Music Video and Aesthetic Communication" (book review). *Journalism and Mass Communication Quarterly* 81(3) (2004): 718–20.

McLuhan, Marshall. *The Gutenberg Galaxy.* Toronto, Canada: University of Toronto Press, 1962.

McLuhan, Marshall. *Understanding Media: The Extensions of Man.* New York, McGraw-Hill, 1964.

McLuhan, Marshall, and Fiore, Quentin. *The Medium Is the Message.* New York: Bantam Books, 1967.

McLuhan, Marshall, and Fiore, Quentin. *Understanding Media: The Extension of Man.* New York: McGraw-Hill, 1964.

McNair, Brian. *Journalism and Democracy: An Evaluation of the Political Public Sphere.* London: Routledge, 2000.

McPhail, Thomas. *The Future of the Daily Newspaper: Public Policy Issues.* Montreal: Institute for Research on Public Policy, 1980.

McPhail, Thomas. "Canadianisation of European Broadcasting: Is an Electronic Berlin Wall the Answer?" *Broadcasting and Research: Experiences and Strategies,* Amsterdam: ESOMAR, pp. 15–30, 1988.

McPhail, Thomas. "Direct Broadcast Satellites: The Demise of Public and Commercial Policy Objectives" (with S. Judge). In Indu Singh (ed.), *Telecommunications in the Year 2000: National and International Perspectives.* Norwood, NJ: Ablex, pp. 72–9, 1983.

McPhail, Thomas. "The Communication Economy Sweepstakes: Few Winners, Many Losers: A Canadian Case Study." *Informatologia Yugoslavia* 17(1–2) (1985): 97–105.

McPhail, Thomas. *Electronic Colonialism: The Future of International Broadcasting and Communication.* Newbury, CA: Sage Publications, 1986.

McPhail, Thomas. "The International Politics of Telecommunications. Resolving the North–South Dilemma" (with Brenda McPhail). *International Journal* XLII (1987): 289–319.

McPhail, Thomas. "Inquiry in International Communication." In M. Asante and B. Gudykunst (eds.), *Handbook of International and Intercultural Communication.* Newbury, CA: Sage Publications, pp. 47–66, 1989.

McPhail, Thomas. *Development Communication: Reframing the Role of the Media.* London: Wiley-Blackwell, 2009.

McPhail, Thomas, and Barnett, George. "An Examination of the Relationship of United States Television and Canadian Identity." *International Journal of Intercultural Relations* 4 (1980): 219–32.

McPhail, Thomas, and McPhail, Brenda. *Communication: The Canadian Experience.* Toronto: Copp Clark Pitman, 1990.

McPhail, Thomas, and McPhail, Brenda. "Television and Development Communication: A Canadian Case Study." In Andrew Moemeka (ed.), *Communicating for Development: A Pan-Disciplinary Perspective*. Albany: State University of New York Press, pp. 191–218, 1994.

"Media Forum Examines Widespread Press Freedom Abuses." World Association of Newspapers, www.wan-press.org/article12549.html.

Melkote, Srinivas, Shields, Peter, and Agrawel, Binod (eds.). *International Satellite Broadcasting in South Asia*. Lanham, MD: University Press of America, 1998.

Menge, Peter. "1998 ICA Presidential Address: Communication Structures and Processes in Globalization." *Journal of Communication* 48(44) (1999): 142–53.

Merrill, John, Berenger, Ralph, and Merrill, Charles. *Media Musings: Interviews with Great Thinkers*. Spokane: Marquette Books, 2004.

Mishra, Vijay. *Bollywood Cinema*. New York: Routledge, 2001.

Mishra, Vijay. *Bollywood Cinema: A Critical Genealogy*. Wellington, NZ: Asian Studies Institute, 2006.

Mitchell, Tony. "Treaty Now! Indigenous Music and Music Television in Australia." *Media, Culture, and Society* 15(2) (1993): 299–308.

Mittelman, James H. *The Globalization Syndrome: Transformation and Resistance*. Princeton: Princeton University Press, 2000.

Moemeka, Andrew. "Development Communication: A Historical and Conceptual Overview." In Andrew Moemeka (ed.), *Communicating for Development*. Albany: State University of New York Press, 1994.

Mohammadi, Ali (ed.). *International Communication and Globalization*. London: Sage Publications, 1997.

Morris, Merrill, and Ogan, Christine. "The Internet as Mass Medium." *Journal of Communication* 46(1) (1996): 39–50.

Müller, Milton. *Ruling the Root: Internet Governance and the Taming of Cyberspace*. Cambridge: MIT Press, 2002.

Murdock, Graham. "Television and Citizenship: In Defence of Public Broadcasting." In A. Tomlinson (ed.), *Consumption, Identity and Style: Marketing, Meanings and the Packaging of Pleasure*. London and New York: Routledge: 77–101, 1990.

Norris, Pippa and Inglehart, Ronald. *Cosmopolitan Communications: Cultural Diversity in a Globalized World*, New York: Cambridge University Press, 2010.

Nostbakken, David, and Morrow, Charles (ed.). *Cultural Expression in the Global Village*. Ottawa, Canada: Southbound, 1993.

Paek, Hye-Jin, and Pan, Zhongdang. "Spreading Global Consumerism: Effects of Mass Media and Advertising on Consumerist Values in China." *Mass Communication and Society* 7(4) (2004): 491–515.

Papathanassopoulos, Stylianos. "Europe: An Exampleary Landscape for Comprehending Globalization." *Global Media and Communication* 1(1) (2005).

Parameswaran, R. "The Other Side of Globalization: Communication, Culture, and Postcolonial Critique." *Communication, Culture and Critique* 1(2008): 116–25.

Park, Hong-Wan. "A Gramscian Approach to Interpreting International Communication." *Journal of Communication* 48(4) (1998): 79–99.

Paterson, Chris A. "International Television News Agency Coverage of Conflict." *Journal of International Communication* 4(1) (1997) 50–66.

Pauwels, Caroline and Lisen, Jan. "The WTO and the Audiovisual Sector" *European Journal of Communication* 18 (2003): 291–314, 2003.

Pintak, Lawrence, and Ginges, Jeremy. "The Mission of Arab Journalism: Creating Change in a Time of Turmoil." *The International Journal of Press/Politics* 13(3) (2008): 193–227.

"Predators of Press Freedom." Paris: Reporters Sans Frontières, 2007.

Price, Monroe E. *Television, the Public Sphere and National Identity.* Oxford and New York: Oxford University Press, 1995.

PWC. *Global Entertainment and Media Outlook 2006–2010.* New York: Pricewaterhouse Coopers LLP, 2006.

Ramaprasad, J. "Content, Geography Concentration and Consonance in Foreign News Coverage of ABC, NBC, and CBS." *International Communication Bulletin* 28 (1993): 10–14.

Rao, S. "India." In A. Cooper-Chen (ed.), *Global Entertainment Media-Content, Audiences, Issues.* London: Routledge, 2005.

Rao, S. "The Globalization of Bollywood: An Ethnography of Non-Elite Audiences in India." *Communication Review* 10(1) (2007): 57–76.

Read, Donald. *The Power of News: The History of Reuters.* Oxford: Oxford University Press, 1992.

Rich, Frank. "Is Obama Punking Us?" *The New York Times* (August 9, 2009): 8.

Ries, Al and Trout, Jack. *Positioning: The Battle for your Mind.* New York: McGraw-Hill, 2001.

Riffe, D. "Linking International News to US Interest: A Content Analysis." *International Communication Bulletin* 31 (1996): 14–18.

Riley, Patricia, and Menge, Peter. "Introduction." *Communication Research* 25(4) (1998): 355–8.

Robertson, Alexa. *Cosmopolitan Narratives. The World of Television News* (forthcoming).

Rogers, Everett. *Modernization among Peasants: The Impact of Communication.* New York: Holt, Rinehart, and Winston, 1969.

Rogers, Everett. "Communication and Development: The Passing of the Dominant Paradigm." *Communication Research* 3(2) (1976): 213–40.

Rooke, Richard. *European Media in the Digital Age. Analysis and Approaches.* Harlow: Pearson/Longman, 2009.

Rosenblum, Morton. *Coups and Earthquakes.* New York: Harper & Row, 1979.

Rostow, Walter. *The Stages of Economic Growth.* New York: Cambridge University Press, 1960.

Rothkopf, David. "In Praise of Cultural Imperialism." *Foreign Policy* 107 (1997): 38–53.

Rugh, William A. *The Arab Press: News Media and Political Process in the Arab World.* Syracuse: Syracuse University Press, 1979.

Sambrook, Richard. "The Poliak Lecture: Holding on to Objectivity." A speech given at Columbia University, October 27, 2004.

Schafer, D. Paul. "The Millennium Challenge: Making the Transition from an 'Economic Age to a 'Cultural Age.'" *World Futures* 51 (1998): 287–320.

Schiller, Herbert. *Communication and Cultural Domination.* White Plains, NY: International Arts and Sciences Press, 1976.

Schlesinger, Philip. "The Babel of Europe? An Essay on Network and Communicative Spaces." In Dario Castiglione and Chris Longman (eds.), *The Language Question in Europe and Diverse Societies: Political, Legal and Social Perspectives.* Oxford: Hart, 2007a.

Schlesinger, Philip. "A Cosmopolitan Temptation?" *European Journal of Communication* 22(4) (2007b): 413–26.

Schlesinger, Philip. "Wishful Thinking: Cultural Politics, Media, and Collective Identities in Europe." *Journal of Communication* 43(2) (1993): 6–17.

Seaver, Brenda. "The Public Dimension of Foreign Policy" *Harvard International Journal of Press/Politics* 3(1) (1998): 65–91.

Semetko, Holli, et al. "Europeanised Politics – Europeanised Media? European Integration and Political Communication." *West European Politics* 23(4) (2000): 121–41.

Sengupta, Subir. "Analysis of Television Commercials from India and the United States." *Gazette* 57 (1996): 1–16.

Shah, Hermant. "Modernization, Marginalization, and Emancipation: Toward a Normative Model of Journalism and National Development." *Communication Theory* 6(2) (1998): 143–67.

Shannon, Thomas R. *An Introduction to the World System Perspective*. Boulder, CO Westview Press, 1996.

Shen, P. " 'It Came from the East.' Japanese Horror Cinema in the Age of Globalization." *gnovis* 2(9) (Spring 2009), from http://gnovisjournal.org/.

Shim, D. "Hybridigy and the Rise of Korean Popular Culture in Asia." *Media, Culture, and Society*, 28(1) (2009): 25–44.

Shoemaker, P., and Reese, S. *Mediating the Message: Theories of Influence on Mass Media Content*. New York: Longman, 1991.

Shukla, S. *India Abroad: Diasporic Cultures of Postwar America and England*. Princeton, NJ: Princeton University Press, 2003.

Slater, Robert. *The New GE: How Jack Welch Revived an American Institution*. Highstown, NJ: Irwin, 1992.

Spark, Alasdair. "Wrestling with America: Media, National Images, and the Global Village." *Journal of Popular Culture* 29 (1996): 83–97.

Splichal, Slavko. "In Search of a Strong European Public Sphere: Some Critical Observations on Conceptualizations of Publicness and the (European) Public Sphere." *Media, Culture and Society*, 28(5) (2006): 695–714.

Staff. "Culture 101: Beyond the Blog." *Egypt Today* (March 2009).

Starr, Paul. *The Creation of the Media: Political Origins of Modern Communication*. New York: Basic Books, 2004.

Stewart, J. *Disneywar: The Battle for the Magic Kingdom*, New York: Simon and Schuster, 2004.

Stevenson, Robert. *Global Communication to the Twenty-first Century*. New York: Longman, 1994.

Swan, Jon. "I Was a 'Polisher' in a Chinese News Factory." *Columbia Journalism Review* 27 (March/April 1996): 33–6.

Taplin, J. " 'Crouching Tigers': Emerging Challenges to US Entertainment Supremacy in the Movie Business." *Observatorio* 2 (2007): 167–90.

Taylor, Philip. *War and the Media: Propaganda and Persuasion in the Gulf War*. Manchester, UK: Manchester University Press, 1988.

Taylor, Philip. *Global Communications, International Affairs and the Media since 1945*. London: Routledge, 1997.

Tehranian, Majid. Foreword. In Y. Kamalipour (ed.), *Images of the US around the World: A Multicultural Perspective*. Albany: State University of New York Press, 1999.

The 9/11 Commission Report: Final Report of the National Commission on Terrorist Attacks upon the United States. Washington: Replica Books, 2004.

Thomas, Bob. *Building a Company: Roy O. Disney and the Creation of an Entertainment Empire.* Boston: Hyperion, 1999.

Thompson, J. B. *The Media and Modernity: A Social Theory of the Media.* Stanford, CA: Stanford University Press, 1995.

Thussa, D. *International Communication: Continuity and Change.* London: Arnold Press, 2000.

"Top Advertisers and Product Categories in Markets Worldwide." *International Journal of Advertising* 18(1) (1999): 123–8.

Trenz, Hans-Jörg. "Media Coverage on European Governance." *European Journal of Communication* 19(3) (2004): 291–319.

Tunstall, J. *The Media Are American.* New York: Columbia University Press, 1977.

UNESCO. *The Power of Culture,* www.powerofculture.nl/uk/archive/report/background.html, 1998.

UNESCO. *Universal Declaration on Cultural Diversity,* www.unesco.org/culture, November 2, 2001.

UNESCO. *Convention on the Protection and Promotion of the Diversity of Cultural Expressions,* Paris, www.unesco.org, October 20, 2005.

UNESCO. *World Report on Cultural Diversity,* 2009.

Van de Steeg, Marianne. "Rethinking the Conditions for a Public Sphere in the European Union." *European Journal of Social Theory* 5(4) (2002): 499–519.

Van Rossem, R. "The World System Paradigm as General Theory of Development: A Cross-National Test." *American Sociological Review* 61 (1996) 508–27.

Volkmer, Ingrid. *News in the Global Sphere: A Study of CNN and Its Impact on Global Communication.* Luton: University of Luton Press, 1999.

Wagnleitner, Reinhold. "The Empire of the Fun, or Talkin' Soviet Union Blues: The Sound of Freedom and US Cultural Hegemony in Europe." *Diplomatic History* 23(3) (1999): 499–524.

Wallerstein, I. *The Modern World System.* New York: Academic Press, 1976.

Wallerstein, I. "After Developmentalism and Globalization, What?" *Social Forces* 83(3) (2005): 1263–78.

Wanta, Wayne, Golan, Guy, and Lee, Cheolhan. "Agenda Setting and International News: Media Influence on Public Perceptions of Foreign Nations." *Journalism and Mass Communication Quarterly* 81(2) (2004): 364–77.

Ward, David. "The Democratic Deficit and European Union Communication Policy. An Evaluation of the Commission's Approach to Broadcasting." *Javnost: The Public* 8(1) (2001): 75–94.

Ward, David. *Euroepan Union Democratic Deficit and the Public Sphere: An Evaluation of EU Media Policy.* Amsterdam: IOS Press, 2002.

Ware, William, and Dupagne, Michel. "Effects of US Television Programs on Foreign Audiences: A Meta-Analysis." *Journalism Quarterly* 71(4) (1994): 947–59.

Watts, Steven. *The Magic Kingdom: Walt Disney and the American Way of Life.* Boston: Houghton Mifflin, 1998.

WebJapan. (2005) "*Howl's Moving Castle.*" *Trends in Japan,* from web-japan.org/trends/arts/art050314.html

Weingart, Peter. "Science and the Media." *Research Policy* 27(8): 869–79.

Westerstahl, J., and Johansson, F. "Foreign News: News Values and Ideologies." *European Journal of Communication* 9 (1994): 71–89.

Wheeler, Mark. "Supranational Regulation: Television and the European Union." *European Journal of Communication* 19(3) (2004): 349–69.

Whittemore, Hank. *CNN: The Inside Story*. Toronto, Canada: Little, Brown, 1990.

Widholm, Andreas. "From Television Flows to Generic Structures: Reflections on Form and Content of Euronews and BBC World News." Unpublished conference paper, Department of Journalism, Media and Communication, Stockholm University, 2009.

Wildman, S. S., and Siwek, S. E. *International Trade in Films and Television Programs* Cambridge, MA: Ballinger, 1988.

Woodman-Maynard, K. "Bollywood and the Indian Film Industry." *Indian Business*, from www.indianbusiness.com/article/bollywood-the-indian-film-industry, 2006.

Wu, Haoming Denis. "Investigating the Determinants of International News Flow: A Meta-Analysis." *Gazette* 60(6) (1998): 493–512.

Xu, G. "Remaking East Asia, Outsourcing Hollywood." In L. Hunt and L. Wing-Fai (eds.), *East Asian Cinemas: Exploring Transnational Connections on Film*. New York, NY: I. B. Tauris, pp. 192–202, 2008.

Xu, M. "New Plan of China Film Overseas Promotion Corporation." *Variety China* (May 14, 2007): 9.

Yash Raj Films. About Us-Company Info from www.yashrajfilms.com/AboutUs/Company Info.aspx?SectionCode=PRO001, 2009.

Yin, K., and Liew, K. "Hallyu in Singapore: Korean Cosmopolitanism or the Consumption of Chineseness?" *Korea Journal*, 2005.

Yoon, J. S., Kang, M., Yoon, H., Choi, S., Kim, Y. D., Kim, Y. S., et al. *A Research for Promoting a Continous Development of Korean Wave*. Seoul, Korea: KOFICE: Korea Foundation for International Culture Exchange, 2008.

Zhu, Y., and Berry, C. *TV China*. Bloomington, IN: Indiana University Press, 2009.

Index

Note: page numbers followed by *n* refer to information in a chapter endnote. The Arabic article *al-/el-* is ignored in the alphabetical sequence; search by using the initial letter of the following element.